THE BROKEN KING

ALSO BY MICHAEL THOMAS

Man Gone Down

THE BROKEN KING A MEMOIR

MICHAEL THOMAS

Grove Press
New York

Copyright © 2025 by Michael Thomas

All rights reserved. No part of this book may be reproduced in any form or by any electronic or mechanical means, including information storage and retrieval systems, without permission in writing from the publisher, except by a reviewer, who may quote brief passages in a review. Scanning, uploading, and electronic distribution of this book or the facilitation of such without the permission of the publisher is prohibited. Please purchase only authorized electronic editions, and do not participate in or encourage electronic piracy of copyrighted materials. Your support of the author's rights is appreciated. Any member of educational institutions wishing to photocopy part or all of the work for classroom use, or anthology, should send inquiries to Grove Atlantic, 154 West 14th Street, New York, NY 10011 or permissions@groveatlantic.com.

Any use of this publication to train generative artificial intelligence ("AI") technologies is expressly prohibited. The author and publisher reserve all rights to license uses of this work for generative AI training and development of machine learning language models.

Permissions acknowledgments appear on page 417

FIRST EDITION

Printed in the United States of America

The interior of this book was designed by Norman E. Tuttle
at Alpha Design & Composition.
This book was set in 11-pt. Calluna by Alpha Design & Composition
of Pittsfield, NH.

First Grove Atlantic hardcover edition: August 2025

Library of Congress Cataloging-in-Publication data is available for this title.

ISBN 978-0-8021-2014-4
eISBN 978-0-8021-9453-4

Grove Press
an imprint of Grove Atlantic
154 West 14th Street
New York, NY 10011

Distributed by Publishers Group West

groveatlantic.com

25 26 27 28 29   10 9 8 7 6 5 4 3 2 1

I forgot that I was a King's son,
And became a slave to their king.
> —The Hymn of the Pearl

εδιζησάμην
> —Heraclitus

"Still, again, I forget myself."
—Padraic Michael O'Reilly

For my fathers, my brothers, and my sons.

The Beautiful Game	1
Frankie, or The Loving One	89
What Pip Saw	175
A Peace	225
Mercy	293
Mercury Days	365

The Beautiful Game

Lord, protect my child.
—Bob Dylan

1

My boy is beautiful.

I write this to remind myself. I remind myself because I am a hard man. I am a hard man because at some point in my life I chose to be. I can be intolerant, quick to anger, unforgiving, and therefore, seemingly irredeemable. I fear my hardness. I am past fifty, and my musculature, like my mind, is losing its flexibility. It's more prone to fatigue and injury when exercised and slow to recover from exertion. I am hard because I sometimes believe I have seen too much, felt too much, and I have made the choice not to feel anymore.

My legacy is of broken men, each of whom, at one time, had to transform their own legacy and in doing so transform themselves and the inheritance of those to come. Each man failed.

But my boy is beautiful. My boy is beautiful in spite of me. He moves with languid grace, which underscores a quiet, peaceful stillness in him that seems unshakable.

Beautiful, not perfect; Alex can be rude, insolent, and subject to wild emotional swings and failures of decorum and logic. Beauty, however, isn't pretty. It isn't a superficial modifier. It demands we participate. It embraces rather than rejects. It's a jangling phrase we hear that we transform into song. It's that which inspires us to toast with and drink from the cup of trembling. It's the heavens leaving. It's a synthesis—if only momentary—of the internal and external forces that threaten to tear us apart.

I have four children now, but Alex is different—to me. It might be that I see him as being so because he's my oldest. I never thought I'd overburden my firstborn male. I'm the youngest of three, and I've watched my brother and father stagger and fail under that load. I know this isn't the case for all fathers and eldest sons. I never thought it would be for me and mine, but there he is, my Alex, alone, fixed in primogeniture, set to receive an inheritance from his hard father.

The estate bequeathed to Alex is a troubled one. His father is a troubled man. And I often feel that because I have not completely freed myself from what my father left me, I will always endanger my son. I feel I cannot help Alex. I cannot protect him from us.

2

In mid-June of 1995, my wife, Michaele, and I found out that she was pregnant with our first child. We were driving north on I-95 near Madison, Connecticut, when she said that she was "late."

"Do we have to be somewhere?" I asked. She turned to me, baffled. We were returning to Boston after having signed a lease for a Brooklyn townhouse for $1,500 a month—three times what we were currently paying. She'd recently received her degree in social work and, having given up on theater, I was about to start an MFA program in fiction writing. Neither of us had jobs in New York, and three months sober, I was having a protracted bout of the heebie-jeebies.

We'd been told by her family and white friends that our children would be beautiful. Physically, they'd be a combination of the exotic and the familiar. Metaphorically, they'd represent the reconciliation of the races. They'd be concrete proof of peace: tan skin, light eyes, that good hair. The gene pool of the muted Black and unexpurgated white. It was lunacy, but the only conclusion I could afford was that they meant well. I had neither time nor space to think any more on it.

None of the practical considerations frightened me. I could always bang nails, haul trash, wash dishes until I found steady work. As for my alcoholism, I'd had what I believed at the time was the lifting of my compulsion to drink. I knew I wouldn't pick up. If anything, impending fatherhood had validated my choice to stop. What I didn't know was whether I could be present and intimate enough to provide the tenderness I imagined a child would need. I didn't know if I could learn how to give or stand receiving affection from a child. While driving, I went silent and wondered what would happen when my child would need me to hold still long enough—soften enough—for him to be able to love me. As we sped north, I tried to script a narrative that would depict and explain the reasons for my condition and by explaining, give us some relief.

I believed that children loathed me, that they could sense something wrong and couldn't stand to be in my presence. "Babies hate me," I used to say—sometimes as a boast. My friends would dismiss this claim until they saw me enter a room in which a happy toddler was playing and see the child stop and look away. Or other times, when someone would give me an infant to hold, it would scream. After repeated instances, I decided that it was best to avoid them.

I stayed away from older children, too. People were incredulous that I refused to be a coach or tutor for Black city boys. "You have so much to offer," they repeated. I suppose, from what they saw, it made sense. I was young, seemed educated, and allegedly came from circumstances similar to those I was supposed to mentor. I resisted, however, because I knew what they saw was only the mask of normalcy. That cover had a dual purpose: not only to keep people out but also to keep me in. I imagined what I could offer was eyeless, mute, and if culled from the deep, pressurized dark, it would soggily pop in the light and free air.

We drove on, and I thought about how growing up, I'd identified with epic heroes, not the anodyne *good* ones but those whose inner pain couldn't, in the end, keep them from doing right, even if the people they tried to save did them wrong. Those who grieved yet acted estimably. But I hadn't a cross or crown, spider strength or cosmic power. And while I knew that I was waiting for that battle from which I'd never return, I could only communicate this to others with a blank affect and proxies from the ancient world.

It had scared my mother, this blankness. I think this is why she used to call me a cold fish. I suppose I was, but not entirely for the reasons she suspected, namely that I possessed some inherent trait that made me distant: shy to some, aloof to others, alien to most. If she could've asked—and I could've answered—the reasons for my remove, I would've told her that the risk of allowing someone to get close enough to touch me always surpassed the rewards. Intimacy was dangerous. Neither of my parents were physically approachable anyway. I didn't trust either of them near me. My mother, just beneath her skin, housed a palpable rage, and my father's cheeks were pocked and rough from ingrown hairs. He smelled like an empty beer-can-turned-ashtray. Sometimes he'd forget about the lit cigarette he was holding. He wore polyester. His belly was large, his arms were small, and his hugs were insufferable.

Even when they were together, they seemed divided: the Northern urban dreamer, the Southern rural pragmatist. To him, her migration from Hampden Sydney, Virginia, to Boston must have seemed like one that belonged to an earlier generation. In him, she found a new Negro: educated, urbane, and comfortable around white people. One look at his lone, dark face in his Brighton High class picture tells you. He hadn't much of a choice.

I never saw them being kind to each other. My early understanding of the two dichotomized them, segregated them into distinct Black American traditions: he, Du Bois, she, Washington; Locke and Hurston; the new and the old; white collar and blue; the talented tenth and those they were charged to uplift. It, of course, wasn't—still isn't—that neat. My folksy mother's tastes were rarified and cosmopolitan. She pushed us into the wider pluralist society that she couldn't, without anguish, enter herself. My father, for all of his altruism and cultural literacy, never moved away from his hometown. He kept us in the same house in which he grew up and, like his father, left us there. His expeditions were to the small jazz clubs in and around Boston. When he was home, the television was always on, the house in disrepair—one dead Pontiac in the yard and another dying in the frost-heaved driveway. He was, simultaneously, honky-tonk and erudite—beer in hand, quoting Emerson to his children while watching *The Munsters* or candlepin bowling on TV.

My mother was hot and didactic. She drank Heineken and got angry. She was a screamer. My father was pensive and Socratic. His

Millers made him wistful. Unless Yastrzemski hit a homer, he rarely raised his voice. My older siblings have memories of our parents being unified. They recall Sunday afternoons spent driving through the suburbs house hunting. I remember fracture—uneasy dinners, grim Christmas Eves and Christmas Days, rages at dirty dishes by her, and his sudden escapes into the Boston night.

I don't remember where my brother and sister were, but at 8:57 p.m. on a Sunday, I was on the couch with him watching commercials, waiting for *The Six Million Dollar Man* to come on. I could always tell when my father was enjoying himself: he'd smile a dopey smile, recline, and stretch his arm along the back of the ratty sofa. Nothing better than to spend quality time, buzzed, in front of the idiot box with your boy offhandedly commenting on a plotline, making fun of this character's hair or that one's nose or how that supporting actor had once been a film star: "What a fall." He was free to do this because he was seldom part of the bedtime ritual, which wasn't much of a ritual at all. There was only a time when the lights needed to be out. His visits to my bedside were usually prompted by his need to share an idea he had on his way home after an early night at the lounge. Beer-and-cigarette-aroma lullabies. My mother, exhausted, would simply tell us to go to bed.

During the teaser, my mother came in. I had been hoping she'd forgotten me. Perhaps there'd been an unannounced referendum on bedtimes. What I wanted was for my father to outrank her. I wasn't quite seven, and my mother and I already had an unspoken and uneasy truce between us. I reminded her of my father. I looked like him, spoke like him, and seemed aloof like him, too.

She stood between the TV and us, hip jutted out to one side, one hand on it, the other gesturing vaguely to the doorway. My mother could always summon a look of great fatigue combined with supreme exasperation—taxed, heaped, vexed—which declared that all you'd said and done, were going to say and do, was part of a burden that would someday break her. Then I'd be alone and *What would you do, count on him?*

I started to get up, but he said, "It's okay. Sit down." So I hovered above the cushion, waiting for her to hiss, "Get upstairs!" She did. And not yet the hardheaded boy I'd later become, I started to oblige.

"You can stay," said my father. She laughed. I started to go. He pulled me back onto the couch. She grabbed a wrist and pulled me up toward the door. He stood and grabbed my other arm. They both pulled—a silent tug-of-war—to Steve Austin's theme music.

Then he was on her: his arm around her neck, locking his wrist with the opposite hand. Her eyes bulged. He dragged her out to the porch, left her there, stunned, gasping, then came back in and bolted the door.

He went back to the couch. I went out to the hall and closed the French doors that separated the spaces. I watched my mother's face in the window go from flat to a wicked grin as though she were planning his quick demise or she were the one inside. It faded, though, her disconsolate face framed by the night. I let her back in, and she paced about on the linoleum, stopping only to stare down at me. I thought she might slap me or crash through the glass, tear the television plug from the wall, then storm out. Or stand over him, arms folded, daring him to do it again. Instead she knelt awkwardly, rubbed my arm once, and asked me if I was hungry. My mother, when she wanted, had a warm, honeyed voice that could charm most children and creditors. I, by this time, was almost inured. I shook my head.

"You sure?" she sang.

I nodded.

"Cold fish," she whispered and stood.

3

The first time I'd seriously considered fatherhood was on my twenty-first birthday. I was living in Madison, Wisconsin, trying to gain state residency so I could enroll in the university for in-state tuition. This was proving difficult. I hadn't been able to find a place to live, so I hadn't an address, so the months I'd spent there had been a waste of time. I should've been entering my senior year, prepping for either graduate school or some profession. I was, however, on my way to being a crazy hobo.

I'd been trying for the last three years to get sober, but every time I went for more than a week without a drink, I'd enter what a psychologist later would call a fugue state: a type of dry brownout. I'd come to in a different city, but rather than sleeping on a bench or a strange floor, I'd be walking down a street and snap back into consciousness.

Some friends had rented a house and given me space in a portion of the unfinished basement where I was supposed to stash my belongings, but I often slept there on my duffel bag. My girlfriend—I still find it unbelievable that I had one—found me in my hovel, gave me flowers, and announced, "I was pregnant."

I stood and inhaled deeply, puffing out my chest, and rubbed my chin as though I had whiskers. I wanted to display confidence and thoughtfulness to her—a strong but gentle patrician demeanor—something I'd only seen in movies.

"What do you want to do?" I asked calmly in a quasi-baritone and looked at her with a soft intensity.

She looked back as though I might be insane.

"I *was* pregnant."

Autumn came and I was sleeping outside some nights. I admitted I was beat and limped back east to Boston. The next nine months—a strange gestation of sorts—I tried to convalesce. I spent my days driving a taxi, my early evenings going for long runs, my nights drinking and writing very dark, very bad poems. When I could sleep, if I had dreams, they were of my dead child.

Michaele and I met in college. I was a sophomore. She was a senior. She graduated. I dropped out. We eventually started dating on my twenty-second birthday, and a year later moved to the East Village together. After four months I had a crack-up, mended, and enrolled at Hunter College. I worked in a restaurant, did well in school, and began, at least superficially, to legitimize myself.

Two years later, Michaele was "late" for the first time. She woke up feeling nauseated. We were at her grandfather's country house. Her mother and sister were there. Looking at them—having them look at me—I heard Langston Hughes's poem "Mulatto" in my head: "A nigger night / a nigger joy / a little yellow bastard boy." Although, of course, *this* was an inversion of the slave master–slave woman coupling. I wouldn't take responsibility for appropriating the text. Instead, I fixated on that bastard and willfully ignored all the raped Black women at least one of whom was my ancestor.

I couldn't stay in the house with them. I felt dread, and I couldn't help but show it. I was a stereotypical young Black man. All of their suspicions about me would be confirmed. I had brought Michaele low.

I grew up in a world in which many white people and many institutions still believed in the notion that the innocence, purity, and honor of the white woman needed to be defended. But I also grew up in an alternate world in which the same was said for the Black woman. And there was no greater injury I could cause my mother, my sister, my sisters than to be with a white woman—or even to try to be with one.

I went outside and twisted shamefully in the winter wind. "What . . . ?" she'd asked, had always asked, and would continue to ask for a long time after. I could never fully explain that unlike hers my actions didn't occur in a vacuum. White and Black people were always judging me for them. And I would never be judged fairly because those actions would always be wed to centuries of inherited truths. She only obliquely understood what it was to represent something—her family, perhaps—most likely herself. But she would never understand what it was to represent a people—millions of people. Contrary to what Eliot wrote, every moment wasn't "a new and shocking valuation of all we have been" but rather an inescapable proof of the predetermined belief in what you are. The content of my people's character, and therefore my own, was already known.

I knew that I would not, could not, be a father. One of the few things I could plan was my next drink, even though that tended to be a chaotic, Byzantine endeavor. I hadn't any notion of the future, no sense of who I'd be or what I'd do—or if I'd be alive.

And though I was sure—most of the time—of where I'd been, I could only obliquely apprehend what it had cost me. When I wasn't drunk, I was dissociative. When I wasn't psychologically and emotionally removed, I was suicidal. When I wasn't despairing, I was enraged—a rage that could keep me up for days. And when I did sleep, I'd gnash my molars to what would eventually become jagged stumps. And when all these states were combined in my mind and body, I would run through the streets as fast as I could for as long as I could. If I slowed, I'd be flogged by the whip of sensations and images that even to this day when it cracks makes me want to throw myself in front of a bus, jab a steak knife into my eye. Drink. There's a rapist in the bathroom. There are junkies in the alleys. There's no heat. There are marauding cops. And there's nothing to do but flee as though escaping perdition or howl as though hunting salvation. Then that feeling of being lifted—saved. Then no more memory. No images, no pain, just weightlessness and the wind on my sweat and tears.

There'd been a hurricane that summer and a lot of tree fall. I went to the woodpile, picked up the ax, and began splitting logs. I tried to imagine our child: how and where we'd raise it. I thought of the strange and cruel places I'd been, all the fucked-up shit I'd heard from the mouths of people who just as soon would praise me, would say they loved me. How ill-equipped she and hers were to deal with me. How I'd introduced a permanent racial apparition that would, as long as I was around, haunt their house and point to their ignorance, their exclusionary practices, their privilege, the bigotry in the people, art, institutions, and legacies they valued. They would have to finally confront the myth of American meritocracy. And when the Spike Lee film was over, the Bob Marley song faded out, the James Baldwin book closed, I, in all my terrible flesh, would still be there.

I continued swinging, wondering if I could produce a shard that would half blind me; how easy it would be to miss the balanced log and drive the ax-head into my shin; how some beast could emerge from and drag me into the wood: anything other than going back into that house as I was. Then it occurred to me that we were finally in our proper places: they, inside by the fire; me, outside, laboring in the cold.

I worked faster, swung harder, sent the split wood flying apart. At some point, her mother stuck her head out, I'm sure to tell me that I'd done enough, but I ignored her. I'd thrown my coat onto the ground. She asked if I was cold, and the sound of her voice riled me. "No!" I grunted. I felt that if she didn't go into the house right then, I'd throw a log through the window. She did, but I still wanted to throw it, and when Michaele came out, I would tell her I was leaving.

Even growing up in their midst, I'd never really considered marrying, living with, or even dating a white woman. I found no inherent quality to them, nothing special about their visage or carriage. What I knew but couldn't as a boy articulate was that if I ever did fall for one, it wouldn't be worth it. It wouldn't be worth it for me. For them, I couldn't say. For me, white girls, women—and I don't really care for anyone's self-serving, revisionist history—have always invoked lynching. That history—oral, written, visual—has had a profound influence in the shaping of my, and I assume others like me, sexuality. It is another aspect of our diasporic pact—tacit and implicit—that we will not forget, and one to which we will never submit. It's a reminder of how cheap my life can be, how corrupt, cruel, and ambivalent the empowered are. It kept me perpetually vigilant. Though while knowing vigilance might afford me metaphorical readiness, it provided little protection in the world of men.

But my arguments against being with Michaele, against the possibility of there being an us, were all the by-products of my being tumidly invested in a cause. And as Baldwin tells us, "causes are always bloodthirsty." I didn't have their privilege, their power, their ownership of value, of morality. But victim or not, despite what I'd witnessed, endured, and the empirical proof I had that my world—our world—was fucked, despite that we were probably doomed either to split and then regret or go forward and suffer, I loved her. I loved her more than anyone I'd ever known. I chopped wood and repeated a mantra—*I love that girl. I don't care*—which over the last hour became *"She loves you . . ."*

I saw her in the doorway of the redwood house, propping the screen door open with her hip and shoulder. The smell of new ash. Smoke billowing out of the chimney. What could she have seen? Brown man, bare-armed in the red dusk. Steaming, ax dangling to one side. What could she have thought? It didn't really matter: faith. She loves me—*yeah, yeah, yeah, yeah.*

She wasn't pregnant. The nausea was due to a stomach bug, and her period commenced soon after. She seemed relieved, and I pretended to be as well, but privately I was crushed. I knew then that I wanted to be a parent with her. I trusted her. She made me believe that there was something in this world, this life, that was, perhaps, if we continued to love each other, within our reach—a condition that countered, outstripped, and, more importantly, outlived fear, rage, and sorrow. And I wanted to raise our child in love. My responsibility, my privilege, was to act as if we could live The Dream, within The Dream in which there was no place for my fear and anger—no matter who or what had caused it. To live in a land to love and be loved I knew began with forgiving—everyone. So, first, I went to see my father.

4

Abortion. Taxi. Michaele. New York. School. Stomach bug. Epiphany. Father. We still had the Honda Civic four-speed hatchback. I didn't mind driving long distances in it, which means my knee wasn't completely shot. We were still living in New York, and it must've been during our first tour—after the East Village, Brooklyn on Atlantic Avenue—although it could've been another time, another set of circumstances that I'll never accurately reassemble. But it was winter, sometime after threatening my father that I would kill him.

    I hadn't spoken to him in close to two years. But when I called to tell him that I was planning to visit the coming Sunday, he responded as if we'd been in regular contact. He was living in senior housing in Framingham, about twenty-five miles west of Boston. It's like many other northeastern suburbs: a highway running past it; an old highway, now a secondary route, cutting through it; shopping centers and strip malls the only points of interest. The backstreets are lined by houses, which, when I was a boy, would make me think, *Who lives here?* The first right off westbound Route 9 after the Mobil station, a quick left after that, and into the small parking lot that fronted the hamlet: four rows of two-story buildings, a place of exile, a place to die.

    My father was a *gentle* man. At least that's what I told myself. He was a drunk, a liar, a deadbeat, a cheat, and I'd seen him choke my mother and drag her out of the house. Once when I was seven, as a punishment for some transgression he'd asked me if I wanted a spanking. I told him no. He nodded, said okay, then started to weep. But he'd also forced me into corrective shoes and locked my foot braces to the bedpost at night to cure my pigeon toes. I have night terrors. I have sleep paralysis. I'll stir, howl or bellow. Eventually, I'll knock the demon off my chest, get to my feet, and wake up when starting to run.

He liked to reminisce about how special I was when I was very young. I do remember feeling special around him and it wasn't that I couldn't do wrong by him. It was that I wouldn't. But this was difficult. My father was also distant and cryptic—not cold, just away in some place of abstraction. He was monkish in his solitude, grotesque in his carnality. I listened to him quote, whistle, and hum. I watched him drink and smoke and screw—all without commentary or explication. Being with my father was both freeing and burdensome. Unlike my friends' fathers, the ones who stayed and instructed or abused as if they were Polonius or Santini, he never told me how to think or feel about anything—even himself, his dalliances, his failings. He left that up to me.

I parked beside a car that I knew must be his: a spent black Mercury sedan full of stuffed manila folders, newspapers, and clothes. I paused for a long while and wondered what I'd say to him. Each meeting with my father was like feeling out a stranger. I imagined mathematical problems with vectors and cubes; pencil sketches in the margins of legal pads and on the backs of envelopes; loud cracks, and baseballs flying over the green monster's netting; the river at dawn; the river at dusk; trumpets and saxophones and drummers sweeping brushes along snare drum skins. He could be so reserved, so quiet and pensive. I felt I had to coax him out of his head—what he was thinking, what he thought of me—in the same way I imagine people have tried to coax me out of mine.

But I wasn't that boy anymore, and those images, over time, changed for me. I saw the gleam from the tiered liquor bottles, smelled perfume in dense smoke, heard him warbling over cocktail chatter, grunting in the dark, the rasp of his jowls on someone's skin.

He buzzed me in without a word. One flight up, he'd left his door ajar. By the time I pushed it open, he'd retreated back into the room and was leafing through a stack of papers on a card table. He looked much older than I remembered, as though his rate of aging had accelerated over the last few years. If what he'd always claimed—that he was six feet tall—was true, he'd shrunk a startling amount.

After he moved out and came for Sunday visits, he wouldn't enter the house. He'd stand on the front porch and, while waiting for us to exit, survey his childhood home: the failing window and door trim and suicidal gutter; the knee-high grass, wild, shapeless hedges, and the black rose bush. My mother's contempt for him was severe, and she defended the house from him with it: moat, wall, and turrets. As the months passed, her hate intensified and his shame grew. He'd wait on the path, then the sidewalk, then in the car. Then he wouldn't show. Then he wouldn't call. In all the years since he left, this was the first time I'd seen any of his homes, and his apartment was close to what I'd imagined. There were stacks of newspapers, department store and supermarket circulars, clipped coupons for things he'd never buy. It smelled like old nicotine and grease from things he'd fried in the kitchenette in Crisco or butter and the visual remains of both—amber taint to the walls, the glowing television screen, everything through a haze of ash.

"You're still growing," he said crisply. "What are you now, six three or four?"

I responded flatly. "Seventy-two and one-half inches."

He nodded, fidgeted with the papers, then set them down. He still wouldn't look directly at me. I don't know what I'd been expecting, perhaps nothing to have changed, that we'd still, in our particular way, act as father and son, but something had. In the best of times I liked to believe that my blankness, which could make me seem like the epitome of equipoise, nihilism, or scorn, never troubled him—at least openly. At one time I believed that because we were so similar, he knew the places, inside, I'd go. Later, I thought he was so at ease because he didn't care. Now I hadn't any idea at all.

I do know that from my sophomore year of high school I'd changed. I would get openly angry with him. I would yell at him, jump out of cars at stoplights. Eventually, I shunned him. I refused to meet, speak on the phone, or acknowledge him when he tried to come see me.

Then he had a heart attack, and although I didn't want to at first, Michaele made me visit him in the ICU. She'd lost her father to one about three years prior and she knew I'd regret not going. I think she was shocked and frightened that I could be so willing to be cruel.

He'd been living on a friend's couch for months. But the woman couldn't extend her charity to house and care for a heart patient, so after he was discharged from the hospital he'd be homeless—at least until his social worker could find temporary housing for him before securing a permanent home. So I said he could come home with me. It was a terrible idea. His doctor had given me specific instructions about diet and exercise. I tried to make my father follow them, but I'd come home from driving my cab and smell bacon or fried baloney and eggs. The only exercise he'd get was walking down the hill to the Brighton Center superette for death meats and cigarettes. He rarely had enough money for anything other than these items, so he couldn't buy beer. I also didn't have a television, so by the time I got home after a twelve- or sixteen-hour shift, he'd be itchy and I'd be edgy.

Soon everything about him offended and then sickened me. Even when he washed the dishes or vacuumed the floors, the sight and smell of him, the way he clicked his loose teeth together made me want to smash his face. The worst of it was that he was sleeping on the floor in the enclosed porch of my second-floor apartment.

Eventually, we had an awful fight. While brandishing a chair over his head, I screamed that I'd kill him. He retreated to the porch and stayed there quietly. I called his social worker and told him that my father needed an apartment—today. He found him a temporary one. I drove him there, carried his things inside, and left without a word.

Now, though I'd come in peace, the way he looked at me, slowly shaking his head and grinning, suggested that he didn't think anything between us had changed.

He pointed weakly at my face.

"You get that from your mother. That anger."

"You don't get angry?"

"Not like that. I haven't seen many people who do." He stared into the past. "Whenever you'd get like that as a kid, no one could talk you down. You had an . . . *incendiary* temper. It would start off a slow burn in the walls. Maybe hours, maybe days. Then, wow." He paused. Smoked. Looked further away. "I thought when you got older, you'd get a handle on it." He smiled, nervously I thought. "But it got worse."

He pointed to the greasy kitchen. "You hungry?"

"No."

"Remember when I used to call you Hungry Horace?"

"Yeah."

"Yeah, I shouldn't even ask. You remember everything."

He wanted to go out, and I didn't want to stay, so we drove to the Steak Loft. He was eager to direct me there via the back roads so we wouldn't have to get on Route 9 and make a U-turn. He was smiling. He seemed happy. I was suspicious. I knew he'd want to show me off to his friends. I hoped that he realized I was too old to be his trick pony or dog. I wondered how many beers it would take for him to be able to sit still and listen to me—how many it would take me to ask.

The waitress, of course, seemed to know him well. "Hi Dave." I hated when people called my father Dave. Her face was narrow and delicate. Her skin was olive and her eyes dark. She couldn't have been older than me, but she seemed work-weary and gravely sad. She pointed at him. He nodded. She looked at me. "Bass." I thanked her. She smiled.

We sat for almost an hour drinking. We ordered food and moved it around our plates. We talked about the Red Sox, of course. He rarely spoke of the present or future. He reminisced aloud. I did so privately.

I used to make packy runs to the corner store for him. I was very young—six or seven—and sometimes they'd sell to me, other times they wouldn't. The Clemente boys had grown up with my father and had always been very kind and gentle to me whenever I went into their store. One time in particular, however, Mr. Clemente stared down at the Miller bottles, and when I asked him, trying to replicate my dad's voice, for a *"pack a Lucky's,"* he put his hands on his hips and slowly shook his head. "I can't sell you this." He picked up the six and went off to return it to the cooler in the back.

Mr. Clemente had been gone from the register for quite some time before I left the store and drifted dangerously across North Harvard Street. There was a commotion at the Merit gas station—where we never got gas, so we never got S&H Green Stamps and so never traded them in for fishing rods or train sets or baseball gloves. Two cops had a man at the pump. One pushed the end of his club into flesh just below the clavicle. He held it there, his partner at the ready on the left flank. The perp didn't seem all that menacing—no one I'd bother avoiding, now or then—just another flayed indigent on the avenue who, before the advent of bottle returns in the east, combed the sidewalks for other forms of income. Perpetually stooped at the waist—searching for something just beyond his stride. They took him down. It was too quick for me to see. I remember that thick, semi-hollow double thud, though. His chest and then his head. Prone, cuffed, and suddenly bloody, he barked something garbled. Then they had him up, but he was legless and dropped to his knees, so they dragged him to the car and threw him, face down, into the back.

"I want you to meet someone," he said after a pensive drought. And for a moment the two of us sat in our booth in the present. "Someone" meant either a drunken buddy or a girlfriend—sometimes both. On visitation Sundays, he'd argue for a particular restaurant. Invariably, after we ordered, he'd look up from the table, beam, then croon, "Hey kids, look who's here!" as though we knew her. "Slide over." Sometimes it would happen down the street from our place. She'd be leaning against the traffic light. "Hey kids, it's . . . slide over."

My mother, if she had any semblance of a romantic life, would never have flaunted it in front of her children. "He must think you all are slow," she'd hiss. "What the hell is he doing, anyway, picking her up at the corner like she was a streetwalker?"

My memory fails with faces: even after meeting them repeatedly, people always seem new. Rather than them all looking alike, one never looks the same. There may have only been a couple of women over the years; there might have been many. They were always white, and they were always of a similar look and disposition—an aging flight attendant or a hostess at a no-star pizza or steak joint with three-star dreams (the kind of places we went). They were always friendly, quick to compliment or laugh. They were always respectful, at least as respectful as someone who, as soon as he dropped us off, our old man was going to ball could be.

"Slide over . . ." Our server was standing at the end of the table, apronless and with three beers in hand. She looked very young and nervous. I felt sick and looked at him with disgust. He didn't notice or didn't care. "Slide over." I didn't.

"It's okay, Dave," she stammered. "I'll just pull up a chair."

We sat through an awkward half round. She finally decided to corroborate some of the stories my father had told her about me—the music, the poetry, the athletics, my photographic memory. It was a setup, as always. He liked to boast—exaggerate my abilities—and have me validate his claims. I wouldn't, however, jump for him anymore. If anything, I'd sabotage his plans, and rather than a wingman I'd be a cockblock for my father.

"So, you're a musician," she asked with a mild Boston accent.

"No," I responded, terse and Anglican.

"Well," my father offered, trying to match my snobbery, "he plays several instruments."

"Wow. How many?"

"Two," I said.

"You sure look like his son." She tried to mimic our speech.

People see what they need to see. They do it, I suppose, to keep that frayed narrative line that moors them to the earth from further unraveling. It's true, though. I do look like him, at least from the neck up, but only superficially in that if one were to do a line drawing of us from straight on, at the same ages, we'd be indistinguishable. I have the same cinderblock head, the same widow's peak. Filled in, though, we are quite different. My nose is a gift from both parents. In profile, I'm much more like my mother's line. I have her coloring—equal parts red and brown—and copper eyes circled by strange blue rings.

But these subtleties were lost on him, as I was his "spitting image." I didn't expect this woman to see them either. She studied me, squinting in that dim, awful light, then turned to him. I looked at my father, too. He hadn't yet had his open-heart surgery, so his chest was still intact as far as the Thomas chest goes: narrow, somewhat pubescent, to match the rounded shoulders, that hairy anachronism above his lip, and the dentures. I looked back to her. I couldn't believe she'd let my father touch her.

I wanted to punch him in his shrunken face, and my rising anger made me remember the epiphany that had brought me here to forgive him, the epiphany that made me believe I possessed some kind of refining—redeeming—power. That feeling was now gone. I was a prick. I responded to their questions in a cold, clipped way. And he looked at me in a way he never had before—befuddled—as though I were now the unreadable stranger.

He managed to compose himself and hide his uncertainty. We spent the next half hour leaning against the seat backs, heads cocked smugly to one side, smirking, gazing into the distance, exchanging quick jabs, quips, and quotes—each trying to outdo the other. She tried emulating us, but the best she could do was sharpen her consonants and shorten her vowels. Eventually, the beer, his health, his age, or any combination caused him to slow and falter, and I hit him with Horace:

"'Clogged with yesterday's excess, the body drags the mind down with it.'"

He didn't flinch. He didn't do anything for a while. Then he tried another tack. He made his face grave while looking down at the table, nodded, took a sip, leaned in, and murmured, "You seem down."

I paused, wondered, almost stayed quiet, but had to ape the poet: "'If you would have me weep, you must first of all feel grief yourself.'"

He sat back, then excused himself and left. I stared into nothing. She stood.

"It was really nice meeting you."

I turned slightly. She'd extended her hand. I stood, too.

"Good to see you, too."

"Yeah, right." She let her accent slip.

"Really," I said, trying to convince us both. She looked ridiculously sad. I wanted to ignore it. I knew, from past drills, that although my approval of my father's girlfriends was helpful in assuaging their guilt and shame, my scorn wouldn't stop him. If anything it would provide him with an excuse for saying goodbye: "My son hates me" is perhaps the best reason for a father to disappear. And I did hate him—so I let him, let her, be sad.

But I didn't hate her. She was, dare I say, sweet. While shaking her hand, and in the awkward silence that followed, I wanted, if I could do so without sounding like an idiot or insane, to tell her I was sorry.

"See ya around." I let my accent slip, too.

"Yeah?" She brightened.

"Yeah."

"So, you make it up from New York a lot. To visit?"

I didn't answer. I looked over to the bar. There he was, smoking, pretending whatever the bartender was saying was funny. Then, as if he knew I was watching, he met me with a wide grin and winked. I looked back to her. She was smiling, too, and with a sudden twist of my guts I realized that she was there for me.

We drove back in silence eastbound with the failing afternoon light. I wore my sunglasses because I was crying. He muttered and pointed, although he knew I knew the way. I pulled into the lot. I didn't park in a space but instead left the car running by the curb. He lingered for a moment, thanked me, and got out.

I watched him enter his building and then pulled around the parked cars to leave. I stopped, though, shut the car off, got out, and sat on the warm hood. I took off my glasses and watched the sky turn. It was a pale, melancholic rose. Because of the chill and the wintry light, I thought I should cry some more, but I couldn't. All I could manage were sharp exhalations, morbid grunts and chuckles, and the beginnings of ways to punish him. I wondered if he knew I'd been crying and if he did, how he felt about it.

I remembered different events and what I'd thought about them, but I couldn't remember how I'd felt. I didn't know why I'd gone so far from him and for so long. I couldn't remember ever being angry at him when I was a child. I couldn't possibly be angry with him as an adult. I knew the man's fall but only in part, and I'd never known his wrestling. And really, what had been mine? I couldn't understand how I'd become so rigid and vindictive. I thought about the music and the books, the traditions he'd introduced me to, and the wider world he'd always believed was out there and had pointed me toward. I wondered what it was like to see me now. I thought about why he'd left. Perhaps he'd spared me a greater hurt. Perhaps he was a hero to have left the son he loved.

I wasn't sad or angry when I left the parking lot, but I was numb from sitting in the cold. I still had a long drive ahead. It would be late when I got home. I decided I could be done with him. I found my anger again. Dark highway, shitty car, no radio: I had come by day to forgive and therefore redeem my father. I'd failed. And now I wondered if I could forgive myself.

5

About two years into our relationship Michaele's grandfather Cecil had asked her if she was serious or just fooling around. She might have been expecting the question but not how much it would hurt. I think she began to wonder then what life with me would mean. It was, perhaps, the first time she realized she'd have to make choices between me and them. The first would be how to respond to him—if she should do so. If she should tell me and how she should.

She was caught among the questions; either/or, yes/but, or yes/and: all of them and more. It can be a terrible condition—if you've been raised to believe that any one of those questions is worth answering or asking—loyalty to kin and kind or loyalty to self. Unlike the fulfilment of desire loyalty to the self isn't selfish—not if the self is part of something larger. And if people—any people—can't or won't see that they are part of something larger why does anything they think or feel extend beyond their person? For me, it was simple: I chose her. Not because I was without a family and a people, it was because—at my best—I knew that my people would never try to prevent my loving someone else. I wasn't disrespecting my mother. I wasn't a race traitor. I was free.

But I know it isn't easy. It rarely is for most. I think one of the two tragic intellectual failures in America is practicing dialectical thought in bad faith. Beginning and ending with the same conclusions, after asking others, literature, the law, and God is veiled didacticism. Its only aim is to corroborate one's personal truth. And personal truth is the abdication of social responsibility. There can be no collective social progress without individual responsibility. The other failure is that America's democracy, truth, and freedom is almost completely dependent on those it has failed the most.

Our country asks us to believe in it and trust in God but it offers nothing empirical to substantiate any belief and it doesn't practice a faith that has anything to do with spirituality. It relies on the good names and wills of individuals who try to live justly. Even partial participation requires self-abnegation. But of course, no matter what one does to oneself, the self is still there with all its fears and needs and pains—and love. It all doesn't just go away. You must constantly decide how to carry it.

What did—does—this have to do with us? It can seem so hard to love a single person that loving two people is impossible. I doubt Michaele's grandfather meant anything rude. And I know, because I'd already seen what she called angry, that their exchange was civil. She told him we were serious and discussing marriage. I can see him nodding and—so *British*—looking into the abstract distance. He then asked, "What about the children?" I don't think she answered, but I can see her cheeks flush to English rose.

When Michaele's extended family heard about his question, some called him a racist—though not to his face. Some thought him ignorant and backward; others thought him cruel. Some tried to comfort me by explaining that he was of another time and couldn't understand how wrong he was. One said that his mind was slipping: he wasn't like that.

Whether he was a racist or meant this, the basis of Western philosophical practice—their tradition and allegedly not mine—demands we consider the other. I don't mean indulgence in personal anxiety but rather deep and rigorous contemplation of ethics, mores, cultures, and practices derived from different experiences and points of view. But asking the privileged to practice fallibilism is to ask them to question their identity. To question their identity is to jeopardize their surety. They must then wonder if they have an identity or merely a series of attitudes. To question their identity is to question the origins of perceptions, beliefs, and following actions. To question like this—which is different than asking me why I'm in this neighborhood—is to threaten.

The question a cop asks with their Glock isn't a philosophical one. And while it may be philosophical to ask me why it happened—happens—it's not to question me if it really did; nor is it philosophical, or even humane, to question how I feel and think about it.

Threatened white people are either dangerous or they feel useless. And in crisis, which we always are, useless people tend to themselves.

Cecil didn't tell her not to marry me, or have children with me. Perhaps because he was too polite—too conflict averse. Perhaps he thought his granddaughter understood the Anglican unsaid. No one asked me what I thought. I don't know if I'd have been able to respond then. Now I'd ask if anyone had been harmed and if not then why the outrage. No one realized that he was the only grandfather I'd ever known. I spent afternoons sipping bourbon and watching golf with him, cracked lobsters at his summer table, took autumn tea in his living room.

Michaele was harmed though. And she was scared. She was scared for us, and I'm sure she believed that she'd either have to carry that fear alone or pass that harm on to me. I think she'd begun to consider what it might be like for me to be among them and subject to their many—what are now called—microaggressions. But I was more concerned with being murdered by the police while driving through their affluent suburbs than being slighted at tea. That would come later.

Cecil congratulated us when we got engaged a year later, and the tense white people relaxed—until his notebook was discovered and the section heading: "must rethink the negro." He'd watched Alvin Ailey's company perform *Revelations* on PBS and had been astonished by what he saw. He wrote of how awed he was by the beauty, power, and elegance of the dancers. It wasn't that he thought Black people weren't capable of such creation but that he was allowed to be privy to it and could be so moved.

Now some of his family seemed *harmed*, angry, and focused on shaming him. They wanted me to feel the same. All I wanted to do was shrug. Though I'd just turned twenty-five, I was feeling old, tired, and limited. I didn't want to spend any of my remaining intellectual or creative capital explaining—by lecture or proxy—that Cecil wasn't the problem. They were. Cecil, along with rethinking the Negro, was rethinking himself. Approaching ninety, he wondered if he'd gotten it all wrong. He openly tried to remember and talk to me, not about his failure to understand the Negro, but that Ailey and his company compelled him to ask himself if he'd failed his entire life.

He'd been too young to fight and die in World War 1. He was too old and also stateside for the Blitz. Because he was a second son, he didn't inherit his father's wealth. He blamed himself for the accident of his birth. He wondered if he'd been a bad father and hinted about the pain of burying his eldest son and his wife. I thought I sensed the pain of his loss—family and friends he'd never see again, places to which he'd never return. And he hadn't use for hyperbole: his personal pain and struggle was enough. When Baldwin writes, "Our suffering is our bridge," he means all of ours. Cecil's pain made mine real to him—or it began to do so. I think he realized that he could begin to "cease lamenting" and, perhaps, act.

He'd sought out Ailey. He put the onus of learning on himself. I believe he did it because he loved his granddaughter. And he loved me or wanted to. It wasn't that I was under probation after which I'd receive conditional status but that he had to earn the right to love me and be loved.

Cecil's personal alienation was the beginning of trying to understand my—my people's—lack of place in this country. There was no hyperbole concerning his personal pain—unlike my white, liberal contemporaries who couldn't seem to understand that my city, state, and country wanted me dead as a child and now a young man. Those same people—and people like them—who were outraged by racist behavior and were hurt when they hurt me expected me to forgive and forget (they are not the same and do not occur in lockstep) their innocence. And to trust them. What they didn't understand—though they spoke of their traumas and their triggers—was their ignorance of what happened inside me when I heard a siren, saw a cop. What they didn't understand was what I thought about a river, ditch, alley, or abandoned house—or prison. Or when I heard Curtis Mayfield exhorting, despite this, to "move on up." The rage and sorrow, the pride and joy, of what it is to know that I always had been and always would be truly beautiful, no matter how dangerous that knowledge is, that I was willing to die for that knowledge—not to learn, take, or grasp it but to let it be, inside and out. That is how knowledge can become wisdom. I see the line of my people. They are beautiful, and I am here because they loved me so.

And Cecil saw me *as this*: a young, gifted Black man who was menaced by white people and loved his granddaughter. Watching Ailey and rethinking the Negro, he saw the inheritance I was willing to share. Black love. Black beauty. Black joy. At his table, we were free. We sat in peace. And we laughed.

He died before he knew he'd have a great-grandchild who we'd name after him. I hope he knows I respect and love him, and I always will.

6

We got married August 28, 1993, on the thirtieth anniversary of the March on Washington and one week after my twenty-sixth birthday. In my vows, I addressed our guests with the importance of the day, why it had to matter to all of us. I asked them—the white people on Michaele's side, the Black and white on mine—to hold hands and consider what was happening and what it said about our past, present, and future. I think most people were moved save for a few of Michaele's white friends. They questioned my bringing politics to the altar. Some of her extended family implied that I was ready to be assimilated. And the Black man on the eve of the twenty-first century—still a problem—didn't "answer a thing."

We moved to Cambridge. Michaele started an MSW program. I enrolled in a free-form postbaccalaureate and did a lot of sneak drinking after she went to bed. We went out often or entertained at home. When we were with her old friends or new classmates, I had to drink or be evangelically dry. I don't blame my alcoholism on anyone or any group. I drank—or didn't—by choice. I felt I had to be extreme in their presence: Dionysiac to counter their rigidity, Apollonian to impose structure on their disorder.

But it wasn't only this. At school, I was working in the Black theater with Black people, producing Black plays. And Michaele was welcome in this collective in a way I would never be in hers. She didn't have to know our culture better than we; she didn't have to audition or perform. We were part of a community I hadn't been in since I was a boy—ever, really. I began to experience the counter to what I'd felt at the woodpile. If I trusted myself and waited I'd remember I was loved—and in love.

There seemed to be some pall over every gathering though, some specter at each feast that kept all of us—Black, brown, and white—on edge. Something was waiting to do us wrong. Hurt seemed inevitable. I couldn't write or say it then, but what troubled us was Whiteness. The stakes were different but no matter our race, religion, ethnicity, class, or gender we were all subjected to its power. And while it didn't *seem* to affect the white people in my life, it did. I suppose it's the belief that white people aren't oppressed by their own assumptions and attitudes that allows them to live in a constant state of criminality, guilt, innocence, ignorance, deservedness and justification.

It afforded the privilege of being obtuse and irreverent about their ignorance. Causality, responsibility, accountability, and morality were concepts by which to judge a government, an employer, a parent, or a peer who'd slighted them. They were codes of conduct for others rather than core components for the self. And they seemed to drift and jerk between selfishness and guilt. And guilt begat the right to self-pity, and self-pity excused them deep civil engagement. Rather than the state of their country, they seemed more concerned with the quality of their lives. The quality of their lives was in direct proportion to the depth and intensity of their fears. And in that, a moral life—even a theoretical one—was unattainable. Their great societal complaints became arbitrary. They'd suffer like that until they got bored. They'd quit acting, painting, writing, or playing music. They'd change partners, move, change or quit jobs, go to law school. You could see them, suddenly, relent to becoming the parents they allegedly abhorred. They accepted their inheritance.

Most of my Black contemporaries seemed set on combatting the Whiteness with Black art. Not all, but many, adhered to a late-twentieth-century version of negritude. Some tried to recruit me. Others thought me a pariah. I don't think they saw me as being white but rather a type of Black they didn't think relevant. I think, like most, that they considered me a threat—not because I openly challenged them but rather because I wasn't as invested in what they believed to be truth. I didn't conform to the Black aesthetics of the time.

My siblings reacted like many Black people of our generation had. My brother—four years older than me—had been gaslit, shamed, invalidated, conned, and abandoned, knocked loopy and sideways. When he lost his way, I can only speculate. But walking what he thought to be a straight and narrow line got him lost some more. He never found his way back.

My sister—who has always been among the most humble, gentle, and kind people I know—was partially paralyzed by "them": the white boys who wouldn't look at her, the white girls who had better clothes, our father who ignored her, our mother who terrorized her into thinking not only that lipstick and a date would make her a hussy but also that if she'd pay attention to her looks she might one day find a boyfriend. It was the bougie Blacks whom we'd always flummoxed, who'd almost—almost—convinced her that she wanted what they had and shamed her for not having—or wanting. She had an MFA but didn't teach and lots of good work but didn't try to show. She rejected her work and herself before she submitted it. When she neared thirty she stopped painting.

The Whiteness had demanded we hate and distrust ourselves. I thought I was too angry, recalcitrant, and—perhaps—obtuse to be affected. It enraged me that white people tried to define me, and it frightened me that a cop could kill me. I had the gift of being the youngest. I'd seen what had been done to my siblings. It wasn't going to happen to me. White people, the Black bourgeoisie—no one had anything I wanted. I was married to a white woman but she had chosen me and we belonged to each other.

We'd been together for six years and married for almost two. We loved each other but didn't trust each other. I can still only speculate why she was wary of me, but I knew why I was of her. In the months before, I'd been drifting away from Michaele. I'd lost the late winter—booze sick in the dark hours. It was hard for me ever to consume enough alcohol to stop withdrawal—the baseline being like a viral infection with a low-grade fever and aches. My mornings were extended headaches and a churning, bilious stomach. I'd try to counter it by chugging espresso-laced coffees followed by wind sprints on the side streets behind Central Square. My late mornings and afternoons were filled with attempts to seem normal. Maybe a sneak drink, but mostly a manic rush through work, school, errands, and then the gym to dinner, where I could, without question, have a few. I'd earned them. While she slept, I could drink.

I drank and, to a degree, also alienated myself from my people. I had to maintain enough privacy to be active without anyone knowing how sick I was. Alcoholism is one of our realities that is truly colorblind. It takes everyone.

My first months of sobriety were worse than my last months of drinking. I was still twitchy and miserable. Most days I woke with a dry hangover. I was woozy and light sensitive—all of the mental disorientation without the physical sickness.

When I ran along the river at dusk, my jingling keys reminded me of ice clinking into a rocks glass. When I drove home from an AA meeting, I'd stare at the neon liquor store and lounge signs and lose sight of the road. When I tried to focus on driving, cocktail glasses, like stock symbols, would scroll across the top of the windshield, and I'd have to pull over.

The vexing paradox of drunkenness is that alcohol helps to filter out the more extreme frequencies. Although I knew they were there, somewhere in the mix, the illusion—that there existed only a midrange—was essential. No shrill highs or dolorous lows, just a middling buzz. I could, to a certain extent, meet the dulled head of the world straight on. It was always easier for me to sit through a job interview (go to one for that matter), submit a poem to a journal, play my guitar onstage, talk to *anyone* at a dinner party, tolerate my family, or be still for my wife, drunk. Most of my life it seemed futile to try to live in an unmuted world: the present was grating, the future was daunting, and the past was full of menace.

Now, only a few months clean, white people appeared to me in a way they never had. I was present in a way I'd never been before. Lucid for the first time in my adult life, I realized—truly—why I couldn't trust the white people in my life. It wasn't that they were the ones killing and jailing Black people. Many of my friends railed against our country's racist atrocities: though they marched and donated and boycotted I knew they would never believe it had happened to me—stopped by two cops, detained by four, then surrounded by six. Cuffed, a shoulder disjointed, your skull seems dented and your brain is throbbing. Other than that, there's nothing going on—neither fight nor flight. All you can do is stupidly lick at the blood pouring from your nose. Then you're in the back of the wagon with boys and men who could be mistaken for you. It stinks—armpit, booze sweats, shit and pissed pants, fear and anger. The police are up front. You can't show your anger to them: they'll kill you. You can't show your fear: they'll press you till your fear turns to rage and then kill you. Or you're so afraid that you have to kill yourself. That it could easily happen again. For me, murder by police was just one stale green light away. When confronted with the fact that though they were generations removed from practicing brutality, there were still people—every minute, everywhere—ready to brutalize me, that the cops who *had* had the chance to lynch me weren't merciful but rather shrewd, my friends either wept and needed to be consoled—or called me a liar. I couldn't trust them. How could I trust them having anything to do with my child?

I got sober in March. We found out about Alex in June. Michaele and I had different reactions to the positive test result. Ever since she was a girl she'd wanted to be a mother. Now, though, she repeatedly screamed *"Shit!"* and demanded I return to the pharmacy for more tests of different brands.

    I ran to the CVS and bought four tests, ran back. I thought nothing of the baby, only of the mission. I stood next to her in the bathroom as we watched each confirm the first. She started crying and shaking her head. We hadn't health insurance, were moving back to New York, jobless, and would be paying triple what we were paying in rent. She wasn't only scared of having a child under these circumstances though, she was terrified of having a child with me.

The only older Black men with whom I could talk about fatherhood were in my head—and they were all dead. And since I could only imagine them, I could only imagine what they would say. I could talk to my closest friends about the absurdity of asking ghosts about the present and future, but that was all. The sum of our fathers' failures seemed to be the only material we could share.

But our child was coming. Forget the itching, the dry mouth, the hairy throat. Forget my mild aural and visual hallucinations. Forget them. Alex was coming. On a bright June morning, we went to the birthing clinic at Cambridge City Hospital. I felt, strangely, good. I couldn't think very clearly back then, and my diminished cognition served me—us—well. Rent was cheap. Life was simple. The days consisted of drives to see the midwife, the gym, or the fancy supermarket. I'd started eating meat again after a long vegetarian stint, and Michaele developed a taste for grilled sirloin, asparagus, and rosemary and garlic roasted potatoes. I set up a small Weber at the bottom of the back stairs. We cooked and listened to Marley and The Band playing in the front room.

We moved into that $1,500 apartment in Brooklyn, found jobs, paid COBRA insurance, and watched her transform—five miles of new blood vessels, and at all times, in all kinds of light and space, a radiant beauty and joy. Whatever doubts she'd had seemed to have faded. Her fear morphed into euphoria, but my *good* turned into fear. I stayed up for days. I refused food. I punished myself on the road and in the gym. I watched people—normal people—and tried mimicking their behavior, their speech patterns. I read the baby books. I prayed.

Michaele watched me struggle and tried to reassure me. "You won't be like that. You won't be able to resist this baby." And when I didn't seem convinced, she'd say, "You'll be fine. Both of you." Those months brought me closer to her. I was content to be still and quiet enough to feel our child kick and hear its heartbeat.

I realized I didn't have to trust her. I had to trust myself. I had to trust what I believed was right and act from there. If I was wrong, I'd admit it and I'd try again. Rather than searching time for offenses and harm I remembered how I did things right—regardless of how afraid I was of being hurt by her. I remember we'd been in the East Village a few months. We shared a lease, a bank account, a cat. We were broke and hadn't much to eat for dinner. She tried to hide it but she was worried and teary. I remembered when my mother used to pull boxes and cans from the back of the pantry shelves and unwrap the foiled contents of the permafrost. She'd always be humming one of her original compositions and we'd have a hot delicious dinner. So in Michaele and my kitchen cabinets I found Minute Rice, molasses, and brown sugar. We had some milk in the fridge. I called it "sugar milk stew." And told her that it was an old family recipe from the farm. I baked it in a CorningWare casserole. It came out looking bad—kind of a loose rice pudding. And we laughed. And it mattered who we were. It mattered how far we'd come to be there and what we'd brought with us to that moment—standing in the galley kitchen of our sixth-floor walk-up a modern dancer and a singer-songwriter. I wasn't going to touch that mess. But she got us two spoons. The first few bites were divine. The next—not so much. But we kept eating and laughing. That was over thirty years ago but I can still feel what it was like to be bound to this life with joy and in love. We didn't get through it. We made something of it. We achieved a kind of freedom. So I chose to be with her.

"*You'll be fine.*" Here was Alex: balls first, pale lilac and gray. We have pictures of his birth. It was an emergency C-section. My mother-in-law was allowed in the delivery room with us, and no one stopped her from snapping away with the camera. I was expecting a girl. It took me a minute to process he wasn't. *He's so light*, I thought as they wiped him down. And then he was in my arms. Then one of the nurses suggested his startling was a product of Michaele's drug use. Then the social worker repeatedly ignored our documented marital status and our rings. She needed our son to be a yellow bastard. There was the pediatrician we fired, the elite who, when she strolled with him alone, knew my mother was the ol' Black nanny. I'd made those white people shiver on the dusky streets, but now with Michaele and Alex, they smiled.

It didn't matter. I'd hold him for hours and never get tired. I wasn't some unfeeling machine or nursery prop as I'd imagined I might be. I'd make up reasons to take him out—emergency runs for a gallon of milk or a pound of coffee. We'd wander through Brooklyn and take the long route to everything. It felt good to keep him close. It felt right that I needed to do so. If he were sleeping, he'd stay asleep. If he were awake, he'd watch me—dusky boy, with the soft curls, hidden by his striped cap.

Because I was so accustomed to temporary states of self-medicated ease—the few hours afforded by the buzz or rush from booze or adrenaline—I kept wondering how long this one would last. But it stayed, or I stayed with it or in it. I felt free. I had no father, no past. There was my wife, our son, and me: him napping in the afternoon sun, waking us in the early morning—wide-eyed—cooing. It was the first time I had lived without dread. I don't know exactly when it happened or how or why, but sometime, somehow, I became a father.

7

He was the first child—first grandchild—on both sides. His early years are well-documented, both in photographs and in memory. They, for me and—I hope—for us, were good ones. They were simple. Our needs were basic and similar—love, giving and receiving. My love kept him safe. His love rescued me, brought me back from the margins. I could wash him. I changed his diapers. I could speak in calm, soothing ways without trying to manipulate or lie. I'd find myself rubbing his back or arms or singing quietly.

He had straight black hair. It grew in strangely—a tufted Mohawk or rooster crop. At first, he was long and thin, then plump. Then he stretched out again and grew thick, dark brown and auburn waves of hair. His face became, essentially, the face he has now. The best I can describe him is as copper that changes with the comings and goings of each season. Alex has enormous eyes and a wide mouth, and they function in an inverse way. When he smiles, his eyes close. When he opens his eyes wide, his mouth rounds to a small circle. There's a picture of him walking with my father, pointing to something beyond the frame.

I worked in a restaurant then, and most nights I wouldn't get home until three or four in the morning. Michaele would have to leave for work by eight, and—fatigue stupid—I'd have to manage a toddler who howled as though his mother were leaving for good.

I'd take him into the kitchen, put Marley on—"Three Little Birds"—and hold him while swaying and humming until he calmed. We'd eat breakfast, then turn the TV on in time to watch *Little Bear*. I'd doze off, and he'd wake me by pulling on my sleeve.

We'd go out and roam the city. I only had one close friend with a child, but she worked, and the nanny didn't like me very much. The only way I could stay awake would be to keep moving. Most days we'd cruise around our neighborhood, stroller packed with enough diapers, snacks, drinks, and first aid for many children for many days. Some days we'd get in the car and drive into Manhattan to the Central Park Zoo or downtown to the Village, wandering the streets, stopping in bookstores, killing time until lunch. We'd luxuriate in diners with plates of scrambled eggs and fries. One of our favorites was Two Boots pizza in Alphabet City. Once he spilled a large glass of my soda on himself. It was cold outside, and I needed to dry his clothes before we continued our wanderings, so we went to a nearby laundromat. I stripped him, wrapped him in a blanket, and washed and dried his clothes while reading to him.

I see him in the Washington Square Park playground, fifteen years after my friends and I used to drive from Boston to buy drugs or find a quiet place to drink, stare, and listen to the downtown night. A hot June afternoon, he's sixteen months old, naked except for a diaper and sandals. I can't remember if the animal sprinklers are seals or turtles, but they're spraying water. He teeters in and out of the spray. He's only been walking for a few months and tiptoes as though he knows how treacherous the slick asphalt can be. The other children dart in and out of the shower and he flinches when they get too close. I want to rush to him, hold him up, shield him from those who don't seem to fear the imminent danger—without regard for other legs and skulls. The other parents urge their kids into the fray. The nannies chat on benches. Except for them, we're the only dark people. Shy brown boy among the others, he moves cautiously—arms up to balance.

It's one of the last times I remember in which my past didn't directly inform my relationship with my son, before I began to—once again—return to what I'd tried to reject. Before he began to apprehend what being bound to me meant, when we were still okay.

Two summers later, we stood on a Brooklyn corner with a white family—a friend of his and the parents—waiting to cross. The light changed, but a police cruiser blocked the crosswalk. The driver looked over to us. "Wave to the policeman, boys," the mother of the other child directed. The two boys obliged. The cop smiled and waved back. I took Alex by the wrist and lowered his arm. He looked up at me. I shook my head, then stared at the cop. He stared back with equal loathing. I wonder if the other family knew what happened or if it was our secret. This first time I asked him—*told him*—to choose between them and me.

Now I can't look at pictures, think of those times, without feeling regret and shame. When I put an album down, when the memory fades, I'm left with the lingering surety that I've done him wrong. Coupled with these feelings is the knowledge that I've had many chances to stop, to remember the early days when we were free. I could've tried harder to keep him free, divested of that poisonous capital that, perversely, kept me alive. It had accrued over time and now I had something to protect. Let them come for me as they'd come before, and I'd pay them no mind: *"Walk right through them."* I believed I couldn't be redeemed and therefore could no longer be harmed. But they were coming for my son, and all the while the white people in his life would ask *"Who?"*—as though my fears were unfounded. Somehow, they discounted the man before them. I was formed—caught, twisted, released, and left wandering along the edges of this mad America. Somehow what I'd seen and felt, in spite of all they knew about our country's bloody past and present, wasn't, in their minds, real.

I too would like to believe that what I've witnessed is divorced from past and future events, that personal and collective experiences are actually discrete. But how can one segregate what a police force means to a Black community and a Black person, what the police, as both individuals and a collective institutional power could, *would*, do to me, my brother and sister, *my brothers and sisters*—from tailing me as I lugged my backpack and bass clarinet home from school, to splitting my "black faggot" head open on the hood of their car. All the times I've fit the description—the years, the bodies, from Birmingham to Soweto. And now, in New York City—from Amadou Diallo to Sean Bell and the litany before, between, and to come, why would I want my son to wave? Why would anyone, regardless of origin, wave?

And yet I still asked rhetorical questions to myself because I still hoped someone would tell me that they knew we were still living in a divided world, peopled by many who with certainty wanted to widen those gaps or eliminate those who inhabit the other side. And we—my family—were a divided house but not in the same way. Michaele and I came from such different worlds that to speak of us as a collective—as a whole—was false. Individually, we were a strange quasi-amalgam of late-twentieth-century America: spiritual but secular, apathetic social activists. She grew up relatively wealthy, although next to many of her schoolmates she felt like a pauper. Upon my first seeing her childhood home, I was simultaneously awed and appalled. I grew up poor—foreclosed home to public housing. But relative to most poor people I knew, I had great privilege. My father, in spite of his failings, was a college graduate, and he expected at least as much for his children. My mother always figured out a way to keep us enrolled in the best available schools. She had a vision of a future for her children beyond the cramped confines of our present world. She tried, every day, to make that vision real.

Where we arrived—a substantial leap for me and a plummet for her—was a tenuous class compromise. We teetered on the edge of financial disaster. For an artist and the child of an artist, who for different reasons were raised to disdain money, it was cruelly ironic that this is what we spent so much of our time thinking about. The difference, though, is that she was intimidated by wealth, bullied by materialism, and as many are, no matter how many times they've encountered the beatitudes, was jailed by the pernicious idea that one's morality is somehow attached to one's bank account. The pile of bills on the kitchen counter, the unknown callers and 800 numbers that made the home phone frightening. They either angered or amused me—or they passed below my notice. High-mindedness, although financially impractical, so I thought, lessened the psychological impact caused by creditors' responses to delinquency.

But the most obvious division in our family was racial. Perhaps one of the reasons we stayed together so long is that we tried to at least acknowledge the gaps between. At our best we recognized that we couldn't claim any certainties about our commonality—our difference. In the urban Northeast our demographic is growing—common almost. But that doesn't mean it's mundane, not in our house, because it—this difference—must be respected. Over the twenty-five years we were together, we sometimes came to realize that we could never assume a unity about how we negotiate the world, how it perceives and affects us. We recognized the divides but did not attempt to name them or what dwelt within them. The only thing we could do is reach down into them, lay our bodies across them, because within and on both sides, our children were growing as foreign to us as we sometimes were to each other.

We are, as a family, unnamable, irreducible. Our children are called brown, white, mixed, biracial, and other, but each label points away from what they are and are not. Simultaneously rich and troubled, witnesses and bearers of the familiar and the strange, in spite of, because of, with no regard to the color of their parents' or their own skins. We are confused and unsure, but our struggle isn't to arrive at certainty. It's, rather, how to live without it, because in certainty is bias, and in bias is dichotomy, and dichotomy is a lie.

Alex feels this more than his younger siblings. He's the most aware—has always been—of his identity or his lack of a defined one. And because he constantly thinks about it, asks the question of me and to himself—*What am I?*—he's the most confused by it, too. "People ask me what I am," he's said. And he lists for the inquirers the different lines that have converged in him, but "They don't seem to understand." On separate occasions three white family friends called him "mulatto." When I asked them why they used the word they responded in three different ways: one was immediately apologetic and too embarrassed to answer. The second used that awful intonation one employs when trying to make a declaration interrogative. The third was annoyed by my question. "It's just a word," he said, as though exhausted by the conflict he thought was to follow.

"Well, what is he?"

"An American boy."

"Mixed?"

"I'm mixed."

"Your father was white, right?"

Each birthday, every Christmas, friends and relatives took care to give him politically correct toys, games, and books—not too white, not too radically Black—that they thought to be melanin appropriate. I let this pass without comment, but I'd be damned if anyone tried talking to him about race: I knew that no one knew what to say. Very few people I knew thought about race in a manner that wasn't convenient or advantageous to them. On both sides of the color line, most theories are self-serving. They assume either humbly or with arrogance a superiority—a certainty. The difference between Black and white being the power and precedence that comes with being white. From white supremacist to Black Nationalist and those in between, most American notions I'm familiar with are insane. They are rooted in an illusory sureness. Their proponents assert an actuality they want or need. These theories engender identities: philanthropist, avenger, or victim. They don't consider that their desire for a favorable conclusion skews the lens through which they observe (or ignore) the data so they can feel good and right.

I couldn't trust white people with my child because they seemed vested in him being more than a child; the *idea* of him was cleansing and healing. But these projections were those of lazy, foolish cowards who, in truth, desired to be led into the waters of the river Lethe and in them be baptized.

My in-laws, on some level, would now have to deal with color on an almost permanent basis. I didn't want Alex to hear it. I didn't want to hear it: the paranoid lament of the eternally wounded and their capitulation to futility or the treacly platitudes of those who, although they refused to admit it—because it was their privilege, their right to *know*—knew nothing, save their oblique need to pardon themselves, weakly, of the West's greatest, longest crimes, slavery and segregation, and all the profits gained, the accrued wealth received by those whom the peculiar institutions benefited, and because of a specific inheritance, still do.

I didn't want to politicize my child—nor my relationship with him. I just wanted to be his dad. But the white people who wanted to claim him as their own hadn't any means or methods to protect him in the world in which they were trying to indoctrinate him. They didn't even know that they couldn't protect him from themselves. Their way was capitulating to entropy—the Whiteness. Even his mother couldn't understand that the places she wanted to take him I simply couldn't follow. I couldn't unsee what I'd seen, unknow what I knew. It wasn't safe. I had to be the cold fish, with my son watching. They got me. They would not get him. If I couldn't protect him, I'd prepare him—no matter the cost to either of us.

When he was about four, Alex began to be troubled by the fact that he might be brown. His white schoolmates started asking him unanswerable questions. He was teased by some. Along with this, he sat through curriculums that introduced him to various historical figures, all of whom were white. But it was more than these local pains. He seemed to have a premonition about what it would mean if he weren't white.

His discovery seemed to take place over time in both the public and private spheres. Although his awareness was gradual, I couldn't help but think about W. E. B. Du Bois's sudden realization—his valentine spurning—or of fictional characters like James Weldon Johnson's X-colored man, who's suddenly jerked from the first world to the third; or Hurston's Janie—Alphabet—who can't identify herself in a photograph, but when she's pointed out utters the regret "Aw shucks, I'm colored."

For Alex, that realization was more like a slow epiphany. The awareness of meaning, or God, in everything, came to him like adult teeth: meaning, rather than illumination, was more like a passing shadow; that God—like Jonah's, eternally dogged—hardly merciful.

As much as he struggled with his racial identity—what it would cost him—he began to embrace brown people. His allegiances ran counter to what he at times sought to reject. When we watched sports, he'd root for the Black pitcher, quarterback, or coach. He wed their local struggle—to win—with the larger struggle to be free, a burden they shared. He found, through the TV screen, kinship with them or at least witnessed, from the relative safety of the shore, those who were in the big sea—neither hiding below the deck of a storm-tossed ship nor in the belly of the whale, nor adrift—but moving confidently through it. He conflated his bourgeoning awareness with them and assumed, whether it was true or not, that they were aware of and grappling with the same things as he. And he was sure they'd win.

As a boy I had many heroes—from Jim Rice to Achilles—who I tried, without much success, to emulate. The right-handed slugger's swing, the warrior's rage. Frederick Douglass was one of them. I'm not sure which came first, me trying to mimic the diction and syntax of his speeches and prose, or if a voice like his existed in my head before I knew of the man. I sounded absurd. But since I was an absurd child with a penchant for mythic, transcendent language and thought, whether or not it was inherent I kept that voice as my own.

Douglass served me well: his purpose, his legacy. He was the perfect synthesis of courage, erudition, and rage—genteel in manner, inspirational in oration, brutal with his hands. When I thought about him, life had a purpose. He helped me form at least a temporary identity. Black people questioned my racial loyalties. I was often called an Oreo or *honky-nigger*. They'd mock how I spoke, and I'd tell them I sounded like the baddest, Blackest man this side of Nat Turner. Sometimes my white friends would refer to other Black people with epithets and rather than apologize or retract, they'd explain that I didn't seem Black or that I really wasn't Black. I'd tell them that my mother was from the Jim Crow South and had seen the burnt cross firsthand, that we lived in public housing, that I was yet to meet a cop who was impressed by my linguistic facility, and that not a single quotation from the Western canon nor my deathless devotion to all of Boston's sports teams would grant me safe passage through Charlestown, Rosi, or Southie—not even the bleachers of Fenway.

By the time Alex was six, he was ready. I was ready. I'd gotten him the abridged version of *The Narrative of the Life of Frederick Douglass*. His brother Miles was three, and after he'd heard his story, Alex and I would sit on the floor and I'd read to him. I'd read the unedited version when I was his age and remembered how it had the unbalancing power of being both familiar and strange, near and far. Alex would stare at the pages, perhaps envisioning the deep clefts in the author's feet, the fields full of dark people, Master Aaron Anthony standing on the porch or walking past the slave quarters, ignoring him. Perhaps Alex saw old Baltimore: the glyphs and ciphers young Frederick scrawled in chalk on the cobblestone streets, Lucretia Auld's cruel transition from educator to slaver, the inches given by good Christian folk and the els taken by niggers.

While reading about the blessing and the curse of literacy and knowledge, I couldn't help but think of Baldwin's words in his short story "Sonny's Blues" concerning the danger of children who know too much too soon. I wondered what conflations were occurring in Alex's mind—whether or not the characters in the book had likenesses in our contemporary world. Was it too much? Parenting, as anything else, requires balance. How much you tell your child and when you tell them—their preparation—can either shackle or liberate them. In America, being the parent of a Black child requires that an equilibrium is struck: the world you and your child inhabit is underpinned by the manual and cultural work of your ancestry, and in part, those contributions, if not celebrated, are certainly obvious. They are undeniable. I feel great pride—Black pride—because of this history, this present day, the potential: *"up ye mighty people"* and this pride can be an incredible force that drives both the individual and the collective forward. This pride is an outgrowth of the underpinnings.

There is, of course, the counterpoint: the bodies—the millions of bodies—which are also our foundation. The other feeling, perhaps equivalent to the achievement-based pride, is that my country wants me dead, if not dead then erased or assimilated. For any Black person who has ever subsisted on the hope that they would, on their own terms, have the right to move through their country with dignity without fear of retribution, such acquiescence to their own disappearance is the same as choosing to be a ghost.

What am I? The question had been coming since that day at the woodpile.

"You're many things." He looked at me in a distant, unknowing way. "You're the descendant of slave and slave master."

He climbed up to the top bunk and lay atop the covers.

"What are you?"

"The same . . . sort of."

"What would you have been, back then?"

"A slave."

"What would I have been?"

"A slave."

He saddened. "Because of you?"

"No."

"Because of Mom? She's not a lot of things, is she?"

I told him about our lines: the history of the Fowlkes, the Allens, the Millers, and the Browns, the Thomases. I told him about Virginia—how my mother had been born only a few hours' drive from the Anthony plantation. I told him how Douglass, in spite of what he went through, married a white woman. I told him that although he was one of our nation's greatest sons, he spent much of his free life in exile; how a man with a mind like his, unfettered from the absurd need to argue for his humanity, could have done great things; how many people with great minds had forgone what they'd desired—their private dreams—or risked what they had so that we could be free; free to be who we needed to be; who we must be—our one true, inalienable right. We were free to choose, free to pay the cost for that choice, free to define ourselves. He could be what he wanted, claim both worlds—all worlds—without fear or shame. *"We, all of us, are so much more than our color."* And when I looked to him for an answer or another question—some kind of response—he was asleep.

8

Alex and I watched most of the major sports. We were loyal—for all the obvious reasons—to the Red Sox, the Celtics, Patriots, Bruins, and Tiger Woods. But in soccer we were loyal to a country, and it couldn't be any one but Brazil.

J. C. Thring's mid-nineteenth-century rules for football call it *"The Simplest of Games."* A century later, Pele named his autobiography *My Life and the Beautiful Game*. And in the Brazilian Portuguese *joga bonito* means *play beautiful*. It is my team from childhood—there was no American team to speak of, and even if there had been, I'm not sure I would've privileged them over my adopted country. The names were almost enough for me to swear allegiance: Manoel Francisco dos Santos became Garrincha—*Little Bird*; Arthur Antunes Coimbra, Sócrates Brasileiro Sampaio de Souza Vieira de Oliveira, or simply, Socrates—doctor of medicine, doctor of philosophy, master of the backheel. I remember watching one of his and Zico's teams refrain from scoring a goal that wasn't beautiful. I'm not sure if this is a real memory, but others I've spoken with corroborate this happening.

Regardless, a well-crafted goal—or no goal—can be beautiful. The way teammates share the ball, trade positions, seem to find, as a group, space in which to move where there seemed to be none. At its best, the series of horizontal and back passes can be hypnotic, like incantation, a slowly gathering leitmotif. We know what the desired result is, but the process, because of the discipline, the nuance, becomes as important as the end result. The celebration of the dance: the dance has a beauty of its own, the beauty of tension, of uncertainty and the beauty of faith. Believing in an end that's out of sight.

My father didn't acknowledge the game and though I started playing at six, he didn't ask me anything about it until I was almost fifteen. He never watched a game. I still love that he didn't. Soccer had helped me socially integrate into the private and then affluent public schools I attended. The club teams helped me even more so. I didn't have to speak. I just had to be good. I could make that space my own field of action. The rules allowed for dynamism. I felt I could safely be me.

Alex started playing when he was four. He quickly became very good at trapping, passing, and sharing. He was hesitant to dribble and more so to score—as though both were selfish acts. Though he played baseball (as did I) I like to believe that he apprehended that because it was so static, it was perversely un-American.

He loved the Red Sox because I loved them and because they were tragic. He watched Brazil because I watched, but I don't think he loved them because of me. They were fucking awesome. Though I ridiculed people's need to do so, in that team he saw himself. Alex looked like the great right back Cafue and he would go on to play the same position of the Verde-Amarela's captain until he was thirteen.

One of my happiest memories I have of him as a boy is watching the 2002 World Cup. We were at a bed and breakfast the day after a wedding ceremony. We were the only brown people. They loudly cheered for Germany and mocked Brazil's style of play. Alex and I sat among them but they didn't seem to notice. We both stayed quiet. When Ronaldo scored the second goal Alex stood, unzipped his sweatshirt, and revealed his National Team shirt—canary with the green number 9. He celebrated the goal just like the great striker did—hand aloft, head down, and lips slightly parted. He ran through the inn with unabashed joy.

When he was hurt or scared he came to me. Perhaps because his pain didn't frighten me. We laughed together. We ate junk food together. After dinner I'd make up stories and he'd stay still and listen. We did nothing together. It was all good.

It could turn though. I could turn. Sometimes those old problems rolled in and I was back where I'd been. But it was different. I was different. I was only in my early thirties but without that youthful dynamic anger felt like a hardened, brittle, bitter edge. We lived in a rapidly gentrifying neighborhood and he went to school with the children of some of the wealthiest people in New York. Few of my Black and brown friends were married and none of them had kids. I felt alone in a way I never had. My loneliness made me feel needy; the neediness made me feel weak. My weakness made me afraid. I could feel suddenly desperate—for money, a future. I had two degrees and not a damn thing to do with them.

In that state of desperation I'd try to love and protect Alex. The only way I thought I could do that was to teach him how not to be lonely, desperate, or afraid, which meant he couldn't be weak. He had to read better, calculate in his head faster. He had to walk straighter. And if he felt physical pain, anxious, tired, or afraid he couldn't show it to anyone—certainly not anyone white.

For *they* were no longer coming: they were here. They weren't going to do to him what they'd done to me: they were going to take him from me. My lifelong fight with the Whiteness had been called a long time ago and it had been a slaughter. I couldn't remember holding him. I couldn't remember ever having felt right.

But that doesn't mean I was wrong. They were going to try to take him and there wasn't anything I could do about it except get him ready. This is of course all hindsight. And the accuracy of the backwards look depends on one's present state of mind.

I feared my son's fear. I'd never been able to allow myself to truly be scared. I didn't know what to do with it. I wanted him to know he was better and be better than it. This must've been horrible for him. The more I thought of my failings the more I demanded that he have none. I didn't make these demands because I thought I was better than anyone. I did so because I felt I was worse. I was so noble. I'd only defended—and usually with a hidden, smoldering disdain—my individual notion of aesthetics. I wasn't a civil rights lawyer or an animal rights activist. I was at best a brooding malcontent who possessed a temperamental twinned gift of vision and language. Something, when closely examined, I'd never used for the greater good but instead as a thin shield to protect me from all social mandates. It was grossly unfair to demand that my son be like me—*that* would be the negation of any notion of progress, more so that he do the things that I could not, would not. He couldn't and cannot take it. He must have felt between at least two worlds—mine, which he could enter only at extreme cost and his mother's which, I'd excoriated—and that he wasn't good enough for me but too good for them.

I kept finding new fears and new anger. In addition to the battles of race and class, there were physical dangers, too. In a way, I realized them before he was born. When he did come, I'd stand over him in the night for hours to make sure he was still breathing or didn't somehow disappear. There was a short list of people I'd let hold him and a shorter list of those with whom he could be alone. Rather than easing, my fears grew alongside him. Michaele tried hiring a part-time babysitter, but when I'd leave for work he'd have such a look that I couldn't leave him with her. I'd take both of them with me or escort them through the day until Michaele got home to relieve me and, with apologies, send the sitter home.

I feared for his safety. In one picture he's five, in uniform after one of his first soccer games. He's on my shoulders. I remember putting him down so he could ride his scooter—slowly and not more than a few yards away—to the car. A young man on a bike approaches too fast, brakes too late, and bumps Alex onto the sidewalk. Alex hops back up, unharmed, but I snarl at the biker. His friends ride up and are ready to defend him. I let them know that they'll all be eating soup for weeks to come.

In another picture, I'm shaving and he's doing the same but with a toy razor. I place mine on the medicine cabinet's top shelf and leave the bathroom for a moment. When I return, he's kneeling in the sink. I yank him out and sit him on the toilet. He cowers. I know he only wanted a closer look at himself, but in my mind I see his skull cracked by the fall and him bleeding out from his slashed throat.

When I realized that I couldn't protect him from all the danger, I knew I had to prepare him to either avoid it or defend himself—a kind of mother wit from the father. But my hypervigilance drills made him dread those lessons as much as the alleged dangers. He couldn't walk, read, or latch his seat belt fast enough for me. I cringe now when I think of the hot lectures he endured about the importance of mastering—everything. *Don't be weak. Don't be slow. Don't be scared.* While he might not have internalized my mistrust of others, when meeting people—adults or children, strangers or friends—he'd first look to me before making eye contact with them. Then he'd mimic my stoic affect—at the ready, prepared for any threat or insult.

I knew I was wrong, but I compounded the injury by repeating the offense. Orwell writes that "an effect can become a cause, reinforcing the original cause and producing the same effect in an intensified form, and so on indefinitely. A man may take to drink because he feels himself to be a failure, and then fail all the more completely because he drinks." I was, though *sober*, that drowning drunk: up once, down again; up twice, back under; up three times—each time with more water in my lungs.

If any good came of this, it was that I made it easier for him to reject me, but anytime I felt him doing so, I clutched at him more. Instead of freeing him of his inheritance, I burdened him with it. Instead of guiding him, I'd marooned him somewhere between Black and white, privilege and deprivation, thought and action, desire and spasm, old and new, broken and whole.

I couldn't be sure that I felt any danger, but rather, theorized it. Yes, there were dangers; children were poisoned and snatched. They tumbled down stairs, dropped from balconies and suffered what seemed irrevocable damage. This intensified my need to be closer to him, but closeness for me initiated thoughts instead of feelings. Thought is abstract. Abstraction is distant, and I compensated for distance with fundamentalist presence. There seemed two obvious choices for the son of an absent father: be absent himself or be smotheringly present. I chose the latter, and whenever I felt myself sink—heavy with the knowledge of what I might be doing to Alex—I was buoyed by a sanctimonious pride that I, unlike my father, could be present for my son.

Sometimes presence is a failing. There was hubris to mine—that I possessed something I could bestow upon my boy. I was full of ideas about his edification. In my mind, at my best, I was a potent distillation of the West. This was good for lectures, for art, for *objectivity*. I walked as both Prospero and Caliban. And while these qualities may have made for an interesting dinner guest or a good statesman or artist, they made for a lousy father.

From the outside, what I was doing looked like great parenting. Those who heard me speak or read what I'd written about my children believed that any elegance of oration or pen was an extension of my parenting. This wasn't so: I spoke well, but that didn't mean I was well. At times I'm still troubled by the possibility that my children, especially Alex, would be better off without me. While I'm similar to the man I was when he was a baby—physically present—my function seems to be to imbue him with Spartan practicality. The irony, and this is my greatest fear, is that I don't see him. I don't know him, other than in the abstract; and abstracted children are easy to raise, their fears are theoretical, their pain is metaphorical, their needs figurative, and their future—their great potential—is whatever you want it to be. I know now that as abstract as he was to me, I was real—solid—to him, in all my terrible flesh.

In the same way my memory meanders to past events, so does my language with particular subjects. I sound diffident, even coy, when answering questions like: What happened? I don't mean to be, but finding some agreement in me, settling the unstill components of time, place, and words and searching for the appropriate larger story to allegorically connect my own (because who wants to hear the myopic narrative detached from history and tradition?) feels like my poor attempt at alchemy: I've little knowledge of what combining these elements will do, and I've little faith that the result will be anything good.

It's ironic: I tell my students, "Don't write around the subject: write to it." I tell my family and friends, "Just ask it. Just say it." But I don't hold myself to the immutable rules that I've declared for others—except when I'm angry. *What happened?* I know I can always rationalize my anger in terms of race and class. There's more than enough—personally and collectively—to support any claim I make. I have been physically and psychologically maimed: I ignore what ignored me. I reject what rejected me. I now shun the Boston neighborhoods I once feared. There are street addresses, coffee shops, and restaurants I continue to boycott even though the venues have turned over more than once, and their original racist owners are now long gone. I scrutinize every store I enter more than its detectives could ever do to me. I hover outside of parties and literary functions—even my own—chin forward, clenching my fists and grinding my teeth. Even walking past a bar, it's not the booze that makes me tense but the presence of rednecks or frat boys. There are institutions I've barred myself from, contests I won't enter, fellowships I won't apply for. There's food I won't, even privately, eat. I continually scan the road behind me for state troopers. When I look in the mirror, my frame seems twisted. My left shoulder is pushed forward; my right, back. There's no symmetry—shape, size, or length—to my arms, because of different violent handcuffings: walking while Black, driving while Black. I will never have these things fixed: no surgery, no therapy, because even twenty years after the last insult, I won't give those motherfuckers the satisfaction of knowing that it hurt. I never used to care what it cost me.

There was something else, though—some brackish feeling in me that made my guts seem like a mire. With Alex, it would take me over whenever he strayed too far. It was segregated from my racial agenda, as though in an alternate arena, another ocean, a different hunt was going on. But if I were Ahab there, too, I hadn't any galvanizing powers. I was without the resource of vengeance. Here my frenzied mission was to run: the whale was hunting us.

I'd have the same sick feeling when he got too close. I'd brace myself. I know he could feel it. I know it frightened him. I could hold him but only in a practical way—after an ankle twist or out of the car and up to his bed if he'd fallen asleep during a drive back home. There was no warmth to my embrace, and he seemed equally chilled. Rather than trying to remedy it, I got colder, more rigid, so as not to feel the growing gap. I remember being jealous of those who could be affectionate with their children, though most of the time I convinced myself that their cooing was vapid, contrived, sickening.

He grew more beautiful with each birthday: longer, more deeply hued. By the time he was seven, I could only look at him secretly, from a distance, because I always felt when doing so that I'd fall apart. And I'd be sure to move too quickly for him to be able to look at me.

It was summer. He was seven and a half. I was about to turn thirty-six. I'd given up film and was willfully being exploited as an adjunct at Hunter College. It was a job I once swore I'd never work, a place I'd sworn I'd never return to. I was writing a novel—*Man Gone Down*—something else I'd sworn against. Though I hadn't an agent, and I hadn't any sincere plan to sell it, I was doing it for the money.

Alex and his younger brother Miles had been in school full-time, but our youngest, Ella, wasn't. We'd hired a full-time nanny so Michaele could work at the school in the hopes of getting remission—our only hope of keeping them in—but at $24,000, we were losing money. We'd spent what we had on the purchase and renovation of our townhouse. Born Black and poor, followed by a spell of quasi-indigence, I'd become a cash-poor, land-wealthy pseudo-WASP.

We were *vacationing* in Massachusetts at the house where she'd grown up in an incredibly beautiful landscape full of natural wonder—along with racial, social, and class peril. I, the once-registered communist, had run down to the beach. I'd convinced people that I did it for fitness. It was a ridiculous claim as it was only three-quarters of a mile to the water. I did it so I didn't have to walk the gauntlet of pale sun worshippers and have to stop with her and say hello. Alone, I could sprint past them—an excuse to skim along the water's edge, shoot an obligatory wave when needed. A freak in motion is in every way for everyone better than a freak standing still.

It was near dusk and I'd run to the end of the boardwalk. I stopped to scope out the terrain. Usually this late in the day it was empty, but it was packed like a weekend afternoon. Double peril. I chose the ticks hiding in the beach grass over the wasps on the sand and made my way along the path behind the dunes.

When I knew I was far enough, I climbed to the top of the rise and looked down. Miles was digging a hole in the sand, and Ella was wobbling up the slope with a pail of water to fill it. Michaele was talking with a family friend. They were all there except Alex. I felt panic and suddenly smelled the stink of dead things in the summer marsh. I scanned the beach break and the swells. Nothing. In my mind I saw him wide-eyed, drowning. I almost screamed from the top of the mound, *Where's Alex!* But he was there, below me, halfway up the dune. He was looking up at me with his head cocked to one side and squinting into the sun setting behind me—about to walk into my shadow. He waved timidly, then as if to pretend he hadn't, visored his eyes with that hand.

I wanted to say hello and make him feel at ease. It was going to be a beautiful evening, and I didn't want to ruin it. I thought we could have a silent walk up the beach to the inlet channel, perhaps along it toward the marsh and float back on the outgoing tide. But the smell of briny rot kept growing, and I couldn't shake the image of him disappearing beyond the swells. I couldn't speak. I couldn't get my breath. Then I felt as though I were being strangled. He turned, made for the water, then stopped and stood in profile as though waiting to see if I'd follow. But I couldn't. Instead, I turned back from where I'd come and slid down into the hollow and I knew what I'd only felt—that he was the same age as I was when I was raped.

I was seven, attending day camp at the West End House Boys Club in Allston, Massachusetts. I was in the bathroom, alone—so I thought—at the urinal when I felt something like a panicked wind rush the walls trying to escape. I heard myself, somewhere, yell, "No!"

I came to walking out of the building. I turned left down the hill toward Brighton Center. There's a fieldstone wall that rises opposite the descent of the sidewalk. I continued along it, past the few blocks of modest vinyl-sided two-families. There's a Burger King on the left corner, the Silhouette Lounge on the right. Brighton Avenue and Cambridge Street cross in an X there. My mother had repeatedly warned us that any child would be killed if they tried crossing alone. I made the far side and turned east onto Cambridge Street. My house was about a half mile away, beyond the turnpike overpass and the train yard.

While waiting for the light at North Harvard, I looked in between the taped-up sheets of butcher paper that advertised the specials—frog legs and chicken livers on sale, half gallons of Hood milk and freshly made subs. I continued past the Merit station, the AAMCO transmission shop, across Seattle Street to the side of our house. We had a secret tunnel in the hedges, which I squatted through.

Earlier that summer, we'd learned how to break into our house. Back then we still had a full hedgerow, so no one would've seen me climb in. Under the dining room window was an unused oil feed in the foundation wall and a water spigot below it. With a stick in hand you stepped up to the second pipe and popped the screen back in to the dining room.

Prince was there. I'd forgotten about him. He would've attacked any stranger but stood silently as I went upstairs. At first, I thought I should wash. I didn't. I got clothes from my room and went to the bathroom. A few months before, the latch assembly had fallen out of its mortise and only the loose knob and strike plate remained. To close the door, you had to snap open a washcloth and shut the door quickly to catch and bind it against the jamb.

I changed. I remember feeling that I shouldn't look at myself—not down at my body or my face in the mirror. And the thought that I might inadvertently do so spooked me. So, I picked up my dirty clothes and went back downstairs. As I descended, a plan revealed itself. The matches were beside the kitchen table ashtray. There were empty Star Market paper bags, lighter fluid, and a spade in the back hall.

We had a skinny strip of land between the hidden side of the house and a long run of neglected bushes. It was more like an alley than a yard. The ground was hardpan, tree roots, and gravel. Behind that ragged hedgerow was an abandoned lot. I slipped through and into the high grass for about twenty feet to a clearing where a house once had been. There'd been two on that lot—both abandoned as long as I'd known. Each had been torched two years prior. Near the foundation of the first, I cleared the broken glass and concrete rubble with my foot, and then dug a hole as deep and wide as the shovelhead. I crushed the bag of clothes down as much as I could, then dropped, doused, and lit the package. I watched it burn. I remember the blue flame. I thought for a moment that the fire might spread beyond the pit and that I should perhaps smother it with the loose excavated soil and tamp it down, but then it would be a grave. Then I felt from my throat down through my guts an awful emptiness, which I suppose is the absence of sensation: there seemed inside me a growing nothing. I started to panic and shake. My skin grew hot as a slow, cold fever rolled in to fill the void. I thought, *That isn't me in there!* I wanted to scream and cry, but something told me that I could not. If I did, I'd die.

I cooled and stilled. The fire was almost out. Soon everyone would be home. My mother would scream at me. She might do worse. She'd demand to know where I'd been, what I'd done, why had I done it, and why was I such a goddamn, stupid, selfish, no-good fool. Questions I wouldn't answer. I'd apologize and promise never to disappear again. And I was sorry, but I knew I would do it again and again.

I buried the ash and the embers. As I started back to the house, I began to feel heaviness, not my weight but a greater one pressing on my shoulders. Something told me to speak, *No.* I did.

And then I remember not remembering how I got to the bathroom. I heard everyone downstairs. One story above her, I could feel my mother's panic, so I opened the door and caught the rag as it fell. I slammed the door three times to simulate the sound of the latch failing. I shut it with a fourth. I heard her on the stairs. I even dropped my pants before flushing the toilet. I pulled them up as she made the hall. I was washing my hands when she crashed in. I knew she was only an arm's length away but wasn't solid. She was only a vague shadow. Perhaps she grabbed my arm and shook me. I'm sure she screamed. But I wasn't in my body's senses. I was somewhere else—witnessing something else that couldn't now or then have been substantiated by anyone else who might've been there. I saw my face: my eyes were partly lidded, my mouth soft and contrite.

Later that night, when everyone was asleep, I got out of bed and crawled under it. I lined up my sneakers and shoes for more cover. I stayed there in the dark. My father came home. I heard him close the front door. I knew he'd stay down there for a while, then come upstairs and look into the room. When he didn't see me in bed he'd enter and, so as not to wake my mother, call my name low. I would not answer. He'd check the bathroom and my sister's room. He'd return, come closer, and finally bend and look under the bed. When he saw me there he'd ask, *What's going on, Mr. Michael?*

I didn't know what I'd say, but I imagined I smelled his cigarettes and his beer. I started to cry, but it was okay, because I'd be done before he found me: done and disappearing. *To be, or to be gone?* There is always only one answer: I'm not here. And while I faded, both in and from the darkness, I began to apprehend the future: the lies I'd have to tell, that I'd never be able to be honest with anyone again and that I'd always be alone.

I've been writing these pages for the better part of a decade, and I've abandoned every draft. I've been counseled. I have tried convincing myself that the difficult subject matter has prevented me from finishing and publishing my account of my rape. Yes, I've wanted to protect my mother and children, but I haven't been able to talk or write about what happened because it seems immutable. I've tried other essays, songs, poetry, and fiction, but it's something I can neither interpret nor render. There's nothing metaphorical. It is real: sweat, semen, and blood. I can't change it, but it changes before me. What happened won't keep still, so I've always killed it. And any attempts to conceive a public eulogy for such ephemera, because I've believed it to be a futile act, have always seemed devious—unrealized artifice is a falsehood. The aborted narrative of trauma has been for psych wards and lab coats, giant pharmaceutical companies and their pills, and for murmuring therapists who ask, *How did that make you feel?* It's been for the night and being too wary for sleep and for the hours before dawn, alone.

And alongside my love for my son—it was there, so woven into any instinct of compassion that I couldn't bear to be kind. But I couldn't bear to be gone. And so, I was back on that verge. That unsustainable nowhere. I could act in a crisis, but I couldn't be peaceful—or at least that's how it seemed to me. Every positive, joyous moment was being corrupted or erased. The past was truly horrible and had such a toxic, malevolent power that it reached from that bathroom, those streets, that grave. It contorted everything. Alone, the post-trauma became trauma unto itself. I wanted to emerge from under my bed—fully grown—and tear my father to pieces, wake my siblings, see them safely out, and then burn that fucking house down.

The only relief at times was to imagine being folded into a vast nothing. Or to travel through space so fast that I outpaced the edge of the universe, and in the nothing, expanded the gap between it and me.

I've also had to accept that my every account has been a lie. Lies are the children of the despairing moment and the desperate heart. The first lie was that I didn't know what happened. I did. And while I hadn't the specific language for it, I knew that what had been done to me was a crime. The second was that I, as though I were the perpetrator, had fled the scene. The third was the fire. The fourth was the grave. The fifth was the promise. The sixth was to hide. And so I came to believe that my body was not my own, that I was a fugitive, that any evidence could be burned and buried, that an impromptu rite could heal me, and that I could become and remain unseen.

I grew up resisting sleep and caroming between the extreme conditions of self-annihilation and self-preservation. I ate Sani-Flush and studied Jeet Kune Do. I often had fever chills and almost always felt that weight. A hole slowly grew in my stomach. There was a nothing around my heart.

I started cutting when I was eight. I needed to feel and to bleed. I cut my hips and upper thighs. When I ran out of skin I could hide under clothing, I abraded my knuckles on the rim of the cast-iron skillet and steel wool pad. I always volunteered to clean it. I'd stand on the seat of "the little chair." The one David and I had to sit in when our mother picked our nappy hair. Up that high I could watch my blood mix with the water and soap. Soon that wasn't enough, so I began to double my sister's hair bands around my toes and leave them until they were in my skin and I'd have to tweeze them out. I had my first alcoholic blackout six weeks before my tenth birthday. Then I started bruising my ribs. I broke my left pinky in a table vise. I wanted to feel something. I wanted to create a body around my pain so I could leave it.

I'd occasionally go deaf and blind—the world around me hushed and dimmed—and be folded into quiet shadow. It can be a relief to be silent in darkness, and silently—unseeing and unseen—surrender to the nothing. I'd feel the last of me disappearing from myself: it longed to be gone. But desiring a person, place, or thing begets the pain of losing all you'll leave behind—no matter how awful. Some part of me would remember what it was to be present and ache to return. And I'd *almost* exist between two realms—where I couldn't remain. The darkness would become crushing and my relief would turn to terror and I'd suddenly be frantic for anyone to find me, but no one would, so I'd flail back. While returning, I'd relive it. That rush of wind took corporeal form. My walk home wasn't stoic. I was terrified and in agony. Concussed and bloody, I'd staggered home where I panicked. I know I left evidence. I know I sobbed in front of my mother. There'd been no plan. All of me had been there in plain sight.

Years passed and the physical evidence with them. It didn't matter that I could feel *it*. But feelings are subjective and cannot be corroborated. I couldn't prove it—to myself—so what happened to me became a mystery in me, then just a vague rumor in my bones.

I look back now and see a boy who resembles me but who's too disfigured to positively identify. I still don't know what my parents saw on that day or those that followed. Perhaps the first lie was that neither they nor anyone else wanted to see. Perhaps they'd hoped that I was okay and had faith that nothing like that could've happened to me. After all, I'd always been such a strange boy—a cold fish.

I realize now I tried to live according to what my parents needed most. I knew my pain would kill them. Growing into a young man I was distant, wayward, wild, drunk. I could be cruel. I'd lie to everyone I knew about anything. And though our family was broken, for us I didn't tell. It seems perverse now. We hoped for *nothing*. But we were desperate and despairing, and for us, hopes, wishes, and desires closely resemble each other, especially those of the parents who cannot help their child, or a child who doesn't know how to live but does not want to die.

9

When he was eight, Alex was ready to transition from recreational soccer to a competitive league. His first travel team was the Brooklyn Patriots. At its worst, the team was the epitome of social dysfunction: discord and discontent; too many voices; too many good ideas drowned out by the loud fury of the mob; too many bad ideas perpetuated or yowled into being. At its best, though, it was what an American institution should be—democratic, dynamic, diverse—with players, coaches, and parents from many different places of origin, who, under the colors of one banner, played with one set of ideas: fairness, community service, dignity, and inclusion. We were a motley bunch. It's easy, when looking at a team photo, to get swept up in utopian fantasies about what this country could be. The tryouts were hilarious—eight-year-olds vying for a spot. Each had been able to dominate their rec games, but here they were in their place.

Alex's game, like his affect, was always reserved. He stayed out of the fray. He rarely lost the ball. Not one to over-dribble, rarely out of position, his efforts were in service to the team. His game wasn't flashy, but that didn't mean he couldn't do flashy things. He loved watching the showmen but he'd lean towards the TV when someone like Emerson or Roy Keane would run down a loose ball, take a touch, and release it.

Michaele got tense watching Alex stay on the edges of the game during tryouts. During a break, she gave him a pep talk. "You need to get in there—mix it up—or else you won't get picked!" Alex looked up at her, incredulous, wondering where his mother's Anglican propriety had gone. He sipped his drink, went back out to the field, and continued to play the same—out on the edge, waiting until those in the center were beyond resource and had to ask him for help.

He made the team. Jimmy, a Saint Lucia transplant, and a very good player in his own right, said, "You have a player."

Jimmy's son, Bradley, was the best player. He could outrun and out-dribble everyone. Alejandro played with swagger and flair. His left foot had been kissed by God. Robey, his father and one of our dedicated drivers, was the son of West Texas oil-folk and Italian masons. His mom's people were Puerto Rican and Venezuelan but he couldn't speak Spanish with Alex Rosas from rural Mexico or Michael Franchesci from Panama. Sam Soule was just a private-school white boy. He was a selfless defender. He was hilarious and exceptionally kind. Theo was the most technically gifted. His mother was a lawyer who grew up in elite New York City and wanted to burn the criminal justice system down. His father, Clay, managed the team. Though we all had our disparate notions of time, he always got us to be where we needed to be and when.

We resembled two of the best teams in the world—Brazil and France. Opposing parents didn't believe we were a real soccer team, at least not until we beat them. Regardless, along with racist epithets, they called our boys "divers" when they were fouled and "dirty" when their children fell on their own. By the time they were ten, our boys knew every away game was rigged.

Despite our pluralism and diversity, we were also homogenous. We had conventional identities and we could use them to explain ourselves to each other and explain each other to ourselves. I am Black. I can say, "Those white people." When I do, I'm not homeless. Even if it is a lie. Alex cannot or he chooses not to. He listens to his deep stillness. On that team he couldn't hide behind the affects and attitudes that his coaches and teammates could. He didn't join in when the other kids told their bigoted jokes. He didn't engage with opposing players when they called his brown teammates spic and wetback, or his white teammates fags, or their parents ape-called at our Black children. My boy was all of us. He was a problem. His only answer, in spite of the refs who often tried their best to stop him, was to be better than all of us.

This burdened him. When challenged on or off the field, he'd often silently pause. As he approached adolescence this seemed like recalcitrance. He became moody. At times he was openly angry at his mother. He would challenge me by sullenly dragging through things I asked him to do and go slower when I demanded he go faster. He moped if he didn't play well but he wouldn't practice on his own. But then he'd have a fantastic game or training session and wouldn't part from his ball. This commitment would last for a week or two. I'd praise him but that wasn't enough to keep him going. So I'd warn him that there was always someone watching and judging him for one small failing and one small failing would confirm to others that he was a failure in full.

There was my boy—beautiful. He was trying so hard to be his father's son. Trying to be seen and loved. I did love him. We still laughed. We still watched movies his younger siblings couldn't and force-fed ourselves pizza and chicken parms. I think he knew I would do anything for him except stop demanding who he was and how he should be.

I told him what to do, how to do it and what and how to feel about it. Work and play had to be approved by me. Home wasn't sanctuary; it was boot camp. I trained him to survive the ignorance and unearned privilege of his white family and friends. I continued to tell myself that I'd been a cool, efficient, fearless child, wholly self-reliant. It was the virtue I'd earned that gave me the right to treat him so rather than my pathologies that hurt him. I told him, implicitly and explicitly, that he wasn't good enough. There's a narrow gap between telling your brown child that he's not good enough at something and that he's good for nothing.

I was Whiteness to my son. Though he wouldn't show it, he was afraid of me.

10

The last time I was weak in front of my father was on an early spring evening in 1979. It had been a difficult five years. Following my rape, he left. We could no longer go to private school and rather than enrolling us in the Boston public system, my mother held us out until she could find something better. My friends would call every night asking when I was coming back. I'd tell them I didn't know.

My mother eventually used her sister's address in Newton. In October 1977, we drove what formally had been my aunt's car, an army-green 1969 Chevy Nova, and took my brother David and sister Tracey to Warren Junior High. After getting them settled, we drove a quarter mile up the hill to Peirce Elementary, where I was to begin fifth grade. We entered Mrs. Aronson's room. She greeted us, then announced my name and that the other students should welcome me. My mother then added we were currently living at 122 Austin Street but would soon be moving to 12 Prospect. Aaron Still, the only other Black boy in the room, looked up in shock and yelled, "Twelve Prospect Street, that's where I live!"

We spent the year commuting, lying, and living in mild panic. Outside the house was Boston in the '70s. Very few places were safe. Inside was unsafe, or at least unsure. Every mechanical system was failing: leaks, broken latches, cracked panes, and peeling paint. It was a relief to come home at night and see the lights turn on. When there was no oil for the furnace but still gas for the stove, we'd sit by the open oven. If we had electricity, we'd listen to the TV. If not, we'd sit quietly in the candlelight. Instead of oil heat, the smell of Prince's fresh poop rose through the floor vents.

This didn't seem like hardship but relatively normal, and what followed, reasonable. My brother became a tyrant. I was dyslexic, had ADD, Asperger's, and had begun exhibiting symptoms of bipolar and panic disorder as well as alcoholism. My sister tried to be my special-ed teacher and ignored her own pain: her kinky hair, changing body, acne, and perversions of and abandonment by our father had started her own self-annihilation. My mother's rage, sometimes alcoholic, sometimes because she was so scared and alone, in part because life is just so fucking hard, was mundane and terrifying. And she was so sad.

Every day we lied about who we were and where we lived. This, however, considering what else I was hiding, seemed trivial. I couldn't be publicly sad. It would've hurt my mother, which would've angered her. It would've told her that she'd failed. It would've disappointed my ancestors. I imagined telling them that I was sad because I couldn't go to a friend's house after school or because they couldn't come to mine. But what was any or all of that next to being hanged, castrated, your screams muffled because your penis is stuffed in your mouth before being set on fire?

And there was something in me that hated boys crying—mine or another child's, the screeches and contortions. I didn't understand why they couldn't keep it to themselves.

We finished the school year then moved from my father's house to a rental in Newton. The Red Sox lost a fourteen-game lead to the Yankees. I started sixth grade at a new elementary school. We stayed there till January, then moved to a third-floor tenement walk-up—the last building on the edge of Newton's two-block Black ghetto where we displaced the Stills. I returned to Peirce School.

Up to that point, I'd grown up playing sports with a pack of kids of whom I was among the youngest. I was better than most. I loved striking them out or hitting homers off the smug older boys, then styling around the bases or in football beating them on a go route and doing a White Shoes Johnson in the end zone.

That had been on our street, and my mother could see us from the back porch or the dining room windows. If she couldn't see us, she could hear us. If she couldn't hear us, she'd walk out the kitchen door to the back porch—a little nervous and almost angry—to make sure we were still alive. I still believe I could see her, from a hundred yards, exhale and soften. Still, I couldn't appreciate how terrified she must have been. Abrasions, contusions, concussions, fractures, and cars and trucks using our side street as a cut through were mundane hazards. The police, at least there and then, weren't as dangerous as, say, if we'd been playing on another street or at the park. If we stayed close to our house, they'd remember that we were *Dave's kids*. In that strangely integrated neighborhood, most of the Black people were second-generation homeowners. But they weren't my father. Dave had grown up there—with some of them. Dave wasn't like his parents. He seemed white.

The Clemente brothers, our uncle Al Mancini, and Bob Sullivan, the white husband of Lois, all knew and loved Dave. He'd gone to Brighton High with some of them. We were Seattle Street kids not Windham Street kids and though we went to that fancy school—not even a Catholic school—we weren't uppity. Yes, one of our cars was dead, but it was shiny because my siblings and I washed it for fun. The hedges, before the blizzard of '78, were still relatively neat because we knew how to use the hedge clippers. The front lawn was *good* because we never played there. And though the back lawn was now beat, they'd seen him every spring, along with me, planting grass. And Dave's children had kept trying.

But neither Dave nor his children could protect my mother. Any second we could vanish. Where, she wouldn't tell. If she didn't have consistent, tactile proof of our safety, that meant we were lost somewhere in that "city of destruction": teen pregnancy, addiction, prisons, suicide, and murder, the wrong places at the wrong times. It was real, as were all the missing Black children from Boston to Virginia. All the space and time in which she'd witnessed some of the many thousands gone, and all the space and time greater than her own lifetime—the many thousands before and thousands more to come. We could not be among them.

So, other than her sister, a few close friends, and certain neighbors, the only people she could trust us with were select upper-middle-class or wealthy, liberal, secular, Northern white people: the parents of our classmates. The professors, doctors, lawyers, and those funded by trusts who lived in the colonial and Georgian houses along Brattle that neighbored Longfellow's, the Dutch, the American craftsman, and mid-century moderns on the side streets near Harvard.

When we moved to the wealthiest per capita city east of the Mississippi, she needed another way to keep us safe. Now it was from the police. They wouldn't know us, but because we were in Newton they'd know how and where we lived.

My cousin had played the prior year in the majors for the Royals, and it was decided by her that I'd play for them too. My aunt or uncle could drive me to games and practices and most importantly they vouched for the coach as a man we could trust. Regardless, the Little League officials required I try out. The first thing they had us do was take grounders at shortstop and throw to first. Other than a few games in the peewee league, I'd never played organized ball. I'd rarely been on a proper diamond or even fielded on dirt. Most of my practice was with my father, who'd skip the ball off the street. Batted balls are different. Strange white men make them more so. In the street, I'd throw directly back to my father, but there I had to do so across the diamond to the strange white men. And in front of so many white coaches, players, and parents. It was a disaster. I tried being the Red Sox shortstop Rick Burleson, but all I could do to keep the ball from getting past me was to kick and flop about like a hapless goaltender. I managed to keep the ball in front of me, but I short-armed the first throws. Instead of being seen as having a weak arm, I decided to hurl the ball over the white man, the fence, and into the bleachers.

Batting was worse. I didn't swing. After I *hit*, a man approached me. He was the coach of the Red Sox and asked me to play for him. My mother was pushing her way through the crowd, looking as though I was about to be kidnapped. By the time she reached us, she was enraged. He tried telling her what he'd already told me: I had great raw talent, and he could teach me the game. Now my mother didn't know much about how to play the game, but she knew its history. Her favorite team was the Dodgers: you couldn't really be Black and root for any other. The Royals were okay because they were from Kansas City, home of the Monarchs. The Red Sox, however, were anathema to Blackness. She loathed the Yawkeys, pitied the fans, missed the Black players who always had to get the hell out of Boston, and of course hated anything my father loved.

The other coach listed me on his roster anyway, but my mother wouldn't let me play for him. So, I hadn't a team. I was conflicted. The Red Sox were better, and they were my team. But the coach didn't seem to care about me, only my raw talent. The real Astros played in the dome, had garish uniforms, and, most important, they had J. R. Richard, a giant Black man who could hold seven baseballs in one hand and threw as hard as Nolan Ryan.

I wanted to ask my father what to do, but I didn't know his number. I don't think he had a phone. He'd call from a public phone or a friend's. I didn't even know where he lived, though I learned later that my mother and siblings did. Still, we all had to wait for him to contact us.

The season had already started when he finally did contact us, but it was only to check in. My mother answered. I could tell it was him because she barely moved her mouth when she spoke.

That was a Thursday. He was supposed to come Sunday at five. Neither my brother nor sister believed he would show. David didn't care. He was about to turn sixteen and despised him. Tracey was in a torpor. They'd eaten dinner and were doing their homework. I knelt by the front window and waited. He called at seven. My mother answered. He spoke to her. She repeated to me. He couldn't make it. Something came up. He continued. She held the phone so that I could hear. He couldn't afford to take me out. I took the phone and calmly told him we didn't have to go anywhere. He said he was out of gas. I told him I'd get to him. He asked how and why. I told him I didn't know but would. I needed to talk. He asked about what. I couldn't answer. After a long silence, he said he'd be there as soon as he could.

I returned to the window. A couple of hours later he arrived. I went outside. I started to open the passenger door but stopped. The way he was sitting—almost relaxed, looking out at the opposite side of the street—told me he wanted to be somewhere else. He finally turned, leaned across the front seat, and rolled down the window. He waited for me to start, but I didn't know how or where to or with what. He sighed, straightened, and cut the motor. I started to weep.

He was looking somewhere past me.

"Michael," he exhaled. "You've put me in an untenable situation." He fixed on my eyes. "Do you know what *untenable* means?"

I didn't respond. I didn't, at that moment, know what any word meant. I stood there in the dark, roaring silence. Though I felt that if he started the car I would die, I wanted him to go. Now I was openly crying: my mouth wide and my chest heaving. I gestured vaguely with my arms. Now he looked out the windshield, down to the turnpike. East. West. Where would he go? He started the car, lit a cigarette, then quarter turned to me. With the butt in the corner of his mouth he asked, "You going to be alright?"

I nodded and managed, "Uh-huh."

"Okay. We'll get together soon. We'll talk."

I nodded again, this time with some vim. He did, too.

He drove about thirty feet then slowed. I remember feeling what I can still only describe as a spectacular ecstasy and an outsized joy too great for me to contain. It sprung me from my body, and I flew down the sidewalk to him. But he didn't know anything about it. He'd merely slowed to roll up the window.

He sped up, but what would I have said? Father, I was raped. I need your care to make me whole. I need your love to know I am still worth loving. I need to feel the substance of your hope and faith. Teach me how to walk without sight yet not be blind, for I did so to my death inside those pisshole walls or if not death, then my destruction—that agony of unliving. Father, teach me how to live with such strife long enough so that I may know beauty. Teach me *"how to care and not to care."* Teach me how to tell you. I do not have the words.

But he was gone. Everyone was gone and I was alone, exiled from my body and absent from the Lord.

11

When he was eleven, Alex was cut during the last round of tryouts for the Eastern New York Olympic Development team and wrongly so, for he'd clearly been more skilled than many of the boys who made it. There'd been some obvious political wrangling to spirit those of marginal skill and questionable temperament through. And Alex, I thought, had been quietly devastated.

I'd been proud that he wanted to try. I hadn't expected him to make it past the first round—he wasn't confident or selfish enough. His game was too practical for him to stand out. He let me pin his number on his back—545—and ran out to join the others.

I wanted to go somewhere else until it was over, but there wasn't much to do in that part of Nassau County, so I was obliged to wait and watch. Since he's been playing sports, I've always tried to keep close to him—the overprotective parent—but none of the parents were allowed within thirty yards of the boys.

He was brilliant—aggressive and daring in a way I'd only seen glimpses of—enough to garner the respect of the strangers he was playing with. Enough so that when they lined the boys up at the end of the night, he was among the first chosen to come back.

The next week he was even better. He earned a few nods from coaches and high-fives from teammates. Near the end though, he took a hard fall, and when he got up he was clutching his stomach. I went to high school with a kid who ruptured his spleen in a basketball game. I wanted to go get him, but I didn't. I watched him hide his discomfort from the others, straightening as best he could until the whistle blew.

He then doubled over and ran as fast as he could to me, pointing to the bathroom as he did. I met him near the door and reached out for him, but he shook me off.

"Just get the door, please."

I did. He almost made it to the first stall before vomiting explosively. From inside, he calmly told me that he needed help. I went in, not knowing what I'd find. He'd stripped down to his underwear and held the rest of his clothes out toward me. "I'm a mess, but I've got to get out there for the lineup." I rinsed his clothes. He swabbed the floor, and somehow we managed to do it all quickly.

Back outside, in the rapidly cooling night, he made sure not to shiver. And when they gave him his slip this time, he made sure to get past the line of anxious parents before doubling over again. When I met him, bent at the waist, he held the slip aloft. "I'm so happy," he mumbled. And we were back in the bathroom for another session.

The last night he was even better—playing out of position with a zeal and flair I hadn't seen before. Some snarky kid had demanded that he wanted to play right back, and so Alex inserted himself in an attacking midfield position and started *dealing*: balls left, balls right. He handled difficult balls, controlled them, sidestepped a defender, and slotted near-perfect passes to teammates. He functioned like a lanky axel tree—transferring small to large, large to small—always spinning.

After he didn't get picked, as he walked toward me several parents—strangers all—offered their sympathy with pats and thumbs-up. One woman, whose son had been chosen (wrongly so), took his face in her hands and told him that they'd made a huge mistake in passing him by. I tried to intercede, but Alex let her keep her hands, which hid everything but his eyes, on him. "This is all wrong," she implored. "You're a good boy, a great player. Do you understand?" He nodded, more for her sake than his own. She let him go and, only a few steps away, began celebrating with her son.

I put my arm around his shoulders and led him toward the parking lot, but he stopped, pointed toward a darkened patch of unoccupied field, and asked if we could walk that way—away from the crowd. When we were far enough away he let out a long sigh.

"You were great," I said. "Absolutely amazing." But he didn't seem to hear it, or he did but didn't believe it.

"Are you disappointed?"

"In what?"

"In me."

"Never, no."

"You look like you are."

"I'm sorry. If I am, it's with them. You were fantastic. I'm not just saying that. You heard what people said. They don't know you. They didn't have any reason to say anything."

"Remember what you said. This summer? About work and being ready?"

"Yeah."

"You were right."

And I wished I had something for him, but at that moment he seemed to have left the realm of my care—my small reign. He shed exactly one tear—near perfect in size, shape, and the manner it moved then lingered on the fading cheek before dropping off and disappearing. And as I watched my boy stare out into the wilds of Long Island, I wondered how many disappointments he had left—not the mundane ones—before the hue of his life would turn blue.

I think Alex believed he'd failed me and everything in which I believed and there was nothing he could do to make it right. Even if he could make himself right *for me*, he'd have to do so without resource. I couldn't be trusted and I'd become a barrier to his inheritance of the wealth our people had left him and a conduit for my generational pain. For him to accept this, he'd have to see himself as wretched. My acceptance and love were contingent on the denigration of himself. However disorienting this country's hypocrisies are and brutal its practices are, you cannot punish and protect your child. This is neither balance nor harmony. It is reactionary and myopic. This is pain. This is the repeated history: this country did—*does*—to me, what my father did to me. I felt it and perhaps I'll continue to until I die.

One Saturday, not long after the tryouts, we had a fight. He had a paper due the following Monday, and his schedule was full until then. We'd thought he was developing bad habits: doing things at the last minute, but worse than that, he wouldn't accept the responsibility of his failings when his lack of preparedness left him hamstrung. Michaele was wondering aloud about how he'd get his work done, and he was doing his best to ignore her. Finally, she asked directly, and he exploded: "Leave me alone!" but she wouldn't, and his anger and volume grew with each rephrasing of the question. Then I stepped in to show him what fury really looked like.

Michaele had once welcomed my intervention, but here she quickly declared, "It's over. It's no big deal." Alex regained his composure, muttered, "I'll do it now." And was off to the kitchen. She gave me a pleading look, as if to ask that I leave him alone, that it was, indeed, over. Later, Michaele told me, "You have to recognize your power." It seemed, considering who we were, absurd for her to tell me that. My *authority*—to me—was weightless.

I can't recall a time when I told Alex, *I don't know*. When he was little, he had to believe that I knew. I needed him to believe it because I felt I hadn't anything else to give him. What dark nights they must have been for him; the path between where he was to where I might be, and what I might be upon his arrival, what criticism would await him, what little praise. But to my boy . . . if I waited years for the affection and approval of a man who chose to be gone, what must the son of a man who stayed think and feel?

I want—as I did then—to turn back the clock, or at least to break it so I could stop, take a breath, and if not undo what I'd done, without pressure choose an unbroken series of right actions into the future. But I'll never have that power.

It may seem ridiculous after all these pages, after all these years, to have finally written to this understanding: what I needed was for someone to show me the way, but that boy is gone, and it is best to let him be. The past has been horrible. My honest assessment begets the same conclusion. It ends with me.

I still have hope. So this is my beginning: whatever has happened—will happen to me—doesn't atone for any other hurt I might cause. To now know this is my gift. I have searched myself and I am not so deeply hurt so as to be faithless, and I am not so wounded that I cannot offer my hand.

When I think this way, my life becomes somehow different. Remembering my father this way, I don't feel compelled to define him. I'm comfortable with him as an uncertainty, that he, in another moment, may become something else.

Our nature seems paradoxical, perhaps we can be led beyond it—if only for a moment—and from wherever we arrive, see back to ourselves tearing at the unions of our worse and better angels. And from there, free of desire and of being desired, unafraid and compassionate, we can act not to repair our rifts but to learn how we might live with them, what we might make out of them, who we might become, and then be moved to try. Perhaps such movement is what we may ask of the spirit, and testimony is what we must ask of ourselves.

To testify is to put yourself in peril. It is the moment when you choose to bind your life to the lives of others. You simultaneously confess and absolve. And contrary to what it may seem, the testimony neither grounds nor defines you but rather releases you from these conveniences. This is not a practical undertaking, especially if you're concerned with your identity, with your standing among your peers, your measurable achievements, your assets in the world of men. Testimony is sacrifice, the articulation of what you have witnessed. It will give us more than what you, individually, stand to lose.

Testimony is the most high because in doing it we seek nothing for ourselves. It is the unguarded, immediate public revelation of where, what, and who we have been. It is holy and profane. To testify is to be of service to something larger than oneself. It is the faithful act, which reminds us that though the world is on fire, and we are the flesh and the spirit of pain and relief, we can live with such strife. It is the substance of what we hope for—that we are not alone.

Forgiving myself—having faith—is the only chance Alex and I have. I've known this. I've had faith in it. I've lost it. I've recovered it, or I have been recovered. So now I know I hope for patience and guidance. And the substance of this hope is my faith. So precious Lord lead me with your love: it is salvation.

This is my choice. The sacrifices, the credo he follows, that which he sacrifices himself to—if it's anything at all—will be whatever he chooses. And I have to believe he will be alright. I know that it will always be a struggle but I know, with his best effort, that he is trying. I hope he knows I'm trying, too.

I hope he trusts me with this. I hope he has faith in himself. It might be all he can take with him; it might be all he can bear. For the night of the peregrine child is as dark as any other's—and as lonely. I pray his journey will take him beyond me, to whatever destination, where he will arrive unbroken.

12

It was a late October Brooklyn morning. I woke and sensed that everything outside was dead. Our street, Pacific, runs one way slightly to the northwest, and whenever there's an arctic front with high winds, hard gusts seem to break off the main squall and tear down it. The gusts ran the deep puddles left behind from the night's heavy rain into cruel gutter rivulets. They rattled my shrunken door. No sun, too cold: a day that makes me wonder still why I came here, why I stay.

Boston, 220 miles up the coast, is colder but never as harsh or bleak. Maybe it's the lack of greenery here, the way the blocks extend without grass or trees, or how the sky is blocked from view by the dim towers. It's strange that the further I remove myself from nature, the greater its impact on me. Cold in the country is different than cold in the city: the tarmac and concrete channels act as echo chambers for the wind.

It was a Saturday, and I didn't want to get up. Even the big game failed to stir anything in me. It was 7:00 a.m., and everyone would have to get ready.

I didn't want to confront Alex. I didn't want to get angry at him—harass him out of bed, harangue him into his uniform, cajole him into eating. And I knew I couldn't motivate him—or me—in any other way. I remember lying there listening to the gusts outside and thinking that his playing days were winding down—that I'd ruined the game for him.

I got up, motivated by the vision of standing next to his bed offering him some kind words—motivational, consoling, apologetic—some corrective that would make us, or at least him, forget. Fortunately, I was too tired and cold to come up with anything. So with rolled shoulders and the softest expression I could muster, I started for his room to lay his uniform out and then maybe make everyone breakfast.

He wasn't in his bed. The sheets had been pulled back roughly so I knew his mother hadn't done it. I walked downstairs to the kitchen. He was sitting at the counter finishing breakfast—water, Gatorade, and Emergen-C laid out next to his plate. He was dressed. The lights were off and the drapes still closed, but the bright uniform and his skin glowed in the gloom. I had to catch myself as I thought I might cry. He spoke without looking up.

"My warm-ups are on the couch. I found my gloves, and I just have to put my cleats on."

He waited for my response, but I didn't say anything.

"Okay?"

"Yeah."

He nodded, pointed at the packet of magic dust. "When should I have it?"

"You don't have to drink that."

"I want to."

"It hurts your stomach."

"Not when I eat first." He nodded at the empty plate then raised the last of his bagel.

"Before you warm up, I guess."

He nodded, and his face closed again, suggesting that I should leave him alone.

Down in the cellar looking for something warm in the dryer that I could wear, I found his gloves. On the way back up, I placed them where I imagined he thought he'd left them. The others were rustling above. I quickly put my coat on and started for the door, but he was in the room before I could leave. He moved briskly, picked up his cleats, sat on the couch, and began putting them on.

"Coffee?" he asked.

"Yeah." I stood with my hand on the knob.

"When do we have to leave?"

"Twenty minutes."

He exhaled, fumbling with his shoes and pulling at the laces with a quiet, controlled frustration. They—or his fingers—weren't doing what he wanted them to.

"You okay?"

In a chilling, deadpan way he answered, "I'm nervous."

"Need anything?"

"No."

"I'll be right back." I sighed.

I walked down the stoop knowing that I was weeping. The streets were empty, but I readied an excuse for my tears. I rubbed my eyes in the hopes of convincing any passersby—myself—that in this lifeless time I was having a bout with my allergies.

I'd never seen him like this, and I wondered if he really believed that everything was riding on this game—for his team, for himself. I wondered if he, like his father, had crushed that which he believed to be good—or not—into this one event. *Thou knowest this boy's fall.* No: I'd deduced my father's, felt my own, but I had not, did not know of my son's and had been blind and deaf to his wrestling. That he'd somehow fallen and that this event, and only this event, could redeem him. If this were true, if I'd gotten my son so wrong, that all this time he'd been remembering it, rolling it all up himself—then I'd hurt him more than I'd ever imagined, and more than I could ever repair. Even so, as I trudged through that wind, I searched for something I could say or do to unburden him—if only for this day—some joy or relief, but I was still so caught up in my mind, my reckoning, that I never could have found it. Nor could I have realized that if he had believed himself to have fallen he might have been planning his own redemption.

We drove through the drizzle for the Parade Ground to meet the rest of the team, collect them, and continue on to Long Island. In the past I'd been open, happy, to give rides, but over the last several weeks my generosity had shrunk. I'd wanted to be alone with Alex: not that we spoke much during those rides, but I'd felt that he might have wanted to, and he never would have if someone else were with us. Though the rest of the family was there, we could listen to whatever we wanted, sing along if we felt, open or close the windows, be ensconced in our own car, immersed in our own culture without having to accommodate anyone else.

We were early, but most of the team was there. The area around the gate was full of players, parents, and siblings, many of whom were juggling, passing the ball, shooting at, or crashing around in front of the chained-up goal. Some saw us pull up, and they waved for Alex to join them. He waved back but stayed in the car.

I got out and moved into their midst to start herding everyone up. Anthony, smiling, juggling, caught me.

"Michael, are we playing on turf or grass?"

I'm sure I said it glumly. "Grass."

"Oh." He frowned and toed at the green plastic.

"Just play the ball harder. Expect bad hops." I don't think he heard, though.

We gathered everyone—head counts, directions, cell numbers. The boys who'd been running about tackling each other had, upon exiting the gate, suddenly cooled. All of the other parents helped Clay and me organize. They were businesslike. Everyone seemed—though probably for different reasons—to share gravitas. Everyone knew what this day meant, a strange collective certainty about the uncertain. The grim intensity made me uneasy, so I got in my car and waited for the caravan to depart.

Trips around New York City—into the ethnic enclaves—were bad enough, but Long Island was something else: the mysterious East that most of us only vaguely understood by the exit numbers of that highway and that which contained it: the houses in the last bit of Queens that give way to the strip malls, the big malls, the ornamental line of trees punctuated by office parks.

The boys rarely played well in strange circumstances and this ride wouldn't help. Our motley group was going to Levittown, where the American dream of home ownership seemed to turn on itself. Somewhere between the gleaming city in the west and the sprawling estates to the east in the Hamptons, property values have flatlined.

Exit 41S, the first and one of the largest mass-produced suburbs, Levittown quickly became a symbol of postwar suburbia—for good and for bad. Although Levittown provided affordable houses in what many residents felt to be a congenial community, critics damned its homogeneity, blandness, and racial exclusivity (the initial lease prohibited rental to nonwhites). Today, "Levittown" is used as a term of derogation to describe overly sanitized suburbs consisting largely of tract housing.

The building firm, Levitt and Sons, headed by Abraham Levitt and his two sons, William and Alfred, built four planned communities called Levittown—in New York, Pennsylvania, New Jersey, and Puerto Rico—but Levittown, New York, was the first.

Our *difference* starkly contrasted with the perceived sameness we saw through the car windows. Without anger, I could do little to allay our fears or inspire us. I wouldn't even be able to go into a store for supplies, ask directions, or exchange platitudes with the coaches and parents of the opposition. I would only feel their scrutiny, their unease. I could already hear their silence upon first seeing us then that first holler accusing our boys of doing something criminal. And if our boys did well, in spite of the conditions, the others would join in—and the boys would have to choose between ignoring them, caving to pressure and fear, or answering them with equal contempt.

There was always some notion of deservedness to these games. Poor ethnic city boys had no business beating, let alone competing with, suburban teams, as though this game hadn't been played—beautifully—in the barrios, favelas, barefoot in the streets of our various countries before any *American* ever laced up boots on Long Island.

It's amazing how even the most chaotic of us require some kind of continuum, something familiar to latch on to. We become so comfortable in our environment—even a place like the Parade Ground—that it disappears, and we go with it, in the sense that we are no longer conscious of it or ourselves. We exist in an Eden of sorts, a shameless place we once inhabited before we realized our difference—our shame. It may be something small: wearing the wrong brand of sneakers, packing a strange lunch, being late to pick up a popular trend, and then embracing it after most have let it go. And once this happens—shame, symbolized by whatever fig leaf we don—the only hopes are to somehow reengage that place or tear away from it completely.

For the child athlete, knowing how alien you are is death. Your limbs become heavy, outsized, awkward. The things that came so easily—where to put your feet, how to breathe, let alone move with speed, power, and grace—become impossible. This quasi-paralysis is the antithesis of equipoise. If the drive on the highway didn't do it, the wind through the streets of sameness, the parking lot did. The field wasn't like anything they'd seen: it was sunken thirty feet below the level of the tarmac that wrapped around its perimeter like the rim of a bowl. And the people talking, gathering gear from SUV hatches, moving through the lot, and descending the slope to the field stopped and greeted us cold and silent as though witnessing the sudden appearance of gypsies on their land.

We unloaded the boys and the gear. Clay and I tried to get them to focus on us. Some were still and blank, but most of them looked about like nervous birds. We made for the fields, down the slope as Robey tried to take charge of the rest who seemed as uneasy as the players. Everyone shivered in the drizzle and wind.

Walking the drop I could tell the field was soaked. All the water from above had run down and collected there. We wouldn't be protected from the wind either. The gusts swirled around the bowl, seeming to collect force as they did. It was hard enough for Clay and me to push our way through it, but most of the boys could lean into it without falling over. They tiptoed through the cold swamp, silent, looking around anxiously as though individually planning their escape.

Jimmy was standing in the middle of the field with his head bowed and his hands in his pockets like some reluctant homesteader. Over the distance and through his coat, I thought I saw him shiver. I remember thinking, *That man is a long way from home.* I started jogging to him, in part to keep vigil with him, in part hoping that the boys would follow. They didn't but continued their slow mince through the elements.

When I reached Jimmy, he greeted me with a slight nod and a weak smile. I nodded back, slapped his arm then looked up. Robey had led the caravan around the perimeter so that all of the cars were parked—engines idling, lights on—above what would be our sidelines. I pointed up to them.

"We've got that going for us."

"Yes dread." He didn't turn but smiled wider. He then looked beyond me, surveying the team slogging across the field. He squinted and frowned. "Where's Alex?"

I looked with him but couldn't see my boy, though he was always the easiest to pick out in a crowd—his height and hair. I felt sick, then a sudden panic. I turned in a circle scanning the field. There he was, slowly descending from where the cars had parked. I pointed. Jimmy smiled again and walked toward him. When they met, Jimmy put a hand on Alex's shoulder and leaned in. Instead of the small, shy smiles he usually gave, he looked up at Jimmy, nodded, dropped his bag, and walked away.

We had to call to the team several times to gather them for the warm-up, which they performed without energy or focus. They tiptoed through their jog and shied from the ground while stretching. Things that would've made them laugh—trying to kick the ball around only to have it stop in a puddle—passed without a joke or a chuckle. For Alex, this was the worst of all scenarios: he wasn't even moving or watching, just standing peevishly like a commuter waiting in foul weather for the bus to take them home. Someone passed the ball to him and he made a limp attempt at it. Although it stopped only a few yards away, he wouldn't retrieve it. Edgar moaned, "Come on." To which Alex answered with a glare. I thought that I should go to him and remind him of how focused he'd been at home earlier. Instead, I clapped and yelled, "Warm up!" But I think my voice was lost in the wind; that's what I'll believe.

It didn't go well. Franchesci was lame from the start, and five minutes in Alejandro's great left foot was maliciously stomped. He wouldn't come out, though—he couldn't—so he hobbled through the muck, diminished.

As we expected, the boys weren't getting any calls. Even the blatant fouls went ignored, while Levittown was given free kicks, it seemed, every time one of theirs lost the ball. Bradley was chopped down three times in the first five minutes and got up slower after each offense. Theo took a violent studs-up kick to the thigh and had to come out. No foul—only a bruise the color and size of a grapefruit for his pains.

But then Bradley scored—one of his trademark solo goals—and energized the team and their supporters above. It was brief though: the ref—inconceivably—called the play offside. Above us, Brooklyn groaned. Jimmy howled. Clay yelled, "The fix is in!" and the boys looked gut-punched.

Levittown scored soon after that: a goal that was clearly—of course—offside by many yards. I thought Jimmy might run onto the field and brain the ref, but he howled again—only once—and stood frozen. Our boys on the sidelines started crying. Clay tried to dismiss the gravity, but they knew. The fix was in; there'd be no winning.

But on the far side of the field, Alex was having a fantastic game. He was doing things I'd never seen him want to try in practice: leaping high into the air to head wind-swerved balls; pointing and barking commands to his teammates; straying from his area to make hard tackles and win loose balls. It wasn't that he was the only one trying but rather that he was the only one out there who wasn't spooked or lame. He was moving with the controlled fury that we'd seen in snatches and demanded that he display. Shit call after shit call, he kept throwing his body around in knowing that he had to stop the bleeding for his team and somehow, without giving up another goal, get them to halftime. In spite of the ref's attempts to undermine the plan, he did just that.

Halftime was a sad affair: lots of tears, some hysteria, accusations of wrongdoing, a litany of bad calls, and a paraphrasing of epithets the other team and parents were calling them. All we could do was tell them that it was a new half and they now had the wind. They had to forget about the ref and not let him take the game away from them.

Jimmy put his hand on Alex's back and with a slight grin whispered something to him. Alex nodded, stoically, and jogged back onto the field before the positions were called out.

U-11 halves are twenty-five minutes, and with Theo and Franchesci off for the start of the second, the task was to keep from conceding an early goal—playing desperate but composed, like a boxer trying to spare himself the indignity of being knocked out. They dumped the ball in, we cleared it—ugly soccer, Long Island style—again and again until Brad or Alejandro would try to make a run at their defense, only to be chopped down without a call.

Bradley finally stopped running. Alejandro, on the far side, was lost in the wind. Even Jimmy had stopped yelling. Not much hope, but Theo begged in and hobbled onto the pitch. He and Alex high-fived gravely. The other team stared at their solemn ritual, and the two stared back. Play resumed. They dumped the ball in again, Alex gathered it up and made a dash up the line toward midfield. He was pulled down from behind, and his leg twisted awkwardly. I gasped, but he popped up, looked to see if a free kick had been given, scowled at the ref when he saw that it hadn't, and instead it was a throw-in for Levittown. He faked as though he were going to drop back into formation, but instead he nipped in front of the throw, foxed the boy in front of him, and was taken down again. No whistle, but the ball was still in play. He sprang up, regained possession, and took off again. Down again, but this time, for reasons I will never know, the ref blew for a foul, and then sheepishly looked down at my son.

He hopped to his feet and straightened his uniform. I remember wanting to call out his name and have him look so I could wave. I didn't. He lofted the ball. No one up front could chase it down. He exhaled, shook his head, kicked at the mud, and jogged back into formation. My son. First, I felt that stab and twist of shame, but it quickly passed. No redemption was needed—for either of us—because there'd been no fall. Along with the rage, the sorrow, there is, almost unbelievably—and I must say to myself again and again—at least an equal measure of grace that lives alongside them: it counters, moves among, surrounds, and suddenly reforms them—a momentary synthesis. And there is no fall from that place because that place is always there, everywhere—high and low, long and wide—if we just remember, if we just have faith. And if it doesn't seem to be within us, if we for a time lose that refining power, it certainly is around us—my beautiful boy.

Rosas to Soule to Newsome: not the Tinkers to Evers to Chance exchange, but as lovely in execution. Alejandro lost his hobble, found his speed, tore down the left flank and into the wind, lofted a cross that had no right covering the distance it did. I think it bounced once, perhaps not, but Theo, with his back to the goal, took it off his chest and prepared to turn, and because he was still a long way out, perhaps make a run at the goal.

I don't know who he saw, but both Bradley and Alex charged at him, looking for the layoff. Alex had the better angle, but Bradley usually got to balls first. Maybe it was because he was injured, or maybe Alex found some new speed, but they arrived at the same time. The strange thing is that Alex was waving his hand at Brad, yelling for him to leave the ball. And strangely enough, Brad did. Theo passed. The ball took a slight hop and Alex took one last long stride, planted his left, and cocked his right.

When you hit a ball squarely in sports like golf or baseball you don't feel the impact and most watching can predict its path and end. A soccer ball struck flush on the laces *feels* the same, but its flight is counterintuitive. There's no spin. It wings like a high-speed butterfly and it's difficult for anyone except the shooter to know where it will go. He swung and, after impact, held his right foot aloft for a moment. And as he lowered it, he raised his hand, pivoted, and ran. He may not have even seen it fly across the twenty yards and still impossibly rising ring the top of the net.

Above us, Brooklyn sang. And I felt my jump—halted at its apex—higher than any in years. When I finally came down, I saw the once-weeping boys on the bench—suddenly transformed—up and hugging each other. The boys on the field, a screech of wild birds, sweep the dead grass in an unconscious form. And Alex, a red and bright brown figure, loping, but also burning and still, forever juxtaposed against and fused into the mist. His sleepy lids over those big eyes, cupped hand held aloft, dulling that wind, and lips slightly parted as though he were set to testify to us all.

Frankie
or
The Loving One

Love your brother like your soul,
guard him like the pupil of your eye.
—Gospel of Thomas

1

The same day Grove Atlantic made an offer on my manuscript, my brother was pinched for grand larceny and possession. It was 2005, mid-May, late morning. I was standing on the corner of Sixth and Waverly in the West Village, hesitant to enter a restaurant to bid on a small construction job. It was an extremely bright day and too hot for the spring. I was itchy and irritated. I'd finished a taping job the day before—sanding joint compound and plaster—and I hadn't showered. I'd slept in my clothes and hadn't changed, and the day-old gypsum felt like it had fused to my skin. I must have looked ragged, smelled funky, and probably, other than my giant key ring, phone, tape measure, and notepad, there was little to distinguish me from the daytime screwheads wandering or loitering on the avenue.

I was wondering if I should leave my illegally parked car, wondering when that letter from the DMV was coming, wondering if my vying for this job was the manifestation of my work ethic—my conviction to at least try to support my family—or an exercise in bad faith: a domestic con.

I was there to take measurements of the bar so that I could then go home to my shop/cellar, fabricate a new bar top, and, when finished, install it in the middle of the night after they closed. I didn't want to do it. I'd worked for these people before at another location. I'd made a weatherproof, solid mahogany menu box for their facade. It had turned out beautifully. They loved it, but I got hosed. What I charged had barely covered my material costs. It wasn't their fault. They had been shocked by the price and gave me a $100 gift certificate, which I gave away because I didn't care for their food.

I hated these jobs because I felt guilty about getting paid. I never marked up materials, couldn't price my time—price myself—or even keep track of my hours. I often wondered how quickly I should be working, if trips to the hardware store or the lumberyard should be included, if returning to buy something I'd forgotten should be their cost or mine, and if the time I spent wandering through the aisles of Home Depot was billable.

And my pay was really a loan. Their deposit would float me for a spell, then I'd go under, and the final payment would bring me back to zero. I was a bad businessman but not for conventional reasons. I could easily calculate the number, but I couldn't account for my inability to ask for it. No matter how much or little the client had to spend, I couldn't budget for my shame. And so I'd begin projects with zeal, grow desperate, and realize that I couldn't, for that price, do it—no matter how well-meaning I was. The easiest, the best thing to do at that point was to do what I'd often done: remove myself from the situation, say fuck it, and go.

I wondered if I was beaten. I was tired—physically, emotionally. My children were growing—nine, six, and four—and they needed to be in different places at different times. Since they outnumbered their parents, Michaele and I were overmatched. I had two regular jobs—adjunct teaching and construction—and picked up random work doing random things like hauling shit and fixing things, but we never covered our expenses. We'd barely made it through the winter: defaulted credit cards, one then two months behind on the mortgage, a tax bill, a breaking car.

I'm not sure when it happened, but something slipped. My efforts didn't seem to have traction in the physical world anymore. I used to walk the kids to school, go teach class, or go to the jobsite. I'd come home and get the kids dinner, coach Alex's soccer team, go to the gym, grade papers, coordinate lesson plans. I'd work on our house—close some gap in an exterior wall, hang a door. I'd play my guitar, record scratch tracks of originals or cover songs. I'd write: poems, the opening paragraphs of an essay, the denouement of a short story, the epiphany of a novel's protagonist, the notes for the preceding events, images, and language that would earn those moments. I'd run through the midnight streets. At the very least, I'd organize the bills and make plans to pay them. Then I'd lie in bed and conjure a vision of some grand synthesis of it all.

I'd sleep in the predawn then begin again.

Then I got scared. I used to boldly answer the phone—all callers—but when credit card companies morphed into malevolent collection agents, I started screening. Sometimes I avoided good news, too, because one must be optimistic to believe in it. To be optimistic is to be vulnerable.

My agent was going to call and I knew my brother was, too. She would relay Grove's offer and he would ask for help. I decided I wouldn't answer either. I hadn't the time, the room, or the resources to react in the way I knew I should. I was deadened to them both. The fever in which I'd conceived and written my book had passed when I'd typed the last clause, and I'd learned to snub David a long time before.

He was in trouble with me and, I assumed by that time, the law. About a week before, two credit card companies had called to inquire about "irregular charges": one for $2,500, the other for $4,500, both at the Brooklyn Marriott, a hotel that was a five-minute walk from my house. "It seemed strange to us," one operator had said. "Have you given your card to anyone else? To your knowledge is it lost or stolen?" I had told both operators no, but I knew that it was David.

He'd been living in Florida, returned to Boston, floated around then dropped in on us in Brooklyn. He'd stayed with us for a few weeks until other guests displaced him. Instead of heading north, he decided to stay in the city. "Boston is dead," he'd proclaimed. "There's nothing there." And although he'd already had two failed runs at New York, he'd thought it was time for a third.

He called a few days after customer service, several times in fact, and left throaty, mumbling, vague messages, apologies in which he tried to explain his condition: a weekend of calls until I finally picked up. He seemed surprised that I did and meandered through pleasantries, asked how everyone was, cryptically described his plans. This latest con, like all of his cons, had no exit strategy, and he was scrambling.

Although he sounded calm and sober, I knew he was scared, using, and sick with shame, but I didn't know—and will never know—if that call was to test my ignorance or my mercy.

I also knew that I could've ended it. I could've tried to pay for part of his $7,000 bill. I could've tried to borrow the rest and found some way to sort it out later. I could've told him to run, to sleep on my couch, and bought him a bus ticket home. I could've kept lying to the creditors until they wrote it off. But I did nothing—or closer—I waited in numb protest, cold rage, practical hurt. Whatever, I knew his next call would be from jail.

2

A few weeks earlier, my friend Mauro had commissioned me to build a cedar fence around his backyard. I'd hired Kelly, an out-of-work carpenter, and Dominic, an out-of-work playwright, to help. We'd worked together before and worked well, because we all sensed when it was time to joke and when it was time to focus. Although I was the boss, our hierarchy was dynamic; whoever knew more about a particular project—a particular moment—was in charge of that project and moment. Kelly kept us laughing with stories of disastrous jobs, crooked bosses, and stingy or crazy clients. And we—American-born men with advanced degrees in the fine arts—bemused him with absurd chronicles of our allegedly refined other worlds. "What the fook is dat mon?" he'd ask as to the behaviors of the cultured and white.

We laughed a lot at white people: the men who delivered our building materials and peered past us while asking for our boss, at our clients who raised their voices and slowed the cadence of their speech for us, at the guys in the bagel store who couldn't recognize me as the same person who'd been buying after-school snacks from them for the better part of a decade. Mostly, though, we laughed at each other, at Kelly's thick Jamaican patois, Dominic's Ivy grad/Jersey hoodiness, my up-South twang, Boston knucklehead, Emersonian verbosity, Mencken cruelty, barroom honky-tonk sleaze. We laughed at ourselves, our individual narratives, and at how they converged—momentarily at least—and formed an odd diaspora. We were Black, but Black in very different ways, so we laughed because we were relieved that we recognized but didn't have to explain our differences, that in spite of them, we formed a strange whole. We laughed at our incongruities and the incongruous places we found ourselves. We laughed when people who knew me as a teacher and writer would see me, ragged and dirty, with my toe-down musketeers, humping drywall into or garbage out of our neighbors' brownstones.

We'd take breaks on stoops with our sodas and watch passersby scrutinize our presence. Kelly would whistle and Dominic would shake his head, make his short dreads tap against it, and I'd curse under my breath. If we didn't have a quip, or story, some parable to explain, discern, or protect us from the inscrutable moment, we'd together and alone stare into the day and the days to come. I'd try to remind myself of something larger that I was supposed to do: something I could still achieve. I'd remember that I revered the life of the mind—*"O dark dark dark."* But often that incantation would widen and deepen the encroaching nothing—the vacant—and I'd feel like I was about to disappear, fold then fade into some forgotten fable: Oisín whispering from the wood, murmuring beneath the hills, mist surrendering the marsh and meadow, the fog, the cliffs, and the dunes. Making nothing—trucking in abstractions like law or real estate, money or art—builds something, whereas manual labor paradoxically builds very little. The word makes flesh, but the flesh is hushed. I'd half dream about those who anonymously raised these buildings, dug that tunnel, spanned that river. How it's Pierrepont we remember, or Roebling with his maimed limb and binoculars, or his wife, watching the nameless workers hoist the cable, rivet the beams. *O, those forgotten*—the dead ones, drowned laying the foundations. Labor: our hands pull us toward a particular kind of oblivion.

Then one of us would stand and we'd all stretch and stand and wander back to work: the smashed wall, the twisted metal, the splintered plank, back and forth through the dust. No more grandiose allusions, just *one, two, three, grunt—over the dumpster wall, thud, and gone.*

We'd spent that particular morning hauling the footings, posts, and links of Mauro's old cyclone fence through his lovely parlor and out the front door. I'd hired a truck to collect the debris, but he was late, so we had to pile everything curbside. We'd nearly blocked the walk when he pulled up—a wreck of a machine—rusty, clanking, noxious. He stopped in the middle of the narrow side street. He got out and walked slowly around the back of the truck. He was a Black giant—old and diminished—but still larger than any of us. He wore sooty fatigue coveralls. Even over the truck's exhaust and the deep stench of old loads, I could smell him—burned motor oil and tobacco. His deep drawl startled us.

"Whose job is this?"

Dominic turned away. Kelly sucked his teeth and leaned his head toward me.

The driver sucked his teeth, too, waved a huge finger. "Where am I supposed to put this?"

I pointed to spaces I'd blocked off. He studied them, nodded. Cars had begun to line up behind him. They started honking. He lumbered to the cab. "Back them up," he mumbled.

I waded into the street and began a ridiculous series of hand signals. No one moved. The truck started beeping and closing in on me.

I got him parked. When I showed him the cash and promised another nearby haul, he lightened. He worked the lever and chatted idly at each of us. We dumped our garbage into the back of the truck and watched the hydraulic press bend and twist our metal and stone offerings.

I'd done a bathroom demo a few blocks from Mauro's and had bags of plaster, lath, and tile waiting curbside. I made a quick deal with the driver. Dominic and Kelly started walking. I hopped into the cab and pointed the way.

I once had a frightening tolerance for alcohol, drugs, and sleep deprivation, but fumes and gases have always punished me. One whiff of oil paint or the suspicion of a poorly vented boiler makes me faint. Even in the open air, I'm left with the poison taste. The exhaust pipe was holey, the gas line compromised, and the driver's stink was overwhelming. He had the windows up and the AC on, and it recirculated the airborne toxins around the cab. We were idling a few blocks from our next stop. Folks were making their way up the street. It was the first day of T-shirts. Some wore shorts. I recognized some school moms walking toward the Heights to run errands and have the first iced coffee of the season before pickup.

I was waiting to die when my phone rang. Eileen Cope, my agent. I rarely got calls from her. I imagined that she'd tired of paraphrasing rejection letters.

"She has it and she's loving it."

She was loud. Although he pretended otherwise, the driver could hear as Eileen recounted her conversation with the Grove editor. I had a manic surge, which seemed to reoxygenate my brain.

"Anyway, I think we're going to get an offer."

"An offer?" I asked. The driver turned to me and winked.

"Yes," she answered. "I'll keep you posted. Are you excited? Get excited."

"Right."

She hung up.

"You write a book, man?"

"Yeah."

"Somebody like it?"

"I guess."

"You're gonna make a lot of money. I know. You think?"

"I don't know." I tried to sound humble, but I was so high I didn't know what I said. I could, however, speculate how much and what I'd do with it: *An advance of $50,000 with half up front less 15 percent will be $21,250. Then we'll pay off . . . okay, $70,000 will . . .*

We still hadn't moved. I felt a new wave of nausea. I pointed up the street.

"Three blocks. On the right. I'll meet you there."

I tripped out of the cab into the path of a school mom. She smiled weakly and waved. I grunted a hello and stumbled up the block, searching the crowded street for a place to throw up.

3

Out on Sixth Avenue, Cope's call finally came. I decided to answer it.

"They're offering ten thousand dollars, but I'm pretty sure I can get them to go up."

"I can't talk right now."

She waited. "Hey, look on the bright side: it's an offer."

"Yes, I know."

"Are you okay?"

"Fine. I'm working. I have to go."

I knew I'd have to call my mother. She'd been calling me repeatedly, but I never answered for her. We never had anything to say. *How are the kids? Good. How's your wife? Fine. How's that house? Same. The book sell? No.* Now I had something to say. News. Good news. Bad news. Paradoxical twins. I hadn't the energy to reconcile them.

I can conveniently reduce our trouble to some biological, psychological, or experiential difference. Something inherent, something lived or not lived. I know now; I didn't know then. I could not bear her sadness and the perpetual fatigue it caused her. As a boy, her sighs made me hide in small places and cry. As a young man, they made me sick. I resented her for trying to guilt me into cleaning up the messes the other men in her life had made—her father, her husband, her other son. I didn't think—and never have thought—myself better than any of them, but I always wrought my havoc away from home, out of her view. I kept my carnage as my own.

What I came to feel, though, was, of course, shame that I'd question her sorrow. Whatever we had been as mother and son had, over the years, under the pressure of piled-up time and action, been compressed and reformed into something alien that could not return to its original state. *Sigh*: a plea. *Sigh*: a siren call. *Sigh*: her blues. Calling for her child. Waiting for my response. And whether I was unwilling or unable to answer, unwilling or unable to hear, the impact on her was always the same. *Where is my child? Where is my boy?* It never occurred to me how small it might be, what a boy feels, who thinks he's lost his mother, compared to what a mother feels who cannot find her son.

I went inside the restaurant to make my bid. It was dark and after being out in the sharp sun, I couldn't adjust to the gloom. I spent too long there.

"How much?" the owner finally asked.

I shrugged.

"Can you do it for less than nine hundred?"

I said yes. It was already a waste of time.

I threw the parking ticket into the back and headed to Brooklyn. I felt lightheaded, gut sick, and removed from myself. I'm not sure how I made it over the bridge without crashing. I figured it was best that I shut myself down for a while—mark time until the kids got out of school. Picking them up always made me feel useful. Paint stained, dusty, it didn't matter. *Shut it down*: no more experience for now, no more feeling. I'd watch the people or the East River. Quarters in the hour meter, cruise back to it, and a half hour more, arrive in time to get all three, an ice cream from the truck, then lead them . . . *Where are we going, Dad?* . . . back to the car—a ride home.

Rolling down the Brooklyn Bridge toward the Heights, I realized I hadn't eaten since the night before. I've never understood how someone can, without shame, attend to their needs. I don't think they should be ashamed: it's my failing. Hunger, exhaustion, loneliness, loss, grief—they don't make sense to me. I don't comprehend affection. Watching people eat, or rest, or receive another's touch—especially when I need food, sleep, or human contact—makes me feel like an idiot. I don't want to feel like an idiot. I can't afford to feel helpless. So rather than being confused and weak I convince myself that I have a moral obligation to reject the essential.

Sometimes I try to hurt myself out of, or away from, needing. I use exercise that borders on self-mutilation and the endorphin rush that comes from it. I crave the light psychosis of sleep deprivation; the tension, the stress caused by procrastination or of putting myself in situations I can't resolve. I seek the thrill of impending failure, rapidly approaching deadlines, covering too great a distance in too short a time; northeast roofing in a winter storm; transporting illegal loads on the roof of the family car through the New York night.

Refusing my needs, though, intensifies my wants. Food deprivation is one of the few ways I have left of getting high. I get amped with anticipation—I like to imagine, before the hunt, the useless vestige of a predatory past. There's the wonder of getting the food, the euphoria of finding a place to sit with it, and the surge of adrenaline before the first bite. When I eat, I feel like I'm swallowing blocks of life, which are instantly metabolized and fill the holes I've made starving myself. My glycogen spikes. Anything is possible, and I stay feeling like this until a few moments after I finish, and then I'm as good as stoned.

I parked on Montague Street and decided to get a sandwich. Nothing seemed appetizing, though, so I got coffee instead and walked the two blocks to the promenade. The May sun was above the Statue of Liberty. It's always troubled me: the river and that vantage point. The walkway hangs over the crumbling Brooklyn–Queens Expressway and you can hear and feel the trucks rumbling beneath, the cars screeching and honking. There's soot and grit in the air—the city's eroding infrastructure—and it settles on your lips and in the corners of your eyes. Below, refracted by the heat and monoxide is the river: the blown-up warehouses on its banks, the garbage scows and tour boats, the city beyond—sometimes in mist, sometimes gleaming.

The direct sun slowed me. I must have dozed off—something I never used to do in public—because for a while I had an idea of how to set things right. My book needed only to be in print for me to start applying for full-time teaching positions, and it only needed modest sales, one or two good reviews for me to be able to sell another. The money, even that small amount, would buy me two worry-free months. Most important, though, it would get me started. During my final attempt at an undergraduate degree, when I was ready to quit—again—my advisor told me to stay no matter what.

"It will get easier." He'd recently made me apply for a fellowship, and we were waiting for the response. I hadn't much faith, but he told me, "Fellowship begets fellowship. Don't quit. Whatever reasons you have for leaving, ignore them. There's a gravy train out there, and all we need to do is get you on it. Once we get you safely aboard, even you'll have a hard time getting kicked off. *But we need to get you on it!*"

I wasn't on the train, but at least, finally, I was at the station: right track, early, ticket. Baggage. Three decades of breakage—home, promises, hearts. Somehow, after the expulsions, the escapes, the failures, the night sweats and the morning shivers, sleeping in the park, bleeding in the paddy wagon, concussed in the holding cell, I'd managed to arrive. I'd held on—to my wife, my children, my home. And they'd held on to me.

A cloud must have passed. I cooled, snapped awake. The river, the scows, the city weren't any more welcoming—or discernable—but I didn't care.

I took a chance and called my mother.

Her phone rang too long. Even though I didn't know what I would say, I was impatient. She answered sleepily. I still had nothing. I waited.

"Hello?" She let that Virginia farm girl sing a little.

I cleared my throat and proclaimed as though I were an English prep school don, "I have two kinds of news."

Still groggy, she did her best to match me. "Will the good news make me feel better about the bad?"

"I don't think so."

"Well, tell me the bad news first." Empty space. She suddenly awoke. "Not the kids?"

"No."

"Michaele?"

"No." Empty space again. "It's David."

"What about him?"

A southbound Coast Guard chopper buzzed the water. I wondered if it was headed to one of those Scandinavian super freighters out in the harbor, trying to gain the Hudson, just out of sight.

"He's in trouble, or he's about to be in trouble."

She sighed.

The few things I'd thought about saying sounded, in my mind, insane. *I've apprehended his demise . . .* I realized why one feels compelled to shoot the messenger, to put him out of his misery of being a fool.

"I can't"—her voice cracked—"hear that now." She sighed again, this one to cleanse the air. "Tell me something good."

I told her about the book deal and convinced both of us that it wasn't, nor had it ever been, about the money. A relatively small advance (if one ignored all logic concerning accrual) was better. I told her about my editor's successes and how I now had a room in the house of Beckett and Miller. While I listened to my borderline veracities, I thought, sincerely, about how I'd finally done at least one of the things that she'd raised me to do: not compromise, not give in. I thought about how I'd come from a long line of people who'd—it seemed, just for me and this moment—sacrificed most of what they had for me to have the chance to do that. I was the first in our family, on both sides, who was free. I'd done something to make her proud, to keep her from going under completely. At least one of her troubled boys had finally gotten over; one of her prodigal sons had come home.

She sighed again—light, trying to sound wistful. And although she wanted to corroborate my rare emotional gushing, and confirm that I was right in feeling what I felt, I knew it was because she hadn't anything to say.

"Let me know what happens."

"You sure?"

"He's my son."

"I know."

"I know it's a lot to ask." Another sigh. "But will you help him if he needs you?"

"I'll do what I can."

She tried to sound chipper. "I'm glad for you." Her tell when she faked exuberance was to repeat herself. "Yep, glad for you." My mother was never chipper.

I signed off with her still repeating the phrase. I wondered, while scanning the irreconcilable panorama, what I would do when he called again.

4

David had first called three months before. He'd said that he wanted to visit his niece and nephews. I'd bristled at his voice, which to me has always been the voice of the obvious con: baritone warbling, drawn out affirmations—*yeah* and *right*—that could somehow assuage the stupid, the lonely, and the desperate. I shouldn't have answered.

I couldn't stand how he said "niece and nephews." Our father had ruined familial labels when we were children by assigning aunt and uncle to his friends who, for him, were too close to be Mr. or Mrs.

My mother had used those terms, too, but sparingly, for the adults who were regular attendees at birthday parties, who asked about my soccer games, who called Monday night if they heard I'd scored a goal over the weekend. They—though members of that nebulous world of strange foods, smells, jokes, sudden bursts of laughter, and bouts of silence—were the people she could rely on, friendships she'd maintained over the years.

As for my father, the only *uncle* was Uncle Albie. He smoked cigars and drove a white Coupe de Ville. I loved to disappear into the forest-green back seat with his two sets of twins. He let us eat back there, play with the windows, and wrestle. When I was sick and couldn't go to school, I'd always choose the Mancini house and stay under the care of his wife, Aunt Patsy. She'd let me watch reruns of *Bewitched* and *The Flying Nun* until her soaps and game shows came on. Later she'd set out lunch—macaroni, meatballs, veal or chicken cutlets—all topped with the gravy she'd been stirring all morning. Red beehive, CorningWare white skin, a Pall Mall 100, and her smoky rasp: "What can I get you, hon?" Housecoat over her bulk—I can't remember seeing her feet in anything but slippers. Her heels needed to be scrubbed with pumice.

But there were too many other aunts and uncles—a litany of strange white men with their cigarettes and cologne, their fishy handshakes and head pats, their creepy winks, their impersonal gifts, their magicless magic tricks, their transparent bravado and hollow largesse, their glances, shrugs, and head tilts to my father, their whispers to him in farther rooms. How they'd make him disappear.

And an aunt was a woman he hadn't fucked.

With my brother, Uncle, it was all this—the swindle of language and the perversion of a name—but also he was my blood and, therefore, theirs.

I should've said no or at least come up with an excuse as to why he shouldn't come. I had plenty of reasons, the most obvious being that we didn't have the space. Our half-built house, which was supposed to have four bedrooms, had only two: the boys shared one and my daughter, Michaele, and I the other. We had one bathroom, a makeshift kitchen, and one living space in which we could gather as a family. Although even that was raw—exposed studs and live pigtails.

I could've pointed to our twenty-first-century busy-ness: kids; school and homework; soccer and baseball; lessons on the ancient, percussive, atonal piano; patchwork repairs of temporary solutions in the bathroom, on the stairs in the cellar, on the roof.

And Michaele and I were barely hanging on. Every month seemed to be the last month before something failed. We couldn't afford our life, yet we were too broke to escape it. She wanted to get out, though—of the house, New York City. The value of our building had increased 400 percent since we'd bought it, but our mortgage principle had more than doubled and our rate had jumped two points. If we sold it—half-built—we'd be leaving hundreds of thousands of dollars on the table. We'd have a profit, but we'd have to start over again—entry-level jobs. Because our credit had been ruined by late payments, we'd have to make a massive down payment for our purchase and suffer usurious interest rates as well for any home loan.

And we didn't have anywhere to go, at least as I saw it. It's enough of a drag being a recalcitrant Black man in a major American city, so I hadn't any interest in looking across the Hudson to some pluralist utopia or up the river where I'd seen pickups flying the stars and bars.

David, things are kinda crazy now . . . Or: *When things calm down . . .* I didn't say anything, though. Instead, in the dead air, I thought about how the arrival of family—a brother—should unburden you, relieve you of pressures and strangers who don't care about those pressures. But it had been so long—if ever—since David and I had been anything like that for each other. Rather than protect me from trouble, he'd introduced me to it. And I can't say that I ever really protected him from anything. Alas: school-night dinner, baths, busy—good night. I said something bland then goodbye.

David had lived in New York, but I don't remember when—or where. Trying to recall makes it more confused. In each decade, there are examples of his flameouts, emblematic episodes, brief and long, which depict him and his always bizarre, sometimes frightening career: when he heaved a cinderblock through the windshield of a car that looked like his ex-girlfriend's; when he became a slumlord in East New York. What seemed behaviorally odd or deviant as a child seemed shady as an adult and, for the last ten years, insane. The stakes, over the years, grew as his ability to salvage something—or merely escape the wreck—diminished.

The threat of him visiting made me moody and Michaele tense. Her tension made me moodier. He was, after all, my brother. It was okay for me, but she couldn't be critical of him. She wasn't, really. My sensitivity to her criticism was only a distraction for me. I wouldn't have to think about him, or how and what I thought *about* him, and whether any of it was right or true. Michaele, in fact, was optimistic about his chances. At that time he was forty-two. He was smart, charming, and still very handsome. I've never understood whether such optimism stemmed from faith or naivete—perhaps a combination.

Perhaps fear. I was a twenty-two-year-old drunk. A broke, broke-brained, cab-driving bum. She thought I was good husband material and so it wasn't a stretch for her to believe that David—though maybe not a husband or father yet—wasn't completely gone.

Being hopeful about my brother, though, or about myself, required a certain kind of faith that I've rarely demonstrated. People, oddly, are only cognizant of faith—another's, or their own—and laud it when it produces something concrete, useful, good. I appear to have faith because I can see the tangible results, and they, like units on a ledger sheet, outnumber or outvalue my blind faith, my bad faith, my lack of faith, my faithlessness. The products of my faith can thereby erase my cynicism. And if one were to measure my brother and me fairly, one couldn't begin with what I have and what he has not. David, by many other measures, is far more faithful a being. He has always believed, and that belief has burned him so many times. This "faith" in the popular mind is "bad judgment." It was bad judgment that made him try to act, sing, write, start a business, or fall in love. It was "good judgment" for me to be suspicious of him. Perhaps it was more his bad judgment to think of me as an unconditionally loving brother.

But there's a point in our lives when we haven't any more potential. It doesn't matter how we appear to others but rather what we see when we look at ourselves. And rather than dream of what we might become, we instead begin to dread it. It seems our future selves can't be anything more than a diminished version of what we are now.

And then we have memory, which we sometimes conflate with the present, the future, or both. This works, perhaps, better on others than on ourselves, because we know that in the end the idea of what we are—could be—is inextricable from what we were, what we had, what we have suffered, what we have lost. And we apprehend that we were never that person we believed ourselves to have been, that perhaps we never had a chance of being anything other than what we are now. This realization—immediate or slow, exploding or creeping—can perhaps, eventually, help us reconcile the fact that we've failed, help us accept how this, we, came to be. Reconciliation and acceptance of ourselves relieves us of the burden of our will, our choice, but it releases us to carry the burden of fate, which is also liberating: we had no choice, and either way, we are free to further erode.

Or we can deny this. Run from this or numb ourselves as to our condition, to, perchance, redream. These dreams, though, however charming, inspirational, or trite they seem when they belong to the young, are something different when dreamed by the older—when they're steeped in delusion or last-chance desperation or both. And because there's little time left for us the way to achieve these dreams has to be a shortcut. The shortcut for the deluded is the long way round; the shortcut for the desperate is crime.

I considered all the outcomes—the inevitable shadow that would trail David's arrival, but I'd overlooked the obvious. He wouldn't show. The date came and went, and I remember getting worried, wondering what had happened to him. He called, though, sometime after to apologize and make a new date. This time I said okay.

He did the same, but this time, somehow, the boys had heard he was coming. Alex was only nine at the time. He nodded and probably said "cool" if he said anything. Ella was four and didn't seem to understand. But Miles, whose sixth birthday was near, has always intuited the unspoken—things he shouldn't know, couldn't have known. "Captain Scallywag," he called David. "He's coming. Avast, ye scurvy dogs!"

I've tried, many times, to erase David from my life, but he won't go away. For Ella, he was a series of funny anecdotes told by her brothers. Their collective memory of David was a good one. When they heard his name they didn't frown, shake their heads, or roll their eyes. They smiled. These might be memories neither I nor anyone else—even David—will be able to corrupt. Their uncle was fun. He was kind. Special. He brought them useless things, and allowed them to be useless in a way they never could be with me.

He was all of this and is none of this. The next weeks were full of his telephone promises—"I'm coming"—their questions, his not showing. Finally he said he'd come for Miles's birthday—March 23—and Miles, who was in many ways the opposite of his reticent brother, openly ebullient, smiled weakly to mask his disappointment when Scallywag didn't show.

Michaele and I were furious with him but I more so with myself: I knew this pattern, the promise followed by the failure to keep it, followed by the shame of that failure, followed by hiding—a strange self-exile from a country that was never yours. My father did this to us. I spent many Sunday afternoons waiting for him. If he showed, he was always at least an hour late. Sometimes he'd call, but he'd usually apologize through my mother who then—venomously—paraphrased the excuse to us. Occasionally, after his call I'd still wait, imagining some reversal—found money, sudden battery power, spare tire, new car—something that would bring him to me.

Sometimes, though, he'd speak directly to us, one by one, trying, I suppose, to be honest. I wouldn't really listen but rather, from the background noises, try to imagine where he was calling from. Pay phone, inside or out. Café. Bar. House. I'd listen for traffic, other voices, jukeboxes. Cocktail sounds. Our father believed that gifts excused one or two no-shows, but when he went missing and finally showed—one month, two—all we felt he could do was present palpable shame. If he managed to get out of the car, he'd be leaning against the grille, looking down at the tarmac, smoking nervously. He wouldn't even acknowledge us until we were well into our drive and he was sure that we wouldn't voice or act on whatever resentment we might have—a benign question to all of us, none of us, silence, then one kid would finally answer and he'd relay and he was our good and interested father again.

David didn't show for Miles's birthday, but he called—somber, serious, that voice, which through its gravity attempts to take *full responsibility*. But neither my father nor my brother ever understood that responsibility—devotion—requires more than the affectation of voice.

He wanted to speak with Miles, but I wouldn't let him—more busy-ness. That voice, so much our father's, whose bravado or humility increased or decreased in direct proportion to his lateness. One hour, he could still smile, joke his way past my mother's hiss and stare. He could defray our questions: "Where were you?"

The next time David called he was in New York—had been for a few days. I perversely agreed he should come over that evening. He entered our house smiling, tentative, with a bag of anachronistic gifts for the kids, who did their best to act excited.

I understand, superficially, why one can't arrive at someone's home empty-handed. I understand the pleasure of gift giving, but what is the gift? It saddens me—not the gift, but the gift as a proxy: flowers and an evening out for sex; cash given by the parent out of guilt; but if these things are stand-ins for care, compassion, affection, then "Where is the love?" I know it's my baggage—my family's baggage. I know people do give out of love, receive in love, but I still feel sickened when adults think that children expect or need anything but you. Especially after I've done it. When we were older, my father would sometimes admit (truthfully or not) that he hadn't come because he was broke. I still wish I could make him see, reinvent the moment prior to his choice, that he could have come to give our mother a break, cook a meal, let her go to a movie—disappear if only for a few hours—the value of that action, that *giving*. He never understood that his children didn't want anything but to see their father.

It's easy to shun, vilify, attack David Milton Thomas Jr.—or his namesake, David Milton Thomas III. But sometimes it's unavoidable and obvious: that one thing the Thomas men share is bottomless self-loathing. We, because of whatever teachings or learnings—predilections, the beatitudes, secular humanism, civil rights combined with the misguided interpretation of Darwinism—house the awful contradiction of martyrdom and self-preservation. We are Thoreau and the drowning man who must gain the plank.

It's almost impossible to live and appease the polarized drives. Good or bad, right or wrong, what you are, what you bring, is never enough: one calling perverts the other. It's easier to depict the hatred and the representations of the hate, or our inadequacies though so familiar as to be cliché—but they aren't. Unlike vapid attempts at provocative language, our actions have power: we destroy ourselves with them; we maim those we love.

It's strange then, that our proxies for affection can be so empty—especially when they come in the form of material. Someone with material wealth can rely on the Western practice of purchasing goodwill, affection, love. Money, rather than Pentecostal fire, is what we baptize ourselves in—that by which we are refined.

But for those without—my father and brother—it was, will always be, an impossible task. Their notion of redemption can't be separated from the materialist conception of winning. Winning is the end and the means. My father and brother shared the hope that they'd somehow score that job, close that deal, hit the number, scratch the ticket that would redeem them, compel those they'd harmed to forgive. Some master stroke to make all well.

I, however, had always been dense about all this—not better, but rather obtuse. I, at that time, was blinded by the smoky haze, drifting ash, the residue of burning altruism.

But of course there is the darker view—that they never felt love and the guilty gifts, the shamed arrivals, were only cons.

And no matter the gospel—God or lucre—I, then, for them, refused to believe in redemption.

The first twenty-four hours of David's visit were terrible. No one had much to say to him, and he hadn't much to say to any of us. I think he was unsettled by what he'd walked into. It seemed to me that he expected to enter some contemporary version of our childhood home but quickly realized it wasn't. We weren't. We were relatively calm. Our kids weren't fearful. They had a mother and father. There was no yelling, no booze. David didn't know how to assimilate or integrate into our life. I suppose that was it, really. We had *some* kind of culture, a routine. We had—and were continuing to establish—traditions instead of desperate individual survival skills. In spite of the fact that we lived in what was little more than a shell, that we hadn't any money and little chance at getting any, we were somehow okay.

My brother announced that he'd be with us for a week, which to us was far too long. The first couple of days, though, he kept to himself. He avoided Michaele completely, spoke to me shyly when he was sure everyone had gone to bed. He had no idea what to do with Ella and, in passing, didn't talk to the boys but rather made a comical noise or face trying to get them to stop and laugh. I eavesdropped on every exchange and made sure that he wasn't alone with any of them for more than a few minutes.

Miles, a few days in, finally announced to him, "You're a scallywag." Remembering some exchange they'd had before, David smiled—relieved.

"Mr. Scallywag to you."

"No. Captain Scallywag." Miles paused, pointed. "Rascal. Pirate, you are."

That was enough. Miles was content to swap pirate jargon or reenact scenes from Daffy and Bugs Bunny encounters. They spoke to each other as though both were Mel Blanc in character.

Baseball season was starting for both Alex and the Red Sox. Taciturn as always, my older son waited for me to show him what to do with David. I'm sure he was confused by my behavior—my distance. David had gotten us tickets to game two of the '04 American League Championship Series. Alex had been watching me for years curse at the Yankees, howl at the umps, rant, dance, high-five, and pray. Alex joined: crashing around the living room, swearing, rocking in his seat, looking at me as if to ask if what he was watching was real. David was with us at home for the World Series. After the Sox won we called my father. Alex took his place in line—the order of the Thomas men—so he could listen to my father: "I never thought I'd live to see it."

David and I must have seemed like brothers, but Alex didn't know that other than the game, we had little else to talk about or share, that I directed whatever anger I felt about David toward Jeter, Posada, the umpires, or Joe Buck and Tim McCarver. And David had to find a way to fit—contort himself to a shape and space I could tolerate.

Nor could Alex have known of the pile of memories for me to sort through, examine, grasp, or discard. That his father was one man—altruistic, magnanimous—with many. But with his brother, he was stingy, judgmental, cruel, perhaps jealous. David, the wonderful thing about him—something I've at times admired but for the most part resented—is that he can be present in a way I rarely am. He is *here*, and so he is subject to the perils and transgressions of being here—carnality, desire. And he suffers the punishment of his sins fully. I am so strangely removed it is almost impossible for me to trespass. Because I am distant I can punish my brother in a way in which no brother should: I can pretend he's not there. But for Alex, it must have seemed bizarre. I didn't know how to tell him that no matter how I arranged the sequence or determined and redetermined the past events, I couldn't trust my brother.

I waited for David to say or do something that would give me a reason to boot him, but he was a great houseguest. He washed dishes, took out the garbage, and walked the dog. He bought groceries. He smiled.

I must have softened. I stopped watching him and started talking to him. I asked him to help me haul in new drywall or throw out off-cut lumber. I held the level and he marked the line.

David didn't know much about soccer, but Alex was still playing baseball at the time. The three of us would go across the street and play in the schoolyard. Practicing with two adults was much better than with one. I could stand behind Alex and instruct him while he pitched and David caught. When I hit Alex grounders, David played first. When it was time to hit, I took the mound and David shagged balls. I could keep the drills focused. David kept them fun. After a couple of weeks, he started coming to games with us, first as a spectator, then as the first base coach.

We were into May and Michaele had friends coming to stay with us. David knew. I was sorry he had to go, but I thought it might be good that he did. I was past—I think—suspicion, but I wanted the visit to end well. I thought we should try something other than the *more more more* so we'd have something left for next time.

David, Alex, and I were driving home from an evening game. We were all buzzed, listening to the Beatles—*Rubber Soul*—on one of those midspring twilights that can make the Fourth Avenue gas stations, fix-a-flats, and fast-food joints seem ethereal. Alex had pitched well and knocked a late-inning double to secure the game. David was to leave the next day. We all, tacitly, wanted to celebrate the victory and mark David's departure. So when we passed the KFC, we all looked at each other and laughed. I banged a U and pulled into the lot.

Dinner for six—three adults, two small boys, and my thirty-pound daughter—but we ordered for ten. None of that new crap—a twenty piece, biscuits, mashies, and gravy. The three of us chuckling, repeating, "Should we get more?"

We got home with our $50 of fast bird and sides, set it up on the coffee table, and turned on the TV—cartoons or game—who cares? Michaele wasn't too horrified to take a piece. Miles was ecstatic. "I'm a chicken hawk and I gotta have me some chicken!" And Ella hovered, drawn to the delicious odor of deep-fried poison.

We didn't finish half. It was disgusting. Alex was disappointed, but David and I made him forget by telling him stories about the Golden Age of fast food. Back then, KFC was Kentucky Fried Chicken. Chicken—and the basic sides—was all they served. The one in Brighton Center was the best. "Everything" was in Brighton Center back then. Next to the Colonel's was a Jack-in-the-Box (the only place I'd eat onion rings). Next to that was Twin Donut. We weren't a McDonald's clan—Ronald didn't believe in mustard and didn't care that you had to scrape those nasty raw onions off their fried, gray pucks. Burger King: they grilled their patties back then and had real fries. You *could* have it your way. "Whopper Jr, please . . . Hold the pickle, hold the lettuce . . ."

It was when Dunkin' Donuts was only in New England, had eat-in counters with swivel stools, and hard-edged white ladies who called you hon. No bagels back then. No sandwiches. No glazed donuts. We called them honey dipped.

He moved out. Michaele's friends moved in. I asked him what he'd do, where he'd go. He told me he was going to stay in New York and look for work. Over the next few days, he either called or dropped by. When one of our parents called, I'd tell them David was fine. We were fine. But rather than be happy for us, they each reminded me of all the things he'd done and that he couldn't be trusted. No matter what they said, I defended him. Whenever I started to doubt my brother, I thought of Florida, that house, the buyers, and the gator. There's a big difference between being a bum and having shit luck.

When Mauro gave me the fence job, I asked David if he wanted some work. He said he'd think about it. He showed up for the first day of demo and then the next to help load in the concrete bags and lumber, but he wouldn't take money for it. I tried to convince him that I needed his help, that there were more jobs waiting, but he said he was busy. I didn't ask. He'd come to the jobsite though, not to work, just to chat. Sometimes he'd hold a board or grab a box of screws.

He brought lunch one day. While we were finishing, Kelly asked David what he was up to. As soon as he started talking, I moved away, then I started to fuss with a warped board, but I half watched Kelly listen and grin while Dominic slowly shook his head.

After David left and we'd been working for a while, Kelly asked, "So he's a businessman?"

I didn't answer.

"Yeah mon." He couldn't fight back a chuckle. "He's got big plans." He shook his head. "Big deal."

Now Dominic was looking at me. He'd cocked his head as if asking, *What are you thinking?* He had an older brother, too. He'd never been a criminal, but he was in his early forties and still lived with their mother. He was jobless. He ordered the lamb stew special in a diner. He was writing an opera that, right side up or upside down, could be played either way.

When I spoke to David later, I asked him if he wanted to join our crew. We could be partners. He could do the selling and I could handle production. He again said he'd think about it. But I knew he wasn't interested. When I asked him how he was living, he said he had money left over from Florida that would last him until a deal came through. I didn't press him. I didn't want to hear it. I was waiting on my own deal to come through. Before we hung up, he promised to give me some of the money. He didn't give a dollar figure, but I believed him. I had to. I didn't want to lose him again. And I needed anything he could offer.

It went bad from there. Very soon after that conversation, Michaele told me that we'd—he'd—been getting calls from Florida. At first, she hadn't answered them, only listened to the messages. Most of the callers sounded like creditors. One young-sounding woman, though, sounded different. Her first message had been shy, the second sad, and the third pleading. Michaele answered the fourth and the crying woman promised Michaele that she didn't want David to get in trouble, that she wouldn't tell anyone anything if he would just give her and her husband their money back, that David had taken everything they had.

Michaele was near tears when she finished. She looked at me as though I should've been, too, but I don't think my face or body revealed anything. I don't think there was anything to reveal. I flipped through the mail, looked through the fridge, and asked what she wanted for dinner. When we decided on the meal and I'd gotten it on the stove, I called David. I asked him about work. He told me it was going well. I asked how long he was staying. He told me not long. When I asked him where he was staying, he told me—after a pause—Marriott. I didn't ask him about money because he'd remind me of the Florida properties. I didn't ask him how he'd secured the hotel room because I knew he didn't have a credit card. I wanted to ask, but I didn't, how he used one of mine without my photo ID.

Florida kept calling. We didn't answer and eventually erased the messages before listening to them. When Miles asked where Scallywag was I told him that I didn't know. Alex watched me grow cold.

Sometimes I don't know why I have so much anger and resentment for David. I couldn't tell if I feel these things or feel like I have the right to feel them. Other than how to drink and drug I don't remember him offering me any guidance. And even then, his end was to get me to puke and pass out. He was never there after the party. He never cleared the vomit from my windpipe. He didn't know that I could've died from hypothermia—more than once—after blacking out in the cold. When I eventually could outdrink him I got no praise. He didn't know how scared I was for and of myself and I feared and hated using.

Over the years people who had been there to witness us told me I should hate him. So did people who hadn't. It didn't matter if their family relationships were extraordinarily good, bad, or normal. I didn't have to be his brother anymore because he certainly wasn't mine.

I can't accept that conclusion for long. Brothers disagree. Brothers fight. But they're always, still, brothers. They deserve each other's loyalty and love no matter what. The appeal to and for brotherhood is just that: Philia must live in the care of unconditional love. It's too fragile to be alone.

If I can't conclude that he was a shit big brother, I have to believe I was a shit little one. Or if not a shit one then a difficult one. I was certainly a strange one. I wasn't whiney or a brat. It's that I rarely made sense to anyone. I counted my steps out loud. Buttons terrified me. I couldn't touch them, but I wanted to handle venomous snakes and crocodilians. I had to have the right food arranged in the proper manner on a specific plate. The wrong cutlery could make meals inedible. I wouldn't complain. I wouldn't say anything: I'd sit quietly and tremble.

I was physically unpredictable. Sometimes I could sit almost motionless, unwatched, without entertainment for a morning but I also at times would fidget constantly. I was obsessed with rules and safety. But if left on my own for long they'd find me trying to rappel out of our bedroom window using a braid of bedsheets, robe belts, and twine.

If I wasn't a shit, then the problem was that he'd had it rough. So much of his trauma predated me. Since I will never know I can never judge. And it's hard to do much without judgment—even when you're too young to render a verdict on anyone. I don't think I'm projecting. I don't know if he was ever kind but there was something in him back then that needed kindness. Kindness and the other things our parents couldn't give. Perhaps we tried parenting each other and we were children, so we got most of it wrong.

I remember it was a Friday morning. We didn't have school. I was six, Tracey was eight, and David, ten. Our mother was unusually tense. She had to work, and we had to stay home alone. I don't know why she didn't have backup. Our father was unemployed, and he should've watched us, but he'd been staying away—often for days—and she didn't know where he was.

We didn't have much to eat but she was getting paid that afternoon so we "could make do until then." After she left David told us to sit at the dining room table. He went into the kitchen to make "brunch."

Tracey and I sat in a long silence. He eventually returned and set the table. He seemed light and assured it was okay to let him do anything. He finally served the meal: Eggo waffles and boiled Armour hot dogs covered by a generous pour of Aunt Jemima syrup and wad of Land O'Lakes margarine. For me topping a waffle was a precise, delicate exercise, and a water-born frank was like a sodden hippo carcass. He'd given me the wrong fork and served the mess on the wrong plate. But when he sat in his chair—the one with the arms—at the head of the table, clapped and briskly rubbed his hands, he looked so proud, so scared, and so sad that I knew I had to eat it all.

I don't know if that's a story about me loving him or hating myself, or feeling what might come; shaming, insults, and violence were all justifiable because I was a "fucking little freak." And I do remember: he was often dismissive and sometimes cruel; he always cheated when he was losing and silenced dissent with a cocked fist.

I don't think he ever considered that I might have needed him. I know he saw me as competition for our father's attention, but I'd nothing to do with that. He never asked me what it was like to be scrutinized and judged. I was our father's *favorite*, but our father left. He left us with our mother, and David was hers. And my oddities vexed her, at times enraged her. He'd join her. *"What's the matter with you? Say it! If you're so smart, say it!"* I wonder if she knew that I wasn't trying to stutter and that her malice made everything worse. Perhaps not. He did.

I was his brother. Where was mine? Where was my brother? He'd so many times told me that he loved me. How many times had he demanded my love? One day in the old house he started screaming at Tracey and me, *"Don't you know I love you?"* He grabbed our hair close to our crowns, forced our faces together, and demanded that we kiss. *"Don't you love each other?"* Tracey seemed dead but I screamed back: *"That's not love! That's not love! That's not love!"*

I remember one of the last nights in our house. It was summer. I was almost ten. He'd just turned fourteen. Our father had defaulted on the mortgage, and we had to move out. He was hauling junk from the basement to the curb. I was on the sidewalk pulling nails from our felled treehouse. They were rusty. I didn't know if our garbage men had received their tetanus boosters and I didn't want them to get lockjaw. He called me stupid, a spaz, an idiot, and a retard and threw me into the street. I jumped up. He swung. I ducked. He grabbed. I dodged. He caught me by the shirt and tried to choke me with the collar. He threw me down on my pile of nails. When I looked up, he was walking back into the yard as if nothing had happened. I wondered what had happened to my dog. I stood. The scrapes on my arms and legs had started weeping. I saw the hammer. I picked it up and threw it high over the bushes. I know I didn't hear it hit his head, but I heard him scream. All I felt was the blood trickling down my skin.

If he loved me like a brother but treated me like a "fucking little freak," what was I to all those strangers out in the bloodless, loveless world?

5

The More Loving One

If equal affection cannot be,
Let the more loving one be me.
—W. H. Auden

I will go back. It must have been early 1999. I was a working partner in a small but successful bar and restaurant—the East Village, just before it was sterilized—lots of smoking, coke, booze, and sex; waiters, bartenders, and patrons maiming themselves with substance and *bad judgment*.

I'd quit smoking a couple of years earlier, been sober for almost four. I worked Wednesday through Saturday, afternoon till early morning. I'd managed to get my MFA, buy a house, and shoot some films, but I hadn't much to show for it—materially. Michaele was pregnant with our second.

David was working in New York, too—managing a large club in Soho. He was running with a bunch of downtown hipsters—or that's what they believed themselves to be. They'd show up in my restaurant, three or four of them—entrepreneurs in their mid-thirties, outer borough and out-of-state pioneers, even a Frenchman—and they all rocked a sort of late-eighties Eurotrash style.

They'd bring girls with them—newly arrived twentysomethings—throw cash around and drink pitchers of cosmopolitans. Get buzzed and loud, bother my staff, and try to introduce me to one of the neophytes if there was an extra one in tow. It didn't seem to matter to David that I was married, had a second child on the way, and had never, even single, during my most heinous benders, been remotely interested in trysting.

I ignored them. They called me a snob or puritanical or cold or gay. "All in good fun." I'd wait until they'd had another round and say something cutting about one of them: their gut, their shoes, their education, or how trite their behavior was—"all in good fun." My responses must have seemed, to them and to anyone listening, disproportionate to their teasing—a knife swipe in a slap fight.

In their suits after *work*, a crew of deluded scammers. None of them could discern between a business meeting and a coke party. They didn't like me, but for David's sake they convinced themselves they did. I was monogamous, a parent, a homeowner, sober—things they superficially respected, assumed they wanted, but did almost everything they could to keep themselves from having. They were so much like my father's buddies—the uncles—that I found it difficult to believe David couldn't see it. My father, though, at thirty-six—David's age at that time—had already started and was about to abandon his family. At least David had minimized damage by not becoming our father in full—perhaps it was the shift in generational expectations. Michaele and I were an atypical urban couple—married in our mid-twenties. I was a father at twenty-eight. Perhaps my father hadn't begun his descent until after we'd been born, and David's carnage—how he treated women, how he treated himself (my father had a straight job and a home, like me), was because he'd had no chance at domesticity. His friends were his family, his *brothers*. They were somewhat loyal to each other. There was a criminal code, I suppose, of not scamming your own crew.

David had wanted me to be a part of this brotherhood. Even when we were young, he'd include me: sports, movies. I was an easy little brother in some ways. I could keep up athletically, outdo many of them. I was quiet and I was an excellent mimic, so when called upon to speak I could sound like one of them. I could perform, lecture about esoteric facts. I was funny, cute, odd.

David was always the best and the worst of the bunch. He'd always run with a crew whose members were beneath him. Class clown, class brain: the same year he wounded Lonnie's ass he'd been scouted and selected as a scholarship student to Buckingham Browne & Nichols. There, he excelled in academics and sports, but most particularly in acting.

In fifth grade, he beat out sixth graders for the lead in *Around the World*. The next year he landed the lead again, in *My Fair Lady*. The irony: the poor Black kid playing the role as the man who transforms the unrefined girl into a woman-gem. I can still see him on the stage during the finale, ringed by the cast. "Congratulations, Professor Higgins, for your glorious victory . . ." So good, my brother. And later, discovered again, he performed at Harvard's Hasty Pudding Club—all of this long before the advent of color-blind casting.

I don't know what happened at BB&N. Just before the start of the 1977 school year we were pulled out—asked to leave. David was entering ninth grade. Things had been going poorly for him: adolescence in an alien environment: white, wealth, dating. He hadn't been *transformed* into that thing he was supposed to become. And our family—the family that he had inherited after my father had left—seemed beyond recovery.

I won't pretend to understand what happened. It seemed then obliquely and seems now directly—but still hazily—that the pressure of having to achieve, of having to make the *best* of his opportunities, hurt him. "Mad Ireland" hurt Yeats into poetry and mad Boston had wounded my brother into cliché. But again, I don't think it was anything as simple as that. I won't speculate about his suffering, his wrestling. I can only, from the outside of his experience, attempt to talk about his fall.

David kept showing up at my restaurant with his crew—though sometimes alone—and I treated him like a troublesome acquaintance, until his visits became less frequent.

I quit my shift when Miles was born and then I hardly saw David—heard from him less and less. When I did he seemed erratic. His stories about where he'd been, what he'd done—been doing—were vague or nonsensical.

I finally got a call from the Frenchman—with his ridiculous coke-affected accent. He was at the club.

"You need to come get your brother. He's sleeping by the cat box."

David had always loved cats. As a kid, he had taken "Cat" as a nickname. I imagined him curled up beside a cushioned wicker basket next to the bar mascot. But when I got there, he was gone.

The Frenchman led me down to the cellar and pointed at the litter box. "I'm worried about him," he said, sniffing, grinding his jaw. I wanted to slap him stupid, grab him by the nape, and force his face into the ammonia stink and the hard little shits, but instead I thanked him. When he asked me what I was going to do, I told him I was going home.

David went from the cat box back to Boston—I think to live with our father. He'd done this before, would do it again. Flamed out in some city, he'd gone to live on one of our parents' couches—illegally, as they were both in senior housing. I still choke when I think about it, the claustrophobia—our father's squalor, our mother's harridan harping, her shrill, perpetual complaints—that even as a child I found suffocating to live within.

Somehow, though, he landed back in New York. It was summer and our town house was falling over. We had to gut it. We found—at the height of the landlord's market—an expensive apartment nearby. Michaele took the kids north to her mother's, and I stayed behind to pack and oversee the initial demolition of what Miles would come to call "the broken house."

I hadn't had a steady job since I quit working in the restaurant.

A year later it burned down.

Summer 2001. No more weekly pay and then no more profit checks. I strung together digital editing and camera work and had started a boutique production company with two friends. We launched a website, made eccentric content for it, and hoped that we could somehow parlay it all into commercial and, eventually, film work. Looking back, that plan was ill-conceived. The work was good but commercially useless: no one could see its application. My two friends and I were wayward aesthetes—relatively large, angry, poor boys who had always been contemptuous of the people we were trying to sell ourselves to. "Fuck it" and "Fuck them" is hardly a good marketing strategy.

But we kept making videos and films—amassing credit card debt—kept stubbornly making unsalable things we'd never sincerely try to sell. In addition, I was helping to build a new iteration of the restaurant—no pay but instead sweat equity for a larger stake in future profits. Michaele had inherited some money, I'd picked a few mutual funds and stocks, and we tapped into our home equity. We had a mortgage, rent, and construction costs. Everything would have to go right for us to get out and escape financial ruin.

I was alone, packing up the contents of our disintegrating house and dreading what was to come. I was worried—almost resigned— that I would fail: three children, no job, nowhere to go. And David appeared.

It was his last chance. I suppose I dubbed it that through some combination of pop culture, pop therapy, common sense, and selfishness.

Whatever had happened since I'd last seen him, he seemed contrite—humble, even. He'd been roughed up. His last jag had left him noticeably older. He'd no gray, no lines, and he had our mother's ageless but ironically rust-hued skin. It was his stiff carriage. He'd lost his elasticity spring. He seemed like if he fell he'd crack.

It was comforting to have him nearby, though. David, unlike me, though a conspicuous houseguest, is happy doing anything. He'll eat anything, watch anything, go anywhere, and do almost anything you ask of him—all without complaint. He can be remarkably generous, miraculously supportive and compassionate—not heavy. Unlike mine, his presence isn't grave or oppressive. He doesn't intimidate or rankle. He puts most people at ease. And while we can both get others to quickly confide intimate details to us, he does so by being jovial and charming. He's an engaging combination: calm but enthusiastic, familial but alluring. I used to think of him as a combination of the

Jell-O Pudding Bill Cosby and Satan. He can, by sincerity or deception, sell you sugary treats or a contract for your soul. People feel good about him and therefore, I suppose, themselves.

I disarm people by making them nervous. Sullen, silent, I say nothing. When I finally ask a question—show interest in another—it seems to be an intimate one. And they are so relieved the silence has been broken that they'll tell me anything.

He was my brother when we moved out of the house and into our apartment. He scrubbed the refrigerator. He helped hang paintings, arranged furniture, ran out for hardware, sandwiches. We watched baseball. It was good to have another Sox fan in New York, someone who knew what the Fenway bleachers were like in the seventies, who could replicate Yaz or Fisk in the batter's box. Who knew how important it was to despise Mickey Rivers.

We ordered an extra pizza, bought assorted family-sized, bonus bags of chips, Doritos, and Cheetos. Cap'n Crunch for breakfast, steak and cheese for lunch. Dinner was Chinese food for five and, in between, hours of basketball on the South Brooklyn hard courts till dusk. Movies and leftovers till the early morning. I think we watched *Shadow of the Vampire* at least three times. David, the clown, hasn't much trouble giving himself up for a laugh. He loved Dafoe's portrayal of the bloodsucker. He'd slink along the streets of Brooklyn Heights, the aisles of the grocery stores, as though he were Nosferatu—*The Unclean*—bugging out his already large eyes, elongating his wide smile. Stooped over, clicking the monster's imaginary dagger-like nails together. *"Snick snick,"* he'd whisper. Sneaking up behind strangers, pawing at their backs—almost touching them, skulking, crouched, then standing erect to bite them. Most wouldn't notice but some would feel his presence, turn with a concerned, half-frightened look, perhaps expecting to find the dread one there but seeing only David, standing tall, whistling, examining merchandise or checking an invisible watch. He'd flash his charming smile, mutter hello, but when they turned away he'd bug his eyes out again, lick his chops, *"snick snick,"* and follow them close behind.

Cat watcher, house sitter, he, for that summer, made my life easier. In my changing world—children, house, career, twenties vanishing, forties looming—he was one of the few familiar, certain people or things. Estranged from our parents in different ways, David was someone who'd *been there*—that distant place, the past—with me. He'd seen and perhaps shared that time.

That summer, even though our roles had changed—my patriarchal status and his diminished one—I became comfortable letting him lead, grew to feel safe with him. I could drift, loosely tethered, as I had when I was a boy. And for the first time in years I thought—and maybe he did, too—that we were brothers.

It's easy to have sublime moments when we're protected from danger. They can even be extended into hours or days. In the summer, air-conditioned apartment, empty New York, and the long afternoons, there is no normalcy to which your behavior is juxtaposed; as friends, new lovers, whomever, we're free from what others demand of us. Within that context, or closer, removed from most contexts, people in a vacuum can harmoniously coexist because at least it seems that we can make our own rules. We can shape the reality of our *now* and that freedom affords us the opportunity to fashion stories that suit and celebrate us—how we arrived at this *now*. We can, if we need, trivialize past acrimony or tell of how we overcame it, lending us at least a transitory power. That person—the other half of the we—in the now, makes us, hopefully, feel grounded, powerful. And we perhaps solidify and empower them.

Together, the future seems different. We face that uncertainty together—a community, a partner, a friend, a lover. But there's nothing like a brother. Brothers: consensus on a past, present, and future. And if not in agreement, then one deferring to the other—unquestioning, without reservation or resentment, with us—wholly, regardless of what the past was, the present is, or the future holds. Together. Brothers. By blood or oath: Hector and Paris, Gilgamesh and Enkidu. We, no matter what, have each other.

I've spent most of my life without this. I have been—had to be—alone, negotiating this uncertainty, crossing—because of race, class, temperament—various boundaries in order to gain access to all the opportunities this country promises its citizens, wondering, *What happened? What is happening? What will happen?* Without a physical place to return to, with the only real traditions I know being fracture, dysfunction, and wandering, having a brother—an older brother—is what I've always wanted. The younger brother, at its best, is the protégé—the protected one. What a second chance for someone who—save for the briefest time—never had a father. That summer, as an adult, I'd never felt so safe or right. So optimistic.

I watched David to make sure that he was "safe." He seemed clean and sober. He hadn't voiced any grandiose plans of entrepreneurial greatness or sudden riches. He spoke of small things: losing his gut, getting a job, paying his bills, and rather than an overly ambitious attempt to erase all his debts at once, he just said, "I need to get my shit together. I need to keep it simple."

We talked about strategies: simple jobs, low costs, regular paychecks, part-time school—a class one semester, two the next, anywhere—or perhaps earning enough doing something legit so he could write, sing, act, whatever. He could re-find the time, the skill, the discipline to try to make one of those muses speak to him again. He, after all, had once been so good.

He repeatedly talked about what I had done. What, from the outside, I'd seemed to have accomplished: city school, Ivy school, fellowships, grad school; bussing tables, waiting tables; management, being a proprietor; monogamy, marriage, children; rent on time, being a homeowner, trying to stay employed no matter how shitty the job; sublimating desire into production; sobriety—staying out of bars, away from drunks. Keeping with the plan no matter what people said or said about me. Swallowing my need for vengeance, renouncing retribution for every person or institution that had fucked me. When I had made my future and fortune then I could tell everyone to eat me. Instead of raging at them or stealing from them, the best way to punish our parents was to give them money, a check from afar, and make them children who had to come to me.

Or disappear.

But most of all knowing which fight was the most important: I kept my family—the one I suppose I earned—safe.

Anytime he'd wander, or wonder about the future, I'd bring him back. *Later, that comes later.* He'd nod. But I'd caution him that the work, the effort, doesn't guarantee anything; he had to disabuse himself of the notion that he deserved something. He'd turn melancholic. Consenting but melancholic as he, perhaps privately, surveyed his life up to then, how he perhaps had missed his chance, and if he still had time, it was limited—and so, was terrified of chasing shadows. I wanted to tell him about work and faith, and how he probably couldn't make amends—fix the damage—in the way he wanted to, that he didn't have the power to make others forgive him. He could only, at least in part, forgive himself.

He could, though, minimize future harm. I wanted to tell him about my shame, how lost I was and feared I'd always be, that the damage I'd done to others and suffered by others was irreparable, but considering where we were at that moment, where we individually had only recently been, and what stretched out before us—individually or as siblings linked, juxtaposed—anything I could've said would've seemed at best empty, probably cruel.

Silence. Until he whispered, "You used to be my little brother."

As much as I liked him being around—needed him around—I looked for signs. He was, after all, ragged. I thought I was the only one who could help and that I owed him as much. He didn't have anyone else. He shouldn't have needed anyone but me. There were his *friends*, but they weren't about to risk anything for my brother's survival. Partners in crime, junkies in arms—they used him as a relative measure to avoid examining how low they really were.

He stayed in New York well past the move in, setup, and the leisure time. He should've been gone, should've taken a ride with me up the coast, hung around the beach, gotten back to Boston, and started on his plan. Or he could've stayed with us. We didn't have the room, but we'd have made space. My sister had lived with us for a year at least when she'd first arrived, why not David? He could've done a lot of jobs. The economy hadn't crashed. He wouldn't have had to pay rent, could've folded most of his food costs into ours. A new Starbucks, cell phone store, or home center opened every month it seemed. I knew two UPS drivers who'd offered to get me a midlevel job so I wouldn't have to start as a package sorter. There was my restaurant.

He'd nod and thoughtfully consider. I'd leave for the weekend and return Monday, hoping along the way that I'd get home to find a note: *at work, be back tonight*, and that he'd enter later that day in uniform, a bit tired but with a paycheck for me to cash for him.

But he'd be there. It would appear to me that he'd never gone outside. He'd preempt my inquiries by telling me what was going on. He'd begun that strange behavior. I did my best to ignore it. I was, in part, trying to ignore my own strange behavior: trying to refinance a house that had already been demolished and, therefore, didn't exist; scamming myself that we were going to make it; convincing others and myself that my searching somehow validated my wayward ideas. I suppose, though, that was it: my searching, along relatively conventional channels, my getting the kids to and from the places they needed to be, each day not picking up, not disappearing, moving my ass regardless of my doubtful, trailing mind.

He was waiting for "a deal to come through," for "money to come in." Ten thousand dollars, I suspected it was an arbitrary amount. But perhaps for him it was enough to delay getting a job and but not so much as to seem ridiculous. When I pressed him for specifics, he'd give me vague outlines of business deals with his coke buddies. I knew he was lying, but as long as he was lying to me and not himself, I didn't mind. I knew what it was like to be pressured to have a plan. We brothers had a century of suggested or mandatory plans that would either defy or ensure our fates; to guide or cajole us to becoming Thurgood Marshall or simply—legally and honorably—feeding ourselves. And grandiose or mundane, the chasm between these extremes made any series of unbroken right actions toward reaching such ends seem impossible. And they weren't—aren't—really ends: every just inch we might gain could be taken back by injustice.

Looking forward we might see potential. Looking back, we might see progress. But I need my brother to brave the eternal valley of death between in which, no matter how young and gifted or ragged and dirty we are, our fate seems to be surviving, any way we can.

When our parents asked, I told them David seemed fine. I didn't want to snitch on him. I thought that by being an accomplice—to his con or his delusion—I could eventually find a way to ask him such that he'd be willing to tell me the truth. But I wanted to preserve the relative safety of the summer and deepen our new intimacy. I wanted to keep being his brother. I left him alone at the apartment for that last week in August so I could celebrate my birthday with Michaele and the kids and bring them back home. Driving back through the thick traffic I thought of conversations we could have—my questions and his answers—but when I got back to Brooklyn he was gone.

I don't know where he went. I think he bounced from friend to friend, couch to couch, much as my father did for—shit—nearly twenty years.

Summer ended and my family returned. The kids began to get over the shock of moving into their temporary home, and I tried to keep busy. I was trying to make use of my MFA—looking for teaching or tutoring jobs, picking up soundtrack work, playing the numbers, applying for grants and fellowships, editing my graduate thesis of long short stories and *trying* to find an agent. The one I contacted told me she wanted a novel. So, I started writing one about booze and coyotes and inheritance and madness.

But mostly I worked on "the broken house." I dug out the cellar, framed the new walls, and did whatever I could to cut labor costs and save time. Sometimes when I was there late at night, I'd let myself consider that the project was impossible and we'd have to sell it, half built.

As for my artistic career I used the illusion of busy-ness. I took meetings with random people. My only achievable plan, though, was getting my mother-in-law's car back to her in Atlanta. It was an old Subaru that she'd left in Massachusetts that summer for Michaele to drive and to later haul our piles of stuff back home. My plan, which would eat up at least two days, was another concrete reason to do nothing, be nowhere, and while appearing responsible, privately twist and fret. I'd drive it and immediately fly back so I could get back to work.

Then our phone bill arrived. I wish I'd gotten to it first because I would've hidden it but Michaele saw it and presented it to me. She wasn't angry but rather wounded I think. She didn't want to accuse David. She didn't want to believe it herself. She wondered—hoped—that it was a mistake, perhaps open to me telling her it was, but I couldn't respond, which of course was as good as any indictment. It was worse, perhaps, because I was, in my silence, complicit in his crime. I don't remember the dollar figure, but I remember equating it to a couple months of groceries or multiple utility bills: too large to blow off, I hoped it would go away.

We got ready for Alex to go back to school—made schedules for us to take care of the other two, which gave me time to pretend to look for David while figuring out a way to pay the bill, to concoct a tale of finding, confronting, and getting restitution.

Alex's first day of kindergarten was 9/11. He saw the second plane hit. He yelled for me. I didn't reach him in time to shield him from the impact and the fireball, which for a long time after continued to explode in his mind. He'd mutter in his sleep, searching for the words that will ground that flight, or wipe the event from his, our, experience.

First, my sister Tracey called. She was in the old Hearst building wondering where to go. She'd heard the panicked rumors of Midtown attacks: planes aimed at the Empire State Building, the Chrysler Building, dirty bombs, C-4 in the subways.

"No one cares about Harlem or the Bronx," she cried. "I'm running north." And she managed to get a call in every hour or so as she made her way uptown.

David called not long after I first heard from her. He sounded different. His voice was high, almost shrill. He was in Brooklyn Heights and rattled off questions and facts to me. I could hear the sirens, people yelling, car horns, and I know now that I imagined the explosions in the background.

"What?" he yelled to someone. I heard a *boom!*

"They blew up the bridge! They blew up the bridge! Michael!" Then he was gone.

It kept churning in my guts and mind: my brother burned alive, shredded by flying debris, crushed, or pinned, suffocating under the rubble of Borough Hall. *David! David!* in the tangle of wires, unable to get free and run. Seared by fire. I knew he was dead. David, I dry heaved in the bathroom, trying to be silent, choking on sobs, repeated the mantra: "I will not cry, I cannot cry, I will not . . ."

It now seems insane—not wailing his name as his life, our lives, rushed before me across the tiled wall. Whether they were of sorrow or joy, all the images corrupted by that moment. *I will not cry . . .* was some survival trait from my childhood: the boy stoic who watched his mother, his brother openly rage against their condition. What kept me from running out to find him? Alex's wild-eyed silence? Miles's terrifyingly remote stare? Weren't they safe? Weren't they together? Would they—unable to articulate their terror—in time have to endure the memory of this moment alone? Would it—how they perceive, experience their experience—drive them so far apart that their later cries for each other would come too late? Baldwin wrote: "Our suffering is our bridge." But for David and I, that bridge—suddenly, again—seemed to have collapsed long ago. And so which of us would "lay me down"? *Where is my brother?*

In the early evening, Tracey turned back south and made it to us, and when we heard that the Whitestone Bridge was open, we left for Massachusetts. Brooklyn Heights—the buildings at least—was still standing. Those who'd survived the attack had made it back across the river. The ghosts hadn't yet risen from the rubble tombs. And David wasn't dead.

When we went back to New York, David called. He'd been staying in Harlem with a friend. His deal hadn't gone through. I didn't ask him about the bill. I didn't press him about his plan, but I did come up with one of my own. Since I couldn't fly back to New York after dropping the Subaru off in Atlanta, I'd have to rent a car and drive. David would be my copilot.

My mother liked the idea. Perhaps she saw her sons sipping coffee, confirming orders at drive-throughs, singing along to the Jackson 5, or simply keeping each other safe like she'd hoped we were when she had to leave us home alone. Safe through her home state of Virginia, and Richmond and its monuments to Davis and Lee. Or south across the center of the state toward Roanoke, across the Nottaway County line and past the Fowlkes plantation—the land of our slaver Welsh progenitors. Perhaps she saw us walking the Farmville sidewalks on which she'd had to yield to white folk, in the movie theater, drinking from the water fountain. Perhaps she saw her schoolhouse, relived her protest there—the burned cross one morning, like a branding iron on her memory. That cream-colored man who haunted the town, who was supposed to be her father.

Michaele wasn't sure, though. She wanted me to take time at her mother's or more driving breaks up or back. I threw some efficiency models at her—how a motel would cost so much extra. She said I should do it later, but I pointed out how difficult it would be to park two cars on our crowded streets and the risk of her mom's car, with Georgia plates, getting smashed or broken into. And we didn't know what would happen with airlines or airports or transportation costs. And I was never getting on another plane again anyway.

Between the time I'd asked him and the time he arrived, the phone calls came. He'd allegedly ordered delivery from a restaurant and paid with a bogus credit card. They wanted their money and a small slice of flesh. Michaele answered the first, the second, and third call. She would calmly deny the charges but after hanging up always felt like she was the deadbeat. She tried to chastise him when he showed, but she's never been very good at that either. And he was there to "help" us. She knew that I, we, were trying to be . . . whatever it was we hadn't been for him.

We were to leave in the evening—post–rush hour—drive through the night, and close in on Atlanta by dawn before the morning's gridlock. Change the oil, pick up the rental, do the drop-off, perhaps a quick meal. Head back to New York and arrive before midnight: a little over seventeen hundred miles in twenty-four hours.

Michaele had nodded through the last of my planning but faced with my departure she looked from me to my brother with open fear. I knew her concerns: crash, cops, and the fact that we were taking the inland route. Back then, on the edge of the last century, before our post-racial society, midnight rambling Black men weren't guaranteed safe passage. Forget the Virginias. She—I—was worried about us slipping through Jersey undetected.

More than that: our children, our finances, the burned old world, and the precarious new. I was six and a half years sober and hadn't, professionally, really gotten anything together. I was about to spend twenty-four hours with my brother, and there was bound to be some fallout. Most likely I'd come home enraged and she'd have to suffer the collateral damage of my anger. The Thomas children aren't yellers. We brood, seethe, and then explode at something that would seem quite small—disproportionate anger in the form of destructive action. I turn that anger at myself: no food, no sleep, self-sabotage, a bender.

She'd heard the stories—our childhood, our adolescence—our bond in mayhem. She'd seen him slip—seen my closest friends drink and disappear. She'd seen, in part, my college drinking, lived with my alcoholism for five years, dealt with my sobriety: the acute withdrawal, the two years of scrambled brains, the sudden clarity after three clean ones. She'd experienced the newer, perhaps more alien form of my narcissism and fury—the psychological and emotional state of my realization of "living among the breakage," a brand-new kind of remorse and shame. But this one, this condition without the buffering or diffusing filter of alcohol and optimism—my history, my repeating cycles, drunk or sober, crazy or sane—they all, no matter the environment or the stakes, seemed to share futility: they had all failed, or I had failed them. Only days removed from a small apocalypse, dwindling assets, growing debt, shaky car, and the past rumbling in my rearview like a pyroclastic cloud gathering speed and size, amorphous, fire and ash. The dark road with my brother would be the perfect place for a fall.

We made it through Jersey without incident. We had time to talk about what had happened, how we got to be here, in the night, speeding west, so much to say but no means to do so. Silence. I'd convinced myself that I wasn't interested in what happened to either of us. I've always thought—even as a child—that trying to construct and articulate a narrative that explains "things," either to demonize or absolve people or events was absurd. I've heard too many: Ham and the rationalization of the African slave tribe; why Black people were inherently flawed or inherently noble; the "up south migration" and the "cities of destruction" in which we came to live. Monolith after monolith. The static to understand the dynamic, our experience as something useful either to others or ourselves: why Jesus is white or Black, why he's real or not, how white people built everything and had dominion over this earth.

But most narratives, because the purpose behind their construction and telling are in the end to assert "facts," metamorphosed to serve a predetermined end rather than a journey—which leaves us, even momentarily, with a new consideration—are transitory. For me, especially with my brother then and now, I could not, cannot, tell it—confounded by the run of blood. I can speak about heredity, environment, our different and same trajectories, but how we arrive at our now, and then how we witness and bear the now, I cannot. We are compressed by the pressure of piled time. We are—or are not—transformed by it.

I had a girlfriend in college who told me *our story*—as individuals and as "us." And it gave her license to dump me. Perhaps this is my story, the defining event that caused me to doubt—or validate—my reality. I have never understood that the aim of story could be communion—intimacy. Because if we really experience intimacy, at best don't we do so alongside another? In parallel? Don't we hear and feel it alone? And if so, isn't it because it corroborates our sensibilities—our own story? If this is true, story is nothing more than a clannish anthem. It functions as sign rather than symbol. It's a didactic claim rather than a longing yawp: *Is anybody out there? Can anybody hear me? Where is my brother?* Even on a dark highway, the story can never mean this or that. We don't manipulate it. It doesn't manipulate our audience. We, at best, wrestle with the devices, those elements by which our tales are attenuated.

But perhaps this is all nothing more than my attempt to explain why I stayed quiet.

Creedence got us across the Jersey border and a soul collection through the eastern Pennsylvania flats. Al Green—"How Can You Mend a Broken Heart?"—took us up and into the mountains. I preoccupied myself by checking the mileage and the time and our speed—calculating and recalculating our arrival. Calculating doing seventy, seventy-five, eighty—which was better? Safer? Within the law but more time exposed or less time? A state trooper would see us only from the side, but perhaps would never get the chance if we stayed far enough ahead . . . at least it kept me from concentrating on him.

I think somewhere on Interstate 84, he took over, but I'm not sure how we made that decision—grunts or nods or sentence fragments—the sometimes magical, sometimes alienating shorthand we use with those with whom we don't need to speak, or to those we don't want to speak but must. Perhaps more than platitude or euphemism, familiarity, along with contempt, breeds and sustains our strangeness.

I don't like talking to most people—and I'm not sure if I can. Most of my interactions, other than with my wife, children, and closest friends, are performative. For me to speak is to engage in a monologue that can morph into a soliloquy, or some improvised audible prayer. Or simply talking to myself. There was an audience, now they're gone. Or, of course, I'm not there.

Or I listen, pretend to—half pretend. I can hear most people's opening lines and extrapolate the rest. The particulars don't matter. If I need them later, I can ask—concerned. From wherever it is that my mind is, it moves my body—or keeps it still—accordingly, enough to let whomever think I'm *there*. "You're such a good listener." Like this, I can appear present to almost anyone for a long time.

This is a product of my great discomfort with others and with myself. It's not that I'm bored or aloof. I don't want people to think I am. I do feel for people, what they say and do, what's been done to them. I feel affection, I think, and sometimes passion, but rarely compassion. There seems nothing we share. It's partial love. I cannot get close enough, I don't know how, and so I will not be close, because when in the middle I feel so lonely and frustrated that I want to gouge out my eyes, tear off my skin.

And I didn't want to be lectured by David. I didn't want to hear his introspections or confessions; I didn't want to be his shrink or his priest. So we drove. He asked rhetorical questions about the Sox and we avoided everything: our childhood, our sister, our parents; our previous, current, and future conditions; even the smoking ruin we wished we left behind.

After Smokey Robinson's *Greatest Hits* I had only Dylan—*Blood on the Tracks*. I was reluctant to put it on. I can't stand listening to Dylan around others—even people who claim to like him. I don't want to be distracted. I don't want them to talk over him. I want to share him with others but when I listen, I want to be alone.

I could never articulate what the music meant to me. My explanations are convoluted, and entirely dependent on synthesizing who I was, who I am, how he and others helped shape me. Dylan, Hendrix, Marley, Green, Gaye, Wonder, Redding, Aretha, Simone, Cohen, Johnson, Guthrie, Leadbelly, Odetta, Holliday, Bessie Smith, Ma Rainey, Armstrong, Davis, Coltrane, Glen Campbell, Hank Williams, Lennon and McCartney, Jagger and Richards, Gamble and Huff, the Motor City, Muscle Shoals. Socrates, Sophocles, Homer, Virgil, Catullus, Anansi, Shakespeare, Keats, Blake, Melville, Whitman, Yeats, Emerson, Thoreau, David Walker, Douglass, Du Bois, Johnson, Toomer, Hurston, Joyce, Fitzgerald, Faulkner, McCullers, Nietzsche, Kierkegaard, Dostoevsky, Ellison, Camus, Saint-Exupéry, Seuss, Marx, Strummer, Cummings, Plath, Hansberry, Parks, Baldwin, Carmichael, Baraka, Jesse Owens, Josh Gibson, Jackie Robinson, Ted Williams, Carl Yastrzemski, Jim Rice, Bill Russell, Larry Bird. Christ, Gandhi, King, Eliot. Eliot. Eliot. They had been there, were there, would continue to be so. Electric, inspirational, healing—if only temporarily.

Whatever I experienced—realized—was enduring enough to span the gaps of my grief. They were there. I was there. We, via some tacit agreement, were there without the anguish of a failed intimacy. The place, the state I inhabited with them was more real than the place I left behind. It was richer in the things I needed and absent the things I couldn't bear. They were my family, my siblings, my parents, my guardians and guides. Alone with them, I was transformed by them. Their stories were beautiful, synthesized, an incorruptible weave of thought, sense, witnessing, and testimony. I could touch the hem of his garment and I could be touched. I could bear the shirt of flame and it protected me from all extremes. I wasn't saved. I was changed. It was a transformation I truly felt. More, more, more than some godhead's mysterious trinity. The hand, the shirt, and the armor, too: a redeeming paradox of carnality and transcendence. Love. Love. Love. I was there. Here. Elsewhere. Everywhere—if only for the briefest of times—I was old enough and new enough to want to live and live again.

But mostly I just wanted to sing. Stereo full volume. My voice full-throated. Following Dylan as he searched up and down for those unreachable notes. Private, decadent, indulgent; those things I couldn't be in the full view of others. Triumphant, I suppose. Stopping, rewinding over and over. A section, an entire song, trying to re-create the ecstatic moment of wholly being me.

And I could never sing around anyone. My voice only sounds any good when I'm alone. For me, David was the worst person to sing around because he's never been afraid to croon or bellow anywhere, in front of anyone, and wanted anyone, everyone to join in. He loved to sing awful songs. Not that his musical taste was all bad—he introduced me to the Kinks, Zeppelin, many of the white groups of the sixties. Four years older, he gave me access to music my friends—white and Black—were yet to or would never discover. He showed me how to listen to whole albums instead of the singles I heard on the radio.

But he also played David Soul: "Don't Give Up on Us" and so many of the awful ballads of the seventies. The eighties were worse:

Billy Squier, Rick Springfield, the early emos—Spandau Ballet, the Cure, Roxy Music—over and over, the robotic treacle, often with a dance. It seemed to me that he hadn't left those performances we'd as children put on for adults at family gatherings. It was as if he were rehearsing for something that none of us watching knew was coming. And though I hated the music I was compelled by him: how bold, shameless, openly celebratory, joyful, sharing or, perhaps like me—since we are brothers and share, deep into our cells, most things—it was, is, his way of living, if only for a moment without wanting to die.

David was the first person I saw writing: composition books of verses, journaling, notes, musings, and things to do. I copied him—the action—believing that this is what one does.

He wouldn't speak to me and wouldn't look up. I'd never know what he was working on, so I'd try to guess by the pressure and speed with which he wrote. When he took to furious pencil grinding I thought he was journaling, his face contorted, as if he were in pain, carving his big, messy print: a record of the triumphs and insults of the day. Then there were those dispassionate, pseudo-sincere lists—Gatsby-like reminders of what normal people did—things that, of course, normal folk never need remind themselves of. Quick hands. Lip bites. Poems were slower. The cues were thoughtful pauses, head nods, and mouthing the initial sounds of words that weren't yet his—that desperate and serene moment before articulation.

Sometimes he'd share with me. I'd never know what to say to his presentations. He'd ask for intimacy without any formal preceding seduction. My guts twist when I think of us then: me mute and still and he, perhaps, seeing and feeling my silence and numbness as scorn.

I never shared with him but he'd read the poems I published in my high school lit mag. Perhaps he'd hear me talking with my friends about artists. Though I couldn't articulate it, I'd always felt that Shelley's poems were sentimental and sloppy, most of the French symbolists artificially decadent, most of the Beats posers who fronted as artists and aesthetes to cover for the fact that they were slack and useless. He loved them all.

Eventually, he started giving me books for my birthdays and Christmas. We, for the most part, admired very different authors. Although I had barely realized it, I'd begun my grinding, monomaniacal attempt to crush Blake's sensibility into an austere form—to speak with the tongue of icy flame.

Auden, however, was one we agreed on. He gave me his selected poems. I knew only a few of his better-known works, and I'd wanted to read more. I think, after I'd unwrapped it, I showed this. I know, however, what I looked like when I read his inscription:

> *Brother, read these poems*
> *with the intention of expansion*
> *Open your eyes and heart*
> *Only then, you can find what*
> *You seek.*
> *You have the potential*
> *But you need the three*
> *D's Discipline, determination, daring*
>
> *Remember,*
> *I love you*
> *David*
>
> *Geeze maybe I should follow my own advice.*

He waited for me to read some right there, but I couldn't fake it. And he waited—days, weeks, months. Later he would, unannounced, talk about them. I had nothing to say. I couldn't, save for with a few people, talk about writing. There was always some gap between us, some misunderstanding that prompted me to talk at them or go silent and suffer their alien concepts. When people told me what art *was* for me, what it did for me, I wanted not to be. For me writing hadn't much to do with therapy, community, curiosity, exploration, hobby, vocation, or commerce. It came as a flash, which seemed an accrual of force and time, reason and viscera, gnostic and epistemological knowledge. And I experienced it alone: my phantom trek to whatever place I went. A kind of dark night of the soul: only for an illusory moment. Art was an ephemeral proxy for something—prior experience re-created in another form—which had never happened. I knew there was little to my writing that would relieve me or anyone else of the suffering.

With David "Tangled Up in Blue" allowed me to be—almost—*not there*. It kept him quiet. We climbed the dark ascent in the diminished four-beater wagon, Dylan wondering what people do with their lives.

"What are you working on?"

"The house."

He grinned, nodded. "Obviously. What are you writing?"

"Nothing."

David nodded again then craned his neck and winced at a high, piercing harmonica note. He waited for the song to end before speaking, but I was moving back to the night. "Simple Twist of Fate." The echoing, open-tuned guitar, the heartsick bass: it kept him quiet long enough for me to face forward and stare at the dark road ahead.

He listened to the blues about sunset in a park, the inexplicable compulsion we feel for another—their lip, freckle, the arc of an eyebrow—and the brief but echoing grotesque loneliness we must endure when our longing seems to coalesce: the juxtaposed hues of her cheeks and a high-necked sweater while there's just enough light to still see color; regret for not having been ready—because of chance, or choice, or both—for this moment, or because the moment has come too late. And knowing what it will cost, however you act on that ache, what else it will bring you, where it will take and leave you. You move, no matter your direction, to that loneliness, to that new ruin.

He listened. I watched him, covertly. His face changed: tickled, bemused, melancholic, blank, that emptiness we see on the face of someone recalling—not strained—passively watching his memory and his hope flash by.

"You know," he said, smiling again. Head cocked. Perhaps trying to suggest that he was being thoughtful. "I never understood why you were so into him." He pointed at the cassette deck and waited for me to look. "His voice . . . I could never really listen to the words because of his voice. Not because it's bad, I listen to a lot of bad singers, but there was always something about his." He pointed again. "But he sounds different in this."

He waited for me to agree.

"Love songs," I said. "With reverb."

He nodded. "I like it. I really like it. I can't pick out all the lyrics, but what I hear is good. I'll have to sit and listen to it again, but I really like the sound."

I returned to the window.

"Ah, women," he exhaled.

"What do you mean?"

"*Woman*. Who was she?"

"There *is* no *she*."

"Who are *they*?"

"There is no *they*," I said, pinched.

"Smart-ass, huh?"

"It isn't about a woman, or a girl."

"Then what?"

"If anything, it's about choices."

"How so?" he asked suspiciously.

I told him about how when Michaele and I first dated, a friend joked that my being in a relationship would kill my art. Since I was "all about sublimation": I'd no longer need or have the power, the drive, to do what I want to do. I'd direct all my focus and energies at a person rather than a construction. I'd be useless, artistically.

"What did you say?"

"I said I didn't care."

"Yeah, right."

"I don't care."

He shook his head.

I told him that we make choices. We live with our choices—whatever comes of them—and, good or bad, others live with them, too. Hopefully we know enough about ourselves—what we can live with and without—to make those choices. Hopefully we know that we have choices, however limited. I told him that I was confident that I was sublimating far more than my libido, that I was aware of much more powerful forces, that perhaps I'd now be able to tame and reshape. When he scoffed I told him, "If all I had is my sex drive and it brought me to her, artless, then I'd choose to be with her."

Back to the night. "I'd rather be a good husband, father, a good friend than a great artist. That is my choice, to try."

He shook his head again.

I was losing my patience, so I lectured on how Dylan, or the speaker, is reflecting on regret perhaps even while regretting the choices he, we, made, will make—pre-mourning our future losses, even. How the album deals with how he rejects the ideal for the carnal, how he has lost, perhaps for all time, his muse, the one thing that can help him—us—grapple with, make sense of, endure our condition. Yes, the girl is gone, but so is that thing that made her radiant, made him burn for her. That thing—innocence perhaps—the transitory power that could help him, guide him, even if it is a lie.

David looked at me.

"I've sold my soul for a mess of pottage."

"Your family and friends are pottage?"

"No."

"No?"

"They'll sustain me forever."

"Dylan?"

"He made his choices and we are living with them."

He seemed angered by what must have seemed smug. "Why do you still make art?"

"I don't know."

"Yeah, right."

I shrugged, stayed with my window.

"There's a reason," he said.

"Probably."

"Don't play dumb."

"I'm not. I don't think about it anymore. It wouldn't change anything."

"So there's nothing, no reason for you to write: protest, catharsis, therapy, expression, love?"

I thought about all of the things I'd made and done for what I thought were reasons—poems, stories, songs, essays—and, removed from the temporary smithy that forged me to make them, especially now, I can't find these reasons. And I couldn't make sense of him—of us—choogling along the Alleghenies' spine, Dylan's "Idiot Wind" around, between, and within us. Another chance, choice, for us: my choice.

"You walk into a bar," I say, without turning.

"Yeah," he mumbles, bored.

"You sit and are about to order when you see a beautiful woman a few stools down."

He turns the volume down. "Your point?"

"What do you do?"

"I might write a poem."

"Then what?"

"I give it to her."

"Same scenario, same woman, I walk in. What do I do?"

"You write a poem."

"Perhaps, but if I do, then what?" I turned to him. He wrinkled his brow—thought or irritation. He shrugged. I waited—one beat, two—long enough to be cruel.

"What *do* you do?"

"I don't go into bars, but if for some reason I do, sit, and see her, and write something . . ."

He spat. I paused then turned back to the dark.

"I put it in my pocket and go home."

Night. More silence. No more music, just the straining engine, the rumbling tires, and the roughly cleaved air.

"We need gas," he finally said, more to himself than to me.

"We just crossed the Mason-Dixon Line," I replied as though I hadn't been an ass to him for the past hours. He nodded, but I wanted a different, larger reaction. Fearful. Resolved. David—openly—has never shared my reluctance to cross lines. His blackness, his class always seemed to trail behind his curiosities and desires.

As soon as I saw the lights from the truck stop, I wanted to turn around and search for something back in the illusory safety of the northern state we'd just left. Brothers, we'd let the fuel dwindle. I studied the gauge and adjusted for my viewing angle. From where I sat the needle was on the orange line, which meant that it was just above empty. The warning light was on. We were into the five-gallon reserve. And most companies were overly cautious about such estimates. I could've checked the owner's manual, but I would've had to turn on the overhead light, and he'd ask what it was I was doing, necessitating an audible or mute response.

So I calculated silently. The next major city was x miles. Five gallons, at twenty-three miles per gallon—I wished I had a topographical map, but it seemed we'd summited and perhaps had miles of downhill in front of us. But again, I'd have to share my theories with him and that might have prompted a debate, or, worse, would give him a chance to see my inner workings, that which he and my mother had ridiculed, scorned, envied, and feared. Or perhaps he'd ignore the chance or not see it. I saw us in the dark, stalled on a shoulder. I heard the criticism—my wife, mother-in-law, and mother: *Why push it? Why the more, more, more?* I calculated the lost time. I pre-regretted why I, in order to delay or escape one grim reality, was so willing to enter a costlier other.

Before I could speak, he was exiting the road. There were several rows of pumps, a large area for cabs and trailers, and a large, glowing store. I almost gave him my card but, remembering who he was, jumped out and swiped it.

I was comforted by the newness of the building, the size and the brightness, the familiar signage. Soda. Cigarettes. Not much different from the I-95 stops in southern Connecticut. Even so, as I approached the door I thought about my posture and stride. Long beard at the register. Truckers at the coffee urns and in the aisles. I decided on a kind of hipster stroll—not a shuffle, but not a high step. Not urban or Northern, but rather like the men I'd known from my mother's family—my uncles and older cousins. Head erect, eyes forward, up-tempo stride in 6/8 time, an efficient lope. Straight line: I knew where I was going.

There was the bathroom: urinal or stall? Were those men in the aisles massing outside the door? Were they about to storm in? I couldn't believe that I'd left the bat in the car but how would I have gotten past everyone without drawing their scrutiny? No weapons. I took the last urinal so I could back up against the wall. They'd only be able to come at me from straight on, one at a time. Had I counted them all? Had more entered? Weren't there others in the trucks in the lot? They'd seen us pull up, watched me enter.

And David pumping gas. Had he any chance to charm them? He wouldn't be standing, like me, in that freak silence: vacant stare, my paradoxical, confrontational distance. Would they ignore his wide smile? I felt sick. I should've stayed with him or held my piss and waited another few miles to pull over. But then I saw myself step over the guardrail into the brambles into some waiting menace. I heard the sudden rustle, felt the blow to my head, then being dragged into the thicket. David waiting in the car, on the hood, on the edge of the thorny twist, quietly calling for me: *Michael? Michael? Where is my brother?* I know he'd enter. Crash through the briars. Frantic. And then I saw him with state troopers, either waving them down or they having stopped on their own. Questioning him. His response: *I cannot find my brother*. And me, now, finally, wholly, disappeared.

But I went in peace. When I left the bathroom I felt calmed. I even thought about browsing the aisles. Finding some junk food peace offering for us. We could snicker at our innocent excess and crunch our way to dawn.

But David was at the register chatting up the cashier. She was clearly nervous. He poked among the gum and candies, perhaps trying to calm them both—as though he had some legitimate reason for being there. She knew he didn't. She saw a creepy forty-year-old rapping to her, blind to the growing scrutiny of all the other white patrons.

I walked past him, out the door, and straight to the car. If I'd had the keys I would've considered leaving him. I paced by the driver's side, wondering when I'd feel that guilt shock for considering it. I waited: one minute, two, five, until he exited, unknowing. Two truckers followed close behind. I knew they were going to jump him. I waved weakly, then openly beckoned, hoping that I looked annoyed rather than panicked. He smiled and shuffled into a lazy jog. The truckers broke off to their rigs. I waved him closer then asked for the keys by twisting my empty hand repeatedly. He shook his head, tossed them. I unlocked the car, cranked the engine, opened his door, and was rolling away before he could close it.

For a moment, I thought we were free, but before we'd made it a quarter mile a truck was speeding up on our bumper. Seventy, eighty, eighty-five. He wouldn't let us get more than five yards away and often closed the gap to one yard. Up and down, twisting through the dark mist. I switched lanes and he followed. I thought about exiting, losing him by getting off and on the highway, but that would be worse. Ninety, ninety-five. David at first remarked only on our speed. But after some miles he questioned the blazing headlights behind us—how I was squinting and hunching over to see. He started swearing at the driver, at no one. It seemed to me that he was waiting for me to join him, as though each curse was an attempt at some kind of fraternity, but I wouldn't.

When he began to doze, half lidded, half smiling, I wondered if he was forgiving me for the miles before or if they were fading away for him.

I was chased for the rest of that night until we crossed into Virginia. He exited, but I waited at least fifteen miles before I cut my speed. The sun had just begun to rise. Hissing dew had replaced the sound of rumbling tires. The engine trilled rather than whined. Rose light and peeling mist. Flint morning. These elements asked me to reconsider my brother and me and think of the coming hours as the start of a new day, but I rejected that. Something so trite could never dispel our hurt, never redeem our *brokenness*, tell us—as two, as one— who and what we were, where we'd been, where we'd been going, that being desperate at this moment, any moment, could transform us, me, for even a short space of time; that desperation, perhaps, had little to do with such a change. *My brother.* Unavoidable. Real. There. Ready to be admired. Loved. But all I was willing to do was look beyond him, beyond the lightening horizon and into the empty sky and its dark wonder.

I couldn't *love more.* I never could or would. I didn't want to be alone with that.

And my gnostic voice told me—still tells me—something, which seems paradoxical. I know that unless I'm driven by a will greater than my own I won't, honestly, let myself get close enough to anyone to try to be with them. I'll fight that drive to be present. I have my stars and my tinkered belief that they cannot see me. This is my choice.

My brother, David: anything I could blame and judge him for, any sentence I could impose, had much less to do with his failings than my own. Brothers. Daybreak. Rolling down into the Shenandoah Valley toward our ancestral home. I knew that story—the past, present, and future of us—and I hadn't any place in me for those words.

6

"But will you help him if he needs you?"

After talking to my mother I left the promenade, got Michaele and the kids from school, and drove us home. They were happy to have a ride. The kids were quiet in the back. Michaele spoke softly about the year ending. The sun through the windows was warm; it, along with them, calmed me. I didn't talk about the bar job. I didn't talk about my book or my brother. Peace, for a moment. I wanted us to enjoy it.

We got home and unloaded. No one's mood dipped, not even mine. The once-new construction was starting to, at least superficially, deteriorate, and I was resigning myself to the fact that I wouldn't finish the house before it started to fall apart again.

The kids didn't seem to mind, though. They'd been negotiating the dangers of our half-built house for almost three years—the deadfalls, the pigtails, the metal studs, lumber, and fasteners—they knew where they couldn't go, what they couldn't touch.

Part of the "remodel" had to do with replacing our back wall. We hadn't managed to install the double-height window, and winter was coming, so I built a plywood, drywall, and tarp barrier—15x20. Living in the back rooms was like squatting in our own abandoned building—dark in the dark months.

Finally, in late March, the glass we'd paid for over a year before arrived. It took a few weeks for us to trust that it was real—that the sodden wood and gypsum were gone. The back garden had been destroyed during construction, though. Michaele, friends, and I spent much of April hauling shit through the house to the curb. And then it took a few more weeks to believe that the garden was a safe place to be—no glass, construction debris, sharp metal, wood offcuts, random saw blades, or drill bits. Yes, there was a two-inch gap between the mullions and the frame; yes the rain, or mosquitoes and flies, seeped and buzzed inside. But the house was light and warm and seemingly safe.

Miles and Ella headed for the garden, Alex went to get ready for soccer practice, and Michaele and I settled in the kitchen. She didn't even bother with the answering machine but rather sat at the counter with the paper. I searched the cabinets and fridge for something to cook for dinner—something to focus on for the next hour until Alex and I left for the fields. I got a pot of water going, put music on, set into some garlic, remembered the chicken cutlets in the back of the fridge: they were still good. Potatoes, green beans. Plenty of olive oil left. *Exile on Main Street.* Miles skipped in, singing his own song, smiling. He rummaged around the fridge until he found that lost cheese stick. Michaele told him to close the door. He did, jump-turned, saluted her, then me. He started to leave, stopped, pointed to the ceiling, and asked, "Where's Scallywag?"

"Out." Michaele covered for me. "He's busy with something." Miles kept his finger pointing up. "When's he going to be done?"

"We don't know."

He marched out. Michaele looked at me sadly. Whatever I'd planned for dinner seemed disjointed, impossible to prepare. I thought I should start throwing everything out.

At five o'clock, Alex hadn't gotten himself downstairs. I barked up at him that we'd be late. When he didn't answer, I barked louder—and again—until I heard his cleats on the metal stairs. Moving quickly, though not quickly enough. He walked into the kitchen, into the guitars and sizzling. I scrutinized him—probably snapped to tell him to move faster, be more ready. I have always wondered what I look like to my children. I think my being or seeming elsewhere is better for them. Children—some, mine—can go there, follow me. There the music and the splutter don't have to cohere. But during trouble, it's the last place I want them to go. Being elsewhere is living only in part. I want them present, making practical choices. I want my children to live, to feel. I want them to be whole. I got the meal to a stage where Michaele could heat and serve. Late, I badgered the boy into the car.

We drove through gentrifying Brooklyn, past the remodeled brownstones and town houses, the massive, now-stalled, new constructions. Like any other day, I couldn't understand how to live with that strange landscape. It didn't—doesn't—matter whether I reject my environment or it rejects me; my dubious truce with it will never be good enough for my children. They will have to make a different, a real, peace with theirs, find how they will live without suffering.

Alex didn't ask where his uncle was. But I knew he wanted to. I needed him to so I could tell him, begin that didactic lecture about choices and deservedness, hard work and practicality. I almost convinced myself to answer the unknown caller ringing my phone.

I didn't pay much attention to the team. I was happy to let them scrimmage, pick their own positions, let them run, try all their tricks freely. They played: no squabbling over dribbling, no teeth sucking about goals missed or given up. They laughed. The sun set. I surveyed the Parade Grounds—Brooklyn's urban pastoral. I fixed on the older boys on the neighboring fields and started counting how many of them wouldn't make it—x percent of Latinos, y percent of Blacks. All children live in peril, but these boys faced dangers sanctioned by the state. Even now, writing this, check the numbers. See who gets over. See who gets through. How many of them, soon, would get netted when the police made their nightly trolls through their neighborhoods? Be in the wrong place at the wrong time? And who, after being detained, would reject the labels placed on them? Who would swallow theirs? Who would choke? Whose holding cell would radicalize them into greater peril than before? Who, after, would be worth less? Which boy deserved better?

My son was out there, too. I knew that Alex was privileged and empowered in a way most of these boys would never be but that on his own—basketball court, bus stop, or candy store—none of this access would protect him, not at the moment of first contact, the moment when you realize that you might not be worth a damn.

Again, I thought of warnings, speeches, and cautionary tales. No. The sun was down and Alex was running with one of those healing smiles, and I wanted to be there with him in that place, smile with him, and have him see me.

Phone call. No creditor. Michaele.

"David's been arrested."

"Yeah."

"They have him across the street."

I don't remember all of what either of us said. I know she spoke gently and tried to get me to respond, but I watched the boys—my boy—playing in the dusk.

"The arraignment's at eight."

Nothing.

"You should come home."

Nothing.

"Someone will bring Alex later. Or take him with you now."

Nothing.

"But you should go so you can get there." We both knew I wasn't leaving. "Are you sure?"

"We're staying."

Our friend Caroline called. She was a former assistant DA and public defender. She was urgent—almost snarling. She tried to convince me how important it was that I get home, was incredulous about how cool I was, how unmoved. She offered then declared that she'd be there—willing to do whatever. She's from a tight clan of sisters who lived within a quarter mile of each other, who speak to each other at least a couple of times a day, who despite their differences spend a great amount of time together: nine children between them, real uncles and aunts, nieces and nephews—open to admitting others into the group. We, through soccer and school and cookouts and watching our children grow, were a part of it. I know she found my stance—in spite of what she knew about David—indefensible.

The boys kept playing. I kept watching and tried, somehow, to hold on to what I'd been feeling and ignore the encroaching dread. I wanted to tell Alex how well he'd played, how good he looked, how much he'd learned, and how proud I was of him.

Home. Michaele heated our food then orbited me—silent—waiting for me to change my mind. Caroline called again to tell me she was on her way, would stop by to get me—paused—asked again. I told her I'd wait and see.

I don't remember when I decided to go. I waited until Alex was in bed, so I wouldn't have to explain to him where I was going. I don't know if I walked with Caroline. But I remember being surprised at how decrepit the inside of the jailhouse was, how gut sick I felt meeting the public defender. His tie was cheap and crooked; his jacket collar was half raised, half twisted. He seemed nervous, without composure, as though briefing the two of us was more than he could handle.

"I'm going to ask he be released on his own recognizance," Caroline said.

Then she interrogated him as to what he was going to say, which unnerved him more. He repeated himself, didn't know which of us to talk to. Worse than Caroline's probing, though, was my silence.

He excused himself, and Caroline and I entered the courtroom. We sat near the back on the hard pew. I couldn't recall ever having been in a courtroom before. The justice I'd received had taken place on side streets, in cruisers, paddy wagons, drunk tanks; we'd always skirted the legal system's slow judgment. I'd take my immediate beating and be done. But I'd only trespassed. I'd never taken someone else's property—or at least never been caught doing so. I'd traveled through New York with shoeboxes of weed, sheets of blotter, enough opiates over the years to anesthetize a Saturday afternoon crowd in Washington Square Park. I was young, and ignorant of the Rockefeller drug laws. It was before I had anything I thought valuable, or knew anyone with power who thought I was worth a damn. It was before the age of my relative privilege. I could be in jail still.

But besides being a shitty brother, what were his charges: possession of paraphernalia? And what, really, is "theft of services"?

Allegedly $7,000 from an international chain: What had they lost? A dozen cheeseburgers? Wet-bar nip bottles? Facilities wear and tear? Occupation of unused airspace? Of course not: this was about right and wrong. David had done wrong, and it was up to the Marriott to demand restitution, for the system to rule and for us to—via the system—ask for mercy, or at least leniency. But how much can be accomplished by going through the proper channels? Adhering to procedure? How could anyone take what he had done seriously?

Rehabilitation begins with humiliation: to be something better in the future we must first be punished. We somehow must be forced to recognize, accept, and confess how low we really are. Then comes genuflection and contrition. And our transformation, our redemption—even after this—can only occur if we are touched by the divine.

I can't honestly comment on what fourth-century conditions were—the nature of the human relationship with the divine—but I do know that in this time, no matter how much judges and juries, pundits and political groups assert their morality, I live in a godless country. Whether or not I believe in a divine being and whether or not I need to be touched by him is irrelevant: I know what my country has done in *His* name. And I know that to assume I know God's will contradicts my faith in Him. If, as Mahalia sang, "God is real in my soul," then I will never comprehend His shape, His nature, whether He will, in the end, be with me, where, if anywhere, He will bring me after that end. I really don't know if "all shall be well."

I do know that the formation, the continuation, the governance of America has less to do with mercy—the good works by men—and more to do with power and possession.

But I also needed to believe—perversely enough—sitting in the ironic church, watching and loathing the pontiff judge, that blind, God-proxy law, that it was going to be okay. Even though Caroline was grinding her jaw, I knew the judge would lift his glasses, pinch the bridge of his nose, rub his eyes, and, fatigued, groan, "Are you kidding me?"

Are you kidding me? Another silent mantra: moving my lips, slightly, perhaps. Perhaps a barely perceptible back-and-forth rock.

There were two peddlers, one purse snatcher, and one man who had broken into a car. Another, I couldn't be sure, but I thought he was brought in for murder. All of them were varied shades of brown. Several were dead-eyed, another wild, a few looked terrified, as if inside of a nightmare. One tried to act hard, chest out like a defiant man on the gallows, but no matter their affects none of them were released: $1,000, $2,000 bail for possession, petty theft, lurking.

The only white man looked crazy. He was stooped and emaciated. He shifted his weight left to right, slowly, every once in a while imparting a subtle twist. The assistant DA read the charges: he'd thrown hot water on his elderly mother and then tried to beat her with a telephone. The public defender made his case for leniency. Bang, granted.

There were two more brown men and then they brought David out.

He was one of the terrified ones, though he was trying hard not to be—as if he hadn't yet agreed that this was his nightmare, that this mistake would soon be rectified. He was wearing my clothes—jeans I didn't remember having, and a navy T-shirt that read: IT'S COMING.

Even from the back of the courtroom, I could tell he was filthy. His hair was nappy and compressed into the dreaded lopsided, pointed afro. He looked small. I got dizzy and threw up a bit in my mouth. I felt the twist in my guts again, the visceral plunge. I knew it was my fault he was up there, and I knew no matter what the PD said David wasn't getting out.

The DA listened, the PD pled, and the judge announced, "One thousand dollars bail." *Bang.* David winced and shrank some more. Caroline whispered something like "So fucking wrong," nudged me, pointed for the exit, and stood.

His lawyer wasn't as nervous when he met us outside. He spoke directly to me, asking if there was any information I could give him. He didn't think David was telling him much and the little he had seemed contradictory. He waited as though I had something to say. I didn't. Then he asked me if I was going to pay his bail—asked if I had the money, and I told him no.

"Can you raise it?"

"No."

"Look, I know your brother isn't being honest with me, but I also know that he isn't a hard case. He isn't a violent criminal. He's—"

"A con."

"Yes," he replied, relieved. "I'm asking him if he has any warrants out for him anywhere else. Some of his answers are no, some are maybe, and some are about misunderstandings. Businesses and money coming in."

"There's no money."

"Are there warrants?"

"I don't know."

"Look. I don't want to tell you what to do, but if he were my brother . . . If you don't bail him out, he sits until trial. If something comes in on the radar, they could keep him for months."

"Here?"

He shook his head sharply, snorted. "Rikers. They send him to Rikers." He leaned, looked at the passing cops. "He could get caught up in all of it, stuck for a good while. I don't know him, like I said, but I know, *you* know, your brother couldn't do hard time. You need to get him out quick. Like now."

He pointed me to a counter manned by a cop who told me to get a money order and get it back to him at that window by eleven that night and they'd let him go. When I repeated the information he sneered at me then pretended I wasn't there.

Caroline and I ran out into the Brooklyn night. Chase: $200 from me, $800 from her. On the way back I was certain this would work. Pay the bail, get him out. Maybe he was hungry and I could take him to dinner, or perhaps he'd want to shower. We could have something at home. Michaele would be up still, and she would help to keep him from any discussion or keep the silence from going too far.

When we got back to the house of corrections, though, the window was closed. The cops milling around it seemed not to know of any such procedure window. They shook their heads. We looked for but couldn't find his lawyer. I didn't have his card. I drifted back to the closed window, saw who I thought to be the cop who directed me before. When I asked him about paying bail there he shook his head. "No, no, no. You do that at the Tombs."

I must have looked blank.

"You know, *the Tombs*."

I didn't want to agree with him, but I did know. They'd threatened to take me there once.

I was eighteen and visiting friends—moving from one to the other. I'd been at a party; it was during one of my sobriety attempts. There was a lot of high-end vodka and coke and my college pals, in their native environment, seemed alien to me. I didn't have any money for the subway, so I walked from up by Gracie Mansion down toward Union Square. New York in the mid-eighties was a very different place than now, especially after midnight. Unaccompanied walkers were, other than in centers of action, vagrants.

They pinched me cutting through Murray Hill—roared the wrong way down an eastbound street. The usual—the siren beep, the curb jump, and then the second car from the opposite direction. I knew how Boston cops saw me and that was easy to accept or counter, but I hadn't any sense of what I was to these four. And I was dry and twitchy from my walk. I either jumped or didn't jump enough. One puffed out his chest, his partner put his hand on his gun, and the other pair took me down. They went through my pockets—college ID, Boston Public Library card, a pen, and a poem to a girl named Heather. They relaxed and decided to have some fun—pay me back for wasting their time. Into the car—"You know the Tombs? Friday night. No one to talk to till Monday."

They let me go—east, under the FDR. And I remember skulking around in the shadows, wondering if I should keep hidden until I got to Union Square or walk along the major roads where I belonged.

Caroline offered to go with me but I sent her home and ran to my car, then sped into Manhattan to the Tombs. I pulled up behind a row of cop cars. I had thirty minutes to get inside to the window. I was sure there would be a line and that whoever was in charge wouldn't be interested in making it move quickly. I thought I should leave the car and run in. Michaele would understand if it got towed. The cop waved me along though and kept waving when I didn't move. But I leaned across the seat, lowered the passenger window, and asked, "Where do I pay bail?"

He looked at me closely then scanned the white Volvo wagon. "Up the block." He kept waving. "Ya gotta move."

I looked from the moving car, but I couldn't find the entrance, so I spent the next ten minutes driving around the perimeter. I finally found a space, but before I could pull in, the phone rang. It was a strange number, but since it was after midnight, I answered. It was David.

"Michael?" I had never heard him so rattled. It frightened me. He sounded like he was searching, and I didn't know how to respond. "Michael?"

"David?" His name sounded strange. I couldn't remember the last time I'd said it.

"Can you help?"

"I'm trying."

"Are you downstairs?"

"No. I'm outside the Tombs."

I heard him talking to someone. He thanked whoever it was and tried to speak with me calmly. "Okay," David said. "The window downstairs is closed. If you pay there, they'll let me out." He paused. "He's been helpful."

"Have you eaten?"

"Yeah. They have baloney."

I imagined the gray walls of the jail hall, smelled the white bread, mayo, and plastic wrap, saw the cartons of milk, imitation juice. I thought, *Can they just slap him around for a while and let him go?*

I told him I was going inside, hung up. I forced my way into my spot, and then, running, searched for an entrance. Once, twice, three times around the block. Finally, I stopped to ask for help. It was the same cop as before. He didn't recognize me. When I asked him where to go, he barked, "It's closed."

I was getting back into the car when David called again.

"Michael?" He sounded desperate now. I told him I was working on it. He was silent for a moment. He told me to hold on and murmured to someone, perhaps the guard, then he was back on the phone. He told me they were going to take him to Rikers. His voice cracked. We exhaled at the same time. He composed himself then told me the bus was leaving at 3:00 a.m., but if I got to the island before they left they'd release him. "Please?"

I didn't answer but instead pulled out into the traffic and began speeding to the Midtown Tunnel. I realized I hadn't said anything to him, but when I called for him he was gone. I hoped he knew. He must have known that this silence was not the same as all the others in the past. Not the tentative or unsure one. Not the cruel, frigid one. Not the one that meant I was elsewhere. I wanted him to know I was there.

I looked for him inside of me but I couldn't find him: not in memory, not even in resentment. I only felt that twist of guts. I roared up Third Avenue, through the tunnel, and onto the Long Island Expressway with only a vague sense of where to go.

I had to call a friend in California and ask her for directions. I'd gone too far east, had to double back, head north, and then east again on the Grand Central Parkway. She had to repeat the directions again and again. I hung up with her before I found the exit, retracing a sort of quarter orbit of the prison isle.

I felt it and I couldn't ignore it. I couldn't deny or displace it. I couldn't crush it into some abstraction—historical, psychological, philosophical—as to how we had come to this moment. Here: he in the carnal prison; me, not only in the prison of my mind but now my body too—*feeling*. I howled, but that did nothing but make me howl more—again and again, first as some futile attempt at a purge and then in growing terror as I knew I was about to be swallowed by the night; not the "dark sublime" but rather the freezing void, that emptiness between the stars.

I finally made my way off the parkway down a tree-lined street at the end of which was a glowing guard shack. I pulled up to the gate, lowered the passenger window, and asked, "Where do I pay bail?"

The guard only barked at me. "You gotta park and take the bus."

"Where's the bus?" I asked. He answered by angrily jabbing his thumb at a parking lot that I'd passed without noticing. I parked the car and waited. The bus didn't show up until two in the morning. I didn't have change or a MetroCard. All I could do was meekly hold up a twenty. The driver rolled his eyes. I walked down the aisle and sat. There were no other riders.

We crossed the three-quarter-mile, man-made land bridge and approached what looked like a small, dark city. The only seemingly living things were giant, humming turbines. I ignored them, ignored the tableau, and set out to find the bail window. It was in what seemed to be an outbuilding. Again, I was confronted by angry guards who, with incredulity, told me to take off my belt and shoes as though going through airport security. I made my way through a bulletproof glass maze to the bail window.

It wasn't a window but rather a small office. A middle-aged woman sat behind a desk. She seemed surprised I was there. I spoke as if I knew what I was doing.

"I want to pay bail."

She looked back down, shaking her head. "You can't do that here."

I told her what I'd been told. She alternated between looking at me and a Sudoku puzzle, shaking her head all the while. By the time I finished, my voice must have cracked, because when she looked up at me again she seemed sympathetic.

"I want to help you, but I don't even know if he's here."

"Where is he?"

"I don't know." She leaned toward me. "He could be here. He could be there. He could be somewhere in between. But I won't know until he's processed in the system."

"When will you know that?"

"Eight. Maybe nine." She paused. "You can stay in the waiting area until then."

I wanted to tell her I couldn't. Then I remembered I had to give an exam that morning at school. I wanted to tell her that I had to get him out. I wanted to tell her that his warrants could keep him here for months and he couldn't do any kind of time. Not even a night. "I can't." I suddenly felt exhausted. I think she saw this in my face. She leaned back and spoke quietly as though sharing a secret.

"Give me your number." She looked around the room and checked if anyone was outside the door. "I'll call you when I find him."

"What do I do then?"

"You can come back here or go to the Tombs."

"I can pay at the Tombs?"

"You can pay at the Tombs. It opens at eight."

I didn't want to question her again, so I gave her my number and left.

I stayed in the waiting area for two hours with a grandmother and her three young charges. I wanted to ask her what time the bus was coming, but she asked me first. I told her I didn't know. She muttered to herself, "I wonder if we missed it." I told her I'd check and went outside.

I had some folded scraps of paper in my pocket. I wrote. Anything to get away from the jail.

> I miss my brother. I've always missed my brother. Even when he's stood beside me I've always felt that he was gone. Grief is a sickening feeling—rancid syrup from your mouth down your throat to your gut and back up again—but to mourn someone who isn't dead is more awful because of the emotional conflict their presence creates. You have to kill them and keep killing them, and while legally double or triple indemnity is impossible to punish, every replicated violence jails you in a different way.

Armored buses passed. I had nothing. It was too late to save my brother and not by hours but by years. *Where is my brother?* I couldn't see him behind the bars, stooped on the metal bench. I couldn't imagine what he'd see or hear when crossing over that dark water, his approach, the whispering razor wire and that turbine loudening hum. I couldn't conjure him in the night sky. I was here. He was not. For the first time in my life I cried for David.

The bus came just before dawn. The woman and her grandchildren emerged from the waiting room along with some prison guards and workers, took a seat near the back, bent over, and stared at the floor. I didn't want to look at the water or the reflection of my face in the window or the faces of anyone on the bus. I closed my eyes, hoping I'd see nothing, but the tableau inside was sharper and twinned to that which I'd refused to see for so long—his terrified face. It hovered over the channel and its shimmering reflections. Whatever was out there—over us, around us—wasn't restorative. Rather than be redeemed, he'd be broken into smaller pieces, and haunted by this place, and this time, and me. He would haunt me. And we, alone and together, had never been so far from the divine.

7

The waiting area of the Tombs was like a small DMV's: institutional linoleum and paint, drop ceiling tiles and recessed fluorescent lights. There were rows of connected plastic black chairs with scratches, white nicks, and gouges made by nervous fingers, keys, knives. They were smaller than subway seats and had less room in between. Some sitting were content with one or two, but most had spread their bags and themselves across three or four. They either sat with their eyes closed or they glared—strategies to keep anyone from asking if they could have one.

There were six service windows—three on each adjacent wall. All were shielded by unbroken runs of bulletproof plastic. High on the far right was a mounted television. It was tuned to a bright, airy morning talk show. Silent. I didn't recognize the hosts. I stared at their mouths until someone opened the door and I heard the clamor outside. I heard a clang in the distance. I didn't know what it was, but it repeated, twice, a third time. I realized it was a church bell. I checked my watch. It was almost a quarter past nine. The door closed and muffled the tones. I couldn't remember any nearby church. Five, six, seven—clanging rather than ringing. I forgot why I was there for a moment, but I remembered and I felt sick again. More people entered and pushed past me to either sit or form lines. I was caught between doing one or the other. A dull shock made me tremble. I thought that if I sat, I might fall into a deep sleep or have to carve my own mark into one of those chairs.

I didn't have to choose though. Two women appeared through a door that I hadn't seen behind the bulletproof plastic. They took up positions at each middle window. The first was tall and thick with a large head and short orange hair that clashed with her olive skin. Her nose was too small and pointy. She seemed angry and resentful about being there, and I thought she might punish us for having to serve us.

The people standing began queuing up in lines. A short, fat, wheezing man approached the angry woman's window. He fumbled with a small fold of bills and a page of notes while stepping forward. Looking at him, she snapped, "I'm not open yet."

I got in the other line. This woman looked young and kind. She wore her hair in a tight bun. Her face was brown and smooth. She neither smiled nor frowned, but I felt that if I asked a naive question she would listen.

I was third in line, though, and so I had too much time to wait. I shifted and pivoted. I scanned the room. More folks had entered. Most of the seats were full: the bags had been replaced by people. I realized that many of the people waiting were parts of larger groups—parents, siblings, and friends of those in line, of those being held. I was one of the few who were alone.

I spied on an elderly, squat woman. She seemed to be as uncertain as I was. She fumbled with her papers while searching the teller's unsympathetic face. She seemed about to cry. When she finished, she turned and saw the full seats. She searched and found someone who was perhaps her daughter with her toddling grandson. They were both long and thin but as dark and featured as she. I wanted the young woman to see me—make eye contact—so that we could nod sympathetically to each other. She didn't. She didn't look at anyone, not even her people. I turned back to the older woman who was stumbling over the legs that blocked her way down the aisle. When she reached her seat, the younger woman had the toddler in her lap and was looking at me. She nodded. I nodded back. I felt that twist and spike. And perhaps she felt it, too, but instead of feeling closer to her—suffering together—it made me feel far away. She continued to look at me, but I stared beyond her as if she weren't there.

I remembered again where I was, why I was there, and that I needed to pay David's bail quickly. I felt the same panic as I had the night before. I imagined a tin map of the country with each state denoted by a small red light. I knew each bulb worked in tandem with a main buzzer. When a light blinked, the buzzer would signal to the jailers that one, two, more, of David's warrants had come up.

"Next," the teller called flatly. I turned to her smooth, brown face. I pushed the printout and cash under the window. She took the document and waved off the bills.

"I fax this to Rikers," she said without looking up. "If nothing comes up he'll post and be let go." Now she looked up but past me to scan the growing line. "It should take two hours. They'll fax back to let me know. I'll call you, then you pay."

I nodded as though I'd known this but had forgotten. I wanted to stay and talk to her about something mundane—make a dumb joke about the plastic. I liked her voice. I wanted to ask about her: how she'd come to be here, what she saw in all the faces, heard in the voices of all the people in all the lines. I wanted to know if she was afraid or resigned to be the woman in the other window.

"Okay?" she asked but didn't wait for my answer. "Next."

I spent the next twenty minutes under the television trying to get my exam together. I dug through my bag. I looked through my books for my margin notes. There were too many. When I wrote them, I'd felt that I'd discovered a novel way of talking about the literature, but now most of it seemed to be a jumble of tumid musings. I searched for something of value and then, after a while, I realized that I was rocking and muttering. No one seemed to notice. One woman nearby sucked her teeth. I knew she'd have to either stop or leave or else I would go mad, so I tried to focus on others. Some watched the muted TV, some checked their phones for a signal, some fiddled with or studied their paperwork. Some disciplined or ignored their children—grandchildren. One young man sat leaning forward wrapped in his own arms. Everyone was brown.

I watched people for the next half hour, though I'm certain I must have dozed off a few times. The bell clanged again. I checked my watch. Late. More people entered. No one seemed to leave. The air grew thick and hot, laced with the smells of our bodies and breath.

There were a few angry exchanges with the cruel woman—the loudest with someone who seemed to be a very young mother. She'd wanted to deposit money for her son, but the teller repeatedly stated that he wasn't in the system. They barked and shouted about each other's attitudes, manners, and tones. The soft-faced teller finally intervened and quickly found him. Silent. Cordial goodbyes. "Next." And it seemed like nothing had happened.

I had to move. The only open space was by the door. I leaned against it. On *The Jerry Springer Show*, a deranged woman waved a finger at no one. I realized that I'd have to move each time someone entered. A wheezing man sat near me. He moved his bag from the end seat and offered it to me. I told him, "No, thank you." I couldn't bear listening to his tortured breaths and weighed taking my original position—back with the teeth sucker—but someone had filled it.

I tried to avoid the room. But now I could see David, his cell, his face, hours, days, months. How would I tell my mother, my father? I tried to picture our parents waiting with me. She would alternate between ignoring him and jabbing him. He would watch reality TV and look absurdly aloof. They'd realize I had to fix it: my utility and distance, my ability to shut down those parts in me that were useless to them. My mother would have to see my dispassion as compassion. My father would have to reimagine my capacity for cruelty as reason. I'd be *good*, for this moment and crisis. And rather than prodigal I'd be my mother's patriarch and my father's prince. When the job was done, perhaps we could have lunch together—the three of us. Perhaps spend the day together—make it to dinner with Michaele and the kids.

And for a moment I felt I was up to it. I'd begin to forgive until I'd realize there was nothing to forgive or that my trespasses against them were as great or greater than the ones I'd suffered. We'd welcome David back, and I'd try to let him be an uncle first. I'd try to relieve my children of their conflicted feelings for him, and show them how to be a brother so they'd never have to ask, *Where is my brother?* Never have to question or resist their blood. They'd have each other and believe without proof that we could be whole.

But I couldn't see it. I couldn't even fake it. It all made me feel weak and vulnerable. Even my tough love was impotent. I cringed—that spike and that twist—but I refused to cry. There was nowhere to go to not feel. I couldn't escape the suffocating room and its palpable grief. So I crushed my guilt into anger, the other ecstasy: over David's frauds and betrayals, my parents' ineptitude and their devotion to—ideal or carnal—their personal desire. And for my pains I had a diamond of resentment, unbreakable and gleaming.

Ten past the hour. *Clang, clang, clang,* went the late bells of the church—the clamor of green, weakened brass. Ring them bells, Julian of Norwich, but we will always be too late.

I called Dominic and asked him if he would come to either take over at the Tombs or proctor the exam. He said he'd be there in thirty minutes. I returned to my questions, but I couldn't write complete sentences so I settled for bulleted notes:

—Huck's and America's coming of age
—Nick's romanticism in a modern, godless world
—Prufrock's rejection of consciousness
—Hamlet and the cost of action

It must have taken a while to write even that. Dominic appeared. I gave him quick instructions for what to do, but as I was handing him the money, they called my name.

It was too easy. The soft-faced woman didn't mention any warrants. I slid her the money, which she took and quickly counted. She gave me a receipt and told me that if he didn't jump bail I'd get a check after the trial, less the city's percentage. I mumbled something about incarceration for profit, which she ignored. I thanked her. And with my friend I left the Tombs.

We tacitly agreed to get a few blocks away before saying anything. I apologized to him, but he shook his head and asked if I still needed him to proctor.

"You look fried."

I said something about responsibility to my students. He said, "Fuck them," then withdrew the comment. He went on to talk about his older brother who was jobless and still living with their parents—how he'd have let him rot. He withdrew that, too, and said—mostly to himself—that his brother needed some kind of slap to wake him up. I shook my head at him; we both knew it was a lie.

I thanked Dominic and walked north in a sluggish panic. I skipped subway stations and tried in my head to complete the vague exam questions I'd scribbled earlier.

I finally went underground at Astor Place. I pulled out my notebook. I decided one essay question would be enough. Multiple texts—the poems, plays, short fiction, novels—one unifying question and answer; a call-and-response, me to they, from Hamlet to Huck, Prufrock to Sonny:

> How do we—if we can at all—live with uncertainty? How do we endure the agony of not knowing? How do we minimize, endure the damage we do to others and ourselves in trying "not to suffer"? "If we are sure of our *unsurety* . . ."

I ran off the train and up the twelve floors to the adjunct office. Everyone inside seemed unreasonably happy—although perhaps they weren't. Warm May: end of the semester, hours left. I typed the question and printed it out. It looked ridiculous on the page—all that white space beneath it, forget about all the dark space behind.

In the classroom, I tried to explain the best I could: open book, use your personal experience to help—a scope, a lens. I was smiling, but I'm sure I looked reptilian and dangerous. I gave a few sample introductions to comfort them.

"It's what we've been talking about all semester. Don't worry." But I quickly realized that I was only wasting their time. I sat.

"One book?" a student asked.

I responded as though granting her a wish. A close reading: one book, section of a book, a paragraph. One poem. One scene. A soliloquy. Be specific. Exhaust the small—or what at first seems small. Condense the vast. Connect the two. No response. "Remember, 'the dance along the artery / the circulation of the lymph / are figured in the drift of stars.'" I smiled again and gestured to the unseen heavens, but most of their faces seemed to ask, *Then why the fuck did you make us read all the others?*

Two hours. No questions. My best students, even the sycophants, wanted to avoid me. No one smiled when they placed their blue books on the growing pile and only a few gave goodbyes and summer well wishes.

Time. There were two left and they looked frantically from the clock to me to their work. I tried to calm them with vague hand gestures, strange facial expressions, but they continued writing furiously. They finished twenty minutes late.

I wanted to stay in the windowless classroom. I turned off the lights and sat in the cool dark. I thought the room was free, but someone scurried in, muttered at the gloom, and turned on the lights. Her face was pinched, more so when she saw me. I mumbled something that must have seemed menacing, because she froze then slowly took the long way around the perimeter of the class toward the desk.

I gathered the exams, left the class, and started up the stairs. I stopped halfway, though, sat, and began skimming the essays. I suppose I wanted to find something profound, even revelatory, but every response was fearful. No proxies for grappling with uncertainty but rather exercises in avoiding it. One had written on Hamlet. She'd been quiet all semester—sullen, almost. She wrote that Hamlet was a selfish coward and that if he'd killed his uncle when he'd had the chance, no one else would've died. I responded with comments she'd never see.

> If our struggle is to live with uncertainty, the futility, perhaps, of whether we can unify our oppositional selves—a people, a person—then we must live under, even in fear of that "total dark sublime" rather than embrace and be embraced by it, be folded into that frozen, empty space between the stars, which neither gives nor receives love. And perhaps no matter our devotion

to anyone or anything, our desperation. No matter our choice, "To be or not to be," to do or not to do, we will never, except for the briefest time, be right.

I rode the F Train around Manhattan. When I got home, Michaele told me I looked exhausted and I should sleep. She hadn't heard anything, but she'd wake me when she had.

I lay down and watched the events of the last twenty-four hours pass. I felt a crack—a fault—run through me, nothing metaphorical about it. I thought about calling a friend, a devout Catholic, to ask about his priest, someone other than me, to whom I could confess. I wondered what was inside David, what he had to confess, if his fault line was longer, deeper, wider than mine, if it was moving, the opposing sides spreading or grinding against each other. But that was useless, even cruel, to spend any time speculating about his damage unless I were willing to mend it, or at least somehow try to endure it with him. But I knew that it was too late for whatever partial love I'd withheld.

I gave up on sleep and went downstairs. Alex was by the door wearing his Sox hat, his glove, and snapping a ball into the leather pocket. He'd placed my glove on the couch. I spared him the anxiety of having to ask me, called to Michaele that we were leaving, and headed out.

Late afternoon. Long shadows and amaranth light. We crossed our street, then slipped and squeezed through the locked schoolyard gate. I skipped grounders across the tarmac to him. He'd point to where he wanted them, move, scoop up the ball, and throw it back. He'd experiment with different arm angles each time—over-the-top down to sidearm. After each, he'd pause, as though waiting for me to correct him, but I kept silent and watched the sun setting behind him.

After a while, he walked the ball back to me and asked if we could practice pitching. I nodded, but neither of us moved. I was looking west still. He turned to see what I was watching: long, gray clouds—smoke on the angry blaze of rose. I looked down at him. The light deepened the red in his hair and face. I wanted to touch him—his head or his shoulder—but I couldn't. And I felt sad, suddenly, so familiar, unavoidable. I remember it deepening as I wondered what, by not feeling—being elsewhere—I'd missed. Sick. I'd never recover that time, those chances to be there even if I were willing to live with the fragility of everything that we'd broken.

I kept looking high to the west.

"I need to tell you about my brother, your uncle."

He looked down, resigned to having to listen.

"Do you know what's going on?"

He nodded, still watching the deepening shadows.

"Are you sure?"

He nodded.

"Listen, our family, the men, the Thomas men, are troubled." I looked down but not at him. "Me too, but that doesn't mean you are. It doesn't mean you have to be, or you're going to be." I hated what I was saying. I hated that way my voice sounded—flat, mumbling. I tried to change it, make myself sound sincere. I told him that life wasn't formulaic. Do this and that will happen. Do that and this will be. I told him that I was trying and would always try to be good to him and even if I succeeded, it didn't mean I was good. We were in a "good" place—this place, this moment. I said that being good now was easier than if we weren't, but if we moved from this place to a bad one, we had to still try our best to be good to each other—to anyone we loved.

"Your uncle . . . is in a bad place."

"I know."

"And I don't mean just literally, physically."

"I know."

"But that doesn't mean he's bad. There are people in this world who do terrible things. He's not like that."

I started shaking my head.

"But we make choices, even when it seems to us we haven't any." I told him—tried to—that the hardest part is figuring out what the right choice is, that sometimes it isn't so obvious and we wait, but that's a choice, too. Even though it seems like we're standing still, we are really moving, and the world we're in is moving, too. The right choice. "And you then have to figure out what's the right choice for you, or for others." And on and on. I knew I should stop. "And you might make the right choice, but everything turns out wrong." I realized I was speaking in my head. "That's the most dangerous moment. Do you know why?"

He shook his head reluctantly.

"Because you think making the right choice doesn't matter." He took the ball out of his glove and turned it in his long fingers.

"Will I really hurt my arm throwing curves?"

"Yeah."

"How do you throw one though?"

I took the ball and he watched closely as I demonstrated the throwing motion start to finish: elbow even with or above the shoulder, palm at the plate, forearm rotation. Don't try to throw it too hard. Let it break on its own. The deuce, Uncle Charlie: it doesn't really curve that much. It drops, 12 to 6. He took it back, paced off the forty-five feet, turned, and motioned for me to squat. I did. The sun had dropped below the apartment buildings, and I no longer needed to squint to see him. He pulled his cap down and peered in for the sign. I flashed it. He nodded. A car roared down the street and clattered over the speed bump. We both looked. On the other side, about a half block away, David was moving—a broken shuffle—along the sidewalk toward our home.

Alex was suddenly beside me, watching me watch my brother. David was walking in my old shoes, wearing my old clothes. As he got closer, he seemed to be in pain. But at the same time he didn't seem to be all there. He didn't seem real. Or perhaps he couldn't be real to me. I almost spoke his name but I remembered Alex. He looked from me to David then to the ground. Now, when I recall that moment, I think of David as a laboring ghost, a spirit who was unable to fully grasp or gain traction in this world but still bore the onus of it. He didn't see us, and I knew that unless I called out to him he'd keep going. But I couldn't find my voice, and I let him pass by. Alex was there, the car horns, the dying shadows, my brother's wake. And parts of me were there, too—my itchy stubble, my sweaty hand in my leather mitt—but those feelings began to fade away.

And if David would see me, cross over, and ask, "Oh, my loving brother, when the world's on fire / Don't you want God's bosom to be your pillow?" I would answer, *Yes! Yes! Yes!* But where can we go, to whom can we turn now that it's gone so dark and cold?

What Pip Saw

He saw God's foot upon the treadle of the loom, and spoke it; and therefore his shipmates called him mad.
—Herman Melville, *Moby Dick*

έκφραση

1

Miles and I were going to Central Park for a bird walk. We'd been planning our outing for a week. Even so, we were late leaving home, and what had been a dry, white morning would soon be a wet, gray noon. I'd dragged behind the day, feeling doom that would move in with the weather. I'd wanted to concede to the circumstances of time, dread, and cold. Miles, though, had been waiting by the front door for some time. I couldn't say no.

He rarely complained. The middle child, he was about to turn nine, and whether it was his nature or that he'd been nurtured into such behavior, he spent much of his time doing what the rest of the family wanted. He went to most of Alex's sporting events, and his younger sister, Ella, was just beginning her extracurriculars. Our social life was dominated by dinners with school chums and their families. None had children Miles's age. So, at birthdays and cookouts he lived in the gaps of his generation. He didn't seem to have much in common with his peers either. He preferred the company of adults and infants, and perhaps because it was easier for us to *"let him be"* he, in groups, was usually alone.

I felt that we'd failed Miles. Though Alex and Ella required more maintenance, their aptitudes, abilities, and willingness to engage in and pursue them—their relative conventionality—made them *easy* children. Miles, though, because he lived so mysteriously, was difficult. Though his terrible twos were tranquil—as were the following years—besides his parents, most people found it difficult to connect with him. I, however, couldn't do so without neglecting his siblings.

They'd fuss or look forlorn: Miles would go off and stare at a wall or play with a stick or a box.

As an infant he was beguiling. As a toddler he was easy. Nothing seemed to bother him. He ate everything. He didn't fuss about going to bed. His ritual was to jump on the mattress a few times ending with a flying headbutt to my chest. He had his terrible lizard figurines and just needed a safe place and some time. Then he'd lie down and close his eyes.

Miles was *"different."* He was long and solid. He was yellow. The delivery team thought he was jaundiced. His eyes were beautiful. White people often remarked on their color. First, they were blue. Then they were green. But for me, their beauty was how constant they were. Most eyes convey one's emotions and confirm one's presence. Miles was born with a thousand-mile stare. It seemed he saw more.

In the summer of 2001, Miles was two and a half, Ella was an infant, and Alex was about to start kindergarten. Our house was falling down, and we had to move out. My brother was running wild. We were struggling financially. While I don't think we did enough to help Alex with what he suffered in watching the second plane hit—feeling the towers fall, wondering if all of New York was under attack, and if we might be killed at any moment—Alex drew and painted the towers and fireballs and displayed fear, anxiety, and loss that seemed normal in such abnormal circumstances. For Miles, though, when walking along Montague Street and the memorials, he pointed at a photograph of the towers and whispered to no one, "The buildings fell down."

I didn't have—other than Alex—a context as to how Miles should be. Alex spoke relatively early and though he mispronounced a few words—*"lah-doo"* instead of water and *"Nina"* instead of Liam—he seemed, relative to his peers, self-possessed and hyper-articulate. He could also pay attention. He seemed to listen, understand, and internalize what was said to him.

Miles made sounds. He'd growl while lying on the floor, whoosh when running—his arms held back and tight against him as though he were a stooping peregrine. He'd hum a soundtrack to most of his movement. He'd stomp or jump from tile to tile. He'd look surprised while in the air and exhilarated—but also relieved—when he landed.

I didn't think Alex's or Ella's life was easier—or easy at all. It's that because they had more purchase in the *real* world, they didn't seem so helpless when presented with conflict. And while they were extraordinary athletes, artists, and thinkers, they weren't bizarre. And Miles, more and more, appeared as such.

To include him I tried to make him like sports. I loved sports. They made sense to me. I liked rules and boundaries. I liked practice and repetition. I was good at them. I didn't have to explain my presence and value, I could just show. I was, relative to Miles, small. But I was quick, and I don't remember feeling pain. Playing even the roughest games against much older kids felt—relative to anything else I could be doing—safe.

Miles didn't experience this. Perhaps because when disengaged from a game, he'd stumble about like a drunken bear. But when he was invested, or when I demanded he focus, he was intense, agile, powerful, and explosive. Like many lunatic fathers, I saw a glorious athletic career before him. His vertical and broad jumps were outstanding. Sometimes I'd catch him shooting jumpers in the back garden with a regulation ball into a toy basket. He was physically fearless—reckless even. He'd little regard for this material world, so it seemed he'd little regard for pain—his or anyone else's. He didn't hurt other children, but he did regularly thump teens and adults. Once, when he was three, at a Christmas party, he'd stalked the host whom I was standing next to. We were in the front room of an open-floor brownstone. I saw Miles some thirty feet away peering between and around people's legs. When he sprang, I thought he was running to me. But instead—with perfect form—he drove his shoulders into the back of our host's knees, wrapped up his lower legs, and brought him, his drink, and his hors d'oeuvres down. This done, Miles walked away. I apologized. My friend laughed and told me my son was a lock for the NFL. Others agreed. I scoffed, but secretly saw an entire hall-of-fame career terrorizing quarterbacks.

I kept trying to get him to comply with my plan. To predict his adult size, I repeatedly measured his height and head circumference. At 6'4", 240 pounds, he would be the perfect size for an outside linebacker; slimmed down, an NBA shooting guard, a slugging first baseman, a lacrosse monster, an NHL terror, a gold medalist heavyweight rower, and if not a pro or Olympian, certainly an athlete who'd warrant a full college scholarship.

Over the next few years though, no one could interest Miles in sports. He certainly wouldn't sit and watch a game on TV. He'd wander off at Alex's soccer matches, and at Little League games he was only interested in the dirt pile behind the backstop. Inning after inning, he'd climb up and roll down. He always left the fields much dirtier than any player. He looked like Schulz's Pig-Pen: filthy, a dirt cloud hovering around his giant head.

If I couldn't actualize his athletic potential, I could his intellectual gifts. He was reading before he was three. I caught him one day. He was watching *Thomas the Tank Engine*. He'd always bounced and chirped out the names of each engine as they appeared on the screen: "Thomas! Percy! Henry! Gordon!" I'd assumed that he merely recognized them by face, size, and color. This time, however, he tooted the name of one new character, then another, then a third. While trying to conceal my curiosity and pride I sat next to him. After the program, I got a picture book and asked him to identify the various animals, structures, and vehicles, which he did with the same ardor as with the show.

I then got *One Fish, Two Fish, Red Fish, Blue Fish*. It was a favorite of ours. I asked him to tell me the title and author. He did. I opened to the first page and he *read*, as he did the second and following pages. Not satisfied, I got pen and paper and wrote, *"We'll call him, Clark."* He was suspicious but read it. I wish I had, but I couldn't hide my zeal. It spooked him. When I wrote, *"and some are very, very bad,"* his face closed, then he leaned back and looked away into the distance. Miles had three states: contemplative, during which he examined dimensions and forms; furtive, in which he sought refuge in them; and hurt, in which he sought to hide his feelings—as though he couldn't bear to upset who or whatever had injured him.

So, there I was with a genius giant who refused to acknowledge and honor his gifts. For the next few weeks, he retreated into a space from which he couldn't be coaxed or bribed. Whatever praise I offered him—for any small act—reminded him of my intense scrutiny and seemed to be a drag. I let him be. Eventually he returned.

We had to assume that there was something more than growling or whooshing going on inside that big Thomas skull; that when he looked beyond us, he saw something out there. That the parallelism in which he seemed to exist would eventually intersect with the *real world*. He started pre-K the next fall. Because Alex had been there, most of the teachers knew Miles. He was already famous, or infamous, for being so openly and unabashedly peculiar: the strangling yellow-white boy who, mostly, paid no attention to anyone else unless he was ready to announce a fact or report on something he'd discovered on one of his internal exploits. I still wonder had Alex not preceded him if Miles would've been admitted to that private, arts-based school. For Miles wasn't openly creative. He didn't really play or even interact with other children. During his preschool admission play group, he sat alone deeply focused on something. When another applicant offered him a slice of Play-Doh pie, without looking up Miles placed his large hand on the boy's chest and shoved him away.

He was admitted and he did well, or well enough. His early school days he would be present with such ease that, to me, he made other people—children and adults—seem dim. He was, it seemed, paying attention. When studying the Amazon Rainforest the teacher asked one day, *"Can anyone name a layer of the canopy?"* Miles, alone on the other side of the room, deeply involved in acting out perhaps the Permian Extinction, answered, *"Emergent trees."*

While academically he displayed enough intermittent brilliance to allay concern, he struggled socially. Miles stammered and children didn't have the patience to wait for him to get it out. They often passed him by—I know this upset him, but it also, sometimes, seemed to relieve him of the burden of explaining whatever he was thinking, and he could return to his thoughts. This felt oddly familiar to me. I had stammered too. I remembered that it was physically painful.

Whenever people asked me simple questions like *"How are you doing?"* or *"What are you thinking?"* the first thing I'd do was imagine the inside of my skull—which I can now say would eventually appear as a blank, dark gray space. I'd wait and one by one images—most of them new to me—would appear, followed by those with which I was familiar. They'd arrange themselves on a circular platform—much like the various creatures and carriages of a carousel with many levels. Then the platters would start to turn and gain speed. The figures would move up and down. My reply to *"How are you?"* would begin there. Trying to follow hurt my eyes but trying to stop hurt them more, as did when I tried to lock my jaw to keep it from moving. I'd get sudden, terrible headaches. Then I'd realize that I'd been standing dumb.

So in playgrounds when other kids would be doing other things together, and Miles would be standing alone, I'd climb to the top of the slide and bellow,
"What do ye do when ye see a whale, men?"
Miles would find me up high and yell back, "Sing out for him!"
"Good!"
Kids and their parents would look at him, then up at me. And I'd holler,
"And what do ye do next, men?"
And Miles, "Lower away and after him!"
And me, "And what tune is it ye pull to, men?"
Kids would be gathered around him, some curious, some excited, some bewildered. Most of the parents would've turned away, but I don't think they thought the boy calling back to me was my son. He saw something exhilarating inside himself. I could feel it pass from him and rise. He'd flap his arms as though he were trying to ascend with it.

By five, he had some friends. A few were like him. They were imps, who with a little testosterone and disappointment might later become hooligans. They were, Miles and his chums, similarly disengaged from norms. They broke rules. They weren't willful or *"bad."* It wasn't that the rules didn't apply to them but that they acknowledged another authority and seemed puzzled by those who complied to conventional orders.

Along with reading he could do many things beyond his age: arrange reptiles from the Permian period to now. He'd begin a lecture on the behaviors of the orca pod but pause to provide essential backstory; Ambulocetus, the walking whale; then guide you through nearly fifty million years of evolution, sometimes with an excursion to myth and star.

But it wasn't enough—I don't think. He often seemed lonely—usually when his audience didn't share in his zeal, or his passion and knowledge were merely entertainment and not a call-and-response; the practice of sanctuary and choir.

Near the end of the school year his kindergarten teacher suggested that we get Miles assessed. She said it as though she were asking about our summer plans. That's how I heard it. It was the end of the day. The room was hot. She was wrong. Almost every adult that knew him had told us he was a genius. Michaele—I think—and I refused.

I didn't want him assessed. I needed to see that he could participate enough conventionally so that people would leave him alone. But I also wanted him to manifest whatever abstractions he entertained. This required discipline. Then, I was only obliquely aware of how competitive I was and that one of my core beliefs was that winning earns one's freedom. While this tenet might be rooted in maladaptive coping devices, it's one that has been constantly rewarded. This is irrefutable. Many of us have had to win by such wide margins and in such unfair circumstances for the chance of probationary and conditional status as a free and equal citizen. And then there are those of us who must win, still—whether or not our victories are recognized—just to survive for today.

His knowledge grew but his ability to communicate that knowledge lagged. At times it seemed difficult for him to say anything. Instead of using his own words he used phrases he heard other people say, and these were mostly passages from books or movies—that which would work for a talk on the late Cretaceous, space epic, or the Ministry of Silly Walks but not conversations. They were formal, ungainly, even anachronistic. They also couldn't express what he thought, saw, and needed—not quickly enough for most people to listen. It seemed, then, before he was six, that for him most human interaction was an experience in how quickly he could ascertain if anyone was willing to listen or if they had something interesting to share, and if not, how quickly he could ignore them before they left him alone.

Left alone, even though he seemed idle, if one looked closely one could see he was doing *something*. He possessed a strange, secret discipline. He somehow learned things on his own. What he learned he loved, which compelled him to learn more. He loved dirt. He loved Thomas. He loved wrestling. He loved us. He loved dinosaurs.

Miles would lie on the floor with his figurines and growl softly. He didn't seem to be playing, but rather, being. He and the animals had a tacit agreement that they animate each other. For me he was a portal to the ancient world; not a static, linear history but one that was moving and now. I saw it through him, and then perhaps with him—the giant sauropods in the fern valleys, the beast foot tread along the shores of inland seas. It was very beautiful.

It reminded me of being a boy. I could sit and do *nothing* for hours with books and music—really, anything that generated feeling, thought, or sense. I still honestly can't discern their order. The tactile wasn't grounding. That which approximated it was—though that's inaccurate. I'd read Dr. Seuss the same way then that I now read Fitzgerald: I can't say it is or ever was an intellectual engagement or response. Whimsy to bluesy, I was moved, not from this world, but gently into it.

2

We got out. Just the two of us. He still liked holding hands, and at the bottom of our Brooklyn stoop he took mine. Until he spoke, people often believed he was a couple of years older than he was. His voice, unlike his older brother's gravelly tenor, was high and thin. His big body lacked gravity, too. But he wasn't light. His skip was more of a lumber. His bones were thick and large. He was painfully solid, and it hurt to collide with him. Still, he didn't seem to be all there. It was how he looked and looked at: He didn't focus on anything for more than a few seconds, not on the material plane anyway. He seemed to be studying forms in other realms that demanded his deepest concentration. Wherever his attention was, so was a portion of his density, and all of this imbued him with a flightiness that belied his mass.

And so, his hand in mine, without shame, he thumped lightly beside me chattering about whatever appeared to him, unaware of what a strange partner he was: too big, too gone, and—at least with me—too white. But he wasn't anybody's white boy. He was mine. And while it was difficult for strangers to reconcile the two of us together it was obvious to us and those who bothered to look and listen that we were father and son.

First grade had been difficult for him. He couldn't *get over*. He had to be present in a way he wasn't used to. He had to participate. This meant he had to share his thoughts and sound like other kids while doing so. Now there were several kids who were as my mother would've said "not all there." They however weren't all together. Even though the school's founder demanded, "If a child is under the desk, get under the desk and teach them," they couldn't be taught as one. Anyway Miles was never under the desk. He'd already learned to escape. Rather than *space out* he'd retire to the bathroom so many times a day that his teacher asked us if he might have a gastrointestinal disorder.

Whatever *it* was about him, we were all to "keep an eye on it." I thought he needed rote practice of arts, academics, and athletics to prove that he could be *normal* enough to be left alone.

For the rest of the school year there were infrequent unofficial check-ins. That following summer he attended an estuarine camp. He made friends, mostly with counselors, and gave a presentation that prompted the director to offer him a job.

In second grade his struggles were regular and apparent. During frequent parent-teacher meetings—extemporaneous or scheduled—Michaele and I were defensive. We knew Miles. What he didn't do well at school—or do at all—he did so brilliantly at home. The only thing he did *wrong* in public was struggle to be like others. The only *normal* pictures of him are candid. When asked to pose he'd contort his face and twist then stiffen his limbs to such a degree that he looked as though he was in farcical agony. We thought he had to be joking. It was a relief for him, I think, to be laughed at and not scolded.

He had texts to quote, but the phrases were even less suited to casual conversation. And he could casually converse about anything. He had to rely on his Daffy Duck impersonation for that. He loved John Akira Ikufube's soundtracks but he shared them by humming them while pretending to stomp Tokyo. He knew this wasn't normal. He was often hesitant to enter a reverie and embarrassed when he left it. It seemed his behavioral choices were limited to *stay* or *go*. Being *here* looked painful. Going *there* was problematic. Not only did it negatively affect his interactions with others, others were now encroaching on his private internal space. He seemed to be hiding within, a fugitive from convention and from himself.

Writing was hard—so we were told. We were often presented with his work, of which there was little. Other kids filled multiple pages, but he would only have scribbled two or three uninspired lines. His teacher couldn't understand why someone with such a vast imagination struggled getting it onto the page. I replied, "Because it is a struggle."

He eventually wrote a multi-narrative, exquisitely illustrated cosmic odyssey about a giant space turtle. He was celebrated for it, but soon after, it was suggested that he continue his quest to normalcy.

I know we didn't drive to the park because I remember being anxious about riding the subway. We might have taken the F to Columbus Circle, but I don't think I'd freely choose to enter Central Park from the southwest. I also wouldn't have chosen the roundabout route—not with him—across Lower Manhattan, north up Sixth Avenue, and then back east.

We probably took the 4 or 5 train from Borough Hall to Brooklyn Bridge. Had I been alone I would've stayed on the express to at least Forty-Second, but even alone I was wary of that station. We switched to the 6 and rode the twelve local stops to Sixty-Eighth Street/Hunter College. I'd been teaching there for over six years and those familiar buildings would've been good checkpoints for me. With Miles this was the safest option. I didn't want him to see how anxious I was. Being privately complex but publicly simple was the only way I could, I thought, seem normal to him—*for* him. I felt I had to take every chance I could to teach Miles how to publicly function. Away from dinosaurs, books about dinosaurs, and other facets of the ancient world or make-believe, he often seemed helpless.

His siblings understood cause and effect—enough. They were aware of their surroundings. Ella could be reckless. I think she believed she could control fire. Danger was her field of action. She saw peril and challenged it. She distrusted most people and assumed most were villains. Had we let her she would've carried a switchblade, a section of iron pipe, and had a wolf or tiger as a companion. Alex didn't take chances because he constantly worried about an outsized result. He had just turned thirteen. He was walking to and from school and about to start traveling the city on his own. I didn't worry about him falling or being pushed onto the tracks. He was gravely obedient, vigilant, and seemed born situationally aware. But Alex was brown. For him my fear was the police. Our fear was the police.

Even though Miles could calculate the potential energy of the Lexington Avenue train and knew that there were 625 volts living in the third rail, I had to keep him pressed against the subway platform wall. He wasn't disobedient. He never tried to pull his hand away from Michaele's or mine. Miles would drift, then suddenly be gone. He could disappear in the middle of a conversation—even if he was speaking. Then he'd *physically* vanish. At home we'd find him in another room. Out at a friend's he'd be behind a chair or in the back garden. At Target he'd be wandering in a random aisle, and at the beach he'd be at the far end perched atop a boulder he shouldn't have been able to climb. We'd call. He'd never answer. We'd find him staring. Not at anything in front of him but rather something that was beyond the view from a window or the bees among the flower beds. He didn't stop to look at the toy displays or endcaps of cookies. He wasn't looking at the beach break, the swells, or the Elizabeth Islands in the distance. He didn't even seem to notice the racket and motion of the waders or seabirds but he did, and he saw and heard something more.

"*Miles!*" I'd have to bark and yank his arm. If he didn't show immediate contrition and compliance, I'd lecture him about the dangers of the *real world*. But other than how to cross the street I hadn't many strategies for negotiating the *real* world. I expected him to apprehend and immediately process and respond to all imminent kidnappers, pedophiles, and murderers. Really though I mostly knew how to prevent, mitigate, or face calamity. So, by the third grade he could lecture on surviving most natural disasters, what to do if shipwrecked over the Mariana Trench, and how to travel through bear country. All of this was useless in the gentrifying streets of Boerum Hill, Brooklyn.

3

His fascination with dinosaurs was acceptable. Most kids liked them. But his intensifying fascination with birds was a *relief*. It made evolutionary sense. Birding was normal. They were *here*. Everyone could see them, though not in the way he could. He knew birds better. When he saw a chicken he'd see its terrible ancestor. He could also see them when he heard them. He had a book with illustrations of different species with a button next to each drawing that, when pressed, would play that species's different calls and songs. He'd sit or lie for long spells, seemingly looking at nothing—not even hearing the tweets and whistles he summoned. But, of course, he was.

The summer before our trip to Central Park Miles, Michaele, and I were walking back to her childhood home from the beach through the dunes. We were listening to the birds hidden among the long grass and the rosehips. At the end of the brush, she paused to hear one bird singing above the rest.

"That's an eastern phoebe," she announced.

"No," Miles replied. "It isn't."

"Then what is it?" she asked.

And not looking at her or anything, only into the open sky before him beyond the dunes, he said, "It's a northern mockingbird pretending to be a phoebe."

We saw it, the mockingbird, appear from the tangle, alight on the highest branch, and sing.

"Will we be able to see him?" Miles asked. I remembered we'd wanted to find Pale Male. I think entering the park had worried him. The hawk's nest was almost twenty blocks uptown, on the opposite side of Fifth Avenue, twelve stories up outside of Mary Tyler Moore's window. I'd seen the nest many times but never the bird. Miles was yet to see either. It was early afternoon. It was going to rain, and we weren't prepared for it. We probably only had time to quickly check if he was home. After a short visit we might be able to get to the Eighty-Sixth Street station before we were soaked.

But on the edge of the park it seemed, to both of us, that we should do much more. There were only a few people out. Most of them were running on the road. We'd have large areas of the property to ourselves. That's what we really wanted. Living in the middle of New York City has often been depressing. In Boston you don't have to look hard to find something more than a pigeon or squirrel. You don't have to plan a special outing to do so.

When I was eleven, I would ride my bike a couple of miles to the part of the Charles River that flows along the outer border of the Auburndale section of Newton down by the old tram bridges. It's narrow there and there are streams and seepages hidden in the trees and long grass. You can hear the nearby highway. When the trees are bare you can see the traffic on the local roads. But it always feels quiet and private. You can sit on a log and watch the bass in the pools, the painted turtles on felled logs, sometimes a snapper in the murk. Snakes cross, slither up the banks, and disappear under the leaflitter and brush. Sometimes you turn and there's a great blue heron poised in the shallows. It was always there. Even if I was supposed to be somewhere else and nobody knew where I was, I didn't feel wrong. If, say, my mother would've asked, "Where the hell have you been?" I wouldn't have to lie.

Miles had a list of birds he wanted to see: Anseriformes, Caprimulgiformes, Cathartidae and, of course, Hieraves. I told him that I wanted to see an owl in the wild—that I'd only seen traces or heard them in the distance at night.

He cleared his throat. "Strigiformes."

He turned to me, looked at the path, and raised an eyebrow. In the distance I heard Leonard Nimoy say, *"Fascinating."* Then, from the window of the Museum of Science, I sensed, behind the mist, the esplanade. I stopped abruptly and stood at attention. Miles slowed and folded his hands behind his back.

"The only diurnal owl in these parts, I believe, is the screech owl." He stopped and softly pointed at a nearby tree. "It's mating season. They will be screeching." He cleared his throat again. I thought he might try to mimic one. He didn't. Instead, he made sure I knew the differences between the regional members of their order. And, haltingly, offered a prosaic ode to the Accipitriformes, though I don't think he realized he was doing so.

We didn't have his Audubon guide or the notebook in which he'd written the names. While I was confident that we'd remember our catalog I was worried what would happen when the birds didn't present themselves in that order. He seemed okay though. The mourning doves and chickadees seemed to have granted him enough time until they did.

We walked casually through the middle of the park. If he hadn't occasionally talked about the birds he heard—either real or imagined—I might have forgotten why we were there. We were alone now. The paths were empty. No one seemed to be coming.

He spoke, "Spinus tristis." I looked down at him. He was grinning. He continued. "The American Goldfinch."

"Spiny sorrow."

Nothing. Then, "They won't be bright now."

"Have you heard one?" I asked.

"Why, yes. Several."

"Which is theirs?"

He paused and leaned back. "Do you hear that one?"

Amidst cooing doves and the clamor of jays, the tweets and whistles were a blur. I shook my head. He seemed pleased. I tried to focus.

"Do you hear?"

I thought I could.

"There's a second too. A second song." He cleared his throat and tried to stretch up to the sound. *"Par-tee-tee-tee-tee . . ."* He looked at me—partially—and waited for my response. I tried.

"Par-tee-tee-tee-tee."

"It's hard for you. Your voice is low."

"Well." I raised my eyebrow and pointed up at nothing. "Perhaps we should keep moving before something we don't want to know responds."

"It's okay." He checked the air. "It's okay."

It's a different thing, when you begin in a quiet place, to enter one that is quieter still. You bring peace with you. We could be quiet and look for things. And he would tell me the birds we saw; some I knew, some I misnamed, some I didn't know. There were traces of other creatures. We had to track them. There were signs of that which might have been there.

We left the path and wandered through the mist and between the trees. Sometimes we held hands. Sometimes we drifted apart. But we were still a part. We knew the other was there. He didn't need to lecture or even talk about what we saw. He didn't tell me what I should look for. We didn't need to share our experiences to make them real. Miles called and sang to himself and didn't mind whether I was listening or not, only that I was listening to something, deeply.

When I was a boy, I wondered if I existed and if I was here. I had to see something that would tell me I was real and present, and I had to wait for it to come. I still wonder. *"Choc-full of nuts is that heavenly coffee . . ."* My parents didn't drink that. My father liked instant. I used to make it for him. I can feel his voice in the lower regions of the boiling water and his wheeze in the punctured can of Carnation. I can feel his razor stubble in the freeze-dried grind. But my mother isn't there. Not in the Taster's Choice. She's not in the CorningWare percolator or its blue flowers. She's in the bacon grease. Hot danger. Sunday mornings—good Sunday mornings. The sizzle. The cast-iron pan. The blue flame. The oily rainbow and soap suds. The lard she'd never use in the Yuban can—like her pupils, soft ivory, salty, and sweet. A Virginia I'd never know is sunlight behind dust. I can't find her. She could still be in the kitchen, near me, but I can only feel her in the popping grease. My father isn't there. He's in his car. I'm alone with him in the front seat. Seattle Street, right on Cambridge. Bear right. Then a half mile along the tracks to the Lincoln Café. The darkened bar with the dark white men. The empty tables. The light in the windows of the kitchen's double doors. I get to push them open. There's relief in the oven's radiant heat. My father is in the thick cut of pepperoni that Angelo offers me still on the knife.

But pizza night was Friday night, and I can't find my way home. Not even through the grease burns. My mother dropped the skillet. My mother threw the skillet when she caught me feeding the dog salami. The handle broke off. There was a V cleft in the side. Back on the stove we moved it by hand with a dish towel.

How do I get to the cleft iron pan and how do I get back? I don't know if I can or want to return to the judgment I'll face. But I can't remain there picking at the flaking metal. I can't hide in the pantry cabinet. I don't know what will find me. I need time to return. And I might return with nothing. I don't know what I need now but then, believe me, if you had stayed where we'd parted I would've come back to you.

Par-tee-tee-tee-tee. The sorrowed bird in the mist. His was a love song not because it celebrated his love but his hope for it. This is how love, sometimes, must be. I felt a sadness that didn't seem to be mine. It felt too old and too great. I didn't want to carry it. Then somewhere in the mounds and trees of the park was Tristan. Alone. But at the beginning of the story. Recounting. *"The first time ever I saw your face."*

From the age of ten to eleven we moved three times in a year and I went to four schools. Beth Klavens. Unlike the distinct freckles on her cheeks the cluster around her nose formed a little cloud.

When I was sixteen, I walked Sarah Morse home. It was Friday, late April, the first day of short sleeves. We were trying hard to deny that we liked and might be liked by the other. I remember I didn't want or know how to be near her so I started talking about the stars we couldn't see and how there's something, always, beyond. I'd been reading Douglass, Emerson, Melville, and Thoreau. I started with a joke about being lost in the middle of the previous century. She laughed but I don't think she thought it was funny. I lectured then apologized then lectured on apology and cosmic humility but that made me feel alien and distant but also known and present. My presence was a burden. My heart seemed far from me, but I still felt it break a little. Somewhere I started writing a tragedy about love that couldn't be. I felt desperate and robotic.

I apologized, again. She laughed, again. She was there because she wanted to be. We walked. We neared her house. I started talking about Walden—red ants and black. We crossed a busy street and stopped on a median. In the thin grass and sand were small anthills. I gestured for her to watch with me. I told her, *"The universe does not make us small."* She knelt and watched the busy citizens. I told her that they were fire ants. She froze. I laughed. She looked up at me, perplexed. I smiled, bent, and gently raised her by her forearm. Our hands came together as we stood. We looked at each other for the first time. For a moment I got to show her how and what I love. She smiled. I think I did too.

Both girls were white. Both accounts are still painful to recall. The hurt, though, doesn't live in being spurned, or dumped. It's in every instance I, for whatever reason, couldn't or wouldn't allow myself to feel peace, hope, freedom, or love. And I don't mean that I hoped for a white girl to love me, or that when there was peace in our land, we could be free to love. It was that I often felt flawed. I lacked basic knowledge most others—white and Black—had, and my life was tragic. I didn't know how I'd inherited such an existentialist belief—it pre-existed my reading their texts—but I'd learn just in time to die. I spent a lot of time seeking corroboration. But I wasn't completely convinced of my fate. I knew, though sometimes only dimly, that the most desperate-sounding songs were hopeful. No matter how grieving she sounds Roberta Flack always reminds me that there's shared joy that can fill the world and last forever.

An older white couple paused behind us. They'd been listening. Miles turned to them. He looked at them as if they were students who'd entered his class late. He cleared his throat and continued to differentiate songs and calls. I watched them. They didn't know why this boy was alone in the park lecturing about a bird who wasn't there. I don't know if they were more confused or relieved when Miles took my hand and led me away. Regardless, the couple followed.

This happened a few more times with different people until Miles was leading a group of seven into the center of the park, explaining the nuances of voicings and plumage, anecdotes about the intelligence of crows and ravens and how to tell them apart, old and new world vultures, and misconceptions concerning owls.

We left the paved walk and ascended a small hill along a winding path. We stopped about ten yards before a makeshift camp of a shopping cart, milk carton, shreds of blue tarp, garbage bags, and sodden cardboard and blankets. Like everything else, the barren branches, the dim air, and our silence made each item stand out. I know he saw it, but I don't know what it meant to him—if he asked the question *Who lives there?* Who did he imagine and why? The homeless and the very poor people in his life were predominately Black or brown. And I think the wealthiest Black person he knew was me.

I could tell he wanted to say something but didn't know what. I wondered if he pictured what color whoever lived there was—if he immediately saw them as brown. He certainly had the data to suggest such, but I don't think he had the apparatus to engage, not in the moment. My father never seemed to have the ability to do so, and at times, the willingness. The *"isms and schisms"* hadn't aesthetic, philosophical, or moral unity. Of course, I didn't think that at the time. I only heard my father idly humming. He was somewhere in those trees. I wondered if Miles was hearing more than the birds and the distant city traffic. I wondered if he'd heard what his followers hadn't said.

What had Miles assigned to race? And if he had assigned anything, what was it? He thought of himself as brown. Had he considered what that meant? If so, he needed more than what the white people in his life had to offer. For it seemed to me that all they could do when challenged was retreat to the sanctuary that privilege affords. How would I begin to talk to my white son about that person or people who might live there? How would I convince him that we were bound to and responsible for them? If one really believed in what was good and right, one could never look away from anything in any world: our first responsibility was to cede the privilege of doing so, our second to know that what we see has consequence and weight.

None of this was Miles's problem. He had two parents, and he was white. But then, none of *this* should've been mine. So, perhaps it was everyone's. Miles told everyone, *"I am brown."* In his self-portraits he's brown. Yet he was praised for how white he looked. And thus would never be imperiled by being seen as Black. But is acute and chronic suffering the ultimate credential for being Black? Or is it what you make of any or all individual or collective pain? I'd been told many times that I wasn't Black. I didn't sound Black. I didn't act Black. I didn't like Black things. Somehow my life resided within that scope and judgment. I was assessed, defined, and filed. If I challenged the conclusion, I was a problem.

I wanted something more for my son. I wanted him to know that there was more than living life in the gaps and on the fringes of anxious white people. They knew only of closed systems in which, if they hadn't already, would spin themselves hollow. I wanted him to know that there was something larger than all of us with which we had to comply: death, yes, but also life—a life among others regardless of who those others were. And the guidance through this life, though it had everything to do with humans, wasn't a product of human affairs. I wanted to tell him that if there's an end to suffering one first must learn to live with it. Everyone's. I wanted to tell him about the soul. We all had one, and he could sing about his and everyone's—even if he was anybody's white boy. He was my white boy and so he was *"young, gifted, and Black."* Mulatto, quadroon, or whatever he was, he'd been given so much: twoness, at least; the one drop, at least. And in the one drop was something old and faithful and triumphant, seemingly not of this world—but of course it was. It's us and our willingness to always look beyond this world while living in it. This twinned life made us deeper and wider. Jesus hadn't, nor would he ever save Black people. Black people had and would. Perhaps we had and would continue to save this country because of what we have given and not taken. I wanted to tell him about the blues.

I remember riding the Orange Line only one time and it was one way. I was five. We were going to visit my paternal grandmother. My father was still living with us, but he didn't take us. I don't know why. I'm certain, however, that he wasn't there. I see him at work in downtown Boston at Gilchrist Department Store. Or I see him in the lounge at the Ramada. He might not have been at either location, but I can't see him on the trolley. I've never seen him on a trolley. He would've driven, but he did not. His car had failed inspection and the windshield was covered with a red REJECTED sticker. But those laws would come three years later—I think—so that probably wasn't the reason. I know, though, that my mother's Tempest was parked in what had been our cornfield. There were hornets in the trunk, mice in the seats, and mosquito and dragonfly larvae in the footwell puddles.

My mother had promised us pepper steaks. I didn't know how we'd get them. There were only two sub shops I could tolerate. Their griddles didn't taint the beef with mushroom and onion. They were only accessible by car and in the wrong direction. Of course, she'd made her own, which were, of course, better than "anything any place had." I was charged with packing the cold, aluminum stumps into a Star Market bag. The subs were too short. They weren't wrapped in waxed paper. The grease couldn't render the foil translucent. There was no steam sharp with salt and mellowed by fat. Fortunately—for all of us—we were out the door before I could speak. On the porch I'd wonder if only one of my socks was right-side-out. I thought to look down and check.

She must have been exceptionally tired, stressed, and sad. And might've been wondering if the lights would be on when we got back home—if she had enough money to *get us back home* and why she had chosen to take us to visit a woman who hated her, the mother of a man who would soon leave her.

I was wondering about our lunch. Wondering isn't the word. I was reliving all the hidden soggy onions I'd bitten into and how it felt to have my mother watch. I wouldn't look up. I'd try to pretend that I hadn't noticed the fungi and vegetables or had suddenly grown to like them. And if I couldn't convince her I'd rather she threaten to slap the food out of my mouth than apologize to me. I didn't want to hurt her with me.

I was trying not to worry that the meat was sliced and not shaved. None of us saw him, not even as my mother passed out our hand-crafted sandwiches. Not even when I opened mine. Suddenly, he was sitting next to me. He was staring across the aisle. I looked away. He looked at me. We did this multiple times. Finally, we looked at each other. His face was very dark. His eyes were pale gray.

He looked away and mumbled, "Can I have a bite?"

I didn't answer.

Still looking at seemingly nothing. "Can I have a bite?"

I would've told him "No." Even now, I can't share bites or sips. Though I will give anyone a piece, pour them a portion, or give them all I have. That was too much to explain, for both of us, so I remained silent.

He turned to me, empty-eyed.

"You won't help anyone. Not even your own color."

He left. No one else saw him. My mother threatened me—something to do with peppers and how I better not look for them. I forced it all down and later vomited on the tracks. Neither my mother nor my siblings saw—though they must have. I don't remember the visit. We took a cab home. My mother paid in change. The driver, a fat old white man who smelled terrible, called her a bitch. But only after she'd gotten out.

When we got inside Neil Diamond's "Song Sung, Blue" was on WHDH. It was wrong. It was and is an atrocious song. It's vapid while claiming knowledge of the blues. I didn't need to feel better. I needed to know how to ask, "What's Going On?" which might have been playing a few turns up the dial but WILD didn't have a cash call jackpot.

But the lights were on, my mother was happy to be home, and in my head, out of a mix of brothers greeting brothers I heard the alto sax rise, the rim shot echo, the bass stroll, and Marvin—tenor and falsetto—show me what I could do and how I could be the next time.

"*The person who distrusts himself has no touchstone for reality.*" If this is still true, which I believe it is, then integration demands we all find the rock and cling to it. But integration, still, is confused—perhaps willfully—with assimilation, even erasure. Be it the Sisyphean, the lodestone, the ragged, or the rock of the soul, this is reality: to assimilate in this country at this time one must habitually refuse to acknowledge facts, surrender any hope for living an ethical life, and capitulate to the attitudes and actions by and with which we cruelly defend our unrealities and brutally multiply and expand them. One cannot trust themselves if attitude, desire, opinion, and fear are the measures by and how they judge themselves and others. The rock is a hard thing. America will be great when its people accept the responsibility (or are allowed the opportunity) of learning how to *"renew themselves at the fountain of their own lives."* This fountain can only heal if we have faith in perpetual rejuvenation. I think we must forget the self to restore the self. Back then, when I'd talk to my teenage friends about Sarah, they'd say I was *"a hopeless romantic."* People say it now. They were and are confused. For romanticism is the substance of the pragmatic, whose first and last action is to hope.

The tour abruptly ended. The white people departed. Miles and I stayed. We stood holding hands. He looked quiet and very sad.

"Icteridae," he said after a long silence. He was pointing at a small patch near a pile of takeout containers.

"A blackbird?"

"A red-winged blackbird." He sculpted its shape from the air. "Though the color pattern through the wings is red *and* yellow."

"Jaundiced."

He ignored my comment.

"The stripes make it appear to be in flight." He looked away. "That's a male."

"It's beautiful."

"Yes," he said. "The colors seem to make it fast. But then they're just red when you see it quickly and from afar."

It flew.

"It's going to be a cold, wet evening," I said.

"Quite."

He looked about, then back at the encampment. My mother used to tell me, *"You don't have sense to come in out the rain."*

"We should keep moving."

His jaw started quivering. I took it as a yes.

We walked slowly and without purpose. If we didn't move the rain wouldn't come. We could stay and wait and recover what it seemed we'd lost, or what I thought we'd lost. We were both looking elsewhere. I didn't know what he sought but I sensed that whatever Miles was seeing wasn't all benevolent. I thought that perhaps it was projection. I wondered what he saw for himself.

I had memories of being frightened in my head. When I was his age on some nights the darkness of my room simply meant the lights were out and on others it meant I was going to die. In between the two, where I think I often lived, simplicity was baffling. I wet the bed because there seemed—at times—a scrim between me and the toilet. I couldn't teach myself how to tear through it and pee. My parents, opposed as they were, both said, *"It doesn't make sense."* That phrase didn't make sense. Reason was intellectual. Sense was a physical experience. I *felt* that they demanded I was an active participant in making it. I felt a failure because I couldn't. I couldn't show them how or tell them that my basic needs were so distant that they could've been someone else's. I couldn't find the bathroom and I couldn't stay in the chilling, wet sheets so I'd try to make another place to be: the past, from which I could extract a gentle memory; the future, in which I could be alone.

Would Miles have to be alone? One of the crueler things we can do to a child is normalize societal pathology. It forces them if they're to thrive to rely on wit rather than gestate in wisdom. All the while trying to maintain the basic principles that separate right and wrong. They covertly practice ethics within themselves. They must somehow find, without becoming a martyr or a sociopath, sanctuary for beauty, dignity, and love. If there is a light inside them they must keep it from going out. And while their inner cosmos is unfathomable, the world outside is dangerous. The problem of the twenty-first century is still the color line, the class line, the gender line, all of them. I see Du Bois, wandering as lonely as a cloud. The line is something we not only must dare to cross but also look up and down and wonder when it will end.

How will we let each other be? It seems still impossible to do so. It will always seem impossible until we choose a life of meaning over a life of comfort. Those who believe that a comfortable life is a substantive life will never discern the difference between fear and danger or offense and harm. Most white people I know—even those I love—don't, won't, understand what a drag it is, not only to see them, but to be with them and watch them fret and grind about everyday trivialities. But, for me, to lament another's lament is to trivialize what I've suffered. So few of us get to travel the road of freedom. Most of us are lost or are waylaid along the way. I made it. I believe that when one is free, onus becomes responsibility, and responsibility is a privilege: we get to choose how we try to help others be free. So few of us get to freely love. For many of us the thought of being in love is perilous because the act of love is punishable by death. But the chance to love and be loved is our birthright. The experience is an honor. And no human can, and no God would revoke this. We might not choose who we are or who we love but we can choose how we act in love. And even if we've never been free or have loved—in freedom—can't we hope it for others?

Miles and I were still alone together. The birds were still singing. The sky didn't threaten rain. There was no fight here. Though I remembered why we'd come, and I sensed our reason was right, I squeezed his hand and pulled him back to the road.

4

The first time I'd let Miles ride in the front seat: early August, mid-afternoon, Massachusetts. We were heading for New Bedford, to Cap'n Frank's—the *other* fish store—for mako steaks, as Westport Lobster—*the* fish store—didn't carry them.

It was unusual for him to volunteer for trips like these, but it had in part been his idea—or my suggestion—which had excited him: shark for dinner. We had the windows down and the radio low, tuned to the Red Sox game. The sun was warm and the mild breeze carried with it the anticipatory purple scent of wild grapes. He was smiling, bright-eyed, watching the birch and evergreen wood.

I'd found him at his usual post, on the retaining wall that separated the upper and lower yards. He'd sometimes stand there for over an hour listening for birds, but rather than up to the sky he'd been looking down for something in or on the wall, examining the fieldstone and the gaps left by the eroded mortar. I'd tried sneaking up on him, but he knew I was there. With a soft wrist and bent finger, he pointed at a large crack.

"I saw a snake this morning."

"Where?"

He hopped. "Right there."

"Garter?"

"No. A garter is striped. They have longitudinal stripes going to their tails." He sketched the lines. "This one was all brown." He paused. "I think it might, I think it might . . . I think . . . well . . . I think . . . well . . . it could've. I think." He stopped, calmed himself. "Well," now rushed, "I think it was a black rat or racer." He lisped. He looked up. "Yeah." He relaxed now that he'd gotten it out. He looked down, sighed. "Yeah." Back to the wall. I'm sure he saw it in his head, basking, bright-scaled, or waiting in its dark den. "Yeah."

"It could be possible," I said, pointing to where he seemed to be looking.

He stiffened, arms rigid against his sides and wrists cocked. He hopped but barely got off the ground, so he flapped his stiff hands. It must have seemed to him that he'd managed to lift, hover, and land, because he relaxed again.

"There are several species of animals that no one believes . . . there are a lot of animals . . . well, there are many creatures that live in this area that people think don't . . . or even exist at all."

We named them: reptiles, mammals, birds, and fish; the timber rattler and the snapping turtle; the sharp-shinned hawk and the bald eagle; the eastern coyote; that which could only have been bobcat tracks in the mud, in-line, clawless prints; the plausibility of migrant wolves who'd wandered back south and learned to live within a smaller range after a century and a half of exile.

And what about the man-o'-war who every year floated farther north? What about the giant shark hunt on the other side of the Elizabeth Islands? If a hundred years ago a bull hunted bathers miles up New Jersey's Matawan, what was to keep it out of Slocums River now that the coastal waters were much warmer? People once believed that great whites weren't coastal hunters, and then they had to revise that and then assert that they weren't coastal hunters in *these* parts—even with all the seals in the bay, even when a fourteen-foot, seventeen-hundred-pound female was trapped in the Nashom inlet the summer before. "It's as long and almost as heavy as our car," a Volvo wagon. We'd picture her marauding form in the shallows. The other adults would tell me not to scare him, ruin the woods and the water. But they weren't horror stories. They charged the world around us, or, better, they reported on how our world was charged. I'd feel my blood heat and pulse, my muscles pump. Miles would try to fly and alone and together we'd see our environs anew—the coiled viper, diving osprey, and like a giant transparency against the sky, that great fish prowling then surging up to a full-bodied breach with a seal in its mouth.

"I'm waiting for it to show itself." He looked strangely blue. "But it's too warm now. It probably won't come back out until dusk." His eyes cooled. Perhaps he saw the sunset: he on the wall and the snake in long shadow.

"I'm going to the fish store." He ignored me. "I'm getting mako for dinner."

He'd startled at this and turned, grinning. Ever since he learned that people ate sharks, he'd been fascinated by the idea of trying it. "I suppose it makes sense. We're really the apex predators." And although I doubted he'd like or even try it—as his ideal rarely jibed with the actual—we hurried to the car and left.

So, we drove to catch our shark. Miles, I think, smiling at our speed. After a few miles, he rolled up his window and pointed softly through the roof.

"There are a lot of osprey, too."

I rolled mine up to give him a quiet stage. He went through the litany of the area's raptors, the differences between them, how one could tell them apart by wing shape, altitude, or silhouette. "I can see," he said while gesturing at the dial for the AC but not touching it, "how people could mistake them for angels." He stared into the dash. "It's the same as thinking dinosaur fossils are dragon bones." He paused, though I knew he didn't need to. "The ancient Greeks thought Typhon was under the mountain."

"Etna."

"Oh yes." He trembled slightly.

More more more: the sperm whale as leviathan; Architeuthis as the kraken; the banshee screech owl, why they fly so quietly; what lives in the thunderclap; what shakes the earth. More more more: the explanation, though never bleeding the wonder of each or any.

"There can be different kinds of angels?"

"Yes."

"Because there are different shapes of wings?"

"Yes."

He was shy now. He softly twisted his hair, realized he was doing so, and stopped, but he didn't know what to do with his fingers, so he pressed them against the window and then began to play some piano melody.

"Wait." Quiet. Now he fumbled, but again he knew what he was about to ask. "Most big birds from above . . . well, red-tailed hawks from below have spotted, light. All of the birds except . . . but gulls aren't big enough and . . . well, gulls aren't . . . all of those others . . . well, gulls mostly have . . ." Now he was truly lost.

"Just say it."

"If, well, why do people always show angels with white wings?" He paused. "They show them as all white."

Because they're racists, I almost spat, but I waited and thought of how I could be generous instead of reductive. I didn't know where to start. *Because white is good and black is bad. Because though Solomon and Jesus are brown, they're shown as white. Because every neoclassical representation of ancient Greek gods and heroes are Nordic not Southern European.* More more more: "all the way from New Orleans to Jerusalem." Dylan's line appeared on the windshield, then maps of the delta and desert—aerial views of Louisiana and Israel. *Because of the misappropriation of light—the sun and other stars. Because of how the dark people of the world to survive slavery and colonization had to swallow all that crap for centuries or create their own crap countermeasure—if there is a "their."* More more more: a synthesis of the last thousand, two thousand, three thousand years.

He waited, frightened that perhaps I hadn't an answer.

"Sometimes," I began, trying not to stammer, "the world, the universe . . . no, always . . . perhaps . . . this life, our lives, are much more complicated. Nuanced . . . do you know what 'nuanced' means?"

"No."

"Yes, you do."

"Not black-and-white?"

"Is that a question?"

"No."

"Then what do you think?"

"Not black-and-white!"

"It takes energy and imagination to think this way, nuanced thought." Now I was the professor, the big one, though. "Fitzgerald wrote, 'The sign of a first-rate intelligence is the ability to carry two opposing thoughts in one's head and still function.' And most people think they do this, but they can't. They say things like 'I don't see color,' but you can see by what they later say and do that this isn't true. People don't realize how constrained they are to their demographics. They don't realize that they belong to them and that those groups determine what they see, how they see what they see." I wanted to stop, but I couldn't—wouldn't. "We should read *Hamlet* together." I looked up. He was pressing his face against the glass. "Are you listening?"

"Yes," he muttered without turning.

"Look at me." He did. He looked worried, as though bracing himself against what I was about to say. "It makes it easier for people to live a small-minded life, while asserting that they *know*. This idea, or lack of ideas, ignores what they don't see, refuse to see. Can't see. Race is what one sees." I told him that most people need empirical proof. The problem is that they haven't seen much and so they can't believe in much. People who don't see race, conscious or unconsciously, don't believe how some benefit and others suffer because of the color of their skin.

He'd gone back to the window.

"Are you listening?" I said, much sharper than the last time.

"Yes." He sounded hurt, but I pressed him anyway. He repeated what I'd said, some paraphrasing, but most of it verbatim.

Then I remembered the mako steaks. We were almost off the back roads, and I didn't want to make a wrong turn or fail to turn at all.

We stopped at a light. Miles turned slightly but kept his cheek against the glass. He at first seemed to be scanning the sky, but he couldn't have had much of a look at it—only the pumps, cars, and customers getting gas in the shade of the corner Mobil station. The only way he'd glimpse a flying creature was in its dark form on the road, but that too was improbable, so he was probably searching his mind. I let him be, in part because he looked so peaceful, but I also had to have my own vision. It came, an aerial view of the other fish store; first the roof I'd never, honestly, seen, then a widening scope to the parking lot, the Whaler Inn, Rosie's: *a good place to eat and drink*. My lens stopped widening and began panning backward down Hathaway Road—up the hill and past the public golf course gate on the left, the ranch houses on both sides, the private course on the right, the carpet store, Route 6, the Dunkin' Donuts, and the left we'd have to take. And finally what I was now looking at: these people holding nozzles and stretching hoses—all in shadow. I had a quick, small jolt of panicky doubt, but it passed, and I had faith that what I was seeing was what was there and that we were where we were.

5

In third grade Miles told us, "I think my brain is broken."

After a series of expensive consultations, we were told by an occupational therapist that Miles had a "nonspecific cognitive disorder." While Michaele and I sat in her office she tried to explain what that meant. Basically, he presented various "strengths and weaknesses" that contradicted each other. He did and didn't present as having Asperger's. He felt for others, but he *"couldn't"* connect with others. He was aware of this, and it confused him.

"Disorder." As if she knew what order was. "Rewire." A term she used as though Miles had to comply to a municipal code. "Remap." To return his brain to a place that never was. What is there to do when presented with such ideas other than stammer or be silent?

Her further explanations muddied rather than clarified his *"condition."* She presented a strategy to help him *"cope."* Most of it was based on using colored folders to help separate his work and keep him organized. Michaele and I were deflated and angry. We were quiet. I think the evaluator wanted to fill the silence. I eventually spoke on the imagination cognition and something about William Blake.

The therapist smiled nervously and looked at me.

"Like father like son, right?"

I turned to Michaele. She looked at me with wonder and a bit of melancholy and asked, "You didn't know?"

I'd convinced myself that whatever anomalies I displayed I'd caused. Too many concussions; too much adolescent drinking; too much weed; too much acid; too many white people. I wanted to think of my brain as something I'd damaged and corrected. I'd *cured* my stammer by standing in front of the mirror and forcing my mouth to move *normally*. I'd script every social situation I could think up along with multiple variations for each. I'd memorize every character's lines and blocking and rehearse over and over so I'd never publicly falter. I'd watched other people be present and realized that for me to ever be allowed the time and space to be *gone* I had to be better than everyone else at being *here*. It had worked. I'd colonized my brain more thoroughly than any empire could. But I'd tried fixing my body and mind long before I'd actively tried to break them. There always had been something wrong with me. The otherness I felt was inherent. My past became much more painful because I wasn't past it. It was here.

I didn't want Miles to ever feel what I had felt and what I was feeling now. I thought his care to be suddenly beyond me. That there was nothing to anchor him to. Certainly not me. I had *survived* but Miles had neither the rage nor the damage to keep him safe. He was at their mercy.

I started kindergarten in 1972, two years before the Boston public school system was ordered to comply to federal law. Bussing was the answer. My house was a ten-minute walk from Thomas Gardner Elementary—my father's school—and bussed or not I shouldn't have been enrolled.

My brother was in fourth grade, and he had negotiated that environment by being smart, charming, manipulative, and, occasionally, acting out. His teachers had tolerated the practical jokes he played on friends and the wisecracks that disrupted class. The administration saw his behaviors as deviant and typical and his intelligence as intermittent—that he didn't really possess the aptitude he displayed: he was lucky, not right. Anyone with any "aptitude" or interest would've seen that he was bored.

My sister was in second grade and she survived by following instructions, being prompt and neat, and staying quiet. But she was savvy—or frightened—enough to avoid becoming the teacher's pet. She earned the euphemism "lovely girl" who was "no trouble at all."

I was born in late August and so was relatively young. But it was more than that. I was, at best, absentminded, middling, not all there, and a mild reproach by my mother was that I'd lose my head if it wasn't attached to my shoulders. She was right. But only in part—because, to me, the physical connection between it and my neck wasn't a guarantee that it was there. I remember having to feel for it—a reflection wasn't solid evidence enough of its presence.

Anyway, head or none, I sometimes went outside without pants. Shirt on backward, mismatched socks, or just looking generally disheveled, I'd start down the back steps with only underwear on my behind. My mother would snap, "Get back inside." And I wouldn't really know why. I'd take too long; she'd come looking and find me trying to pull my pant legs over my shoes. That day, for me, would be lost, and there was no way to find it again.

I could read but I couldn't speak—not in any way that was coherent to most people. My father, when I was a tween, often told me that people had to be reminded that I was "exceptionally bright." At least by then I could remember to put my pants on, even before my sneakers, though I still struggled with tying them.

I think, now, I would've been labeled as delayed. Perhaps I was and, if so, I still am. Speech has been the laggard in my cognitive order and placing me in an environment in which talking, regardless the quality of diction, was privileged meant I hadn't a chance to succeed.

Had I been able to scout the class, given time to process the environment, and the chance to speak I would've told my parents that the air boomed and clicked and was too yellow and green. Perhaps they could've translated the sensorium and located the phenomena for me in the hard, echoing surfaces and the cycling fluorescent lights.

Perhaps they would've warned me that the desks were bolted to the floor and I should try to keep my legs still like theirs, that I shouldn't move my mouth when I counted the items on the walls or the imaginary steps I took to pace the perimeter of the room. They might have told me that scissors would look strange on my left and to not luxuriate in the look and sound of the word—scissors, safety scissors—that the same words would be different if I wrote them with the other hand. Or don't let anyone see that you switch between the claw of the beast and the hand of God.

They might have told me not to think but just answer the questions about Spot's exploits or the habits of Dick and Jane. To treat every question like arithmetic. To not clear my throat before comparing any other child to Hyperion or pinching my nose to stop stammering or slapping my thigh to recall what I had for dinner, remember as easily as you can remember the Pledge of Allegiance—or just say pot roast.

I wonder who I might have become if they'd told me not to stare beyond the teacher's head to answer a question which to the other kids seemed simple. Like "Who needs to use the bathroom?"—because by the time I realized I did, they'd already returned. And to keep from pissing myself I'd have to look into the space where monsters and heroes dwelled, or where Achilles wept and raced alone on a foreign shore, or where the strange figures in the linoleum were evidence of Cerberus and Hades.

If they told me that I'd wind up standing in the corner with my back to the class and the dunce cone on my head, I might not have bothered trying to be normal and right: I would've fit the crime to fit the sentence.

Or if they'd told me it would only be a year, I would've found a way to last.

The anxiety of kindergarten kept me up and roused me from whatever sleep I had but kept me motionless until the edge of violence. What little third-level sleep I got was inhabited by mythical beasts, the Hancock Tower collapsing, and a Cheerio stuck to the edge of a friend's kitchen table.

There was something wrong with me. And I suspected it was something I couldn't correct—mostly because I didn't know what *it* was, though everyone else seemed to be functioning with *it*. My teacher couldn't understand why things that were intellectually difficult for older children or even adults—say, long division in my head or wanting to share my father's opinions of Nixon and the betrayal of Madisonian democracy after reciting the preamble—came easily to me, but I found *Go, Dog. Go!* astonishing and, if it was a sunny Tuesday, I couldn't remember how to spell "cat."

In order—I suppose—to protect myself, I assigned different values to objects. The blackboard was good because it was easier to understand the words in white than parse oral instructions. I could keep checking to see if what I'd seen was real. And cleaning the board was the one task for which I was consistently praised.

The clock became an enemy. It always changed. The hands moved too quickly for me to finish a project and too slowly for the day to end. Time took on a value—or I began to see how others valued it. I still don't know what could've been done to help me, because if I'd been given twenty minutes to color in pumpkins neatly instead of fifteen, I still would've wound up in the corner with the cone on my head. Sometimes I'd still like to speak for that boy and say, I can't begin to comprehend how you understood time.

On some level I realized that I could no longer wonder about the Milky Way and should just color in Saturn's rings exactly as I was told. I didn't have the time to wonder about anything except how to get over and how to get by. I had to be clever. I had to modify desperation into ambition. Proxy couldn't be a way to illuminate. It became a place to hide.

I became a useful boy. I was *"good with my hands."* In my father's absence I clipped the hedges and mowed the lawn. I'd fix the toilet float chain. When the car did run, I could reassure my mother that it wasn't broken again. That we weren't out of gas, but that the engine lacked air, fuel, or spark. And even though I'd never learn how to employ a shopping list, I was excellent at retrieving items for my mother wherever we shopped as well as spotting a deal.

I could help. This was partially endearing to my mother, and wholly to her sisters, aunts, and the Black women from the rural south. I think it was because they didn't fear for me in the way she had to. She would always be worried when I was beyond her care and knew what would happen to me. She could neither leave me alone nor let me be.

We were, mercifully, pulled from the Boston public school system and enrolled in Buckingham Browne & Nichols. I knew it would be a good place for me because the name sounded and looked right.

The lower school was located near Harvard Square, which was a place I always felt peaceful: the red bricks, the rotary, and the newsstand. The tempo of the circling cars; the angles and elevations of tree limbs, lamp arms, and farther steeples. There was a Rix Drugs: my father had worked for its parent company and that store's light and glass offered me glimpses of what he might have done. I have space and time to see the Charles River wind through the western suburbs; to here, then beyond—the BU bridge. The MIT bridge then under the Museum of Science, where I would sit in the space capsule after regarding Tyrannosaurus rex. I could see the river in all its seasons. I liked when it ran under the ice past the snowbanks or in the late fall twilight rain.

Away from them and school, though, I was still completely dependent upon my wits, and my wits were usually employed on matters other than my immediate safety. White people were dangerous because they were extreme. They tried to either aid or block my passage into their segregated world. *Benevolent* whites didn't think I was Black. Whatever native intelligence I possessed had nothing to do with my race. Blackness was something they were helping me overcome. They, allegedly, gave me culture as though it were theirs to give.

The other extreme: no matter how gifted I was I was still seen to be a nigger and subject to most of the chronic and systemic, acute and arbitrary violence the republic or the individual believed I deserved. This, however, wasn't shocking. It was expected.

The Black bourgeoisie, in many ways, were awful. These weren't my mother's people. They hated her because she was Black in a way they could never be—I think because they didn't want to be. My father's family were—largely—awful, but he had distanced himself or they'd cut him off. He thought too much. He was too eclectic. He was too weird. He was too white.

They weren't the neighbors we were friends with. They were the extended families and in-laws. They were at the AME churches for weddings and funerals. They were at the *community* cookouts and the parents of the few Black kids in school. They were at the events that celebrated *Black Excellence*.

They seemed obsessed with how we represented our race. When the man on the train accused me of being a race traitor, I knew what he had against me. It was my responsibility to share my wealth. I threatened their children's social standing. I made them think about what they didn't want to know—what they refused to know. They attacked my mother's Blackness, which was the very thing they celebrated but desperately wanted to leave behind so that they could succeed in the urban and suburban North and amass material wealth. Yet, had they read any of the great Black texts they supposedly revered, or practiced any of the most basic Black American sociopolitical theories, had they truly appreciated art, they could've looked at me and seen Du Bois and Washington, Hurston and Locke, King and Carmichael. If I survived, their descendants might be good enough to attend a school named after me.

The contradictions abounded. Our raggedy car made us too Black but listening to the Beatles made us white. Education was the great equalizer and valued above all else, but we were scorned for going to an excellent private school. They were jealous of us and, looking back on it, scared of me because by their measure I was the whitest of the too-white Thomas children. Then and now I could never tell a cop that many people think of me as white, or *"It's okay, officer: I'm gifted."*

I suppose I could simply ask why anyone would be mean to a little kid? Also, why couldn't they recognize the similarities—along with the differences—between the white poetry I loved and the Black spirituals we all knew? If not criminal such ignorance allows for criminal acts. I wasn't white. I was American: a Boston Celtics-faithful, Kansas City Monarchs-loving, Woody Guthrie-singing, James Brown-dancing American whose last name could be replaced by an X. I'll continue to be above and amused by such absurdity. This is a hurt I'll admit: they also racialized my strangeness. *My people* called me "dreamy" or at worst, "not all there." No one used the term back then. "Simple." It was, ironically, the most polite. I was autistic. Autism was white.

For the weeks that followed Miles's quasi-diagnosis I was overrun by memories—though they didn't present as such. They were more like reenactments of the past altered by knowledge, time, and hurt. I felt a sudden backlog of alienation, estrangement, and otherness. I saw me not *get it*. I felt, in a way, for the first time, how I felt. What emotion was for me. What sense was for me. I felt the absence of a life I might've had. And I felt years of loneliness and scorn. I felt the incredulity of others when they'd ask, "Why don't you eat something?" *I'm not sure if what I'm feeling is hunger.* "Why don't you sleep?" *I don't know how to go to bed.* "Why didn't you use the bathroom?" *I didn't know that I had to pee. I can't remember what that's supposed to feel like.* Am I hungry when Tony the Tiger floats just above my head? Am I tired when lights become comet tails? My teeth itch and I can't sit still but I can't remember the number of steps to the toilet. I can't see how I'll get there, even in my home. I don't know if I'm real.

But I was real, again, and still didn't know what to say.

The boy's club was loud, smelly, and crowded. I was one of the youngest campers and spent most of my energies winning at pool or contributing to my team in fast-pitch Whiffle ball. We were in a break between games of bombardment—a more violent dodgeball, like MMA fighting is to boxing. My mind was full of sweat, smells, echoes, or shouts, screams and pinging balls, welts and tears and celebrations, but mostly the hot spot on my chest from when I caught one of those big red rubber balls.

I shouldn't have left the gym, but I was exhilarated by our win and my performance. I got caught. It must have been easy. I wanted to tell my mother the worst of it was that I got caught. And that was my great shame and embarrassment. I didn't want to tell the camp counselors because I couldn't see or hear how to do it. Everyone—even my siblings—was unapproachable. The only clear tableau for me was telling my mother in which she'd have one of a series of reactions: rage at the camp, offender, or me. No answer, a rapidly intensifying headshake with a loudening feral cat growl to screech. Or a blank faced "You should've been paying attention."

How can a stammering idiot speak of something so grave? Even now I feel *wrong*. Sometimes I stutter about it in my head. And sometimes in those moments I hate myself for never having been right enough. I wonder what I'm going to do with myself. Bury it. Choke on it. Stumble in public over the word again and again. Sell it. Sometimes I want to tell people I love why it's so hard. And that's why I have to begin with what someone else saw and spoke. At least for myself. I quote. Sometimes it's defensive; other times it's an attack; but most often it's all, in the moment, I can offer—even for myself.

I see it. There are two spaces. One is blank but I know that forms might appear. Some slide into view from the periphery. Others rise out of the nothing. The space is crowded and frantic with colors, shapes, script, faces, and still and moving flashes of memory. Through it all is the auburn rumbling of a didgeridoo. The spaces are separated by a broad, black band. My feeling is somewhere in that border.

Sometimes I'm quiet. It's okay to be a mystery to the self. At least now it is. And if I wait long enough, I'll see the sea and hear the yawp from above, *"Thar she blows."* And the men over the rail and into the boats and how they row. That's how I can explain myself—all of myself—to others, but first, to myself. That's where it begins and sometimes ends for me. I wait, then see. Sometimes I don't want to report to anyone. Sometimes I only apprehend the larger entity in whatever form it appears and it's, at the time, too large for my language. And I see myself when I was a boy.

Then it's no longer me at any age. Pip is there to fetch the rum, work the tambourine, and keep the beat of killing light. There's something in it for him to go along with the men and to keep them pulling. And singing. He fell, once. He was brought back and cautioned that he wasn't worth another rescue. But then he was in again. They couldn't comprehend why he'd jumped so they had to believe he fell. Though they were partially informed of what was below it didn't matter. For some, information nourishes wisdom, but to the ignorant it's merely prey. They pressed on and left him amid the swells.

Perhaps the men didn't consider what being alone in the deep would do to the boy. Perhaps they didn't realize that for those who've been cast out fact and apprehension mix like water and brine, that memory is driven by time and so time can compel the past to heave what is and crash it upon what might be. Again and again. Perhaps they believed that when they returned to Pip, he would be as he was. Perhaps he'd know better. But did they recognize he'd already been marked to a degree he couldn't reason? Would any knowledge have righted their actions? No. Pip had been warned. Whatever could happen to him he deserved. They saw the whales fluking and breaching and their purpose for being and doing.

What Pip saw was the hunt—the men in their longboats, the blood before their eyes, and their chant on the wind as they tried to sync the stroke of their oars to the roll of the sea. In the rhythm of the waters he sensed the sharp horizon. He saw the silver clouds, then the sun and domed sky beyond them. He saw the wobble and spin of planets. He saw stars and streaks of ancient light. And in their wakes, he thought he saw eternity through his inner eye. In eternity is our fate.

But he couldn't join these visions and he could not hold them apart. He could neither speak of them as many nor as one. It might take him a life to say what he couldn't yet. And if he could not speak, he would never be real to those who'd left him behind—at least not enough to keep them from leaving him again and again. Though it seemed to him he should never want to be recovered Pip knew he could not float adrift for long. Eventually his silent nature would take him down.

I spent at least an hour every school day in the square, most of which was in front of the Harvard Coop, waiting for the bus to Allston. Cambridge was one of the few places in my world that made any sense aesthetically, cognitively, emotionally: the newsstand, the traffic hissing round the rotary, the rosy taillights down JFK, and the river, out of sight, but still present at the bottom of the hill. And I know that I was a poor Black boy, strange and alone, but the politics of the day could never intrude on my sensory experience. Even now, the topical, the sociopolitical *reality* is, for me, always outstripped by the sublime. And those moments in November's early dark and drizzle—even with a greater current understanding of my condition—affect me the same way today. The political realities between then and now have never bled those—these—moments of their power, their wonder. A critic might argue that I suffer from a coward's nostalgia, but haven't most battles, aren't most *just causes* centered on the belief that all people have the right to pursue a simple dignity for themselves? And doesn't that simple dignity begin with honoring that small, strange creature inside us—protecting it from scorn—that being who is moved and hopes to move others because of the way the electric lights are refracted by the evening rain—in spite of what has happened? What will happen? One must preserve whatever it is within them that allows them to experience the sublime. This is not a naive position. After many years of *"living among the breakage"* I've come to believe that the effort to make something beautiful—and only the most sincere effort, unaffected by potential outcome, material gain or loss—is the only thing that can prevent us from falling into darkness.

6

We knew the rain was coming. We'd been heading in the opposite direction of Pale Male's nest and were a long way from it. We turned northeast. Sometimes we kept to the paths; sometimes we cut across the grass and over drumlins. It wasn't long before we crossed Seventy-Ninth Street. I decided we'd cut through the trees along the south of Turtle Pond, cross East Drive, and hop the wall near the south wing of the Met. But I kept us in the trees and instead of continuing to Fifth I turned us north. I don't know why. I stopped but he took several more steps then stood.

The first drops fell. We heard them patter the few leaves and bare branches above. Miles tried to turn his head around, to the left then to the right as if he were an owl, but when he realized he couldn't, he arched his spine and tried to look up—over—so far I thought he'd tumble backward. He held that pose, though. The boy seemed like he was waiting to feel the water on his cheeks and let it permeate his skin; that he was wide-eyed to absorb what he saw; open-mouthed so he could inhale the moment, but also exhale to return what he'd been given, but because it had passed through him, in another form. I thought that he might be ready to suddenly appear for whomever and whatever had been waiting and watching for him.

I was open to becoming a part of what I was witnessing and for it to become a part of me: a part and apart. I wasn't frozen in that time, nor did I attempt to freeze and save it for nostalgia. Instead I felt, really, free. *We* were free: alone and together, parallel and forever interwoven. No struggle. No shame. No hiding in remote places—inside or out. Wild. Free: the rain, the finch's song, the red bolt in the blackbird's wing that reminds us of its speed through the air, and the gesso sky, waiting. More. I could see it in how Miles's bowed back suggested a complete circle. I could see it in his face as he could see it in the trees and feel it in the nearing break of the hidden clouds: that which feels and knows us, that which we've always felt and known.

> *The monster 'neath the mountain,*
> *The haunt amongst the cane,*
> *The spirit on the water:*
> *"God is in the rain."*

We crossed over into the meadow. The sky hadn't changed and because of this it seemed as though no time had passed—except that we were now cold.

Although he was walking with me, Miles was still looking up. I thought he was too far gone to call to. But when I was startled by a shrieking siren out on Fifth Avenue, he calmly lowered his gaze and—as if he'd been present all the while—spoke.

"No hawks." He reached out and gently twisted the air. "It's okay though." He opened his hand and waved as though offering a blessing. "We did see so many other birds."

I suddenly felt weak and uncertain. I'm sure my voice betrayed my state.

"I'd like to see a hawk."

"Oh, me, too!" He paused, then, looking across the meadow, pointed skyward. "We can look for Pale Male and his mate." Now he pointed over the trees to our east, which hid the south wing of the museum. "Their nest is right there."

I looked in that direction but struggled to see what he did. I was worrying about whether to cut across what seemed like a small grimpen. The yellow grass would surely be soggy and cold and full of hidden depressions.

The path, though dry, wasn't direct, and there were people: jogging, walking on the wrong side, going too slowly, or not moving at all. I knew Fifth Avenue was waiting beyond, and now I felt drained and unable to come up with even a bad plan.

I grabbed Miles's wrist and pulled him along with me through the bog towards the back of the museum. He stumbled. I tugged him harder.

"Pick up your feet and walk right." He did. And then I snarled, "Keep up."

I sped up to cross the path, zigged through the pedestrians without causing any to stop or slow. Now the building was too close to use for navigation. It had become, rather, a barrier. I slowed, wondering whether to turn south, where I couldn't see or imagine an exit, or north, the long way around, thereby admitting I'd made the wrong choice and requiring more grinding aggression from me.

Now there was a large dumpster before us, so we stopped, and I thought I should pretend that I wanted to study it up close—that it had been my destination and on a warmer day or in another mind we could've stayed there watching the rats and squirrels, pigeons and sparrows and the odd gull foraging. Waited for dusk to see a raccoon, skunk, or opossum—even a coyote.

Then I saw, in my mind, Miles alone, staring at the green metal hull until long past dark.

I pulled him south and dragged him through a row of juniper bushes. We made it out but were only at the delivery bays. The sounds of the real avenue were loud and confusing. I looked at Miles. His face was turning. I dropped his wrist, barked, "Come on," and pressed on. But by the time we'd rounded the wing, I'd become more hesitant and confused. I tried to hide it from Miles, but he knew. He looked frightened. We stopped at the bottom of the Met's stairs. Fifth Avenue was blurred by walkers, bikers, the traffic. The limestone and granite seemed to shudder. Some of it looked, sounded, smelled—felt—like what I'd imagined earlier but not enough. I hadn't fully considered what being on this side of the museum would be like: people walking up and down the giant stairs and through the doors, boxes of metal pins and all the fingers pinching them onto the lapels, the coat check lines, the security guards, alabaster nudes, golden sarcophagi, Van

Gogh's heavy brushstrokes. Miles was there beside me with his arms pressed rigid against his sides—wide-eyed now but with a different kind of wonder. Straining to keep it out or somehow make any kind of sense of it all.

Perhaps his tableau consisted of me leading him out, so I took his hand and led him north along the bottom stair. I realized, though, that I didn't know where I was going. Had we driven? Had we taken the subway? I couldn't concentrate because an aerial view of the city's grid seemed to morph out of the rush, the real, around us, and then I saw underground chambers and tunnels of the subway, each tinted by their respective colors—4-Train green, A-Train blue, the dimmed caution lights of the F, and through them all, long lines of hitched numerals—linked twos and threes clattering under Broadway. I knew I had to stop and wait for it all to pass, but I didn't want to frighten him more, so I pretended to search the line of vendors—despite the fact I couldn't really discern much of it all—for something.

A woman was selling unframed photos of animals—some noble images of eagles and wolves, grizzlies and polar bears, cute photos of koalas and kittens. One stood out: Miles saw it too. It was an 8x10 of an orange tabby looking into a mirror and seeing its reflection, a snarling tiger's face. I knew I had to buy it. I believed it would anchor me, clear my head, and if not ground Miles, then at least provide him with a tether to where we were.

I pulled him through the walkers. I pointed at the print. I felt my jaw tighten. I couldn't speak, but she didn't seem to care. I had to shake his hand loose to pay. He startled. I took the bag from her and told him that Ella would love it. I wanted to get something for Michaele and Alex but knew that trying to browse all those stands would be folly.

He scanned the tumult. "Ella *will* love this," he said weakly.

He followed me south down Fifth. I held his hand to cross Seventy-Ninth but once we did I let it go and started walking south aggressively. It took him a beat, but then Miles followed. I kept checking behind me to see if he was keeping up. He was. He was wide-eyed, but his face was blank, and he didn't seem to be looking anyplace. Rather he did as he'd done when he was born. Unblinking Miles, O Miles, O Miles, my Miles—strangeling child of the endless stare.

We walked a few minutes more when he suddenly stopped in the middle of the sidewalk. He didn't seem to see those who jostled, brushed, or dodged him. I jerked my head southward. He neither moved nor looked at me and instead stayed. I stepped to him to grab him, but he turned to the street. I looked down into his face. His eyes seemed to snap into focus. He was looking up—across the street.

"It's up there, but he isn't in it."

He pointed. I followed the line. Twelve stories to the top of the stone gable was the edge of a large nest. Miles took a step toward the curb. People knocked his arm, but he continued pointing. I tried to grab his collar, but he stopped before he reached the edge of the slab. Still pointing, he checked to see if I saw what he did. When he was sure that I was present, he spoke:

"I'd love to see him on a day like this because in the gray you can see his red." He cocked his head to check on me again. "Do you see? I mean, have you seen?"

"Yes."

Now he had his impish grin. But it faded as people began to stop and follow his point to see what he was seeing. Others broke his line, and indifferent or annoyed were vexed into the gutter.

One woman stopped and quietly asked what we were watching.

"Pale Male's nest!" Miles exclaimed, still focused above. "But he's not there. He must be out hunting or stretching his wings." His face went blank. "Hawks in the wild can live up to—" His face was blue. "Maybe he's dead." He lowered his arm. "I don't . . . well, wild hawks." He tried to point again, but it seemed he no longer knew how. "I don't exactly know his age."

She grunted. I turned to her. Her eyes were rolled halfway up under their lids. She smiled a stingy smile and scurried away.

And as if he suddenly realized the gravity of his thought, he frowned. His head trembled as he fought off tears. He sighed and composed himself, then arched his spine so he could look straight up.

"Where do you think he is?" He looked calm but sounded worried. "What about his mate?"

"Somewhere."

"Do *you* think they're alive?"

"I do."

"They mate for life, you know?"

Without looking down, he found my hand and held it gently. He stepped back and I followed. I thought we should make our way back to the wall, but his face though not yet open was no longer blank, frightened, or blue. I realized the rain had come and gone. O, my Miles. The taxis honked. The bus brakes hissed, and their diesels rumbled and stank. The barkers yawped, and the rushing crowd—uptown, downtown—parted around us and rejoined on their opposite sides. Miles tightened his grip on my hand and pulled me closer. Now I looked: across the street, up the wall to the lintel and then the ledge, past the nest and the mansard and up to the dimming white sky. No one touched us or tried to move us from where we were. And alone and together we watched above, waiting for a dark-winged angel.

A Peace

Remember how long you have been deferring these things, and how many times you have been granted further grace by the gods, and yet you have failed to make use of it. But it is now high time that you realised what kind of a universe this is of which you form a part, and from what governing part of the universe you exist as an emanation; and that your time here is strictly limited, and unless you make use of it to clear the fog from your mind, the moment will be gone, as you are gone, and never be yours again.

—Marcus Aurelius

1

This would kill him. Up to that point, he'd suffered sicknesses of the heart and mind. They'd crippled him, but they hadn't finished him. Thirty years—he'd lost nearly everything from his teeth to his children, but he'd lingered on and it seemed to me that he would forever. This was different: he couldn't breathe. I knew my father was going to die.

It was Labor Day weekend 2005, and I was trying to cram the end of a second construction job into that Sunday and Monday so that I could finish one I'd started the month before. I hadn't really a chance at finishing either, nor would I be able to start or even look for other work. School had already started. I was an adjunct with three classes, and I'd be locked into that schedule. It was a regular paycheck, but it was about a quarter of what I needed to make. We were two months behind on the mortgage, soon to be three. We had a $10,000 credit card bill, and that account was about to go into collections. I'd sold my novel in June but was still waiting for the first payment: 50 percent of $12,500 less my agent's 15 percent. And while $5,300 and change equaled ten weeks of work, which was almost a month of bills, it was a month that had already passed, not the one we were in. And then there was October, November. I'd have to sell a book every few weeks for some time to come.

I was beaten. If I could've envisioned a way out, I hadn't the legs for it. Whenever Michaele needed me to tell her everything will be alright or I won't let us lose, I couldn't. Nor did I have any fiery sermons about eternal optimism. I couldn't speak with the "tongues of angels" because I hadn't any real charity and so everything I said sounded to me like tinkling brass. A patrician smile and nod or a comforting look was beyond me, so I'd be sullen and resentful instead.

Sarcoidosis. He'd called the day before to tell me. "I'm sick," he'd said. "It's in my lungs." I couldn't respond. I listened to his weak breathing. It seemed as though being honest had taxed him.

He'd never—in my life or from what anecdotes I'd heard—been so direct. From preadolescence to young adulthood, I'd had few ways of responding to him. When he lied, I'd ignore him. When he offered euphemisms, platitudes, or vague narratives as to where he'd been, what he'd done, and why, I'd angrily stare at him and dare him to look at me. When he felt salty and thought he could reclaim his authority over me—be a father—he sounded at best Socratic, at worst like a troubled adolescent's social worker.

But even through middle school, though my older siblings wouldn't, I'd still go out with him on visitation Sundays. Parked, he'd relax on the bench seat of his shitbox like some professor in his quarters, humoring a lost student. He'd gesture with his cigarette, gentle spirals to start his rhetorical musings, soft jabs to dot the question marks.

"Have you given any thought as to what your anger will profit you?" or *"You seem angry."* A failing man: kinky, thinned hair, widow's peak, gray-brown skin perforated by decades of ingrown stubble, a weak 1950s mustache and welfare dentures, skinny-fat and potbellied under his dime-store clothes—always a clay jacket and slacks and the dimmed-white shirt of the smoker. David Milton Thomas Jr. the nomad-sage in his jacked-up American coupe home. Trunk wired shut. Rear seat and floor lost under a dump of old notebooks and business suits. And me across the bench seat hating him, wondering if he thought the pile of mail and empty and full packs of cigarettes between us could protect him from me.

When he'd quote Plato, I'd counter with Machiavelli. When he'd offer Nietzsche, I'd mutter that living was the true test of a philosophy. He'd lecture about art as catharsis or that sublimation was the only method for transforming passion into achievement, beauty, and peace. And I'd remind him of his heroes: that Poe died drunk in the streets and Van Gogh blew a hole through his guts. I'd never mention *his* carnality, but I'd mock his endorsement of the ascetic life by mumbling something like: *"Rage, goddess..."*

He'd assert that I'd proven his point: *"Homer is, indeed, someone to emulate."* And I'd get all Boston punk on him—cock my head to the side, squint, and grin. *"Fuck that pussy. I'm Achilles."* He'd sag. His voice would change. *"Oh, Michael..."* like he was some toe-down jazzman begging for one more gig. *"What?"* I'd answer, like I was now a Homer scholar. And he'd go Boston townie: *"You're just like your mother."*

But when I was a boy, I'd listen, not even to what he said, but how he said it—his cadence, syntax, diction, and pronunciation. Those elements weren't separate, but rather the distillation of where he'd been, what he'd seen. His dreaming eyes and liquid voice sometimes made me feel what I thought it was like to be loved like a son.

On the phone I was a boy again, but he spoke to me, finally, like a man. And through the years of anger at him—compassion and contempt for him—I'd never been afraid. Now I was.

"I'm sorry" was all I could offer.

"My prognosis is excellent."

I said nothing, and then finally in almost a whisper: "I'm sorry."

"Thank you." A beat. "You're busy. I can tell you're about to run out the door."

I couldn't answer.

"Chin up, Mr. Michael."

That morning, it took me an hour to do things that usually took less than ten minutes. I couldn't find anything. I'd pick up a tool and put it down or lose it in a pant pocket or my belt. I was perplexed by the task of plumbing corner bead, and it was harder still to fasten it. When I finally relearned how to mud, I realized that there wasn't time for it to dry: forget about priming the new walls. There was no way I could even skim.

After what seemed like hours, I scanned my job. I couldn't tell. My clients would be home in an hour. I had to clean and load out because their kids slept there at night. I had to cut and install some flooring because there was none under the walls I'd demoed. I tried to fit the planks in their places, but I was like a toddler with puzzling blocks, so I sat on the bucket of joint compound and cried until it was time to go.

The best thing I'd ever done, according to my father, was marry Michaele: *"She really helped you get turned around."* Before I could ask how he knew so much about my life, he'd tell me that he'd always been watching, concerned. Whatever I did accomplish granted me probationary status or went unnoticed. This isn't something I intuited; it's what he explicitly said. Nothing I'd done as an adult had been good enough for my father. My first college was the wrong college because it wasn't an Ivy. My rebound school didn't merit comment because it was public. The awards and fellowships I won at Hunter didn't matter because it was a commuter school and all he knew about it was that it was once a teacher's college for women. He openly wondered if my sobriety had caused me to forgo a PhD at a prestigious institution for an MFA at a *"mail-order program."*

I was never good enough for him as a child either. He wanted me to be right-handed. And until I learned to drag a pencil across the page my penmanship was "sloppy." He disapproved of my pigeon-toes. I wore corrective shoes outside and wore them wrong-footed at home. At night, I was locked to a bar in turnout. Now our house was haunted, and I had an expansive imagination. These elements, combined with the books I read, which were too mature for a child not long out of diapers, made for nights of terror from which I've yet to recover. My knees, ankles, and toes are in chronic pain. I sleep like an infant, have the nightmares of an adult.

He didn't understand what was beyond me. My brother was four years older and my sister, two. They were "remarkable" children. Still, he measured my physical, intellectual, and emotional maturity against theirs and theirs against the older kids in our neighborhood. I think his judgment hurt them because, unlike our mother, he never explicitly told them the cost of failure. For her it was simple: success equaled potential safety and tenuous peace with white people. Failure equaled death. Her fears were corroborated by centuries of empirical fact: we were always in danger, and she had to warn us and to the best of her ability prepare us for a life of peril—for a life of being seen as niggers, being seen as worthless, and being treated as such.

My siblings were, I think, practical or real in a way I could never be. I think they suffered his presence and abandonment conventionally. Their reactions made sense. Mine didn't. My brother would rage, my sister would remove herself, and I would either do nothing or try, emotionally, intellectually, and sometimes physically, to do as he asked. I tried to understand the incomprehensible. I think that's why he pushed me in a way he wouldn't my siblings. I think they might have experienced this as favoritism. Perhaps it was. When either of them struggled with homework, and they were working well beyond their grade level, he'd ask them a series of rhetorical questions, which must have seemed mocking. Then he would have me solve the math problem or answer a reading comprehension question that they, given the time, would've been able to. This made David resent me and Tracey want to protect me. He, early on, gave up on them.

I don't know why, but I understood that he wanted more than the answer. He wanted the answer and the doubt that would demand another question. For him, in the life of the mind there was no rest. I still don't know what it was that he saw in me—something to support, correct, or exploit. My understanding depends on my state of mind. Perhaps he saw a budding philosopher whose mind he needed to train; perhaps a born alcoholic who by the age of five already seemed restless, irritable, and discontent. At times, then, I felt special. And feeling special compelled me to be closer, though he repulsed me. So, I tried to be near and far. And in trying to be—wherever I was or wasn't—I was rarely with myself.

When my mother told me that I "wasn't all there," I didn't hear this as cruel. It was comforting. It located me. However, I didn't know why it was so, other than it was difficult for me to be so. Whatever term is used for me and people like me, I lived in a world of wonder. I don't mean the popular notion of the word. My mind seemed a nexus of the sublime, ridiculous, horror, relief, and questions and answers about it all.

It could sometimes be a sanctuary, but I was often very lonely there—and afraid. Few living people could reach me, and I couldn't seem to reach them. The closest I could get to were the prose passages and poems he had me memorize. They seemed to be, if not touchstones, at least landing spots. When he was at work or in bars with his buddies or his mistresses, I tried to reach him through them. Reaching my father was conditional, and I didn't know how to create one that would shrink the distance between us, so I'd read to and for myself. Alone, though, prose and poems were launching pads. Reading "Batter my heart, three-personed God" to myself would make me frantic. And the apprehension of returning, even in part, to the real world with metaphysical exhortations was distressing. It still can be. I suspected my father wasn't conventionally grounded, but I thought he was at ease in the unreal and that somehow gave him purchase in the real.

I was wrong. There wasn't a place for him in either. I think he sometimes got a pass because he was smarter than most of the people in his life. He didn't try to sound smart. I don't think he referenced his heroes of the western canon to intimidate or belittle people. I think he did so to share what he had to offer. He was a philosophy major at Boston University and all of the Harvard Classics in our front hall bookcases had worn covers and broken spines. The pages were lined with his elegant notes.

I think he was lonely. My romantic take is that he'd always felt that way. His mother was second generation up South, and I remember her being clipped, dicty, and bougie. It seemed to be true of her line—at least the way she spoke of them, with misguided reverence. I think the North either bled or exposed them. She confused middle-class striving with middle-class pretense, obstinance with perseverance and snobbery with dignity. If you're going to be that unpleasant, you'd better have something beautiful inside to protect. Her rigidity didn't serve any other purpose than hide that she'd little to offer.

I've never seen a picture of his father. My father rarely spoke of him. David Sr. was dark, squat, drank a lot of whisky in his convalescence, and, at least once, hit my father hard enough to knock him from his chair at the dinner table to the floor, where he woke up wondering what he'd done to deserve it.

He was first generation from a line of Charlotte-area free people. I was told he was also the first Black graduate from the Massachusetts School of Pharmacology. He worked, though, as a janitor. During World War II, however, there was a scarcity of pharmacists and he filled prescriptions in the cellar of Garb Drug in Kenmore Square. After the war, he was allowed to work aboveground until he suffered a heart attack. He was a neighborhood handyman after that. He left Boston for North Carolina. I'm not sure when. He died there in 1979. I didn't know this until a few years back, when I saw a photograph of his tombstone online.

I didn't call him again for over a week. I told myself I was in shock, too busy, or so resentful of him having been a terrible father that he didn't deserve me. I'd never learned the habit of phoning him because I never knew his number. I had to wait for his calls. When he'd moved out when I was seven or eight, I think he lived with his mother until she burned down her house with a faulty toaster. After that, I think he lived in his car.

I was twelve before I knew how to find him. My mother—fed up with his absence and the fact that he only showed up when he had gifts—finally leaked the information. He was working at Lechmere, a department store on the Boston/Cambridge line. It seemed exclusive back then, like a combination of Saks and FAO Schwarz, but it was more like Target. I'd ride the D to the end of the line and make the short walk to the store. I was, of course, followed as I searched for him. Eventually I stopped, told the white man my name, and inquired where I could find my father. "Oh, Dave! You're Dave's kid!" He put his white hand on my shoulder. "You must be the youngest one. We've heard all about you!"

Dave was the assistant manager of the seasonal department. It said so on his name tag. He was surprised but seemed genuinely happy to see me. I think it had been weeks since I'd heard his voice. He acted as if we'd eaten breakfast together before he'd left for work. He introduced me to his coworkers. They were all white and didn't seem like people either of us could relate to. They seemed happy to meet me. An unnaturally blonde, gaunt woman touched my father's shoulder and while trying to look deeply into my eyes asked, "Wait, this one is Michael?" She reached into a bin of Super Friends plastic balls, pulled one out, held it before me, and asked, "How much air does this have?"

In the months that followed, I visited at least biweekly. Sometimes he beamed. Other times he seemed indifferent and said that I should call before coming. So, I would. The operator would answer. I'd ask for the seasonal department. Sometimes he'd answer but would have to rush me off the phone. Usually someone else did. They'd take a message, but he wouldn't return my call. I started going back unannounced, but he was never there. Eventually there were new people who didn't know who he was. I learned where he lived when he had to recover from his first heart attack with me.

I finally called. He seemed happy and relieved that I did. He didn't want to talk about his illness—only Michaele, the kids, my house, and my work. He wanted to know what I was writing and if my graduate studies had helped hone my craft. I told him I was, it had, and I'd made a few good friends. He told me that they must be some special people: "You're a hard one to reach."

I tried calling him every day. And, thankfully, he didn't reminisce about my childhood. He used to tell me about a life that I hadn't experienced. When I'd say something particularly sharp or judgmental—even about the Yankees—he'd be silent and look to someplace far away as though there he'd find an answer as to why I was the way I was. Eventually he would say or even intone: "You know, Michael, when you were a little boy, you were so full of light." He'd started to say this when I wasn't much older than ten. Sometimes he'd say it wistfully, as though he hoped there was a glint of that boy left; other times he would say it as if he was grieving something in me that had died.

But he didn't reminisce, so I kept calling, and each time we spoke instead about writing—who I was reading now, who I best liked to teach. The first lie between us was mine. He asked if I was working on something. I told him I was, a novel. Then he asked questions so quickly I hardly had time to answer. *What's the POV? Is it contemporary or historical? What's the plot structure? What are some of the central themes? To whom are you most indebted?*

He eventually stopped to laugh at himself. It hurt him, but he continued. He apologized for his excitement. He said he was proud of me.

"I'm so happy you're taking a run at something. No more marking time."

I didn't respond.

"Are you there?"

"Yes."

"Are you okay?"

"Yes."

"It seems I might have offended you."

"Not at all."

"Thank goodness. I am very proud of you."

"Thanks."

"Okay, Mr. Michael. Chin up."

2

For as long as I can remember, my father cautioned me about marking time. *"No good can come from such waiting."* When I was small and scared of getting into bed, he'd tell me that I could put it off, but the lights will go out. Though I was horrified by the smells and textures of all frozen vegetables or didn't want to go to kindergarten where I'd sit in the corner wearing the dunce cap, I had to face it because it would only get worse. Later it was homework, then applying to the right college, then being a college dropout. I was marking time driving a cab and delivering pizzas, even though those jobs helped house and feed him. The most engaged he ever was with me was when he lectured me about how I could no longer put off being engaged.

This came from a man who postponed every responsibility he had to his children. While my protracted hiatuses weren't profound, I didn't think I was avoiding life. I was just trying to get my shit together so I could live it. I thought he minimized my struggles and exaggerated his own. But his was not Hamlet's delay. He wasn't wrestling with Judeo-Christian morality or Greco-Roman ethics. There were no paradoxes to suffer. He wasn't a prince. There were no ghosts. There was nothing to settle before action. He left us responsible for his failings and his pain—so many and so much that we couldn't begin to account for our own.

When I finally got up to Boston he told me more. He'd learned about it in the summer. "I've been in for tests," he told me in his now-wheezing baritone. He looked awful. It seemed that every time he went to the doctor for a checkup, or to the hospital for a test or a blip, he'd leave looking worse off.

The biopsy had hurt him. And though it was weeks later, I could tell he was still in great pain. When I visited, he would usually stand until I sat, apologize for his squalor, light a cigarette, ask if I minded while exhaling, then joke about quitting. He didn't smoke, though, this time. He lowered himself into his easy chair, muttered a curse on the way down because he'd forgotten to turn on the TV. I found the remote and gave it to him. He thanked me, turned on the television, and dropped the remote on the floor. I knew he'd forget it was there, but it seemed wrong, demeaning, to pick it up.

He pulled at his sleeves and pant legs. He shifted his feet.

"Are you smoking?"

"Hardly," he answered quickly, as though he'd been waiting for the question. "Hmph." He tried to chortle, but instead he began to cough in a violent, grotesque way. It looked and sounded as though he were gagging on axle grease and broken glass—viscous but rasping—all the worse because he tried to suppress it. He stopped, stifled a moan. He shifted, cleared his throat like an orator, and began again. "Hardly." He raised his hand to his heart. "I haven't had one in days, and then it was a few. And only every once in a while."

Sarcoidosis. It hadn't sounded like him. He'd said it as though he didn't understand the word—something a doctor had thrown at him, followed by an oversimplified explanation or none at all. But my father—the man he'd once been—would've at least been familiar with the disease, at least as familiar as I. He'd been the one who'd watched my growing fascination with the bodies of all creatures. He'd given me the children's and then adult anatomy books, the charts of exoskeletons and segments—abdomen, thorax, and head—the perceptions of the compound eye and the fixed eyes of the *not bug, arachnid*. The layered model of the human form—dermis to organ. How they work and fail to work because of trauma and disease.

When I was in first grade, he'd talked the headmaster, Mr. Curtis, into letting me take a first aid course at school, which was meant for middle schoolers. He also, somehow, managed to get me the required books, which I realize now he couldn't have afforded. And over the next few years, I went on to treat a burn victim at a birthday party, keep a girl with a broken arm warm and still while she was in shock, diagnose a concussion under the jungle gym when our teacher had thought that my puking classmate had been hit with a stomach bug. I won an argument with a substitute teacher, proving that one doesn't disinfect a puncture wound the same way one would a laceration. Mr. Curtis had called me into his office—told me that my open recalcitrance was out of character. He then stood and shook my hand. He waited until I had crossed his threshold and just loud enough for me to hear said, "A fine doctor. You'll make a fine doctor."

When my father still lived with us, when I was sick, he'd take my temperature, use my stethoscope to listen to my heart and lungs. He'd rub his whiskers and tell me his diagnosis. I'd do the same for him. And whatever medicine I brought him—properly milked and sweetened coffee, a fizzing glass of Alka-Seltzer, a Lucky Strike, which I'd light for him, a Miller High Life—"Your bedside manner," he'd croon before sampling the antidote, "is excellent." My dad and I were the best quacks we knew.

"Sarcoidosis, do you know what that is?" I'd been hurt by this question. Of course I did. But I let him continue, "There's a cyst or cysts, the plural, I'm not sure." He seemed to be looking into his chest cavity. "They can't operate. They want to dissolve it, or them."

He'd debate his cardiologist about stents, angioplasty, and open heart surgery. He'd understate the complications of each. Lying in the ICU he'd boasted, "My prognosis is excellent." His doctor hadn't corrected him, nor had he pulled my siblings or me aside to tell us what his real condition was. I hadn't pressed my father. I knew he said it to protect us—but more to con himself. I hadn't cared either. We were different then. He was a jobless couch hobo and I—at that time a drunk cabbie—was only months away from having been one too. I was twenty-two, raging, and impossibly far from whatever I or anyone else had thought I'd be. I was a French fry vegetarian with perpetual strep throat, which I'd thought was sudden full-blown AIDS. In my head I had various cancers and was days away from my own stroke, cardiac arrest, or schizophrenic break.

I thought I hated him. I took him in, though, after he was discharged, I think so I could torture him. I let him stay for two months. I kicked him out and ignored him for three years, saw him once or twice, went another year, went another two, and saw him briefly at my wedding. I endured a hug and tuned out his toast except the last clause: "And may you and your love stay evergreen."

I was married with children when he was in for his second heart attack. His fear, for and of me, felt more like sincere affection and guilt. I was still very distant, but I wasn't angry. I listened to him while he considered what he might need done: nothing, stints, angioplasty, or open-heart surgery. He discussed the last two—enthralled—as though they were pure abstractions, or if real were to be performed on some faraway stranger: the snaking camera and inflating balloon; cracking the chest open and moving blood vessels from his thigh to bypass the clogged ones around his heart.

He talked about his nicotine—though not booze—withdrawal. He openly, extemporaneously, meditated on the metaphysical nature of arterial plaque, blood thinners, ventricular predetermination, and the environment in which one—he—had been raised: "The collision of our nurturing and our natures."

My father had always been a shit liar and he knew it. His strategy had been to lie to the end of the other person's or people's tolerance and—when they called him on it—to repent. If he couldn't charm them to feel compassion, he'd feign forgetfulness. When that failed, he'd try to blur memory. His, yours, or whatever the two shared. If that didn't work, he'd ask for forgiveness, and when that failed he'd tacitly agree to retreat into silent exile.

But he'd never forget—like most—and put it behind him. He never tried to reduce or justify whatever we, because of him, had suffered. He lived fully aware of his mistakes and failures. He suffered that unabridged story of whatever mercy, regret, or shame had to offer—if any. At least, I needed to think that, then.

But now he was forgetting. "Sarcoidosis," he muttered again. Now I knew more than he did. He had no more theories, local philosophies. He couldn't lie. He couldn't be true. All he seemed capable of was announcing small veracities.

He seemed to think that he'd told me everything he knew, so he settled into watching *Regis*. He asked me to sit and so I did on his dusty couch, but when he frowned at the screen, I hopped up and grabbed and handed him the remote. I sensed it was my chance to stay up, get out—at least get out of the room.

I went to his bathroom and wondered for a moment if I could clean it, but the old whiskers on the sink and the shower rail on the tub wall made me shiver. I exited and from the doorway I guessed at what he needed. I went to the kitchenette, where plates from days before were stacked in the sink. Two greasy pans were on the stove. A small pot for boiling coffee water, brown rings from his odd mugs and cups, which seemed like burn marks in the counters. A jar of Taster's Choice, a can of Carnation Evaporated Milk, beige sugar in the sugar dish.

There were more open cans in the fridge, pickles, Gulden's spicy brown mustard and no-name yellow. A half gallon of no-pulp Tropicana. An untouched donated tin of box-store lasagna. And an assortment of other foods and condiments I thought had been discontinued long before: Peter Pan. Hollywood Bread: "Life Is Beautiful." I caught myself wondering what fake wheat bread had to do with Never Never Peanut Butter.

I had to leave, but I had to leave him with something. I made a list of food, drinks, and toiletries and told him I was going. He protested weakly, but I cut him off. He turned away from the TV.

"Since you insist." He started to clear his throat—like in our younger days. Even that hurt him. "Would you mind stopping at the pharmacy?"

"No."

He turned his head to me but not his eyes. "Are you sure?" Shallow breath. "My medication is very dear."

"It's fine."

He waited, frowning, but then suddenly brightened.

"Do you know the back way?"

"Yes."

"Because you don't want to go down Route Nine."

"I know." I knew there'd be more so I waited.

"Oh." He turned back to the TV. Looked above it, then into nothing. "If you don't mind . . . if it isn't too much trouble . . ." He was back to his slow, full Emerson. "Get some beer." He waited, then spoke quickly—suddenly he was a low-end salesman. He tried to suppress a grin. "Not a lot, you know, it takes me forever to drink one now. Sometimes I leave half of it, pour it out."

"Yeah."

"Just a six-pack." Like he hadn't already sold me. "Bottles if you can."

"Yeah."

"And would you mind . . . we both know I shouldn't . . . but you know how I like a frank."

"B&M beans?"

He smiled openly. "Absolutely not."

I waited.

"And I haven't had a Reese's in the longest while. It must be years."

I knew he couldn't see me, but I nodded. I left—down the stairs into the hot but fresh air. I wondered how he'd interpreted my quick responses. I almost regretted saying yes. Whatever I returned with would be tainted by his need and my guilt.

I wondered how I'd pay for everything: how much for the meds, whether to sacrifice the beer and candy for the fresh fruits and vegetables I knew he'd never eat. I saw myself conning or pleading with the pharmacist, shoplifting from Whole Foods. I wondered how it would feel to pull a rack of Miller bottles out of the cooler. I wondered how I would choose, for him, for me— know the difference between what we need and what we want.

His meds weren't as expensive as I thought they'd be so I felt I should do more. In the fifteen years since I'd kicked him out, I hadn't done much for him. I'd dropped him off at the doctor or picked him up from the hospital. I'd given him some money or paid a few bills. I'd listened to him lament about his namesake, fabricate stories about Tracey's life, and—for the most part—celebrate me. According to him, Michaele saved me from ruin. He knew I was struggling financially, but I was honest, hardworking, and relative to the rest of the family, doing great and would only do better. I was ascending.

He, however, could chart his life as a downward vector—shallow in his youth, but in the last decades, a steep decline. He was toothless, had three-quarters of a heart, and his lung capacity was rapidly shrinking. He was on multiple drugs for his various physical and emotional maladies. The illnesses exacerbated each other: his heart made him blue and the blues burdened his heart. His shallow breaths were constant reminders that they'd soon stop. The drugs seemed to anesthetize and confuse him. I suspected that they were contraindicated, but I'd never bothered to research their side effects. He was, after all, dying, and though I was the most powerful person he knew I'd never advocated for his health care. I'd rather help a friend's father than my own, just as he'd always chosen to do for and be with others.

I drove east on Route 9. I passed the Steak Loft and remembered some of the awful times we had there. Now though, the bad times weren't so bad. They seemed to me isolated incidents, meetings we perhaps shouldn't have had during our acrimonious times. Most of them however had been in our indifferent hours eating fried foods, drinking beer, and mumbling.

Alone in the car I admitted to myself probably for the first time in my life that my parents' split had hurt and confused me and was something I'd only pretended to have thought about.

I kept driving well past my turnaround into the next town past the strip malls, trying to sharpen some of the hazy images that were pulsing in my head of lounges and piano bars, dark steak houses and grilles, places we'd been together which were now gone or soon to be—his world, lazy days, soda fountains, tin and chrome, lipstick and beehives, cigarettes. When the jukebox in your booth at the Italian restaurant wasn't cute but as ordinary as the decanters of oil and vinegar on the table. When things weren't retro, they simply were what they'd been, or if they were dulled or diminished, it wasn't because they were "poor replicas" or "affects without content."

I'm not nostalgic. I wasn't then either. Memory, now and then, is and was inescapable perhaps because the world was different. We could lose that which could never be replaced. We missed phone calls and *The Wizard of Oz*. Records skipped. Photographs burned. When I thought of people dying all they were died with them.

My mother was a link to Jim Crow and the family farm in Virginia, Reconstruction and slavery. World War II and the soldiers weren't in the past but present in a way Vietnam isn't for my children. That war's veterans were discharged then forgotten. Life, their lives were cheap in another way. Today our boys die no less horribly than before but because their names, faces, and stories can be recalled with a point and click they paradoxically are so much easier to lose. No more MIA's but lost in a cyber world of readily abundant information, which because it's so common is so cheap. But I of course, then, didn't think about a century of war and the superficial ways in which we try to understand it, how we—hawk or dove—ignore or use it for our personal, political, and corporate gain.

I'm still trying to understand though what, if any, of these criticisms are mine. I've thought them and written them and therefore they are my responsibility. I just don't know if they're—really—my thoughts, my father's thoughts, my attempt to preserve his thoughts, a pretense that I had a thought about anything so that people would leave me alone so I can continue to mark time. I don't know if it's a sound analysis of my country folk or adult language masking the protracted reactions of my wounded inner child. Driving East on the old Boston to Amherst highway, I thought about what my father had given rather than taken from me. Unmitigated experience. While he censored or hid most of what perhaps I wanted to know, his phone number and address, he tried to protect me from his ugliest parts.

I thought perhaps that the loneliness I'd felt had less to do with his absence and more to do with my character defect to want more. Perhaps I should think more on the good he gave me by his presence. I lived with him for only eight years but those hours amounted to a large percentage of the times in my life when I felt safe and sure.

We'd sit in his junker car or his lounges or greasy spoons and he'd let me talk about anything, everything. He could follow me. What others thought to be free association, randomness, flakiness, madness he understood to be linked ideas, images, and stories. Fenway, the warning track bread clay, the red mulch of the school playground, the cedar seesaw plank, cedar siding on the second and third grade buildings, Ms. Causey who became Mrs. Hamilton, my clammy stomach and hot heart. I thought she would wait to marry me. And in the smoky womb of lonely people—cocktail glasses and Charlie on the piano playing "You Are Too Beautiful" and me running out of words—my father nodding and gesturing with his head toward the bandstand suggesting that I listen. I would. My father's friends, Martha and Charlie, white folks singing Black music not trying to be Black but honest, talented, beautiful fingers and throat, confident but not glib or smug, suffering but not maudlin, sure and unsure, broken—destroyed really beyond my comprehension but so familiar and so real. The song would end, they'd thank us, we'd clap. My dad would refill his glass, signal for another, then stare into what seemed to be oblivion. He'd find his cigarettes, I'd light him, shake out the match. Someone would pass and say, "Hey, Dave." He'd let them get far enough away so they'd know not to stop, then return their "Hey." He'd check on me with a quick look and return to the smoke. I'd fold my arms on the table, rest my head on them or lean back in the booth. "Are you getting sleepy?" "No." "Sure?" and "Yes." Charlie would start again—a chord or a run, "Another one by Duke you all know." And while Martha sang about the lush life, I'd see the familiar and strange people, places, and events as linear and layered thought, sense memory, and foresight—multiple chronologies converging, in a reverse kaleidoscope.

That was me. It hasn't changed. That moment is one of overwhelming peace. Driving East I know that anything good or worthwhile I'd ever done was conceived in moments like those. Silent, cool epiphany. My father had brought me to those places so I could have those moments and witness how people witness and testify in their own way. Perhaps he knew that those seemingly dangerous places were really the safest I could be. Later I could survive because of what my mother gave me, and with his gift, thrive. When I became a man, I would make what I'd seen and felt real. So that I wouldn't be lost to them or in them. Sometimes I'd feel like a traitor or a spy because the music made me very happy. But that was only sometimes. That music was often sad but never grim. And within it was the right place to be real. I just listened. And in listening I had room and time to hear and I didn't need to force myself into the song and change the words.

They didn't have a saxophone. Why bother? Martha was a mezzo-soprano. She couldn't match the weight of Johnny Hartman's baritone. She didn't even try—but she tried to sing. And that wasn't McCoy Tyner at the piano. Charlie knew who and where he was. He played—it seemed—for Martha so that Martha could sing for us, and we could all be fools "for beauty." Charlie held a chord just a little longer and Martha let a different note turn blue. The first way's not the only way but a start to make the old song new.

It gave me peace, and, in that peace, I sensed my purpose. There was a reason for who I was, where I was, and what I was meant to do. I had a responsibility, to these people, my parents, this audience, those players, the composers, and whoever had come before who I didn't know. They didn't tell me what to do, just that there was something I could do. I *had more*. Because the night was coming, the night is here, for me and for us all.

Instead of going to Stop and Shop for groceries, I pulled into the Whole Foods parking lot. The food would be healthier. The beer would be better. I couldn't buy the beer though. I stood at one end of the aisle and looked down the row of coolers. First I felt high, then I felt drunk. Then remorse—not that which follows an actual bender but rather the state after a drunk dream, then liminal shame after which you begin to remember.

I pushed my empty cart through the giant, bright clean store and thought about drinking with my dad, what it would be like now: baseball, belly laughs, deep philosophy, then, of course, a malapropism—his—or some instruction, nostalgia, or lament; me drinking faster and implying he should match me. He couldn't in my imagination. He never could "in the real," in his early fifties when I was at my best—worst. As I turned into the produce aisle, I grunted something unintelligible. My father was broke, dying in squalor, yet he could still drink. I wished I was a chronic drunk: the happy hour two, the dinner wine, the weekend kickback, the bimonthly tear.

I picked through the apples and pears and wondered if I'd stopped too young. Twenty-seven. I tried but couldn't remember any "wrong" thing I'd done. My thirties in many ways had been my poorest decade. I hadn't really done anything. I couldn't socialize. I lived in practical isolation. Alcohol—*it's the booze*—had always been the answer to: *What happened?*

I headed back to the beer but still couldn't turn down the aisle. Instead, I watched a young man open the glass doors. He took out a six of expensive-looking ale, placed it in his cart, and left. I stopped short of calling him a fucking asshole, called myself an asshole, and left to find the butcher.

Since I couldn't buy him beer I could buy him an excess of other things: organic fruits and vegetables, fresh OJ, prime meats, artisanal bread, natural peanut butter and preserves. He probably wouldn't be able to taste any of it, not without all the additives, not through the fifty-year layer of smoke on his tongue.

All those years and chances: I could've helped him in simple ways. When I lived in Boston or all the times I'd visited it. I could've modified his diet. I could've taken him for walks or to the gym and set up a routine for him. I'd done it for other people—why not him? How I felt shouldn't have mattered. How he'd felt was why he'd left. And the best of him and me didn't begin with feeling. The only way he could connect with people was by talking about ideas and I was his son. I was the same as he. And there were so many things to talk about: free radicals and antioxidants; the error of focusing on BMI; septuagenarian muscle mass; crossword puzzles; sobriety. It didn't have to end here and now. It didn't matter if any of my actions were driven by guilt or spite. I could figure that out later. Today I'd help him start to be new.

I went back to the aisles for garlic, herbs, whole spices, pink Dead Sea salt. He'd always liked hot, spicy foods, so I got split yellow and green mung beans for dhal and a ten-quart stockpot in which to cook it. Back in line, I thought I should cancel classes so I could stay with him, cook him health food, clean the apartment while things were roasting and simmering.

The debit card went through. I helped bag everything, whistled and hummed in the car, drowned out Van Morrison singing "And It Stoned Me." Played it twice more—louder each time. By the time I pulled into his lot, I was stoned.

It took three trips to get everything inside. He smiled. "Hey, look at this," he said on the first trip, and on the second he joked, "Are you moving in?" Nothing for the third as though he didn't want to acknowledge it. As I rustled through and tried to organize all the bags on the kitchen floor and began to assess how much of his old stuff I'd have to chuck for the new, I heard him call my name. "Michael." I didn't answer but instead kept shuffling boxes and bags, opening and closing cabinet doors. I heard him say to no one, "This is too much."

While he watched the news, I cooked, cleaned, and organized. I made brown rice, blanched sugar snap peas and carrots, and seared a medallion of pork loin. No salt. No butter. I plated the meal and brought it to him. He thanked me like I was a little boy. Forget another week, I didn't know if I could stay another hour.

I did, though. He tried to force down as much of his dinner as he could. He employed the child's trick of cutting it up and moving it around, saying that it was a lot of food, that he didn't have much of an appetite.

He wanted orange juice and coffee, so I poured him a glass and made him a cup. I sat with him and watched TV. When I thought

I'd been there long enough, I asked if he was alright—if he would be alright. He insisted he would be, that it was late, and I should get back to my family. After an hour of silence, just as I started to leave, he started to talk.

"TV isn't the same." He chortled. It hurt him. It seemed he wanted to say something more. I thought perhaps he was about to ask for money. But after the pain had eased, he mumbled, "I know you're struggling, financially." He almost cleared his throat. "I'm proud of you."

All the way home, I thought of how Michaele would react to how much I'd spent on gas and groceries—no—how I'd react to her telling me that she was glad I'd done it. I drove and thought about her father—how after almost twenty years since his death, nothing had really changed: she'd always loved him, and he, her.

I had huge gaps of not loving, not feeling. And no matter what I bought him, or how I tried to comfort him, or if I kept driving and never went back, I'd never get far enough away. Or if I turned around and sped back I'd be too late to stop or change anything—there's not much you can do with retroactive love.

3

I have a recurring dream about my father and me. I know it seems convenient but because it's one of the few welcome dreams I have about anyone or anything, I'll tell it.

We're both in our late thirties, though he's fitter than I remember him ever being. We're in Fenway, out in the right field bleachers, several rows behind Williams's red seat. It's back when they had metal benches out there.

From my sleeping POV—a close third—I can see both of us. What serves as a camera is high and to our left—a three-quarter profile full body shot. It's close enough, though, to show detail: the ridges on the aluminum benches, the bulge of the cigarette pack in his shirt pocket, our hairless arms, our faces—how similar they are. It always surprises me, perhaps because since I was a boy I haven't wanted to look anything like him, but awake in the dream or asleep, watching from the outside, I don't mind looking like his son.

The stands are empty. No game. No batting practice, but we're watching something. It's bright enough to be day, but it feels like night—like late August. I can't see more than what the frame allows, but if I could look up, scan the sky, I'd see my city's stars, the ring of lights like the circle horizon.

I started having the dream when there was talk of the Sox leaving Kenmore Square for a new sports complex near the harbor—a glorified outdoor mall—that so many sports franchises have opted for. When I see them on TV, all the attractions and distractions, they seem more like amusement parks, consumer traps, and corporate offices than a place to watch a ball game. But this is Fenway: the way it was and the way I want it to be. It's for us.

Someone is hitting now. I can hear the crack of the bat to ball. My watching self feels the anxiety and anticipation of what might happen, but the two of us seem tranquil even when an unseen ball dongs the metal rows or clatters against the hard, plastic seats. He bounces down the rows, using the benches as stairs. He's light and agile—moving as I'd never seen him. I know he's going to collect the souvenir for us. He disappears. I wait.

More than sharing books and songs, fetching him beers or snacks, lighting his cigarette, visiting him at work at Gilchrist department store. Having lunch at the counter: franks in split-top buns butter-browned on the griddle, crinkle-cut fries—all served in those red-and-white-striped paper boats. I've never felt closer to my father than when watching the Red Sox with him.

He understood: on weeknights we had to stay up—just a few more minutes—to watch their ups. My mother, though, would turn off the TV in the middle of any moment—or potential moment—the moment we'd been waiting for all night. *"But Yaz is up next."* It never worked.

When my father was around though; after lawn mowing, hedge clipping, or prepping for a home repair that would never get done, we'd watch the game from start to finish.

> *Kick your shoes off*
> *Put your feet up*
> *It's time to meet up*
> *With the Boston Red Sox*
> *Boston-born and Boston-bred Sox*
> *Relax (relax relax relax)*
> *And be a Sox watcher*

Saturday afternoon game with a homemade Italian sub on your lap and a cold glass of grape Funny Face. Plenty left over in the fridge because unlike Kool-Aid, it came in a two-quart package. Wise or Ruffles—or Fritos. All the windows open. The bees in the rosebush.

The infrequent car along the weekday busy street. Sleep. Wake. Outside to gather our neighbors for Whiffle ball. As good as those weekend pig-out, pass-out days were, TV was never comparable to going to a game.

It was always a surprise for me. There'd be a bustling in the house, and my brother would tell me to get my glove. At first, I'd think the two of us were going to play catch in the street or our dad was going to take us to Smith Field and hit us grounders and flies, then go for pepper steaks from that place on Western Avenue or pizza from the Lincoln Café.

But if he told us to "bring coats 'cause there might be a chill," I knew we were going to Fenway.

I was four when I went to my first game. It was a Saturday afternoon—back when they played during the day on the weekend. It was hot and hazy. We walked east along the Charles: my father, brother, sister, and I. I was in one of my half dreams, which if I stayed close, my father never minded. Summer. Downriver along the drive, cutting over to Beacon, Commonwealth, up the Brookline Avenue hill—over the turnpike and left on Lansdowne. Through the hot asphalt, sausage grease, sharp and sweet green peppers and onion, peanuts. In the Monster's shadow. The silent net above. The deep resonant organ pulse, which felt like it emanated from my insides—through the mull of fans and the calls of vendors. "Git ya hats here, git ya yeah-ya books! Programs hea-ya! Programs!" Through the turnstile and tunnels. That bright sun at the runway end—the growing, collective murmur—and then—out.

We sat in the lower grandstand (now box seats) just outside the overhang's shadow. They played Milwaukee (back when the Brewers were in the American League). Roger Moret pitched—though I might be combining multiple early memories into one. We didn't lose to the Brewers at home that year, and Moret never started a game. But does it matter? I do know that they lost. The players were small. I was used to seeing the pitcher, batter, catcher, and ump through the center field camera's lens—Yaz's profile instead of his back. But his 8 was so red and sharp. All the colors, even in the dominating sunlight, were brilliant. Our RCA CRT console never came close to reproducing them: the high, bright stirrups, vivid white socks, the vibrant elastic waistband of those double knits, which were more like outfits than uniforms. Not tawny dirt, but instead rusty, granular clay. And the green, green, green: the faded teal walls, the emerald and pine double-cut grass. All of the black became blue.

The PA announcements were like instructions from one of Charlie Brown's parents or teachers—"wah, wah, wah"—but louder and in my belly not my ear. John Killey's organ song sounded like the Phantom's best attempt at a pastoral ode—a wild, haunting freak blues. Though I'd never been around so many people, I didn't have claustrophobia. We sat. The Red Sox took the field. My dad and David opened their programs. Tracey studied the player photo—Bob Montgomery, I think, who she very much liked.

I heard the pop of the first pitch. Hiss. Pop. Murmur. Cheer. Mutter. Groan. Boo. A singular bark, a choral response. I didn't know what to do, so I watched my dad. Someone would get up, get on, or get out, but he'd take his time scoring at the bat. He'd go one batter—two, three—sometimes half the inning without recording anything, then quickly draw those stat glyphs that I still love studying. It doesn't matter, Little League or pro game. They're a record. I can see—feel—the knee-buckling two-strike curve, F0-9-2. Dewy gunning down someone at home who'd try to tag from third: you can't run on his arm. May 2006: Alex's. Little League. His base-clearing double.

Most of the day, my dad sat, smiled, and enjoyed the sun—even when the Brewers scored or when the Sox failed to. When an ump made a terrible call on a pitch, he'd grumble "hey" or "come on." But even so, it seemed he couldn't have been happier.

The result was obvious, but we waited for the last out. Then he got us up and led us through the crowd. I didn't get sick from the crush. I stayed calm—serene, even. Perhaps it was him. He had a way of slowly moving faster than everyone else: zigzag passing into the open spaces without cutting anyone off. Up the stairs, in, through, and out the tunnel, down Lansdowne, down Brookline, across the square, west down Commonwealth—to the Charles. I tried to look at everything but keep up, too, and I didn't do either well. He stopped, threw down his cigarette, then lifted me over his shoulders. From up there, I watched: on the left, Storrow's slow mirage traffic; straight ahead atop the redbrick bottling plant, the dormant Coca-Cola sign; to the right, the picnickers, sunbathers, and orange-silver river, which we followed home.

Other than the '77 July Fourth game, in which the Sox hit a record eight homers, we sat on the first-base side: sometimes grandstand, sometimes box, sometimes those bizarre, wrong-facing seats out by Pesky's Pole. It was always hot—even night games. I liked them best—the silver along the roof, the Monster, the towers, the invisible net and giant halogens and the Citgo sign flashing in the night beyond. We'd drive into town—always past the Kenmore exit, then back east, because it seemed no one drove to Fenway from downtown.

I don't want to ever live there again, but whether circling in the dark over LA's electric fires, approaching Manhattan's skyline from the east, west, or a shallow angle from above, or sitting on the stairs of Sacré-Coeur while night falls over Paris, I've never anticipated, wondered about, or loved a city more than Boston when driving into it at magic hour: the scullers skimming over bright, dark, dirty, silver-and-gold water; the brick or steel bridges that span it; the walkers, runners, and cyclists along the paths; the picnickers on the green banks; the walkways and the overpasses; the red sun on the tower. You can see the sky. You can feel the sky: the city doesn't obscure it but lives within it. AC off. Windows down. Open the sunroof if you have one. Drop the top if you can. No grids. No direct lines: the river and roads wind, so there's always something around the bend just beyond your sight.

I'm not sure if my father knew there was such a thing as public transportation. He drove the Catalina. I don't know what model year. It seemed, though, to be in its midlife. I've never seen one in any other color—amber ale—though that's probably melodramatic. But it was back when car paint oxidized and had chrome bumpers and door handles. Those reflective surfaces tinted each other. It had that Pontiac nose and a black vinyl roof that looked like close-cropped hair.

He never seemed to worry about traffic. He was one of those drivers who didn't stop. He'd ease along shoulders or speed down side streets—the routes of his childhood. He always tried to get "closer." The farthest I remember were the alleys behind BU—never south of Boylston. I remember—though I'm not sure—him parking along the Fens. Whatever—going other places, too—he dared the city to tow him. When he couldn't find a spot, there was always some secret lot or an old buddy's gas station nearby.

He'd have the radio on WBZ for the pregame, none of that bullshit we have now: analysis—filler between commercials like cornstarch, hoof and bone, even, between ground meat.

It seemed impossible that we could hear John Kiley's organ drift over the walls and across the AM wires—the echo, louder than the original—trailing just behind.

We were never early, and so we never saw batting practice or got to walk down to the bottom row and ask for the autographs of the players walking back to the dugouts after warming up on the field. Sometimes we were late for the first pitch, but usually we were taking our seats just in time. Maybe my brother and sister knew where we were sitting, but it was always a surprise to me. I'd try to guess by watching his face: flat for grandstands, a grin for upper box, which widened to a full smile as we made our way down to the field.

I was never scared. Kiley, no longer a wounded phantom, gave the crowd a pitch and rhythm for later chants. Gloves in our laps, programs ready. I trembled and had to check my tears when over the PA, Sherm Feller—the monotone voice of God—bid, "Ladies and gentlemen, children of all ages: welcome to Fenway Park."

It was always the same: nothing for the first three innings. He ignored the vendors. He ignored us. There was the game only. Before the fourth, he'd ask, "Hungry?" We'd nod timidly and mumble our yeses. He, sometimes with David, would disappear under the stands. I don't know why he had to go to the booths. Just when Tracey and I would start getting worried, they'd return: hot dogs with long squirts of French's yellow. Sometimes David would have a pizza. Sprite was okay, never Coke. I'm sure he had a beer, but I can't see it.

Cracker Jacks a few innings later then sport bars. We only got stuff on giveaway days, and we rarely went to those. Bat day. Helmet day. Banner day. No caps or shirts—those were birthday presents or things our cousins brought back for us when they went to games. Rather than be covetous of other kids, I believed what he told us: "Not the real stuff. Not worth it."

I can see him smoking—seventh-inning stretch—though he must have been doing it all along. When we seemed to be drifting off—because of the sun or approaching bedtime—he'd tell us to stay awake for foul balls, because "you never know."

There were never more than a few Black people scattered in the stands—and, of course, so few on the field. There aren't many that come to mind if I think quickly—not chronologically—Tommy Harper, Reggie Smith, George Scott, Cecil Cooper, Fergie Jenkins, Moret, Jim Rice. Tiant was Cuban. Yawkey was still a force—the man who'd demanded "get those niggers off the field," and who didn't roster a Black player until 1963, Clifton "Sweetwater" Brown. "Get those niggers off the field" meant keep those niggers out of the stands too. But there we were, Black. My father, one generation removed from Jim Crow. His children, too—our great-great-grandfather had been born a slave. Fenway—the Sox—should have been terrifying. But in those days it wasn't.

With my father, being Black around white people meant—felt like—one thing; with my mother it was another. No matter the situation, both my mother and father demanded we be polite: proper greetings, table manners, please and thank you, complete sentences, precise vocabulary, flawless enunciation, immaculate public personae, respectful private ones, too.

But she demanded, tacitly and explicitly, that our behavior defy stereotype: "Don't act the fool." Which in angrier moments became "Don't act like a . . ." she'd whisper the first *g*, mumble the second, and stop before the *er* as though if she said the word she'd conjure the specter—make it flesh. No holes, no stains, no off-brands: Levi's,

Carter's, Lacoste. No dirty fingernails, funky pits, or nappy heads: "Don't leave this house looking like a street urchin." After which, she'd hiss one of her—now charming—unique and bizarre threats if she ever caught us running round looking ragged and acting wild: "I'll snatch you."

Her rules could seem arbitrary and stifling, but later I realized they weren't superficial, fearful, or shame-based. She wasn't ashamed of being Black and poor. She believed, rather, that neither should ever be a factor that determined our fates. It was clear her rules hadn't anything to do with assimilating and becoming white and upper-middle class. Neat and clean hair didn't mean we couldn't have picks with folding red and green handles, or fists. Just as we weren't allowed to act the fool, she insisted with a greater intensity that we were forbidden to shuck and jive, let someone lay a hand on us, or *"call us out our name."* We were free—and therefore paradoxically obliged, as long as we kept our dignity—to fight for our rights and for anyone else's that had been threatened.

There were threats everywhere—real or imagined—and she tried to defend us against them all. The alabaster monoliths of our capital, Aunt Jemima, Uncle Ben—the Gerber Baby—it requires constant vigilance to keep those things from doing us and our loved ones harm. And whether these things are real, the onus of such vigilance is costly. It cost my mother almost everything to keep us alive. And although she "laid her body"—and soul—down for us to connect us to all the privileges—the freedom—neither she nor most of the Black girls and boys of our generation and generations to come had. Her hope for us was humble—again, crossing over wasn't assimilation or integration. It was choice: the freedom to choose. "I don't care if you dig ditches. If it's honest work and you support yourself, it's okay."

When I had children of my own, I asked her—obtusely—how it had been raising us. She spoke of my childhood as she'd spoken of hers—she'd lament, but only superficially—about where'd she'd been, what she'd seen, but never what it cost her. And though as much as she said she "didn't notice," her hurt was real: from the burned cross in front of her schoolhouse to the foreclosure of our home, she lived in, and suffered, the *real* world. Suffered more because in spite of all she'd done, she knew she couldn't protect us from much. I wonder if she'd known: you can't cross the bridge your body built. You must return to that hither shore, while your children have gone on to the farther—the further. Suffering is the bridge and the flood.

My father never seemed to suffer that *real* world. What afflicted him was inside—trying to reconcile being flesh and bone, present or gone. All except his contempt for Republicans and the Yankees, like my mother, he hid his pain from his children. But the pain he suffered seemed to have little to do with being Black. While his manner seemed like a man you'd see drinking brandy and tooting snuff at the Harvard Club in the mid-nineteenth century, he had a Dizzy Gillespie cool. Brighton knucklehead and used car salesmen, but he only dressed the part—mud-toned polyester, short-sleeved button-downs. Not a collage or mosaic, the mix was deeper—something I could never understand by rationalizing the time or place in which he'd been formed.

With my father, I wasn't afraid of other people. He wasn't physically intimidating. I doubt that he could fight, but wherever he was, whether anecdotally or with us, he sat amid or moved through the throng—white, Black, or other—with a jazzy acceptance and defiance of his surroundings. He lived seemingly easily within the "wider society." Boston was his town and with him it was mine. I could get a burger in any part of Dorchester, pizza in the North End, walk the Freedom Trail through Charlestown, or listen to any kind of music in any lounge anywhere.

The white boys I knew only mimicked white players and most Black boys rooted for other teams. My mother was forever loyal to Branch Rickey, but I could pretend to be Boomer and blast a tater off the left center light tower, openly adore Tony C, be Dewy throwing out a runner who was trying to score from second on a single to right, Fisk with his interminable pre-stance ritual, replicate El Tiante's stuttering hand drop, head bob, look away, and twist, Reggie Smith's menacing acute angled bat, Tommy Harper stealing second, Fred Lynn in center making shoestring catches or crashing into the wall; Yaz recalling '67 by turning his bat in a counterclockwise wind.

My father was simple to me at Fenway. He was my father and I was his son. The Sox were our team. I could heckle the other players. He wouldn't, but I could join other fans—all of us with our discrete Boston accents. Calls and responses. I'd yell something at Chambliss or Reggie, and when the crowd echoed me I'd get the double jolt—his and their approval—the thrill of belonging. This was before beach balls and the wave. No prerecorded, piped-in music: my generation's winky celebration of vapid '80s pop. It was before the mass insanity of singing along to "Sweet Caroline."

I know it wasn't a golden age. What people of this "post-racial age" don't realize or understand is that I lived in it. I had to find a way to live with it. While the white fans needed only to find room for me. I couldn't have threatened anyone. I was a boy. Back then it seemed that the white/Black ratio was 500:1. And even in my most private, wounded moments I had yet to say anything about them. What do white people—as a collective—have to do that's so damn difficult? What the fuck do they have to forgive?

But then, it was okay with my dad so it was okay with me. Love determined by demographic isn't love at all. Ours wasn't blind. I knew—even then—that it violated de facto segregation treaty. Isn't that—in part—what love is? I loved my team, every past and present player—no matter their production or what they might have thought of me. They weren't heroes or icons. They were humans. Like my father, they were flawed. I never excused Yawkey's dismissal of Jackie Robinson or that they were the last major-league team to integrate. I knew Yaz loved him for what the old man did for him. I knew that Williams was a garrulous crank, and Bill Lee was a "middling intellectual" who smoked those "funny cigarettes."

It mattered. It didn't matter.

Everything changed when he stopped taking us. Other than when we went with my cousins, it was all wrong: the wrong food or the right food at the wrong time. I hated how those days and nights began. I was usually an afterthought; someone got sick or decided at the last minute they didn't want to go. Worse, though, was when I was invited weeks in advance. I'd say yes and then forget about the date until the morning of. My mother would remind me by openly fretting about how to get me to their house. Of course, if they weren't picking me up they weren't driving into town.

My mother's anxiety would provoke my own and I'd begin to regret my decision. I'd search for an exit: illness, injury, transgression, or I'd be honest. I'd tremble and almost cry, "I can't go." I'd ask her to call them and say anything, tell them I just can't figure it out. It doesn't make sense. It'll hurt too much.

It never worked. If she dropped me off early, I knew we'd be eating dinner before leaving. Of course, I wouldn't have eaten that day; I'd be skittish enough to faint. On the edge of consciousness, I'd play catch with my "friend" and dread dinner.

Sometimes his father would play. I could never perform, although I was a good baseball player, certainly better than them. I couldn't—at first—get it together. I'd boot grounders, misjudge or drop pop flies, and short-arm my throws. The dad would feel sorry for me. Sometimes, he'd try to give me a tip or a quick clinic. My anxiety would heat and become rage. I'd want to tell him he was a fucking idiot and that he and his kid threw like monkeys, but I'd choke it down, use that force to find my missing skills, charge them and spend the rest of the time trying to break his hand with a fastball into the palm of his glove. I'd watch him wince. I still wonder if any of those fathers and sons ever saw me grinning.

If I was lucky, they'd order pizza, sometimes plain or pepperoni, but often with toppings like black olive, onion, mushroom, or some combination. I could understand how adults ate it, but I'd watch my peer suck and chew—braces bared—in horror.

Usually it was a "proper meal" because we were going to eat "a lot of junk" later. Summer, early evening, with an organized white family and their strange food: meats with fungi, fishes with sauce, casseroles bound by pungent cheese, and oniony salads. The car was for driving to the train, where we'd wait with the growing inbound crowd. I'd taste the ghostly cheese or shallot or remember the sight of spinach juice seeping into the once-edible potatoes. I'd feel sick.

We usually had to stand for the ride in. They'd start their familiar jabber. I liked, usually, the boy, but the crush of other people, his father, and the dinner bits in his dental wires would make me hate him. Eventually he and his father would take turns asking irrelevant, obvious questions and take turns answering them wrong. Patrician wink for his son, charitable smile for me: "Do you like baseball, Michael?" I'd scan the car hoping no one was listening—think me ignorant like my hosts. I'd want to scream, "I'm a fan! I'm a fan!" I'd announce facts and stats: the origin of the team, the first field, when Fenway opened, its seating capacity, field dimensions, the Monster's height, and how over the last forty years we'd had only three regular left fielders.

I'd share my projections for what Williams's career stats would've been had he not missed four and a half years of his prime flying missions in WWII and Korea. He finished with 2,292 games, 7,766 at bats, 2,654 hits, 521 HRs, 1839 RBIs, batted .344, and slugged .634. So he averaged 37 home runs, 188 hits: multiply those figures by 4.5—846 more hits, 138 more homers gives him new totals of . . .

I'd go on to Yaz's triple crown year: '67 the year of the Yaz, my birthday, how we were born a day apart: Carl Michael Yastrzemski. In '68, he won the batting title with a .301 average—the lowest figure in the live ball era, which epitomized how the great pitchers dominated the mound in '69, which led to the American League DH—Danny Carter in '72—because casual fans came to watch hitters hit and not pitchers pitch.

All I'd get was a "wow." Maybe a nod. I'd search the car again, this time hoping someone had heard and even silently understood.

With these escorts, the park was oppressive—and dangerous. Everyone was a threat. Sick in the morning. Sick at dinner. Sick on the D Train, on the walk, through the gate and turnstile. Sick being with them but also with the thought of being lost or left behind. Dead-legged to our seats—always good—but on the wrong side of the field.

"Popcorn and peanuts?"

"No, thank you."
"Sure?"
"Yes, thank you."
"Did you get enough dinner? Yeah?"
"Yes, thank you."
"Good seats, huh, boys?"
"Yes, thank you."

No heckling. Empty cheers. Contrived talk. Scheduled observations, mundane ruminations of the casual thinker, feeler, fan.

I'd shrink, be sullen. There was no comfort in the crowd. The colors, the waving flag.

Unbelievers: they'd leave early, before the late-inning rally, no room for me to pray: "Please, give all my power to . . ."

But this was only a couple of years. By the time I was twelve, I didn't need anyone's father. I found new friends and we could go on our own. They were fans that understood the nature of baseball—of being a fan: observance and prayer, memory and extrapolation, hope. Friends who knew how to talk about the game and those who didn't but were willing to watch, listen, and learn.

Back when teams played weekday games, we'd leave immediately after school and head inbound on the D Train. I didn't mind it—liked it in fact. Other than us, it was usually empty. The fare was cheap. If someone—usually me—was short, we'd pool our money: 75 cents for the ride in, and the outbound from Fenway was free; $3.50 for bleacher seats. We'd usually have enough for food but rarely more than three hot dogs for two guys, and a small soda for each.

Sometimes we'd have to reallocate our funds. Train fare was the first line item cut. We'd get on at once, four or five boys, and stuff all of our silver into the meter—too much, too fast for the conductor. I remember some delaying the train and eyeballing us in the rearview. We were barked at a few times, lectured, twice we were told to pay or "get the hell off." Sometimes other passengers would sponsor us. Sometimes we'd hitch on the back of the last car. Once we ran along the tracks halfway to the park the second half we ran the streets. If on the train, we'd argue the merits of Tony's and Giorgio's pizza, the best players position by position, and rank the Yankees, bottom to top, from least to biggest d-bag. If we didn't have enough for tickets at the window, we'd push our bills and coins under the glass and try to guilt the vendor into letting us in for a discounted rate.

If we didn't have enough money to eat, we'd sit, woozy, in the bleachers under the midafternoon sun or the raw early spring drizzle. We'd never smuggle in food: it seemed wrong. But fully fed we'd cheer and stomp for our Sox. This was back when you could move down from the cheap seats and take the better ones in right. You could even stand in the aisles if you didn't do anything stupid: don't throw trash or beach balls; be a fan. Try to talk to Evans while he was warming up between innings. Get a reliever in our bullpen to wave.

Our most important job was heckling the enemies in the visiting bullpen. With extemporaneous chants, limericks, and songs. Sometimes they'd ignore us; sometimes they'd laugh or yap back. Most of it was playful, but we could rankle some guys. We'd remind one guy that he got shelled the last time he faced us, another that he had nothing but junk: "Hey, Rag! Rag arm! Hey, Rag!" Which would morph into "Rag-gah! Rag-gah!" Slow and rhythmic. Heckling back would only make us taunt them louder—we could go on for innings—holding down the languid groove: one of us could solo over.

We had rules: Our players were off-limits. No swearing: "You suck" or "You bite" was the low end of our dictum. Poems and songs the high—maybe a satirical monologue or prayer. No family jokes. I once told the Yankee closer, Rich "Goose" Gossage, that he looked "more like an ugly duck" than anything else and to give up on ever being a swan. He stood on a trash can or ball bucket to see us and identify his assailant. I made sure he knew it was me by quacking "Rag-gah" like Donald Duck. He snapped, "Watch it, punk," and slammed the dugout roof. Gossage was famous for his 100 mph fastball and handlebar mustache. I yelled in my best Bostonese: "Hey Rag, give that poor squirrel his tail back!" My boys howled. We all roared now: "Rag-gah!" He jumped back, got a ball, cocked his arm as though he was going to beam me. I yelled, "Go ahead, Rag! My baby sister throws harder than you!" And the people rejoiced: "Rag-gah!" His pen mates laughed. So did some of the Sox. He pump-faked, pointed at me then all of us. He smiled. Perhaps he respected that we weren't hiding in a crowd or throwing beer or talking about his mother. We were boys who loved our team, the game—all of it—as much as he did.

The ragged '70s ended and the authoritarian '80s began. Suddenly there were rules: No this or that. No cutting through yards or fields. No hanging out in parks. There didn't seem to be interest or need for adolescent Black poet-philosopher-kings. School changed for me. Teachers and administrators seemed impatient. I didn't "forget my homework." I was accused of not doing it. If my math teacher couldn't decipher my numbers—recognize a 2 or an 8—it wasn't sloppy penmanship, the concepts were beyond me.

Most of my life at this time seemed a struggle for me to be understood—at least to have someone admit they didn't understand. The people who controlled my life—and tried to make choices for me—didn't have time or ability or desire to understand. My mother's perpetual question, tacit or explicit—"What's your problem?"—was the only thing she was willing to ask. My only response was "Leave me alone."

My "concerned" teachers noted that I seemed "distant," or "lacked enthusiasm." I seemed "confused by the material," or in a few unofficial conferences I was told that I was lazy.

Where once, academically, my mistakes had been overlooked or dismissed as aberrations, my good works were now considered anomalies. At times they went unnoticed. As I seemed to be underperforming in school, school was definitely failing me. Even in my liberal suburb, education seemed to be nothing more than the celebration of white materialism. Art was now the mundane reportage on the mundane. The poems and poets were reductive and not expansive. The fictional characters were limited, the authors more so. And when I read something engaging the class lectures and discussions were not. Somehow they flattened Beowulf, and made Shakespeare literal and dull. Ironically, the '70s had offered far more diversity. It seemed most English teachers thought Richard Wright was the only Black author in the world. I didn't know which was worse: an idiot lecturing on *Hamlet* or adolescent racists talking about *Native Son*.

Almost every white person I knew—teacher, coach, friend, or parent—no matter how generous or kind they were or wanted to be, seemed impossibly obtuse. They either didn't know I was Black or they thought my goal was to be white. I couldn't explain to them how insane that was—mostly because they couldn't listen. When I tried to write critiques about Wallace Stevens or William Carlos Williams they wouldn't help me with research or how to focus my argument. They'd say, "I don't think you understand their poems."

But it wasn't *white of me* to understand the strategies of a game. I didn't need anyone to slow their speech for me to understand the plot of a movie or story in the news. Unlike for my classmates, everything was a big deal. Most was life and death. They couldn't understand why everything for me was so freighted. It seemed for them that everything vital—beautiful or horrible—was going on over there. You could pay attention if you wanted, but anything that made them really look at themselves and how they—especially their ambivalence—affected others was like a television program one might linger on then click past.

I was about to start tenth grade, which in the Boston suburbs was the first year of high school. It would be my sixth school in five years. I was trying not to drink and struggling with what would much later be diagnosed as clinical depression. Though in the '80's, certainly for poor, Black teens, there was no such thing as that.

The more I tried to explain—anything, really—the more alien I felt. And of course I couldn't explain it: I hadn't yet turned fifteen. I couldn't speak like Dr. King and I couldn't write like him or Toni Morrison. And I damned sure would've tried dismantling the master's house but I was lacking most of his tools. Back then there was, really, not a solitary ass to talk to. I didn't read Ellison out of some racial obligation, and I wasn't going to use him as some polemical hammer or crowbar. How and why the fuck would you do that anyway? I just wanted to talk about *Invisible Man*. No one seemed to understand I was there with over two hundred years of Black American literature

The Broken King

and thought and I hadn't anyone to talk to—except white people, my teachers, my friends' parents. And they believed one could use *The Fire Next Time* to solve the race problem. Even I knew that the people who wanted me dead or in jail weren't going to be told what to do by a book—certainly not a good book. I was hoping to figure out a way to tell my mother exactly what the matter was with me. Because I didn't know. I just wanted to know how they did it—how they lived and wrote so much rage and love and joy and beauty without blowing up or falling apart.

We got older, got jobs, pocket money. We could go to night games. My friends started smuggling booze and smoke into the games: nip bottles and pinch hitters. Baseball didn't matter. The game was something going on over there. And they were white and never realized I was Black. I couldn't get caught with drugs and alcohol. I couldn't use drugs or alcohol. It was the summer of 1982 and I was almost one year sober and that was after "not drinking" for five. I didn't think about it like that then but the two times that I'd drank I'd almost died.

Going to Fenway was becoming dangerous for me. Not in the childish sensorial way but because of the real physical peril. I was open to stares, taunts, and threats. It was bad in the park and worse outside it—walking the perimeter before games but especially after. Everyone seemed white and every man other than the fathers and the very old seemed tanked and—win or loss—belligerent. If I was singled out—called any number of racial epithets—my friends wouldn't help. They never ran; they froze. I understand: unless he's crazy, has a weapon, has little regard for his well-being, is used to violence, or is delusional and lucky, there isn't much worse for a boy than to be challenged by a man who has little regard for "fair fights." You can see it in their eyes. They're both blank and blazing and give the sense that behind it all is a burning nothing.

Sometimes my friends pretended they hadn't heard the word or asserted it hadn't been directed at me. I imagined the men who blocked my path and stared down at me. I was "paranoid," too sensitive, a drag. They refused to believe that Brookline Avenue was perilous, walking past the Cask 'n Flagon stupid, and any plan of stopping in Kenmore Square suicidal. If, later, anyone admitted to the earlier danger, they spoke of the group's not mine or that our individual stakes were equal—I was their "equal."

I went to fewer and fewer games with them. Their parents started giving them money for the grandstand or even box seats. As for night games in the bleachers, I'd be better off spending the same hours in a West Roxbury bar. I turned fifteen in the summer and only went to a few day games—makeups for rainouts—and only with a couple of friends—still white, but working-class, and who weren't scared to fight. They'd get stoned and we'd sit in the sun—more a day at the beach than the ballpark. But I was okay with that. And I would've kept going with them, but they started talking about girls. Or I started listening. They'd probably been talking about them for a while.

I still had four years until puberty. Most girls in our school were relatively wealthy and white. Lynching was real. Sexual trauma and abuse were real. My father and his promiscuity were real. And I was never going to hurt a girl the way he hurt my mother. Her pain was real. But I wasn't. Or I didn't want to be. I think I've gotten it wrong over the years. Girls didn't frighten me, the results of interacting with them did. Even my standing next to a white girl could be seen as a criminal offense. Standing near one of the few Black girls seemed like we were at the altar.

Most of my friends had started to date and if they saw me speak with anyone but my sister they'd ask, "Dude, are you into her?" I hadn't any idea what that meant. I didn't want to. When I thought about a girlfriend, I'd hear Catullus evoking Sappho. I'd see Sappho *"paler than glass."* And I'd feel *"a little short of dying."*

I didn't want to grope someone or gag them with my tongue. I just wanted to talk to someone—about anything. But I knew I couldn't—or shouldn't—talk to anyone about anything so I decided I would listen. I just wanted to *be there* for someone in need.

Someone, though, couldn't be anyone. I was an aesthete with OCD and I had standards.

In late August I decided I could fall in love with Stephanie. She was appropriate. She was a teacher's daughter, liberal parents, athletic, good student, cute—perversely all-American. Everyone thought she was "great," not one of the cross-eyed, gap-toothed beauties I privately favored. She wasn't Angela Davis or Roberta Flack. But she was brown haired, brown eyed, and, in the warmest months, had vaguely Mediterranean skin.

I met her behind the high school. She was walking with two other girls. One I knew from middle school; the other was a stranger. They both, though, to me exuded the sneaky contempt that comes with unearned privilege. I could tell their parents were wealthy. But Stephanie seemed unnaturally interested and kind.

I had just leapt from my father's moving car. We'd been on our way to the Barn, a sporting goods store, to buy some back-to-school sneakers. It sold only the popular brands. And saying its name would make my mother pace. I was long past wearing PRO-Keds and P.F. Flyers. Whenever I tried to buy a new pair with my money, my mother wouldn't allow it. But to be able to afford Nike or Puma, she had to go to Marshall's and put irregulars on layaway.

My father seemed happy to be with me. He'd picked me up on time, asked me if I wanted to grab a pizza. "Yeah, but later," I told him. And he didn't ask, "Don't you mean 'yes'?"

I couldn't remember the last time I'd seen him, and I didn't know why we'd been apart, what the big deal had been. He didn't question why I hadn't played baseball that summer but instead asked me if I was going to run cross-country or play soccer. He couldn't help asking, "Letterman?" I let it go.

He asked me where I saw myself going to college. I categorized my response. When I got to his alma mater, he told me I could do much better than that. When I reminded him that King had gone there, he stuck a cigarette in his mouth and shrugged his shoulders. I knew he was trying to be, in his way, supportive, but I wanted more. I didn't want him to tell me where to go, but rather where I might go and why.

It was the age of Reagan, the beginning of neoconservatism, conformity, materialism, sound bite, pastiche. This post-love, post-funk

America looked nothing like the country I'd been ready to die for. I wasn't going to trudge through the swamps and jungles of the third world to spread or preserve democracy. I'd seen the vets return home from Vietnam. I didn't need to survive live combat in order to become a junkie. And since I'd nothing to die for, I wasn't fit to live.

I wanted to ask my father about being Black or to be near him while I asked out loud. I wanted to ask him about thought and being Black, about sports and being Black, about girls and being Black. I wanted him to confirm that even though it was all rigged, if I were smart enough, good enough, thoughtful and gentle enough, that I would be okay. I wanted him to tell me that while teachers could disregard test scores, coaches could ignore stats, their actions could never define who I was. I wanted a girl to know that no matter what anyone said I would never hurt them and that everything I said and did was a proxy for unconditional love.

I wanted to tell him that I'd been reading Malcolm and listening to Marley. I wanted to tell him about my vision of our country's future and my place in it, that I'd realized all of my thoughts on Black liberation, power, art, and beauty were all in my head, that I'd never spoken them to anyone. I wanted to tell him what it was like to have even a partial understanding—even a juvenile one—about who we are, where we'd been, and where we must go. I wanted him to know what it had been like in all of those white schools among all those white people and all the white cops who'd put their hands on me—who'd terrified and hurt me, who'd threatened to kill me. I wanted him to know what it was like when the suburban, bougie Black parents and children whispered that Thelma's kids weren't really Black. I wanted him to know that I was so at home in my Blackness and part of a long line from Douglass to Davis that I could write a poem like Phillis Wheatley or Amiri Baraka to anyone and for any reason.

But I stammered and could only offer sentence fragments. I got frustrated with myself, then angry, which I'm sure he felt was directed at him, because he tensed and closed. All I could do was whisper, "I'm so angry," and hope that he didn't see a petulant teen but rather a young, gifted, and Black man full of rage and love.

But he was the reason I choked and stammered.

My father wasn't Black—at least not Black like me. I was a light. I was *the* light but not a beacon for him, rather he saw my flaming sword that he couldn't know was my way. It had never gone out. It never would. With it I'd cleave a place in this world or I'd die trying.

I wouldn't be good. I would be better. He had nothing. He stayed still and silent and in that vacuum everything rushed from me to it. And I was locked by my feet to my bedpost and I couldn't run. And it was too quiet in that house to scream and too loud to cry and be heard. And among grieving horns, I heard my mother weep and pray. She thought I was asleep. Something happened in that house. He took something from me and gave me less. I carried it, but I knew it wasn't mine. And it was so apparent to me that my father had no love for me and I was ashamed I ever thought I could for him. Then all I seemed to have inside was rot and fire. I wanted to kill him again and again or kill myself. It was him or me.

I opened the door and jumped. I remember sitting on the curb with my head in my hands. I was concussed, had bruised ribs, three dislocated fingers, and abrasions along my elbows, forearms, and knees. I must have been knocked out by the fall. My body was rigid and felt on fire. I looked up. He was standing a few paces away. He held a cigarette in one hand and a matchbook in the other. He looked terrified.

He sighed as if he were about to say something, perhaps calmly shame me for my behavior. I was, after all, a Black boy on the street of a wealthy white suburb. I'd just publicly lost my mind and was sitting in the gutter while his shitbox car idled nearby.

"What do you need?"

"I need you to go."

"Will you be alright?"

"Does it matter?"

He tried to be cool and light his cigarette but was trembling too much to strike the match. This made me hate him.

I screamed, "Go!"

He looked away from me then waved off a car that had stopped. I stood and gathered myself. He got in his car and left. After that day,

I'd experience a series of firsts: the first night I slept on the streets, the first time in a drunk tank, the first time I had to hide protracted benders, the first time I *knew* I wanted to die.

That would come a little later. First, I saw Stephanie—so open to my projections. She seemed so out of place. When she smiled, I thought, it was because she realized I saw a pain in her that her friends could not and never would. I saw long hours of her telling me the truth. I felt how she would eventually break my heart. And that was a hurt I could hold.

Of course, none of this happened but it bought me a few days.

By spring, I realized I could drink, neglect any schoolwork I didn't want to do, and still get good grades. If that didn't work, there were always makeup exams, rewrites, and extra credit. I could always "participate" in class: close read a paragraph I'd skimmed in the hall, preempt embarrassment by demonstrating how I'd solved for x and y in the polynomial equation—pretend that what I'd hastily scribbled in my notebook was what I'd done the night before. It was better to deal with the momentary pressure of living extemporaneously.

The Sox were awful in '83. Anyway, they didn't feel like my team. I didn't like watching them on TV because of the people in the stands. I hated the way people talked about them—baseball, sports. Most broadcasting was blatantly racist—this was when Blacks weren't considered to be capable of management, playing quarterback—they weren't "intuitive" or athletic. Jimmy the Greek and Al Campanis—their "philosophies," their statements, to me were old—hardly revelatory—but they demonstrated how clueless everyone else was—that they were ignorant of the pervasiveness of their theories in sport. It was as if I were back on the D Train trapped with that boy and his father—except every rider was as ignorant and privileged as they were.

Free agency—along with cost-cutting trades—had and would continue to destabilize the Sox. The players I'd loved—Tiant,

Montgomery—had retired, been traded, or signed elsewhere. I found I was more loyal to the remaining individual players than to the organization. When I read the sports page, I deliberately blurred my eyes so as not to read the op-ed pieces by the *Globe* writers who were—mostly—idiots and went straight to the box scores to see how the sullen Jim Rice did or if Yaz was any closer to his three thousandth hit or four hundredth homer.

In the later summer, I started going again—for Yaz—sometimes with my father. No box seats, lower bleachers. As a boy, I would've hoped to catch that ball but it seemed a bit much to ask him to clear the bullpen at this late in his career.

I could be drunk in the park now—but I wasn't ready to be when he was there. Yaz would fail, and my father would want to drive us home. But I was itchy and wanted to go out and get hammered with my friends.

After Yaz hit his benchmarks, I stopped going. In '84, the Sox were—except for nationally televised games—on cable, which we only intermittently had. I had also found a girl—or she found me. Part of the waiting was over. That spring I tried to impress her and her mom with my achievement. I quit smoking pot and struggled with sobriety. I worked hard in school and tried to become conventional, desirable, responsible. I entered April clearheaded and in love.

She, however, didn't love me or couldn't in the manner I needed, which was absolutely transforming, redemptive. And I couldn't love her in any manageable way. I held her hand a few times, sat leg to leg, but I never tried to do anything else. When I thought I should—in the best of times—my head seemed too large and my arms felt like stumps. When my head and limbs were normal, I felt incurably ugly. Instead of pulling her near, I imagined what she saw—my face looming before my eyes. I started drinking again, but by the time I was confident enough, it was time to go. If I started earlier—after school—I was more interested in beer than her. I was thankful that drunk or sober, like anything else, having a girl was futile. I could be fatalistic, again. One late-May day, I was sore about missing the lunchtime beer run. I was in math and a classmate had offered me a few hits of mescaline. I popped them at my desk and was tripping before the period's end. By July, I'd taken several hits of acid. Things were "right" again. I could pine.

By my senior year Harvard Square was the only safe place to go. Traveling there by day was okay, but at night the metro cops who patrolled the drives would see me and pull us over. Newton had its cops, and parties were full of my antagonists. The girls reminded me that I'd never be a boyfriend and the giant houses underscored that I lived in, albeit suburban, the projects.

I listened to the '86 season on the radio. First in my dorm room at school and then that summer at work or following the Grateful Dead in my friend's van. I took the fall semester off and spent it watching and listening in the Heartland Drug storeroom and the kitchen of a gourmet food store where I'd suffer my friends' and acquaintances' mothers' questions as to what I was doing this fall. From the kitchen of that shop, standing over the sink, I listened to Ned Martin's call of Henderson's homer against the Angels. I'd been trying to get sober again, and I white-knuckled it through the first six games of the World Series until the end of game 6; as the Mets celebrated, my "sober" buddies and I doused our cigars and cracked open beers. We wound up performing improv blues to whomever would listen in the midnight streets of our grieving city. "I'll give you the straight dope, I'll sing you the song of my eternal hope." A blackout, home, bruised and broke, we watched game 7 from the lawn of one of my brother's friends' houses. We'd been too sloppy for his living room. So all we could do was stare at the TV through his front window. Then I went on a three-month bender, most of which I spent missing in Europe.

I returned to the states that Christmas. I should've gone into rehab but I went back to school for the '87 spring semester. The next fall I was asked to leave.

My brother and his friends got tickets to opening day in 1988 and they brought me along. There must have been twelve of us, fantastic seats, about fifteen rows up behind home plate. They were an odd bunch of intellectuals and angry Boston dopes. Whitest Boston Irish, dark

Trinidadian, they were all in their mid- or late twenties and roamed the city as if it were their own. David, as an adult, had always done this, much like our father had, but he didn't do it with our father's élan. It seemed to me more of a challenge to those who wouldn't have him. He was certainly well aware of the dangers Boston presented, had seen enough bar fights, been accused of enough by cops and civilians. And here with his UN baseball group of fans, he certainly wasn't safe. I wasn't safe either. I was four years younger than any of them, underage, and probably the worst drunk of them all. But I was like their mascot and often got caught up in their revelry of "what the fuck?" Some of these guys I'd just met and some I'd known all my life. The ones I'd known forever had been smuggling me into parties and bars since I was a preteen. So there I was under my brother's care, red Mohawk, crucifix earrings, back when it meant something to wear these. Clemens started, pitched well, but of course the Sox blew the game in the end.

The Cask 'n Flagon was a place I always avoided because it was full of angry Boston fuckers. It was dangerous after a win, but after a loss, many patrons were drunk, angry, and violent. Or at least that's the way it seemed to me. Whatever the case, my brother and his friends decided it was a great place to warm up after the game. Off we went, past the bouncer who didn't check for IDs and over to a table at the back. I was cooking in a pizzeria then and I was scheduled for the evening shift. I sat there watching the clock, making up excuses for my tardiness, getting drunker, listening to my brother and his friends cuss and boast. I was wondering if I should call the whole day off when I heard them joking about me, little cat. Somebody nudged me and whispered, "Just go talk to her." I looked up across the bar to see the quintessential Boston bonnie lass, obviously like me too young, in a throng of sisters and friends, who were giggling and poking her and looking my way. They sent shots over. Of course the rest of the bar picked up on our budding romance. There were curses and shouts and the inevitable muttered epithets until I heard "Little cat, you better go." So I got up and ran out east down Commonwealth Avenue to work.

Two years later, I went with Michaele and two friends, sat uneasily in the bleachers, and then it was ten years until I went back to Fenway.

Throughout September I drove up to check in on my father. That my siblings and I couldn't coordinate our father's care was indicative of how each of us saw him. Tracey was living with my family and stayed at home to help there. David was living with him. He'd clear out when he knew I was coming.

But he never wanted me to take him to his appointments. He'd insist that he could get there on his own and that when I was free I should come "just to visit." I would, but we did almost nothing. I'd shop a little and cook meals. But mostly we'd watch TV and not talk. Sometimes I'd say I had to run out. I'd get in the car and drive out far enough from his building so he couldn't see me just waiting in the car but not so far as to use much gas. But also a spot where I was least likely to frighten residents, prompt phone calls to the cops, then be detained and questioned outside of my Volvo for sitting while Black.

When I was in Boston, I felt it was wrong to be away from home. When I was in Brooklyn I felt I should be doing more for my father. So I thought of each location as poles of duty and I would do more work, have more focus at each one. I would drive when the road was empty. In the predawn from my home and midnight from his, I would mark time with liminal dreams of what could have been and what might still be.

My advance from Grove Atlantic had come and gone and I was deep in debt. Still, northbound I pictured finishing our house, buying a new car, and buying a life for us five. Heading north—I'd buy him a small house full of books, records, and audiophile gear. Maybe not as good as mine, but still fine. I'd get him a flat-screen TV that I'd hang from the wall. I'd get him a nurse, a valet, people to muse with and at, tickets to Symphony Hall, reserve a table at the regatta bar, an escort to Wally's, an evening at the Wang, and of course Fenway—box seats—to watch the Sox.

Then I couldn't visit him for two weeks. It was mid-October when I finally did. His living room was relatively neat. There were three oxygen tanks by his chair. He was connected to one. He told me he had lung cancer.

"It's advanced." He wheezed. I could see his shrunken, cluttered lungs. "They're not sure, because of my heart, how to treat it. I'm too weak for chemo and if they operate, they say I might not make it off the table."

I asked him what I could do. "Not much." He just wanted to see me as much as possible, and if possible, to "smoke every once in a while." He gestured at the hidden cigarettes.

"If you got 'em . . ."

He waved at the oxygen tanks. "You don't mind."

I shrugged. "Do us all a favor."

"Oh, Michael, that's quite dark." He paused, had a private thought that made him grin. I picked up the pack. Merit Ultra Lights. I think he saw my disdain. Somewhere inside I felt enraged and vindictive, but that place was so deep it felt far away in space and time. It would've been too great an effort to find it and use them.

I opened the box and extended a smoke. He asked with his eyes if I wanted one, too.

"Nah."

He nodded.

As I was about to light the match he held up his hand.

"With a bang or a whimper?"

I lit him. He tried inhaling, but it was too hard. I took the cigarette from his lips, snapped off the rigid filter, then put it back. He inhaled deeply. Coughed violently.

Calmed, he said, "Thanks. Much better."

We sat. Silent. I told him about my book. He didn't ask why I'd kept that news from him. I wished I'd told him sooner. I wished I'd helped him more—looked harder for him. He'd always been like this: at the mercy of something I couldn't see, and he hadn't the protection of his own rage. He'd been alone at least almost all my life.

But he didn't look alone. He was beaming.

"May I ask who's publishing it?"

"Grove."

I'd never seen him so happy.

"Michael," he crooned, "that's the house of Beckett."

I let him have it. I smiled, too.

"May I read it?"

I lied. "Yes, as soon as I get bound galleys, I'll give one to you."

He closed his eyes and nodded. Between drags and coughing fits, we talked about structure and influences. Each coda he offered a variation of "I'm so happy for you" or "I'm so proud."

After that day I'd drive up whenever I could. Each visit I bought him whatever I could afford—franks and beans, minute steaks, orange juice concentrate, instant coffee, and Reese's. I bought him a case of the champagne of beers and a carton of Lucky Strikes. He'd ask me about the galleys. I'd tell him, "Not yet. Soon." We'd watch afternoon game shows and talk shows. After the evening news, I'd drive back to New York.

I didn't know when and if I'd get galleys or even when my manuscript would be returned. I didn't really know much about the publishing process except it moved slowly. What I did know was I couldn't let him read it.

The only unchanged autobiographical character in *Man Gone Down* is my father. Only a few people knew this. Every other character or event seemed to be chained to the facts of the real world and couldn't have a life in any other. It used to anger me. I thought that the white readers who claimed that what happened to the protagonist had happened to me said so because I was Black, and therefore I didn't have an imagination. If one doesn't have a mind then one cannot have a life of or in it. I believed this until I thought of what my father might say, something like *For many, some things are too false to be fiction and some things are too real to be true.*

So little of that time I watched him dying felt real to me then. I often question it now. I was employed, I was sober. I was a good husband, a present parent, and I owned a home. People were listening to me and they liked what I said. I was caring for my father. I had a book. And given the choice, the one person I wanted to share that with was him. He never sat in on a class or heard me rehearse a lecture. He thought he knew my wife and he'd never seen my home. As for my kids, it seemed to me that to him they were abstractions: only when he spoke of them were they there.

I think he would've loved it. I wrote it for him. I wrote it at him, despite him, and because of him, and to hurt him but I think he would've loved it—all the discursive allusions, unlikely conflations, and bizarre collisions of formal syntax and monosyllabic grunts. He would've loved it. Regardless of what anyone else said he would've thought it a success and I don't think he would've claimed that success as his. It was mine. It would've been empirical proof that I'd done something with my anger and my pain—with his pain too. I'd made a place for me, perhaps for us. He would've known his son could—at times still—be at peace and share that peace with him.

But I did talk with him about it—it and writing. He could listen to me talk all day. I'd brought a French press and a grinder up there by then, and every trip I'd bring fresh beans. Neither of us would make him drink it. He'd sip his instant. Sometimes we'd both grin when he'd light a smoke then quickly glance at the compressed air tanks. Neither one of us seemed tense or uncertain. It was different from being in the jazz clubs back then. He was hearing what I'd learned in that music.

When he'd ask me to recall a passage from my book and I said I couldn't he knew that I was lying but he let it go. Instead, I'd talk about the origins—the history, philosophy, literature, or baseball—I'd drawn from. Whenever I'd err in organizing my influences chronologically, intellectually, or by poetics—he'd patiently wait until I corrected myself. But it wasn't like an oral exam. He wasn't listening to test me for the answer, he listened because he didn't know.

I started to bring our favorite books—things we'd read alone but never talked about together. He'd watch me *not* read. I'd walk the room waxing philosophic, reciting passages and poems while he smoked. We had a ball.

I think it was the Tuesday before Thanksgiving. I'd canceled class so I could take him to his oncologist. He looked, suddenly, deathly sick. I didn't know if something new had happened. It had been sixteen years since his first heart attack, and before that, how many years of homelessness, beer, and weenies fried in butter. And the cigarettes: three packs a day for almost fifty years. How had he made it this long? Perhaps I'd grown accustomed to his constant demise. I wheeled his oxygen tank while he smoked as we walked to the car.

"My doctor, you really wanted to sock him in his mouth?"

We were back in his apartment. I was about to make us both Taster's Choice. I walked from the kitchenette to the living room. He said, "Futility breeds tears and violence." He smiled. "Perhaps both."

"Among other things—a fat lip."

"Yes." He gestured to me to sit down. I did.

"What are your aspirations—politically?"

I didn't pretend that I didn't understand.

He tried to help me. He told me that he knew I wouldn't politicize my work, but that all work is political. A character is politicized because of his own place in time.

He was looking through the television. "Your protagonist is Black?"

"Yes."

"And the story is contemporary. Not modern—contemporary."

"Yes."

"I'd think he'd face many conflicts that you wouldn't have to embellish. Just look." He gestured to me and then brought his fingertips to the area of his heart. "I've been meaning to ask you for a while now." He looked at me. His eyes were wet. "Do you think race has had something to do with my life?" He paused. "Would you mind?"

I handed him a cigarette and lit it. While he smoked and coughed I told him why it had and why it still did. From Jamestown to his oncologist. "It has never stopped." I lectured about his father, unrewarded excellence, the Sisyphean boulder of *opportunity*, wage discrimination, financial stress, hypervigilance, and the constant threat of violence. I told him about labor unions, missing income, and unrealized wealth. I told him about what it was like to face absurdity after absurdity, suffer crime after crime, and still be expected to believe that there's some reason to be good. "*And if* you last long enough you end up right here!"

I realized I was raging. He looked scared—again.

I started again. I told him to picture all the places where he was the only Black man in the room. He closed his eyes. He smoked. He opened them again.

"Do you think my being Black perhaps limited my professional advancement?"

"Perhaps." I was so disappointed. I hope he didn't see it. If he did, he still went on.

"Do you think it affected my relationship with my father?"

Gently, I said, "I do."

"He went back to the South, you know. David was a baby. I think." He stubbed out his butt. "I never saw or spoke to him again."

I wondered if it was true.

"He died in seventy-nine."

I wanted a cigarette. I wanted to quietly smoke and drink away the afternoon with my father.

After a long silence he asked, "Shouldn't you go?"

"If you'd like."

"That's not what I meant." He shook his head. His smile looked sardonic. "I know what you think about therapy, but as you know I've been somewhat depressed."

"And?"

"And my therapist thought it might be a good idea if you came in for a session."

He wanted a cigarette. I pretended not to notice. I glared at something, somewhere. And as my father tried to continue I felt anger and numbness growing together inside. I started to panic, so I began to drift—west on the turnpike and to the Berkshires. No music there this time of year but perhaps up high there might be snow.

He coughed, horribly.

"Perhaps not." He wheezed.

"Perhaps not."

I stood and turned to say goodbye. He was crying. I sat. We both looked to the TV.

He didn't cry at his mother's funeral, nor did he at my wedding. He reacted to the news of the birth of each of his grandchildren as though I'd told him I'd won fifty on a scratch ticket. I remember once when he tried to save my bread from our failing toaster. Often slices would get stuck and, if left too long, combust. My mother believed it was my fault. I'd cut slivers of cold margarine and gently press it into the slice. "What I tell you? Stop doing it like that!" She'd snatch it all and scrape as much as she could of what I'd spread away. Then she'd jam it in the toaster and slam the lever down—once, twice, maybe more till it latched, then mumble while fuming away, "If I ever catch you . . ."

But she wasn't there, my father was. He was soft boiling eggs. The toaster jammed and started to smoke so I pulled the plug from the wall and picked up the knife. I used to slide it in between the slice and the coils then either pry up the bread or spring the latch. He stopped me though and barehanded tried to pinch the bread free. He gasped and stumbled back. He was weeping. His fingertip was on fire. He blew it out. Soon after that he was gone.

"He thought it might help us talk," he said as if there'd been no break. "Maybe I could explain . . ." He waited for me to respond. I didn't. "You're busy." He tried to stand, but couldn't. "I just want to be able to tell you how proud I am of you. And I just want to hear what you'd say back." We turned to each other. "I just don't know if I have the right."

"Why not."

"Because I can't help you." He found the cigarettes on his own. "I couldn't help you."

I wanted to ask him, *"Why not?"* but I just put my head in my hands. If I could've spoken I would've told him how hard it was to read. How I struggled—not with meaning, but with words. It hurt to see the words on the page. Their words hurt. My words hurt. I told him that when I thought about writing I felt my head was always cracking and mending.

I looked up.

"Catharsis." He closed his eyes and defined it. "I guess that's why I always hoped you'd play. To have your audience before you. So you could hear them release that breath." He exhaled. "I always have wanted that for you." He was weeping. "I know." He pointed at his temple. "Sometimes it seems it's all up here." He opened his eyes and looked at me. "You must feel—must have been feeling so—so much pressure."

"No."

He sighed, sadly. I offered him a Lucky. He shook his head. "You're so hard on yourself, Mr. Michael."

I shrugged my shoulders and looked away, but there was nothing in the distance. I wanted to leave but I didn't know how or where. It seemed every space would be closed.

"Michael." He repeated my name until I sat up straight and looked at him.

"I'm sorry," he said. I nodded. He raised a finger. "I'm sorry I couldn't help you. But you were beyond me in every sense of the word."

I can't honestly remember where or when I told my father that I'd been raped. I know it was after I had told Michaele and my siblings. I was twenty-three, some sixteen years after the event. I'd only recently told her, but I'd always suspected, even hoped, that she knew. It'd been four years since we first met, and we'd been together for two of them. Unlike many people I'd met since college, she never thought of me as a lothario but rather seen me as shy, even skittish, and perhaps gleaned that my emotional and physical distance from others was a direct result of some kind of early abuse—that I lived in a perpetual post-trauma, in a constant alarm not triggered but heightened in the proximity of others.

Physical and emotional intimacy, witnessing strangers kiss or whisper across a table, a sex scene in a movie, even a fade to black provoked in me an awful response. Cavalier conversations about casual sex sent me into rages, brooding silences, or waking comas. We were living in the East Village and though it was the beginning of the AIDS epidemic, free love was still the dominant discourse. I worked in the service industry, bussing and bartending. I was still drinking, going to after-hours clubs and parties and watching all kinds of hookups. I'd feel gut punched when I witnessed even the most debauched characters' carnality. Women, men, boys, girls, gay, straight, bi—any union that I knew wouldn't become a lasting one would leave me sick.

Mine wasn't a moral judgment. I'd always denied my carnality and of course had to ignore everyone else's. My freshman year in college I'd lived on a co-ed floor. There was a couple I was fond of. I thought they were talented actors and interesting people. I was at best their acquaintance, but I enjoyed our quick chats in the hallway or stairwell or longer conversations in the dining hall. I didn't know or I pretended not to know what was going on in his dorm room where most nights they stayed. By the end of the year, I'd figured it out but not really. Through that spring, summer, and into the start of what would have been my sophomore year, I maintained my virginity and willful ignorance. My sister was a junior at the same school. She was told fictions by upper-class folk about my sexual exploits. She of course knew her younger brother well and knew I was in no danger of getting anyone pregnant or acquiring an STD. She was frightened of me crashing a borrowed car, falling off a roof, drowning in the arboretum pond, being bludgeoned to death by the New London police, or, like some hapless artist, dying in my vomit.

She'd seen me at parties avoiding women. Sometimes, when I was too drunk, I'd get cornered and have to resort to drastic measures— verbally abuse my admirer or just talk her into a stupor. My male friends thought I was insane, gay, or both or hoped for all our sakes that I had a long-distance girlfriend somewhere.

One time, I pretended my sister, who I look exactly like, was my girlfriend by hovering close to her—ludicrous on a campus of sixteen hundred, which at the time was 1 percent Black. After these parties, I would often go to her room and sit at her desk in near tears murmuring things like *I hate this* or *I can't do this*. By day, I'd see people making their walks of shame, listen to my buddies brag about who they were boning, boned, would bone, who were tramps, who was frigid, who required beer goggles to bone. Women would say things like "fooled around," "went with," the more brazen using words like "hooked up." All of this made me grotesquely blue. The euphemisms and clichés to describe adult longing, action, and consequence sounded like child's talk; again, I don't think it was wrong in any moral sense but rather misguided. Sex seemed less an act of independence than conformity, and the only way to cope with one's inevitable and ensuing loneliness was to use sloppier language, promote dimmer theories as to why.

None of it seemed to deal with the repercussions—the life after the small death. All they could do was dull themselves, convince themselves that what seemed to me to be the most profound act two people could engage in was no big deal. Of course, I had doubts about my theories. There's a chance that I was a pseudo empath, a bogus martyr or monk. I was chicken, weird. There was also race and class. White girls were folly. It was futile to be with one. It wouldn't end well. And if I objectified white women and thought their maidenhood should remain unblemished, then every Black woman was a queen of heaven.

One day in the fall, I decided I had to get it over with. I'd taken the semester off and, while preparing for a trip to Europe, visited campus in search of romance. I'd alerted some friends. They were thrilled and organized an impromptu get-Mike-laid keg party. It was a beautiful September afternoon, and they'd scheduled the event for seven. But I arrived just after lunch, started in on the hard liquor, and was on the edge of a brownout by dusk. By midnight, I was in some senior's room and got it over with. She left early the next morning for class, I wrote a boozy, guilt-sick note about a lovely evening and that perhaps we should meet later. I ran into her that afternoon and she told me I was sweet. The "sweetest, prettiest boy I'd ever slept with." She laughed scornfully and said goodbye.

I left for Europe soon after. I made it from London to Crete without a peck on the cheek and returned to school for the spring semester. I met my first girlfriend. We played apartment in her dorm room. I rarely drank or did any drugs. I tried my best to be a moderate, responsible young adult. I thought I was in love, but I think now I was only thankful that I could—with what I thought was little damage—be sexually active.

It didn't work out. Coupled with regular physical and emotional intimacy, my lack of self-medication left me vulnerable. I felt things I never had—those "inveterate scars." Those that weren't only the initial insults but also the following environments, experiences, and behaviors. I became erratic, and she began to confide in mutual friends that I was crazy, delusional, or at best a pathological liar. I was crazy. I simply couldn't handle wanting to be close to someone and loathing it at the same time. I learned later that mine was typical behavior for a survivor of sexual abuse, especially one who doesn't perpetuate the crime against others.

Back then, I thought my greatest—perhaps only—qualities were dissociation and mimicry. Growing up in an unstable, dangerous environment I learned how to read people. So, in our throes, most of me wasn't there. Part of me was partially there. I could watch and respond to her needs without really getting entangled in the mess. I learned to delay then fake orgasm. I eventually even learned how to take pleasure in not having one by giving one. That's what I convinced myself was love.

This, of course, was doomed. I was good in bed but terrible at everything else. When we were having sex, the world was chaos. She found it charming, romantic, then sad, frightening, vexing, and finally hopeless that someone with my supposed gifts was incapable of doing anything—class, administrative work, getting to the dining hall on time. I couldn't get it together, so I was always foggy, twitchy, lethargic, paranoid—and now defenseless.

I wanted to tell her. I doubt now that I would have made any sense. I suspect that even my most lucid account wouldn't make up for experiential gaps. For me, physical intimacy was violation. Not only for me but for her, too. It all seemed a violent crime. Emotional intimacy, after a point, exacerbated the fact that though I desired to be close, physical contact was brutal. What I really needed was gentle verbal and physical affection, something I'd never felt. My most intimate experience was rape. I wanted to tell her, but I also knew it wouldn't explain anything. And I knew it would drive her away. I also didn't want to be weak. Speaking would be a confirmation that I was. And she couldn't help me. I also knew that I couldn't keep up with the sexual relationship because I began to need. Still, I would almost say something, but every time I began I'd question myself. I'd wonder if I'd made it up. Sometimes I felt it had just been a dream. What I did know, real or not, the moment I spoke of it, my life would no longer be the same.

Four years later, Michaele and I were at a dinner party suffering the usual topics: sex and art. No one knew what they were talking about. I sounded like some midcentury relic. My last contribution was "Just because you want to be an artist doesn't mean you are one." Which turned out to be inflammatory and prompted howling, gnashing, and outrage. I was asked if I thought I was the only artist there, to which I replied I was a line cook with perhaps an artistic temperament. I was told I was elitist and evasive. I said I didn't know about that, but what I did know was that I was the only one here who didn't believe he had the right to be an artist. More howling and outrage. But I was unreachable. I felt something turn off inside me. I could scarcely see or hear them. All I could make out was Michaele watching me with great worry.

The conversation moved to the cinema and sexy films. I had a dual experience of feeling nothing and wanting to vomit. At evening's end, I couldn't speak to say goodbye. Halfway down Second Avenue, when I could speak again, I reassured Michaele I was okay. I mocked some of the other guests to prove it. We walked up the six flights to our rattrap and closely fell asleep.

The next few weeks I was lively. I was cast as a boxer in an off-off-Broadway play. I landed a new job at a caterer's. I spent most of my off time training, as I was to appear shirtless on the stage and wanted to flaunt a vascular eight-pack.

Michaele went on a family vacation for Christmas. The day she left, I felt myself coming down with something. I didn't exercise, called in sick for work and rehearsal, got in bed, and began reading Baldwin's *Just Above My Head.* My mother had owned the hardcover and in middle school I tried to read it, but it had been above my head, so I'd quit. The week before, I'd picked up the paperback, and there I was plowing through it. People believe that they experience certain events, view art, meet someone at the right or wrong time. They were or were not ready for it or them. I'm still not sure how I'll qualify those hours in the winter. I remember feeling heightening tension and that something terrible was going to happen, but I kept reading to the end of Book II.

> She made one last effort to rise but he slapped her back. She heard the heavy belt fall to the floor. She knew one thing clearly. She had never wanted this. This rage and hatred. She had always wanted his love . . . Every thrust of her father's penis seemed to take away the life that it had given thrust deeper anguish into her into a place too deep for the sex of any man to reach into a place it would take her many years to find a place deeper than the miracle of the womb deeper almost than the love which is salvation.

I put the book down, went to the kitchen to get a drink of water, took a sip, swallowed something hard, saw that the glass was chipped, and spiked a fever. I was trapped in our apartment for days hallucinating. I couldn't answer the phone. I couldn't get outside. A friend of mine finally checked in and rescued me. She was returning home for the holidays to Boston and took me with her. I had to live on my mother's couch for a week. Then I finally went to the ER, where I was diagnosed with double pneumonia.

I lost thirty pounds. I convalesced in Boston, made it back to New York. On our first night out, it was another dinner party with sex talk.

This time I didn't say a thing and walking back I couldn't speak at all. I didn't talk for three days after, then I finally told her simply, "I was raped when I was seven."

I remember almost nothing about the time around telling my father. The event exists either out of time or so deep within it that it defies my attempt to place it into any manageable chronology. I know the sequence of the hour, but not the day in which the hour belongs. And the place—the larger is vague but the setting in which it occurred is clear. A portion of the room is all I know. These uncertainties give me pause, make me wonder if it ever happened. I remember it being Manhattan, but I can't recall my father ever visiting me there. I do however remember being with him in Midtown and his telling me of his travels to the city—the supper clubs and music halls and how vibrant the streets were.

I know I'd been to the Robert Miller Gallery and walked west on Fifty-Seventh toward Sixth thinking about those bright white, thickly lacquered plank floors, wanting them in the home I dreamed of buying, and what kinds of paints and sealants to use. I know it was spring, I was in class at Hunter, off Prozac, and it was one of the first balmy days when you're reminded of what it's like to feel moisture in the air. I don't see him walking with me, but if my story's true, he must have been. It was 1991. Neither of us had cell phones, but there we were in one of those Midtown coffee shops. Again, really, it could have been anywhere, probably suburban Boston. I don't know. What I do know is that along with his ubiquitous brown suit, instead of the usual cream shirt, he wore a paisley-patterned button-down that looked like a pajama top from the bottom of a Goodwill bin. I wasn't ready for it. It made me furious. We sat at the counter. He ordered a burger, no fries but instead the daily vegetable medley, which enraged me more. He cut his meal into small pieces, chewed slowly, carefully as though all his mouth was a sore.

I don't know what I said or how I said it, but I know my intent was to hurt him. He placed his fork and knife on his plate and looked past me. He held his hands above the counter and slowly turned his wrists in opposite directions as if with his left hand he was trying to turn time forward and with his right hand wind it back.

The last day I saw my father before he died, we didn't speak much. It was December 8th. I neatened the space, heated up a Swanson Salisbury Steak, and poured him a glass of beer. He seemed as repulsed by the TV dinner as I was, so I opened a fresh sleeve of peanut butter cups, pulled up a chair beside him, sat on the arm, and fed him candy as he needed.

I wanted to recite "Little Gidding" from memory—not for anyone else, only him. But that seemed distant, so I thought I'd quote a short passage as a way of talking to him about how we were about to pass through the "unknown, remembered gate," how we were both "children in the apple tree," but that, too, seemed wrong. It wouldn't have been about *us*. We'd left so much of us unspoken—used so many proxies for where we'd been, what we'd seen and felt—that if we'd ever, really, been trying to speak with one another, we'd never said or heard anything that directly had to do with us.

I remember Christmas Eve of 1978. It was our first since we'd moved. He had nothing to give us but he still came. We lived on the second floor. He waited downstairs on the porch. We went down to see him one at a time. He asked me how I was doing. Said "Merry Christmas." And "I love you."

That night, I knew I'd never see him alive again, but he wasn't dead—not yet. He wasn't a memory. He was still my father. I had one more chance to try. So I stroked his cheek with the back of my hand a few times then laid it on his shoulder. He settled, exhausted, but finally at rest. He'd been waiting all the years between this one touch and the last. We waited, alone and together, for the night.

But it was a moment. I took back my hand, left his apartment, and drove back to Brooklyn where there was the semester, the bills, and no room or time for feeling anything. David called on the ninth. Our father was dead. He'd woken in the night, blind and afraid, called out twice for my brother, then passed on.

Sometime after my brother and I had spoken, I stood up and paced the house. I wished I'd told my father, "I forgive you." I wished I'd told him how much I loved him, how all my life I'd missed him. I wished I'd told him how much I'd needed him but didn't want to hurt him. Even if they were lies. I didn't want to punish him for what he had and hadn't done—because that *is* the judgment and the sentence: I neither need nor want you.

We were more than what we'd done to each other. We were better than that. That I could recall him, us, with any affection, be grateful for whatever he tried to give me and have compassion for his struggle—no one took care of him either—lent both of us peace. I knew I was still a ways away from owning it, and I didn't know if I ever would. But I do remember: once I did forgive him. Though I didn't know what for.

I saw an impressionistic arc of his life. It ended with his face, which was horribly contorted in anguish and grief. I felt that pain. I felt mine: sitting on his lap, not daring to move, held fast by the Miller High Life in his breath, the stray cigarette embers that found my bare arms, and under me his reluctant desire. I stayed on his lap because I wanted him to love me—more than anything in this world. I wanted it so badly that he *did* love me more than anything in this world. I stayed because I knew he needed me more than anything in this world.

What a thing—that you can't wind back time and undo hurt, or forward and be past it, or make the wheel stop for a moment to think, or feel, without the pressure of time. I wanted "You are my light" to be the first thing I remember him telling me. And "You've been my light. I love you, Michael" to have been the last.

I received my edited manuscript that day. I read the letter. My editor Elisabeth wrote that there was little to do—it was very clean and needed minimal edits. Along with her notes were instructions from the production manager. I had two weeks to return the corrected work. I don't remember the rest, but I assumed there was an "or else" attached.

I called her. I told her that I didn't understand the deadline. She said it was a guideline and not to worry. I told her my father had died and that I might need a little more than the allotted time. She told me, "Of course." I should take whatever time I needed to grieve. She seemed sincere, so I trusted her—not that I should be affected by his death but that she wouldn't cancel my contract.

We had the service three weeks later on my father's seventy-third birthday. Tracey and I had spent what we had cremating him, so we had the service outside on the bank of the Charles, not far from our childhood home. It was a bitter, gray day. We hadn't a program. All the attendants stood and watched as we released his ashes into the water. I spoke to the river and whoever was listening: "What we call the beginning is often the end."

We had pizza at my aunt's. I did my best to keep the kids free from all my—not feeling.

It was late when Michaele, the kids, and I started home. Nearing Connecticut I realized I hadn't said anything about my father to anyone—about his dying or his death. Years later, a friend would tell me of the difference between grief and mourning. Had that same person been with me then, I would've agreed but also told them, *Later. Later. There might be time.*

When everyone had fallen asleep, I put on Coltrane and Hartman's duet album. I thought it might help me feel close to my father, but it didn't take, and I wondered if I'd ever be moved by it again. Still, I didn't turn it off.

"Lush Life" came on. I tried to make myself listen. I wanted to open the passage between this world and that and enter, even if I had to force my way into the song, into the lounge as a part of the band, a patron, or the bartender. But nothing opened, and I obliquely understood that such places would now be closed. Perhaps after grieving and mourning, I'd find somewhere else for us to be, either before the first hurt or beyond the last, but that place wasn't near. It was *down the road a piece*. I felt I should be northbound, but that night on the highway we were headed home. My family was sleeping undisturbed by Hartman's crooning. And though I still tried to listen, deeply, I sang another song: down the road, down the road; a peace, a peace, a peace.

Mercy

*Keep me as the apple of your eye;
hide me in the shadow of your wings*

—Psalms 17:8

1

My plane landed in Kansas City, and I was confused. I heard what the captain said, but I understood very little of it. While trying to grasp one announcement, I'd miss the next. He welcomed us, but to what city I didn't trust I knew. I worried I'd boarded the wrong flight and was in Cincinnati, Indianapolis, or Dallas. I wanted to ask someone, but I couldn't shape the question. No matter the phrasing, it would've sounded ridiculous.

We stopped, the tones chimed, and all the other passengers began moving. I sat still. I didn't know if I should unbuckle my seat belt or keep it fastened, if I should remain seated or stand. I was sure, though, the crew would reprimand me for anything I did.

The night before I left New York, I'd admitted to my wife that I was scared to fly. I usually hid my fright by being sullen and grunting something like *I hate flying*, but I wanted to be honest. I'd hoped she'd laugh at me or at least commiserate about airline incompetence, but instead she replied, "I know. It is scary. It sucks." This allowed me to indulge my fears: midair malfunctions or explosions or nihilistic pilots. And though it was mid-November, I couldn't discount the late migration of a flock of high-altitude geese and death by stratospheric waterfowl.

While saying goodbye to everyone I told myself, *Calm down. It's simple. It's a business trip. People do it all the time.* The car honked. I strode down the stairs. The driver took my bag. Michaele watched from the stoop. I waved and got into the black Lincoln.

During the ride, I kept checking my watch, phone, and itinerary. I answered the driver's questions about where I was going and what

I did. I usually thought career talk sounded self-important, but not saying anything was rude. When I replied, "I'm a writer and a professor," he asked the genre and subject. "Fiction. English literature and creative writing." It didn't sound arrogant. He didn't seem to think so either. He told me what I did was "important" and "good."

I was fine through security. I bought gum and muscle, golf, and two car magazines. I found my gate, sat, and resumed checking things. Whenever I started to feel anxious I thought, *Move your ass and the rest will follow*, which worked through the wait, the boarding line, the breezeway, and down the aisle to my row just before the wing. I stowed my bag and sat.

The plane was half empty. No one else was boarding, so it seemed I'd be sitting alone. While the other passengers settled and the attendants prepped, I flipped through my magazines. I couldn't concentrate. I put them away. I slid across to the window and watched the luggage train drivers and loaders. I wondered what it was like to wear earmuffs and reflective vests all day. I remembered how as a boy baseball and football helmets and cheap uniforms could sometimes induce a claustrophobic panic that rendered me senseless. I could feel the tarmac rumble. I could taste the diesel fuel. I wondered how many workers were run over by planes each year and if the woman with the glow sticks at her sides was in danger of being sucked into the engines. She walked to the nose and disappeared, but I could see her hanging on to the baggage cart, her body parallel to the ground, unnoticed by her coworkers.

I got out my muscle mag, looked at the cover, and immediately felt ashamed. I told myself to nut up and searched for the exercises that promised to blow up my biceps. While the crew locked the cabin, taxied us to the runway, and demonstrated how to stay alive in the air and water, I devised ways to add an inch to my arms and significantly increase my squat and bench press max but still retain enough flexibility for an elegant gait and a full, fluid golf swing. As soon as I got to my hotel, I'd alternate between push-ups, ab work, stretching, and unpacking.

The turbines whined. The captain mumbled. We sped down the runway. I closed the mag. I twiddled my fingers and scratched my arms. I bounced and jiggled my legs as though I were going to piss myself. I looked across the aisle, past the suited man and out the window. He, of course, pulled down the shade. I wanted to stand and pace. I wanted out. I knew if I didn't get help I would suffocate, but I wasn't able to tell anyone I couldn't breathe. If I screamed, the crew would have to do something. I wondered if there were sky marshals aboard and if they had tasers as well as guns so they could shock instead of shoot me. They'd drag me off the plane and hold me in custody in the terminal. Federal lockdown was better than aerial death. I'd deny having had a breakdown: *It was a misunderstanding*, and I'd have a legitimate reason for canceling the trip.

We were suddenly airborne and ascended and banked at what I knew to be an impossible pitch and yaw. Just before our nose broke the clouds, we seemed to lose our thrust and lolled above Queens like a fat, lazy bird. Before what I knew to be our fall, I whispered, "Pray for us sinners now and at the hour of our death," felt at peace, and welcomed the idea of the plane dropping earthward, tailfirst, into a backward three-quarter flip, then flat bellying and, just before impact, rolling over to the crown. But then we were enveloped by white and were soon above the cloud cover and in the sun.

It's the flying, I told myself. I tried reading a car review but couldn't concentrate on it, so I got out my notebook and wrote:

On Flying, or, How we use our common neuroses so that
we may believe we are unique.

I couldn't think of an opening. I closed my eyes and saw Montaigne, nose up, rubbing his beard, strolling through his estate gardens, musing about smells, anger, and duplicity. I tried to recall favorite quotes for the epigraph and body. Nothing came, but I was sure I'd be able to knock out a partial draft before I returned home.

My first flight had been during the summer between my junior and senior years of high school for some youth enrichment program. I traveled from Boston to DC with a classmate who'd already crossed the Atlantic several times. He was a tough, brash loudmouth, but I liked him and I didn't want him to think me a coward and fool. I couldn't speak, but I covered well by coolly snorting at his jokes about the flight attendants and nodding while half listening to his anecdotes about hot girls and pinhead boys in our class.

A year later, I traveled from Boston to Northern Ireland. Logan to Heathrow, then Heathrow to Belfast: those seven hours aloft scared me more than walking past the gauntlets of heavily armed British soldiers in the airports and on the city streets.

After a week's stay, I left Belfast for Glasgow by ferry and made London by train. There, I spent several days on long runs, visiting museums and galleries, writing in parks, cafés, and bars, and getting drunk. The last day, I ran for an hour, had two plates of sole, potatoes, and summer peas, and got shitty. I was messy on the tube, sloppy for check-in. And I spent most of the flight in a brownout.

Eventually, I theorized that there was a direct correlation between diet, sleep, booze, and time in the air. I had to refine it, because there was always some variable I couldn't account for: afternoon, evening, and red-eye flights; California flights; insomnia; an eating disorder, overexercising; caffeine addiction; alcoholism and my diminishing ability to process drink.

What I wound up with were some basic rules:

1. Never board a plane drunk.
2. Eat enough to keep the bile down.
3. It's better to be undercaffeinated than over. Be sluggish, but not pained.
4. Don't smell. (Sweat or booze.)
5. Don't puke—before, during, or after.
6. Don't be hungover—before, during, or after.
7. Violate any or all rules if needed, as it is better to be sick and/or embarrassed than know you're going to die.

I had to change when I got sober. I never got the sleep, food, or coffee right, I rushed around trying to find something edible and anything other than scalding dishwater to drink. I'd find brief comfort assisting people who were struggling with their bags, but once seated I'd behave like a listless child. When with Michaele, during takeoff I'd strangle her wrist until her fingers were bloodless. Over land, I'd mutter about how we should've driven. Over water, I'd say that I'd rather be tethered to the plane by a seven-mile line and dragged across the ocean. Drowning or being shark bait was better than this.

Later, when I traveled with my children, I had to seem patrician. Still, I searched for outs—feigning a sudden illness or smashing the window and squeezing my way through. I secretly filled takeoff, landing, and the dread time between mumbling Hail Marys and fragments of the Lord's Prayer. After 9/11, I didn't fly for six years.

By my late thirties, any form of public transportation unnerved me: I couldn't ride Amtrak without thinking about the Christmas massacre; the bombing of the Rapido 904 in the tunnel between Naples and Milan; buses, well, were buses. I avoided the subway whenever possible and when I had to take it, I stayed on for as few stops as I needed. My inbound commute to Hunter College was a straight line on the IRT from Borough Hall in Brooklyn to Sixty-Eighth and Lexington in Manhattan, but I'd disembark at Union Square—fifty-two blocks or two and a half miles south of campus—and walk the rest of the way.

When I took the subway, I'd take the F or the Q, which—because of their routes and riders—were less likely to be attacked. Though they were the more likely to fail, and their tunnels more susceptible to collapse, I thought I'd have a better chance surviving a cave-in than nerve gas or Uzi fire.

I traveled with a survival kit. While my two clasp knives would've been pointless against airborne toxins or gunmen, I could wield them against lightly armed or empty-handed foes. And they were useful in many other situations. I kept two in my bag, along with two Maglites (large and small), water, Clif or Power Bars, peanuts, a small first aid kit, bandannas (to tie off lacerations too large for bandages), paint-grade dust masks, safety glasses, work gloves, a utility knife, folding sets of metric and standard Allen and hex head wrenches, a no. 3, 2, and 1 Phillips screwdriver, large and small flathead vise grips, large and small needle-nose pliers, a small hammer, a lighter, Ohio blue-tip matches, an eight-ounce can of WD-40, duct and electrical tape, and a wind of light-gauge, sheathed copper wire.

One way to stay calm was imagining leading the other passengers through the rats, rubble, and darkness to safety, then disappearing before anyone could thank me. Daydreaming helped prevent mild anxiety, but beyond that, I needed something more. Intermediate bouts necessitated reading: usually some of Baldwin's work or a small section of "The Bear." Or I'd sing to myself: what I'd most recently listened to or wanted to hear. However, when there was police activity in the next station or a breakdown in the car or on the line I'd turn to Eliot.

First, there was Prufrock, after that, "The Hollow Men," and the last of the trio was "Ash Wednesday." Sometimes the poems ended my panic; other times they slowed it. At least they distracted me until the ride was over: then off, up to the street, space, and air.

Those poems, too, had their limits. They were useful when my anxiety made sense, but there were other conditions when, even though the conductor told us that we were being delayed by an errant signal, faulty fuse, or divorced connection, I suspected the wait wasn't caused by the malfunctions of machines or triggered by the violence or failings of men, I needed the *Four Quartets*.

I was twelve when I started reading my father's abandoned copy. It was just before Thanksgiving break, and I'd recently suffered some kind of adolescent humiliation. I'd walked from school through a cold rain to an empty house. I was going to shower, change, hide in the bathroom, and read a comic book anthology, but I couldn't find it. I found them—or they found me—and brought them in with me.

I didn't shower or change. I turned on the electric heater—temperature and blower on high—sat next to it, and read. "Burnt Norton" was beyond me. Though I hadn't intellect for his thoughts, I had feeling for his senses. And so "thought and sense," I knew were one.

I felt the dry pools, heard the talking birds, and saw "Garlic and sapphire in the mud." I knew the spinning wheels of "this twittering world."

His voice "echoed in my mind." He was showing me how to incant: "The light is still at the still point of the turning world." His circles and cycles were akin to my need to return and return, again and again, to the start of the movement, stanza, or line; repeat, even The Word, which would not stay in place. The poem—directly and obliquely—calmed, reassured, and empowered me. It explained, countered, or even incorporated what would later be diagnosed as dyslexia: the word that moves. OCD: the search for the one that is perfectly still; synesthesia: the scent word that makes sight, the sight word that makes sound, the sound word on the lips and fingertips, the touch word that makes sight again, and the storm of senses, which at its eye is the still word.

I never wanted to put the book down or leave the bathroom again, but I knew I'd have to. Soon my mother would unlock the dark house, turn on the first light, and curse my swampy footprints down the hall, my unseen breakfast dishes in the sink, my unknown homework not begun. She'd hear the fan, growl, then bang on the door to hammer me out. And when I opened the door, she'd howl about the cost of electricity and how only idiots stayed in sopping clothes.

But I was not ashamed. I was not afraid. I turned off the heat, stood, unlocked and opened the door. She tried to yell but I spoke first: "'The loud lament of the disconsolate chimera.'"

"What?"

"'The loud lament of the disconsolate chimera.'"

She said nothing and went away.

I quickly memorized all four and spent the next few years committing them to my bones. They rescued me—at least in part—from previous conditions and deflected the impact of immediate traumas. Those poems were with me "through the dark cold and the empty desolation," when it seemed no one and nothing else was.

I tried not to abuse them. I didn't want the book to be a bottle of booze. I'd quote them to illustrate a point, but I had to be in danger or despairing to allow myself to invoke their power. When I did, I'd feel myself—mind and body—transform, become what I needed to be. That transformation was painful and frightening, as though the time it should've taken to undergo real physiological and psychological change—losing weight or psychotherapy or sobriety—was compressed into one moment and coupled with the fear that perhaps many of us have: whatever we become, wherever we go might be worse than what and where we are.

So here I was, nearing forty, with my giant orange bag of tricks and books of poems on the subway—using them all the time. I could still recite them from memory, but I preferred to hold the rolled, ragged paperback[1] and read from the text—over and over. I'm still not sure what was the cause and what was the effect—but sitting or standing I'd imperceptibly (hopefully) rock and recite.

Sometimes it was enough to read long passages that were directly related to the moment. More extreme flare-ups required theme-relative directives. Most effective were metric and sonically appropriate lines, like "it tosses up our losses" or "the distant rote in the granite teeth." I said these—wordlessly—while exhaling. Hands always moving—sliding my thumbs across my fingertips or using one hand to caress the other's knuckles.

Another defense was to reread the passages just before the end of a quartet. I'd do this until I forgot what was coming. "The wave cry the wind cry The wave cry the wind cry." I'd usually have to weep and have to cover my eyes, rub them and pretend there was something in them, but I wouldn't stop rocking and repeating: *The wave The wave The wave The wave*, then whisper, because I had to hear:

> *We must be still and still moving*
> *Into another intensity*
> *For a further union, a deeper communion*
> *Through the dark cold and empty desolation*
> *{The wave cry the wind cry The wave cry the wind cry}*
> *the vast waters of the petrel and the porpoise*
> *In my end is my beginning.*

---

[1] My bag copy. I had one for my car, office, bedroom, den, parlor, and kitchen. To replace lost or retired books, I kept three or four on reserve. (I left one in a rental. When I called to inquire, I was told by an unsympathetic customer service agent that no one had seen it: I'll never patronize that company again.) Anthologies not included.

I became so accustomed to the practice that I scarcely noticed I was doing it. I'd wake to find that I was rocking and mumbling. I no longer cared. My coping to me seemed less invasive than all the overtaxed headphones, clicking and beeping handheld devices, sloppy bacon and egg sandwiches, mundane conversations, and disturbing monologues of my fellow passengers.

So I'd rock, incant, and weep. And I'd collect myself while climbing the station stairs, then into school and up the building stairs. By the time I reached the twelfth floor, I could exchange pleasantries with colleagues. If a friend, after scrutinizing my face, asked if I was okay, I'd tell them I hated the subway.

One morning, they weren't enough. I purposely miscalculated my door-to-door time and stayed in bed as long as I could. When I finally got up, I tried to convince myself that I had a migraine or the flu. By the time I hit the sidewalk, I had fifteen minutes to get uptown. I had to take the IRT. I jogged to the station, skipped most of the stairs, passed through my terminal, made it to the rear of the far end of the platform, and pressed against the wall. I wasn't anxious. I wasn't panicked. I was spooked—suddenly—not by anything I'd seen or heard. There was something awful in the station. Something no one else could apprehend. I looked down at the tracks. A few rats scurried across them and disappeared under my platform. I looked back to where they'd come from. There was a filthy yellow mitten pressed against the rail. I left the station, called the English Department office, canceled my classes, and went home.

Over the next few weeks, I avoided the subway. I walked, took secret taxis, or parked in garages when I had the money. But I felt pulled to the underground. I had to know what that feeling had been— why I'd felt it. Not only that, but I'd been embarrassed—humiliated— by a feeling and a mitten. I had to redeem myself. I went back down. I tried to prepare for what might happen. I'd sit or stand with the Quartets and wait until I felt scared enough to open it. While turning to what I thought to be the appropriate words, I'd come across a passage I couldn't resist stopping for. I'd get caught up in debates about what to read and how to read it or if I should read it at all. Then I'd be confused and feel ashamed. I'd look up to see someone tonguing their dentures or I'd look down at a stain on the floor and feel as though I were being dragged behind the clattering train.

Still, I rode—now motionless and with nothing to say. I watched, listened, waited. There was something out there—just before or beyond coherence. Every train ride, it got closer—almost tangible. I whispered, "This is bad" or "Terrible." Some days I cringed; others I was angry and defiant. Some rare days, though, I felt serene. I didn't have to mutter incantations. I was, simply, well. I traveled like this for months. The presence became mundane.

One day there were presences everywhere: They lurked in the vents above the platforms. They moaned from the brimstone tunnels. Their gnash was the clatter of the wheel and the track. They stared at me from the passing trains. They balanced between the cars. They clutched the poles and suddenly rolled their eyes to me. Or they sat and stared at nothing.

Hand tools wouldn't work against whatever was out there. Neither would stories or melodic lines. No poetry. No prayer. No magic. First I stopped packing survival gear, then familiar books. I refused to sing or even think about songs. I left the Quartets at home. I went under unprepared—unarmed. I kept riding, any line, wherever I needed to go. I couldn't stop. They called me to the station and challenged me to enter, coaxed me to the edge of the platform—to look down, to imagine my lips on the third rail. In the train, they snaked their hands down my shirt or raked their nails across my nape. They were ragged forms in the periphery that rasped strange tongues in my ear. But I kept riding—no early exits—all the way to my stop. And as I emerged they made me forget—*we are not real*—so all those rides seemed like one. I kept going down.

It's the flying. My feet and legs were numb, and I had only a vague sense of my torso. When I finally reached for my bag, I found I'd become part squid. I fumbled out of the plane. Halfway to the gate, a loose wind began gusting inside my skull. It blew from back to front then began to twist, gathering speed as it did. I stopped and stepped to the side. I told myself that I was in the right city, and my fear was really an indulged, mild anxiety. Most important: the reason I was in Kansas City was a good one. I'd been invited to read and speak at an important institution. My literary and academic career had begun. People admired and respected my work. They wanted to hear what I was thinking. They paid me to hear what I had to say. It was all good. I should be proud. The squall in my head eased, and I continued down the jetway.

My host met me at the gate. He seemed happy that I'd arrived. We walked to the garage exchanging pleasantries. When he started the car, a Grateful Dead song resumed playing. It was a live bootleg so I couldn't tell which, but at least it was familiar.

He suggested that we get dinner before dropping me off at the hotel. It was late and by the time I checked in I wouldn't be able to find food. Besides, he knew a good rib joint by the Missouri. Though I didn't eat pork, I agreed. They had a great beer list too.

I wanted to get to my room until I remembered him saying that I'd enjoy the hotel: "Artists tend to." I hadn't researched it until the week before I'd left. When I checked the website, it seemed like a quality establishment. The photos reminded me of the Eliot in Boston—although only the facade and main dining room were available for scrutiny. A few days later, though, when he called to make sure that things were in order, he told me that I would like my accommodations: "It's funky."

"Funky" sickened me. When it comes to hotels I did not—do not—like the funky. I need the ordinary. I'm funky enough. I don't want to wrestle with, figure out, or adjust to foreign rules. I want to stay at a familiar chain. I need to see the familiar signage, walk through the automatic revolving doors, encounter the same check-in desk, the same uniforms. I need the same sounds and smells, the same elevators, hallways, doors, and door hardware. I need to know the layout of my room: the places where interlopers could hide so that I can do a quick sweep for them. I need to know where the light switches are; the closet, bathroom, bed, desk, and bureau; the location, size, and brand of television; if there's a balcony with sliding doors and how to secure them. And if I can't I need to know that a bellhop will bring a broom and steak knife so I can fashion a suitable system. The room's psychology and mine must cancel each other out. I can't suffer it; it can't suffer me. And riding with the stranger through his dark, foreign city, no orienting ocean or tower and Jerry's meandering solo the only familiar marker, I started to feel those shocks again.

We parked and walked along the river. It was lined by a row of restaurants. Most of them were dark. The banks were deserted. It seemed as though we were in a noir film, and he was leading me to a mysterious informant or an ambush. When he gestured to a doorway, I thought he was mistaken, but we entered. It was large and empty. He motioned to a wraparound bar.

The bartender greeted us before we sat and smiled while handing us the menus. "You're eating?" He told her yes, quickly ordered a pint, and turned to me. No Coke—Pepsi—so I asked for a seltzer. My host asked, "Are you sure?" I wanted to say yes and leave it at that, but instead I told him, "I don't drink."

I didn't want to eat. The weather in my head had become a tight vortex, lengthened, and touched down in my bladder. It had gathered up a broken power line there and begun to whirl it. I was hungry, but I didn't want to add anything to that mix.

He got ribs and I ordered some arid chicken dish. He drank a half pint before talking about my book—the last thing I wanted to discuss. It had cooled for me. It seemed to be of another time and place—alien. I could feel the sticky wood, hear the '80s rock, hear him, see him, smell his beer. None of it had any effect on me. What did frighten me was that it didn't. I knew some part of me appreciated his praise and questions about process and technical intent, but I could only answer them flatly. Grunts and shrugs were my only choice unless I confessed that I rarely felt anything except sad, angry, confused, or guilty for not being able to feel. I sometimes was lonely because I couldn't admit it to anyone.

He waited for me to answer. I tried to remember what had happened. I wanted to tell him that I didn't remember writing it—that I wasn't even sure if I was the author. But all I could muster was a line from Eliot: "when I left my body on a distant shore." I needed to rock back and forth on the stool, spin, flex, and stretch my fingers, then move them as though I were spastically playing a piano and mutter repeatedly: *"when I left my body on a distant shore, whenileftmybody whenileftwhenileft whenileftmybodymybodymybody . . . when I left my body on a distant shore."* I couldn't do it in front of him, so I tried to think of someone I could, but my half thoughts were fleeting and my mind was too slow to follow them or too fast to stop and settle on any one.

Our food came. I asked him a question about his writing and cut into my desiccated fowl. While he talked, I pretended to eat. After a lull, I realized that I'd been staring at the long tiers of liquor bottles. *A drink. A drink. A drink a drink—all Mickey needs is a drink. A wee dram of the mellow.* The last drink I'd had was Bushmills, neat. Beer had become pointless. I'd get bloated and sick before I got drunk—"quick and messy" as a friend once had recommended.

I scanned the bottles. He asked if I wanted something. I shook my head this time. In my mid-twenties I'd discovered high-end booze, how you could con others—your spouse, perhaps—into believing you didn't have a problem if you chose from the top shelf because drunks drank swill.

The next phase was booze-specific drinking: no white wine, champagne, or prosecco for toasts. Gin was repulsive. Jug or box wine wasn't *winky* but sad. High school girls drank rum, college women, Kahlua. Blended scotch was for the ignorant. Gold tequila for the duped. Mixed drinks were for amateurs and ice cubes, except with vodka, were for lightweights.

Then there was climate-specific liquor. Vodka when warmer than 60 degrees, whisky for cooler days. Then came the deals: No drinking Monday through Wednesday, except out at dinner, and then only beer and wine. No drinking before dark except at a wedding.[2] No drinking without prior exercise. No drinking at home, except beer and wine

---

[2] Unless dinner was before dusk.

with dinner. No more than two drinks in front of my wife. No drinking with my mother or brother. No drinking with drunks.

Michaele believed I followed my rules until her grandfather died and we inherited his liquor cache. We brought it home and stashed it in a closet. But she'd noted the inventory—drawn mental lines on each bottle—and so when she found a near-dry half-gallon bottle of blended Scotch one Sunday, which on Friday night I'd just opened, she confronted me and told me she was scared. It wasn't the quantity alone. It was that I'd never seemed even buzzed.

I agreed with her. I told her I had a plan. I think she felt relieved. She'd seen me stop for months at a time—seemingly without a problem. I told her I'd quit if she wanted me to, but she said she just wanted me to slow down. I implored that I could "stop anytime," and for emphasis I showed her an already-aged bottle of small-batch Islay Scotch and declared that if we had a daughter I'd hold off until her wedding and open it then.

I realized, suddenly at the bar, that I'd ruin my daughter's wedding. I saw myself standing up at the reception, knocking the table while doing so, looking for a knife with which to chime my glass—seeing Michaele's sad, anxious face, dismissing it, then slurring my way into a toast: *"A toast..."* my daughter having to endure my rye breath while we danced and, later, finding her crying to her spouse or her mother, Michaele refusing to acknowledge me, waking to silence—still drunk—and having to choose between facing what I'd done or beginning again.

I had to leave. Fortunately, my host announced that I might be tired. I wanted to get to my hotel, turn on the TV, watch loops of SportsCenter until dawn, and maybe do push-ups, crunches, and a movie.

Outside the bar, I started feeling better. On the drive, he talked about the old jazz district and the history of the city's white flight. I could tell we were close to my lodgings. The neighborhood looked like a forgotten urban renewal project.

"The cattle was run past here to the slaughterhouses." Then he was quiet.

The Hotel Savoy wasn't funky. It was decrepit. It resembled an old brick public schoolhouse with a few baroque flourishes on the lintels and cornice. It had been built in '33, perhaps had a midcentury heyday, but been in decline ever since. He rang the bell, and we were buzzed into a small foyer which opened to a large, dark, empty dining room with lightless chandeliers and feeble sconces. There was a chipped terrazzo floor. The red banquets were yellowed.

Reception was a shadowy depression in the far wall. I looked at my host's face. He was shyly smiling. "This is cool." He said it for himself. We crossed. The desk and the mailboxes behind it were wooden and partially lit by hidden incandescence. Before either of us could ring, the night clerk was suddenly there. He was tall and looked like Boris Karloff.

Evil basso: "Your name?" He sounded like Karloff, too.

"Thomas," I mumbled. He checked the register, asked me to sign in. While I did, he turned to the boxes to get my key, which he placed on the counter.

"The elevator is to your right then left." He looked toward it though it was out of sight. "Be patient with it, please." He looked—lidded—at me. "Or, you have the stairs." Smiling, he gestured my path. "Enjoy your stay."

My host asked me if it was okay, muttered something like *bohemian*, offered me his hand, shook, and hurried away.

The clerk had disappeared. I walked to the back past a kitchen that couldn't have produced anything other than a bleak tea service. To one side was an elevator. I knew its cables were ready to snap, but the stairs were lit only by a single bulb and led to nowhere, so I decided to take it.

My hallway was sinister. More naked, yellow bulbs hung from above, and a grim strip of carpet waited along the plank floor. My room was just to the right of the stairs. At the far end of the hall, something shuffled in the gloom. I mocked myself. I counted—*one, two, three, four*—long enough so as not to look like a fool. I paused. I forced a laugh, then unlocked the door, opened it, and entered a two-room shithole.

I froze—and then began to panic. I knew I should run for it. But I was also furious with myself for being afraid. I dropped my bags, slammed and bolted the door. Two large windows on the opposite wall. An armchair and love seat. A CRT TV on a rolling stand. I crept along the wall of the parlor and peered around the corner then cleared the closet, the bathroom, under the covers and beneath the bed.

I tried to calm myself, but the air smelled sweaty, smoky, rancid, and sweet, and the carpet had grunge one couldn't vacuum or scrub away. I knew I couldn't sit on any fabric surface. I'd never lie in or even sit on that bed. I wedged the hard-back chair under the knob of the front door, lifted the nightstand over the bed, and pushed it against the one in back. I got the ironing board and pulled off the lining so I could get my bag off the carpet. I turned on the TV. Although it was wired to a cable box, the reception was no better than using rabbit ears. I turned down the volume because I might, while searching for sports, stumble on a horror movie and peripherally watch the screen.

I found a college football game and calmed a little, until I realized I hadn't any place to sit. It was just after midnight. First light was around 7:00. I'd have to stand until I could get out and search for coffee. I could get another hotel the next day, fulfill my morning commitment, and sleep through the afternoon. Exercise before dusk, then dinner and the reading in the evening. TV all night and sleep the flight home.

I walked the room and watched the game, but I made it only two hours before I got tired. I'd tell myself that I was crazy, but every time I thought about sitting, even on the bathroom floor, I could feel bedbugs crawling all over me. Over the next half hour I argued with myself about stacking books for a platform, standing in the tub, or opening a window, scaling down the wall, and wandering the streets until sunrise. Mostly, though, I fidgeted. I was too anxious to scratch.

Gradually, though, the small parasites made way for larger ones. There was a vampire downstairs and who knows what else in the other rooms. I could almost see them—the eyes of one in the elevator, the tail of another dragging up the stairs—but never any in full or any one place. They were nearly whole, almost there, and so they could be anything, anywhere: the vibrating windows, the creaking hall, the hints of guests in other rooms, those ragged-nailed fingers circling the knob—and that smell.

I wondered about the folklore concerning the supernatural, not if demons and dark ones existed, but if what we had against them—holy water, dream catchers, evil eyes, rings of fire, garlic cloves—worked. Vampires could only enter dwellings into which they've been invited, but was that the hotel or the room? I wondered what to do if one got in. I tried to remember how to challenge a púca or confront a duppy, but weren't these protections all, really, like superfoods, or quotes, proverbs, prayers you'd read on billboards or a spoiling tapestry hanging from someone's kitchen or bathroom wall? If I lost my fight to a supernatural creature, what would I become? Would I die and the coroner declare natural causes? If I had a soul and it was immortal, where would it go? Would I become a demon or a haunt? I wondered if they all feared the sun? Or were they like me—day and night always afraid?

This was ridiculous. I slapped my face twice, called myself a fucking chickenshit idiot, and phoned my best pal, Mike.

"What's up?"

"I'm in KC."

"What's doin' there?"

"Traveling windbag, you know? Have bullshit will travel."

"Yeah. Sweet."

Beat.

"I'm alone. Fuckin' losin' it."

"Head turnin' on you?"

"Yeah." Beat. "It doesn't like me, so it's having its fun."

"Mental mutiny can be problematic." Beat. "What's it doing to you?"

"There are bugs everywhere. I can't touch any of the fabric, and even with my boots on, the rug is suspect."

"Yeah. That's a problem. Any nonporous surfaces?"

"I've used them to barricade the doors."

"Doors?"

"It's a suite."

"Well, that's fancy."

"It might have been. Fifty years ago. The dude who brought me here told me I'd like it 'cause it was funky."

"Gotta watch that. Funky's good with James Brown and such."

"It smells"—I realized it as I said it—"like my dad's armpit."

He said something like "that's tough," then told me to remember that in spite of his flaws my dad wasn't a violent or angry man, and so his scent might be a "benevolent manifestation of his spiritual self," and that, considering his life, this was what his ghost had to offer. There was comfort in that.

"Yeah." I suggested. "It's only been a couple of years. Maybe his powers will grow over time. Maybe he'll smell better." Mike agreed.

"But there's other things. In the hall." I looked at the couch. It seemed to be collapsing into itself. I told him that I could always dry-clean my clothes, take some sort of chemical bath, and shave my head, but that the couch seemed to be a trap—no—a portal and if I sat in it, I'd get sucked in and disappear.

"I hate when that happens." He spat some chew juice. "What troubles me most is whether or not I should go through it."

"Hamlet."

"Yes."

We both wanted to review the play, but we also knew that I didn't need tangents or conflations. I needed him to be frank.

He then was. He'd told me that I'd been like this as long as he'd known me. And while he didn't want to reduce the spirit or metaphysical realms to an atypical psychology, I shouldn't discount that there are wraiths of a different order, inside my head. "They're pernicious and will certainly punish your mind, but they won't take your soul."

"You know what it is?" I asked rhetorically. He waited for me to answer. "I don't want to be here. I don't want to read, teach, or fly. I'm isolated in a strange place having powerful sense memories of my father." I waited. "And this is the perfect place for a bender. I want a drink. I have every excuse."

"It's high time for self-sabotage." He spat. "You haven't been paying attention to what you've been achieving."

"I've fucked up." I chuckled. "Unawares, I've taken on tremendous responsibilities. I have too much to lose."

"Yes sir."

"Alright."

"You good?"

"I'm good."

"Call if you need."

"Yeah."

"Don't drink."

"I won't. Tonight. Nowhere to get it. Safe until morning. Run. Write. Teach. Sleep."

"Eat. Don't fuck with your sugars."

"I do have a touch of the sugars."

We laughed and said goodbye. I was still rattled, but without the dread. I thought about my class. I needed to prep. I wanted to do well. "Have a good time," Michaele had said. "Blow them away. I know you will." I would. I got my notebook and jotted down prompts for a lecture and soon realized that they could be the basis for the piece I'd thought about on the plane.

> I once thought that most fears were
> —The event removed from the moment is no longer the event, but a mutation—the additive of narrative (conclusion)

It became difficult to follow those partial thoughts. I let them go and chose the epigraph:

> *It seems, as one becomes older,*
> *That the past has another pattern, and ceases to be a mere sequence—*
> *Or even development: the latter a partial fallacy*
> *Encouraged by superficial notions of evolution,*
> *Which becomes, in the popular mind, a means of disowning the past.*

I didn't know what else to write, so I began documenting the prior hours. The images were still vivid, but their impact had faded. I was—new. *"This is what I do."* As I wrote about the room and months that had led up to being there, I realized that I hadn't felt right in a long time. Now I did—because this is what I do. As the last night hours passed, I felt better, stronger—though still I never sat down.

At first light, I changed and ran. I was tired, stiff, and still troubled, but as I made my way uptown, I loosened and the effects of the night before lessened. I cruised for a while and tried to review my night. I couldn't. I couldn't recall my room—only the hotel's facade. I always assigned these gaps and blips to the residue of old bong hits, microdot accumulation, or atypical wiring that allowed me to remember it all in sharp detail later. But this was different. My talk with Mike seemed like an overheard conversation of nearby diners in a crowded restaurant. Dinner, the bar, the flight, the fear: it hadn't been me.

I listened to my breath and my footsteps, studied the dog walkers, early commuters, and rising sun. Coleridge's poem came to me: "On Pains of Sleep." I mused on De Quincey: "There is no forgetting"; and then a line from a poem I'd written: "My body is my only memory. My body is my only mind." It sounded right, so I repeated it for a few blocks until I found a rhythm for my gait. I was fast now, and starting to sweat in the cold dawn. I remembered what it felt like to be powerful, with all my parts and functions synced. Whatever had happened—if anything had—had been an aberration. My baseline was and had always been good. That's what I'd often tell myself. Sometimes I'd even felt it.

I continued uptown and started to think of all that had brought me here.

2

The year prior my novel was about to come out. I was excited and looked forward to updates from my agent. I quickly answered her calls. I answered everyone's calls: friend or creditor. I trusted my publisher's handshake, the publicist's planning, and Elisabeth's notes. I trusted her smile. I believed that she genuinely loved my book. She liked me, too. I liked her. When other writers asked me about my experience with her, I told them, "She's great. It's great." I meant it.

Mike had produced the artwork for the cover. He'd sent me a few sketches, mostly of winos passed out under the Brooklyn Bridge. There was one that was serious—star men plummeting from the sky. I showed them to my editor. She laughed at the goofs but nodded at the cosmic twins. "That's good." It was easy: I got the cover I wanted. O'Reilly got a check.

The pre-pub reviews came. One was pissy; a few were cautiously positive. I chuckled and quickly forgot about them. One though made me cry a bit as I read. She loved it. More than her praise, it was the last clause: "a ravishing blues for the soul's unending loneliness." She'd heard it. She'd gotten it. I got it, too. I realized and accepted that my book could do for others what the ones I loved did for me.

In December, I received a box of books. Michaele suggested that my friends might like signed copies. Initially I disagreed, but when I thought about it, I knew I wanted to give Mike one. I also wanted one for Ben Russell, who'd taken my author photo. Then there were my colleagues in the adjunct corral at Hunter. Instead of signatures, I found myself writing notes I didn't have the room to finish on the books' title pages. There was so much I had to say. While handing someone a copy or sliding one into a mailbox at school, that old familiar distance—now seemed foreign. There wasn't anyone I wanted to stick it to. I didn't think about haters. My mother, my sister, and my mother-in-law were all proud of me. I got teary every time I thought about their approval. I was proud of me. For the first time since my daughter was born, I felt worthy.

The way my kids and Michaele reacted made me feel good too. When people asked them, they'd say, "My dad's a writer." Or: "He wrote a real book." And Michaele had been vindicated. She'd proven me wrong. I wasn't a failure. She playfully gloated, "I told you so." She'd always believed that if I spoke, people would listen. They'd been waiting. If I took a chance—put my work out there—people would like it.

I was high through the end of the fall semester. I met with multiple students every day to help them redraft late assignments, stayed up late grading or working on house projects, and while I did, I'd feel euphoric, like I was on one of those twilight runs I used to take through Boston and Cambridge.

I decided to shop early for Christmas. It was a gray, beautiful afternoon in mid-December. I'd finished everything. My grades were in—nothing lingering. I took the F to Second Avenue and walked up past our old apartment building along the same route I took during my first years in New York. The old East Village was gone. Many of the people we'd known had moved or were dead. The places where we drank, laughed, and cried together—where Michaele and I had grown up—were closed. I didn't chafe against the new environs. I didn't pine for the old. I drifted north in the gentle, mild wind realizing that I'd loved a great many people and that many of them had loved me, too—and still did.

Ninth Street was inviting. I stopped on the corner. The wind was blowing east. It was going to snow—the first of the year. I thought how perfect it would be to walk to the West Side and buy gifts along the way.

While waiting for the light at Third Avenue I glanced at St. Mark's Bookstore's window. It was a good place to start—to browse, at least. I scanned the display, saw titles I'd read about. I decided I should get a few and determine later who got what. I scanned the rows of new fiction and saw my book.

It started to snow—slow, dry, lazy flakes that disappeared before they touched down. I kept looking—snow to window. I realized that I must have looked daft, so I checked my watch then turned to the avenue and pretended to search north and south. I couldn't remember what I was doing, how I'd come to the corner, where I was going. The light changed. I didn't know what to do. Stare? Take a photo? I certainly wasn't going into the store. I thought of the people I should call: Michaele was still at work. It seemed ridiculous to call Mike or Dominic. All I could hear was us mocking the cognoscenti or ridiculing pompous scholars by being deep-voiced, taciturn, and dour.

I was ashamed that I hadn't thought of calling my mother. I didn't, however, have her number. I always called my sister for it, but I didn't want to do that. And then I had sharp pangs remembering how Tracey had spent a good deal of her childhood helping me through moments like these. I knew she'd be happy. I knew she'd care, but when the light turned again, I jogged west across the avenue and took the train back to Brooklyn.

When I told Michaele, she exclaimed, "That's great!" I must have looked at her suspiciously, because she repeated it. Then people began telling me they'd seen it in this local bookstore or that chain. Some followed its Amazon rank. The Grove folks told me it was great and that I should visit particular bookstores to "sign stock." If I saw a copy in a window or on a shelf, I should introduce myself and offer to sign their copies. This sounded preposterous: few stores knew anything about it, and my being there seemed disruptive. I felt like an idiot as the staff scurried around looking for stock and an ass when I uncapped my pen. But I did it.

Even as a child—save for a few dead people—I never wanted anyone's autograph. When Ziggy Marley became popular, people mistook me for him. When my hair grew longer, they sometimes mistook me for Milli, sometimes Vanilli. But mostly people mistook me for Lenny Kravitz. People rarely believed me and were sometimes angry when I told them I wasn't. Sometimes my license was insufficient proof that

I was me. Some men wondered why I didn't pretend to be the rock star. Once on Lexington Avenue, a woman ran out of her work and chased me. I thought she was pursuing a customer who'd forgotten something or hadn't paid, but when she caught up she shoved a manila envelope and pen at me. "Who am I?" I asked. She suddenly realized she didn't know. Embarrassed, she lowered the envelope and pen but made a quick reversal and brightly asked me to "sign it anyway. You never know."

A few acquaintances told me to check my local bookstores for copies and subtly shame them into ordering a box if they didn't. I was supposed to grow and manage my career by creating a website and maybe a blog. I had to submit to journals, go to conferences, and pitch panel discussions. I told myself that I'd been preparing most of my life for this particular personal diaspora. I'd made many before: child to adult, raceless to race man, aesthete to activist, drunk to sober, potential to actual, amateur to pro.

There was my graduate degree and my thesis, three-sevenths of a collection of long short stories that my advisor and other faculty had told me to send out immediately. It was the time of big advances for little books written by unknown brown people. My career—literary and academic—should've been a cinch.

I tried to review my new life positively, but everything I constructed seemed like spin and any attempt to map a course there and back was a lie. I'd been a young poet and a hopeless child aesthete; a rape victim and a rape survivor; an accomplished student athlete and a dropout; a potentially great man and a good-for-nothing—a nigger; a free citizen and a ward of the state. Sometimes I felt like Horatio Alger and others like a reclamation project—a product of many people's charity.

I was still a drunk who simply wasn't drinking. Sobriety hadn't anything to do with willpower. My faith in my talents, self-indulgent and narcissistic. And *literature* was evidence of obstinacy not ability. What critics saw as literary merit was just another example of white people's guilt-driven response to my subject matter: I hadn't produced a work of art but rather a didactic validation of a cause, a demagogical pamphlet, an intolerant screed, that masqueraded as an aesthetic triumph. If I really looked back, I saw myself as petulant and selfish, one who appropriated myth, co-opted art and history for my petty devices. My novel was empty, and I was a phony.

These fugues would inevitably leave me angry or sad, but I kept conflating my condition with some archetypical tale or character: cussed Caliban, Cool Hand Luke, Achilles, or an etherized, heartbroken ape who'd been baited into a deadfall and stowed in a ship's hold: a simian fool asea. Soon I'd be on display—docile but chained. And wonder or monster, I was the epitome of the humble, the defeated, the former king of a realm that had really only been a dot in the ocean. Two deaths: I could stay pimped and gutted or try, at least, to tear whatever I could apart.

I wondered if I could simply disappear, or fake my death, or even—die. That seemed reasonable. That would be the best marketing strategy. But whenever I concluded this, I determined I needed at least one more manuscript—a discovered text. I thought it would be better to have a second. Then someone could archive my creative oeuvre into some kind of multimedia offering. And dead I wouldn't be able to undermine any of it. I thought of Fitzgerald in Hollywood. He'd cracked, but I wasn't him. I'd given up my debauched, decadent life years ago. I was sober and healthy. My wife was sane.

I'd always blamed my inability to pursue any ambition on my dysfunctions—or on others': institutions, administrators, parents, girlfriends, assholes, white people, Black people, phonies, hacks—*them*. Now, though, I thought about the artists I admired: Dylan moved from Hibbing to the Village and had let Hammond find him and Grossman sell him; Hendrix gigged his way through the chitlin' circuit and played the flunky on New York bandstands until Chas Chandler took him to London and dressed him up in Sgt. Pepper's best. Baldwin, Brando, Marley, they'd all been discovered. They'd all accepted someone's help, but they'd all, as far as I could tell—no matter what their critics or fans demanded they make or be—kept some part of themselves.

Yes, I was much older than all of them had been, but in a way hadn't they risked more? They'd gambled their futures. My stake was my past—what I'd wanted it to be—so I really hadn't anything to lose. From then on I entered stores, small and large, with my fine-point Sharpie and announced that I'd come to sign stock. On one occasion, I visited a random store hoping to find a few copies—but no, not even in the African American section. I was disappointed. Hurt.

An employee caught me staring at what should've been my space. Embarrassed, I pulled a Tolstoy from the shelf. "Great book," she said, then asked me if I needed help finding a specific title or if I'd like a suggestion. I told her no.

She was young and bookish. I lingered. We chatted. She talked about works she loved, then asked me about my favorite writers. Instead of listing them, I quietly lectured—perhaps too long—about a particular group of contemporary books I disliked, which then of course demanded I criticize the critics who praised them. She stayed quiet. I thought I'd insulted her, but she reassured me I hadn't and that she was pausing to "take it all in" and that she'd "never thought about those books in that way."

She said she was trying to be a writer. I asked why she wasn't one. "Do you write?" She said yes but that she wasn't published and so—

"Publishing doesn't make you a writer. It makes you a published writer."

She shook her head but smiled. "And getting paid makes you a professional writer."

"You're a writer?"

I shrugged.

"What have you written?"

"A book."

"A novel?"

I nodded.

"That's great. What's it called?"

I shook my head. "Nothing."

"No, you should be proud."

I told her the title, which she thought was "great". She started walking away, then waved for me to follow. She stopped at a computer station and began to search for the title. She asked my name. I pretended not to hear. "Never mind," she said. "I found it." She shook her head. "We don't have it. I'm going to order it." I told her not to. She told me I was crazy. Getting published was almost impossible.

She asked about genre and plot: if I was "pumped," if I was satisfied. I hoped I hadn't sounded dismissive. I wanted to tell her that I could only quote what others said about it and me. I wanted to tell her that the thing doesn't matter, only the making, but I didn't want to sound like a self-important ass. What had I done? I'd filled notebooks. I'd typed words and now I had this—thing. I wanted to tell her that an hour before I entered her store I felt different. I *had* been proud.

I stayed quiet too long. Perhaps I seemed smug, creepy, or odd, but I didn't say anything. I didn't want to hear her tell me that what I felt wasn't true.

She was nodding gravely, but it didn't have anything to do with me. She was concentrating on the screen.

"We have to carry it," she said. "We need better African American representation."

And I was off.

Two weeks later it was Christmas and then the New Year—I stayed home, kept quiet. I almost forgot about it all. I started working on two novels. I had ambitious plans for the spring semester—new books, a new pedagogy, really. New workout routine and diet. New home construction projects. It was difficult to do anything more than scribble notes though. If I got past that initial state, I went shopping—Staples for office supplies, the library for scholarship on the books I was writing, sporting goods stores for gear, after which I'd search the web for deals on sporting wear, and Home Depot or the lumber yards for tools and materials. I'd envision a desk, shelves, modular wood-lined closets, but by the time I'd make it to the parking lot that picture would fade. I'd try to resummon it by seeing me working—cutting, fastening, finishing. But it had been over four years since I'd framed all the spaces for the built-in millwork. I couldn't remember the measurements. I'd get frustrated, then sad. Then I'd get angry, which would help get me moving, and I'd grab tools and materials I didn't need. But if the check-out lines were long I'd leave it all and go.

Back at home, if I managed to buy anything, Michaele would sigh at the load, and the future midnight project, the week or more of racket and mess, or nothing happening. Just more shit in the cellar, where everything, to me, seemed to disappear.

In late January, Grove's publicity director Deb asked me if I was free for a photo shoot. I panicked and wasn't able to think of why I wasn't. She gave me a date and time. I agreed but I was already coming up with ways to blow it.

It was to be an early session. I didn't sleep but I stayed in bed until fifteen minutes before the shoot. I felt bloated, wretched, and filthy. I drank my cold coffee. Under the lethargy I felt a panic attack mount, so I jumped rope for two minutes, did as many push-ups as I could in five, put on the clothes from the day before, and went outside.

It was cold and dark. They'd set up just south of my corner. The morning rush had just ended and because it was mid-January, no one was out. There was a pair of non-white men waiting across the street inspecting their gear. I stayed on my stoop for a moment to watch. They were both at least ten years older than me. They seemed comfortable with each other. I couldn't tell who was in charge.

I crossed. The lighter of the two, without looking away from his camera, said, "Hey," and asked, "What's up?" I felt calm.

While they took tests we talked about different things—their careers—how they'd started to where they thought they'd finish, how I was just getting started, and that they wished me luck. They broke on the few people who stopped to watch, some waved and smiled. The lighter man asked if I knew any of them. "Yes. From around." To which he asked, "They ever stopped and waved before?" I laughed—he caught me. "You're hard to read, but you ain't scary." He waved. I knew this meant step forward.

When we finished, we wished each other well, and they said they would be looking for me out there. I didn't want to disappoint them. I ran up my stoop, changed into my workout gear, and then ran around Brooklyn in shorts and a T-shirt for almost an hour. I went to the gym for another two, picked up some bread and garlic, went home, and made red sauce to Marley—*Survival*—on the verge of a proud cry.

Over the next days I ate better, slept better, and thought more clearly. I got more—anything—done: syllabi, exercise, calls and emails to people to alert them of my readings. I felt ten years younger. I liked talking to parents while we waited in front of the school at pickup. They sounded interesting, and I believed they were interested in what I had to say.

When I got the call to meet Bob Harris, the *New York Times Book Review* editor, for lunch, I looked forward to it. It was Wednesday, and I was set to leave for San Francisco on Friday to start my tour. I was looking forward to that as well. I had dear friends who lived in the Bay Area, but I only saw them when they came East.

I met Bob Harris in Midtown. Though we ate at the bar, I didn't mind. I didn't mind that he was paying. I ate my cheeseburger without incident or shame. (I'd eaten breakfast that morning, too.) We talked casually about the book, our personal lives, how we came to be where we were at that moment, but mostly we ripped each other about our teams: he said my great-grandchildren wouldn't live to see the Sox win another series. I questioned whether A-Rod had gotten enough iodine as a fetus and questioned the intelligence of anyone—despite his talent—who'd root for him. "He looks to be on the verge of an ether binge."

We walked over to the *Times*—still digging each other but talking also about work—finally, inside, he briefed me on what was to happen—a podcast interview with him and Sam Tanenhaus. "No big deal," he said. "Just a conversation."

I was fine until we got to the offices. There were so many piles of books—galleys mostly—that it was a challenge to see anything else. Paper hedges. They were on desks, the floor, and rather than follow him through the hedge maze, I stood wondering who made sense of this. Harris snapped me out of it by calling me to the back.

There were introductions. I think Bob noticed I was anxious and repeated "no big deal." While they talked about what would happen, I chased fleeting thoughts of fortune, and accidents of birth. I heard my mother yelling from miles and years away to "get my butt upstairs," to "clean up this mess."

Apparently they'd been asking me questions during my fugue. I tried to get my shit together. The tape, however, had been rolling, and I couldn't recall what I'd said. Neither Bob nor Sam looked bored or alarmed. Since I couldn't find a proxy, I decided to be "me." I didn't know what that was, but I decided to be honest, to be open—to share. Someone would edit out my gaffes. They seemed to like me and I hoped they wouldn't allow me to sound stupid, dim, or crazy.

It went on for a while. I can't recall much of it. I think they asked about process and literary ancestry. They neither fixated on nor avoided race. I think the autobiographical questions they asked were about children, baseball, and golf. The one memory I can honestly claim having was Harris asking me if I could hit a six iron 240 yards. There was talk of Brent Staples and the Brooklyn gym we'd both gone to. They were confident that I could bench-press more than he. They gave me a stack of book reviews. I left.

Outside, it was dark and misty. I felt empty and numb. I started south down Fifth. I realized that I should bring a pre-pub copy to my agent. I didn't want to go there. I liked her very much, but I didn't want to explain to security that I wasn't a messenger. I saw the tableau—the lobby, the glass doors, the receptionist, the abusively bright light. Her office though would be dark, calm. It was just behind the front desk. I wondered if I could get across to it. Perhaps it would be better to, like a messenger, leave it up front and run.

I began to run. I didn't clear my head, but I liked the click of my shoes—how sharp they were in the cold air, *click, clap*—down Fifth Avenue, crosstown along Thirty-Fourth Street. Once there I didn't even have to explain myself to security. I don't even think I was perspiring as I rode up to the thirty-sixth floor where, upon exiting, I pimp strolled to the door because it felt good.

I jogged from my agent's office to Grove. They knew about the review but hadn't seen it yet. Handshakes and arm pats, then I was gone. On my walk back to Brooklyn, I hoped I'd feel something before I showed Michaele. I didn't want her to question her joy. I told myself that if one could suffer post-traumatic stress—the feeling after the experience—couldn't it be the same with happiness? "Later. I'd feel it later."

When she yelled, though, I couldn't help smiling. "Oh my God!" she repeated while she scanned the review. "Yeah. Wow," I responded.

I called my friend, Mauro. I didn't tell him what was up, only that there was "something big I need him to see." He said he'd come by later. After he hung up, I wondered how I'd sounded: Good news or bad? Plumbing emergency? Lawsuit?

While I waited for him I called Mike.

"I'm on the cover of the *Times Book Review*."

"Hah."

"Really."

"Shit."

"Shee-it."

"Shit. Goddamn. Shit."

I waited. "What does this mean?"

He cleared his throat. Serious now. "Is it a positive review?"

"That's what they say."

He took a second to process this.

"Who?"

"The *Times*. My agent. Grove."

I tried to process it. "But it's as though . . . that doesn't matter."

Michaele had been listening. She shook her head.

"Right." Beat. "Are 'you' on the cover or is the 'book' on the cover?"

"Me."

"Big?"

"It's the cover."

"Good Lord."

"What does it mean?"

"Wow." He coughed. "It means someone made a huge mistake." He started chortling—fake, but it quickly became sincere. I liked it. I've always loved his belly laugh. He composed himself. "You're in."

"Yeah."

Mauro came. Michaele went upstairs to put the kids to bed and give us room. We stood, surveying the spread—cover to review, slightly nodding. Eventually, he smiled and spoke.

"What do you think this means?" I almost answered, "I don't know," but I was beginning to know. I told him what O'Reilly had said. He agreed, but then, rhetorically, I suppose, began to question where "in" was and what it meant to be there.

I told him. Together we went through the pros and cons, the short- and long-term benefits, whether or not it would be leverage in future negotiations with Grove, and if that mattered.

"Do you act on this now or later?" What and when is my market high? He left with a "congratulations," followed by "You don't have to do anything." He paused at the bottom of the stoop. "You got another one in you?"

"Four."

"Do you want to write them?"

I didn't answer. I kicked at some loose mortar. He knew I was about to say, "Fuck it." He preempted it by raising his eyebrow, which I knew meant no.

Dominic was next. He came fast. "What the hell is up? What have you done now? Didn't I tell you to leave it alone?" Then a counterpoint. "No. Really. Congrats. Shit. That's cool." And like Mike and Mauro, Dominic didn't try to tell me what I felt, or discredit what I thought.

Dominic tapped the review. "Yeah it's complicated and simple. Yeah, you're in." He slapped the copy. I thought he wanted to roll it up and swat me with it. "You're in, but you still have to deal with *it*. You always have. You always will. You're gonna kick yourself for staying here." He pointed at my head. "You're going to kick yourself"—he swatted the review—"for going there. For moving to the next room, the more *exclusive* one." He pointed at nothing. "But you've kicked yourself no matter where you've been . . . So, fuck it. Do it. Fuck it." He calmed again. "I'm not you. You know that."

I nodded. "Ready for dem."

"They have no idea." He snorted, closed the paper, gestured at my picture. "You know they ain't ready." He poked it, shook his head. "They never are." He grinned. "You know what this means."

We stared at my face for almost a minute. I looked up, but Dominic didn't. He went from cover to inside—reading and shrugging. Finally, he cocked his head to me. "You know"—he looked back down—"you're that Black guy now."

The next day I was on a plane to Oakland for the first leg of my book tour.

I didn't sleep the night before, carried my necessary effects and studied the Jet Blue Flight Tracker. My best friend from graduate school, Elise, picked me up. *Exile on Main Street* over the bay. I met her cat, saw her living room, and could see the tower atop the silhouette of Telegraph Hill. The Haight was still bright but quiet.

She knew my habits. She'd set up a futon on the floor but knew I might opt for the couch. She went off to bed, and I browsed through her DVD collection and stayed up until dawn watching the first season of *The Mary Tyler Moore Show*.

I didn't think about the fact that I was to read at City Lights until we parked. When Elise gestured to the Flatiron Building and asked, "What do you think," I sincerely answered, "Wow."

I was greeted warmly by one of the managers. As we chatted, Elise grew increasingly excited. After a few minutes, she took my wrist and led me through the stacks toward the stairs. We climbed and stepped into the reading room. People were already seated. As we passed to take our seats in the front, some of them turned and smiled. We sat in the front row.

"You're reading at City Lights," she whispered. "Can you believe it?"

I nodded and answered, "Yeah. I mean, no. No."

She elbowed my ribs. "Yeah. Yeah."

People began trickling in. Then after a few minutes they entered in numbers. The intermittent floor creaks became a consistent note along with shuffling, murmuring, and folding chairs scraping the floor. The air grew thick and warm from the bodies. Elise turned and reported, "It's full. Totally full." She stood and turned, then bent to me. "People are still coming in." She whispered a hello to someone, waved, and then sat. "Your people coming?"

"Some."

"Don't look."

"I won't."

"What are you going to read?"

"I don't know."

"I think you should . . . Never mind." She knocked my leg again. "You're not nervous? You're never nervous."

"No."

"You'll be great."

"Okay."

The room had gotten warmer and louder. I tried to picture how many rows were behind me and how many seats were in each. I could hear voices and feet ascending the stairs. Elise leaned in. "This is great." Then, "Do you know who's read here?" She smacked me with a backhand. "This is Ferlinghetti's house."

I nodded.

"Sorry."

"It's fine."

My introduction drew loud applause. I think I had to borrow a book. I stepped behind the dais, turned, and looked over the crowd. The seats were full, the back wall lined, and there were folks still on the stairs. Many of them were my friends and family, and many of them had brought friends. I hadn't had so many people smile at me at once since my wedding. Some of them wriggled in their seats as though they could barely contain an urge to yell something—to cheer.

I read, answered people's questions, and smiled while the house applauded. I wanted to stay up there in the corner—not with the clapping. I didn't need to keep talking "at" people but rather with them. I even wanted to stand there among them. Then I wanted to be folded into them. I wished Michaele and the kids had been there. Everyone—at least the people I knew—seemed to have shared an experience with each other. I was a part of it. It was real. I was real. I had a place and something to offer; however awkward, inconvenient, or alien I might have been, in that room, at that time, I wasn't rejected, which was all I really ever wanted. I loved and felt loved.

About twenty people went across the street to a lounge. When I entered I started panting, I was feverish, and thought I'd been clubbed in the head. Most of the crowd assembled in the back. I skulked along the front wall and hid on a deep, low windowsill.

I stayed put there, catching vomit in my mouth and swallowing. I was relieved because I thought my sudden episode was food poisoning or a stomach virus. I could tell that to Elise and collect myself in a bathroom stall. A few of her coworkers found me. Elise did, too. We sat in the window and tried to talk, but the music and chatter kept the exchanges to: "Sorry?" We took a few photos, decided to join the party. When we approached the men's room, I excused myself and left them.

I entered a stall and made myself throw up whatever food was left in my stomach and whatever bile I could conjure. I washed my face and hands while repeatedly calculating how long we'd stay. Two hours, max. I could do anything for two hours—or, better, not do anything.

Everyone was kind, and it seemed that whatever they'd experienced at City Lights had carried over to the bar. My companions though let me sit quietly. I imagined my dad sitting at the bar. I felt right: with him, out of time, in dim light, jazz, old and new booze—silent.

I carried that with me through the rest of the night—supper in Chinatown followed by five or six episodes of *Mary Tyler Moore*.

Two days later I landed in Burbank. My sister-in-law Caitlin picked me up and took me to her house. I had a reading that evening. I sat on her couch, enjoyed her company, snacked, and didn't have a thought about any other place or time. But I was flat all evening. I droned through the reading, mumbled through the dinner, and upon arriving home, wished my sister-in-law owned a TV. I spent the night reading *People* magazine.

I dozed for a few hours and woke up to the West Coast dawn. I poked around the kitchen, saw that Caitlin's boyfriend had made coffee. I poured a cup, went to the dining room. He had left his open laptop at the head of the table. I wanted to check my email and decided that if the computer was on and the screen saver disabled I would.

It was on, open to the *Times Book Review*. And there I was. I closed the window and logged on to my email. I had almost fifty new messages. Some were from people who I didn't know or who I hadn't known had my address, others from colleagues and acquaintances, but most were from people I hadn't spoken with for years. I logged out, reopened the *Times*. Went to the kitchen, poured and guzzled another cup, did a few sets of push-ups. I returned to my room, changed into my running gear and shuffled out the door, down the hill and into Elysian Park. I tried to run, but felt disjointed. I slowed to a walk. Instead of exercising, I thought searching for basking rattlesnakes, coyote scat, and a big cat's trail was what I needed to do.

When I got back to Caitlin's house, I called Michaele. It was late morning in the East. Our phone had been ringing for hours. She'd answered the first few calls, but then left it to the answering machine. When it was full, she jotted down names and numbers, but by the time we spoke she wasn't doing anything other than listening to the messages.

"This is crazy," she declared. "It might be a good thing that you're out there." She laughed, quieted. "How *are* you?"

"I don't know."

I drove around LA. The sun wasn't working or it had done too much. I listened to *Exile*. Between Echo Park and West Hollywood, I must have stopped at a half dozen coffee shops. I made two visits to In-N-Out Burger. After the second, I leaned against the car, smoked a cigar, and watched the Hollywood freaks enter and leave the drive-through.

Coffee, cigars, burgers, driving, and sun. Other than calls from Michaele, tour logistics, or what to have for dinner, I didn't answer my phone. And then I was off to the next tour stop.

Atlanta. My mother-in-law Sally had moved there several years before and established a network of community artists and activists. I was to read at the Atlanta Center for the Book, and she'd spent the weeks prior to my arrival organizing friends, neighbors, and others to come to my event.

The phone calls and emails kept coming, but, sitting at Sally's kitchen table, I began writing back. Most of the messages had either said, "Don't worry about writing back," or "I know you're busy." I answered a few dozen. Got a run in, read to a hundred folks, and did two interviews. Sally wanted to drive me everywhere, and it was good to have her. She listened in on my conversations. When she heard words like "bestseller," "movie," "film agent," she cackled, screeched, and once had to pull over to keep from crashing.

The minute my flight home took off I got sick. I didn't bother trying to diagnose it. I left it at "sick." "Sick, sick, sick. I'm sick. I'm sicky-sick." I sang to myself until I was allowed to go to the toilet. I just wanted to get home, sit on the couch with Michaele and the kids and watch cartoons, and order too much pizza—for a few days at least.

The first day I was back in Brooklyn, I was stopped at least ten times by strangers. "Were you on . . ." "Are you a writer?" "You're not the guy . . .?" Most of them were polite. They'd wish me the best. I didn't know which me should respond. My sudden "celebrity" allowed many folks I'd seen around for years—folks who'd avoided eye contact—to say hello and people who'd been casually friendly to go blind and quiet.

School was worse. When I entered the building that morning students and faculty alike—up the escalator, by the elevator—looked at me or looked away. Loners smiled. Couples covered their mouths and whispered—not with a look of excitement or wonder but—almost mockingly—as though I'd come to work pantless.

I didn't want to go to the adjunct office. I took the stairs halfway up—to the seventh floor—and waited on the switchback's landing until class time. I did the same for my second class. I skipped out on office hours and spent the midafternoon wandering the side streets between Madison and Park.

I came back a few minutes late for my last class and ended it early. My students filed out—they didn't know or care—and when I thought the hall was clear, I left.

It wasn't. The department chair stood outside, waiting.

"What did I do?"

She shook her head and smiled. "Nothing."

I must have given her a quizzical look because she added, "Not nothing . . . something."

We entered her office. She closed the door and we sat. I still suspected that someone had reported something about me—I was a profligate, a fraud—that I wasn't who I said I was.

Instead of being fired, reprimanded, and counseled or advised, I was offered a job. The proposal was:

1. A tenure-track assistant professor for the following fall semester at a midlevel salary.
2. A promotion for the current semester from adjunct to substitute professor—retroactive to the semester's start.

All I could reply was "Thanks. I don't know. I have to ask my wife."

Michaele was as stunned as I'd been. "I don't know. What do you think you should do?" I was confused as to why I was having difficulty deciding. Nothing would change. My schedule would stay the same. I'd teach the same classes. The only difference was that my salary would more than triple.

I had to respond by the following week. I knew, also, that I couldn't avoid my office. Most full-timers ignored me. Some adjuncts with whom I occasionally chatted pretended I wasn't there. Others with whom I'd never spoken used "congratulations" as a means to finally talk. My friends were still my friends.

The next day on campus after my last class, the department chair was at the door. We walked to her office. This time the dean of Arts and Sciences was waiting. She presented another offer—with a 5 percent increase in the new salary. Again, I replied, "I don't know." I went home. Michaele and I repeated our exchange from the prior week.

At the third meeting the chair presented the final offer—a slightly larger salary plus two summers of "start-up money." I asked if I could continue to teach summer school. I was told yes, and I would be paid on top of my regular salary—at a substantially higher hourly rate. So I said yes and was a tenure-track professor.

The best way for the reluctant and unambitious to handle the expectations of others and themselves is to plan. I was no longer crazy. At worst I was eccentric—not naive or foolish, but savvy. My plans were reasonable, even to me.

For the rest of the spring, I gave readings, taught, and waited for the semester to end. June was near. Summer school meant I could triple-dip. I now had a biweekly salary, summer school pay, and start-up money. I figured I could coast from Memorial Day to Labor Day. Summer hours are concentrated—fifteen weeks compressed into six—but because it spanned half a season instead of two, it seemed manageable. And there was the afternoon—the light and the empty museums and galleries. I wanted to visit one every day. I wanted to enjoy the city in a way I hadn't since my first years here.

I walked everywhere. I stared at art. I kept a small notebook with me along with a copy of the Quartets, Baldwin's short story collection *Going to Meet the Man*, and Joyce's *Dubliners*. Whenever I had to wait for coffee or a traffic light, I'd read or write—sometimes both. Notes, notes, notes in my book and in theirs. Each day, I studied a different section of one of the texts—page, paragraph, or sentence—and tried to re-create their effect with my writing. By the time it was time to start home, I felt confident that I had done serious work that was the beginning of a long essay or short book—a treatise on my aesthetics. I began to incorporate literary critics—Aristotle and Longinus,

Montaigne, Nietzsche. I obsessed over "Tradition and the Individual Talent" and Ellison's "World and the Jug." I celebrated contemporary critics like James Wood and B. R. Myers and even drafted letters to them hoping to begin a correspondence with each and establish a sort of neoclassical, neoformalist school that would counter the half-wit academics and artists who seemed unaware that their derivative treacle was market driven and that even if I died blind and alone, I'd at least be on record that this age was dominated by myopic fools.

But after a few weeks, this wasn't enough. I had to corroborate my theories by rereading Douglass and Thoreau, Mencken and Orwell, Du Bois, and Baldwin's nonfiction. I needed a sociohistorical backdrop, so I scanned various histories of the West—the Greeks to Howard Zinn, philosophy anthologies. I drew family trees of thinkers and artists from Socrates to the present.

But that wasn't enough, so I'd call Mike and Dominic and tell them my plan to weaponize all of Western thought and use it against the "tumid" and the "puerile." If I couldn't reach them, I'd follow Michaele around the house or trap her in the kitchen and tell her about my day, my thoughts, and how I planned to manifest them. She'd nod, but that wasn't enough, so I'd tell her again in a different way—another voice. She'd always tell me I was right.

But that wasn't enough. I could hear myself. I could hear the lie. It wasn't that my theories were unsound, but my motivation was to publicly humiliate people whose work I didn't like.

By the Fourth of July my captive audiences—family, friends, and students—had to listen and agree or pretend to listen as though they were placating a child who was on the verge of a tantrum. And no matter their reaction—commiseration, indoctrination, submission, recalcitrance, or boredom—I'd repeat myself. Quoting, then conflating the artistic, critical, philosophical, and sociopolitical archives of the West.

If that didn't work, I'd apologize by asking, "Do I sound crazy?" And they'd respond no.

Mid-July: I'd flipped and gone almost silent. If I spoke, I'd preface and conclude whatever I said with "I'm sorry" or "This is crazy" or "Operation Shock and Awe." But self-deprecation seemed to be another lie—or a part of the big lie—so I eventually shut up.

I wouldn't talk so I had to move more. Whenever I stopped, I'd get a quick shock in my chest cavity, stomach, or groin. It felt as if a frayed nerve ran through each of those areas, and when I idled that spark failed to jump the gap. I tried to think of the jolt as a prod rather than as punishment. By late July, I calmed, did simple things—grocery shopping, an oil change for the car.

I played guitar more, practiced fingerpicking and solos. I still, however, wasn't writing formal prose. I didn't pressure myself to do so. It was fine to only think about writing—while watching a ball game, on a run, or sanding a cabinet door. It was okay to go to afternoon movies or search the internet for plumbing fixtures or build a virtual Maserati on their website, write silly poems and songs. Their playfulness and mundanity didn't enrage me. I didn't think there'd be any harm in publishing them. I decided free writing was a valid endeavor. I didn't feel compelled or burdened to extend metaphors, concretize images, unify them via allegory or allusions to what I'd always believed to be the larger narrative. I didn't feel obligated to accept my role or place in any kind of lineage—literary, political, racial, whatever.

None of this caused me to regret having done or trying to do this in *Man Gone Down*. That had been my choice then—perhaps because it was all I'd been capable of. I just wanted to experiment now. I thought I'd write some short stories, perhaps employ Cheever's preferred process of not taking more than a week to complete one. I'd write nonfiction too—not memoir but a scholarly biography. I could write op-eds, or reportive journalism, even. It seemed for the first time in my life I could do what I wanted and more so, that what I wanted to do wasn't drastic, desperate, or doomed. And I wasn't ashamed about pricing my work either. I didn't feel like a punk or a chump or a con for wanting to try.

At midsummer my energy was gone. I wondered how it could be. I tried to retrace the prior weeks to find where and when I'd lost it. I thought back to the spring, but I couldn't remember. I only heard my voice mumbling at readings and in class. I never could hear what I was saying, but I knew it was stupid.

Time seemed to compress. Nothing had happened between February and now. School would soon begin. I needed to start a new book, and the thought of making a syllabus frightened me, as did anything that had to do with writing.

Simple tasks were confusing. They required a multistep process to complete. I'd give up on something like changing batteries and try to revive an old computer or appliance. Sometimes I'd muck through but most of the time I'd wind up standing over a disassembled machine I couldn't fix or even return to its original, broken state.

I couldn't sleep for more than a few hours at a time. I wasn't afraid of things in the closet or under the bed, nor was I worried about my heart stopping. Sometimes, when trying to lie still I heard random clauses of Michaele confiding in her friends about how I was impossible.

As the summer ended it—I—got worse. I avoided people, and people seemed to avoid me. I felt my presence was oppressive. Projects, games, and outings with the kids usually ended prematurely with me correcting them about how they were doing it wrong.

August 21st was my birthday and I was sullen throughout and after. We were always in Massachusetts. My sister-in-law's birthday was the day before, and we often had a joint party. I'd never minded. I'd liked it even—but that year I grew indignant. I'd always had Mike come up from New York or down from Boston, but this year he was in LA. Michaele read through a list of other local people, but none seemed a friend. I either snapped no or curtly explained how I'd never really been close to them. I knew, though, that I would've refused any of my real friends too. I still loved them and I knew they loved me, but rather than trying to help me, I thought Michaele was giving me permission to invite someone. I protested by going silent.

It was decided that the dinner would be held at Michaele's godparents'. I told my wife and sister-in-law, "Whatever," which upset them. They thought I was trying to undermine the evening. I scoffed at their insecurities—that I had so much influence over their emotional states.

I hated the dinner. As we drove over, it occurred to me that I wanted barbecue, potato chips, soda, and hilarity. What I got was oniony, olivey, pretentious food, dreary, forced anecdotes about exclusive trips, and, of course, booze. I hated the separation of adults from children, the hiss of *jokes*. More booze. There were shouts about a particularly exquisite wine and insistence that everyone try it. For some reason, a guest I'd just met called for a reading of "'Fern Hill' . . . for the birthday boy and girl." No one knew or bothered to ask what my thoughts were on Thomas's poetry.

So I sat. I watched my bored children stare into the empty fireplace, the uneaten food on my plate, the wine bottles empty, disappear, and be replaced. I brooded. I growled and grunted responses and never asked a question. Everyone except Michaele was too drunk to notice or care. She smiled at the rest—enough to seem engaged—but she looked at me as if we knew secretly that I had a terminal illness or that she was saddened by her action, or inaction, and that she was trying to say how sorry she was, that she was searching for some way to make it better. I couldn't change my face. I had to be angry. And I couldn't forgive her—anyone—for their trespasses. I wouldn't. It was her fault that I was spending my fortieth birthday here with drunk, wealthy white people celebrating themselves on the bones of the Wampanoag. That's what we'd come to—or hadn't it always been this way?

I spent the last week of summer exploring new routes to and from New York. When I was in Brooklyn, alone, I muddled through the cellar debris that had been soaked by the late summer storms. I bleached and rebleached the damp floors and walls to prevent mold growth. At school, I prepared for my fall semester by looking out over Lexington Avenue from my twelfth-floor window for birds of prey.

Then we were all back home—work, school, soccer. Everyone else was busy, and I should've been, but I moved through those first weeks of September as if under ether. I think this break from my anger was a relief for my family. I got them to trust me again. I walked Miles and Ella to school, picked them up when I could, made dinner. I stayed at school late after classes to grade papers and organize, but I really couldn't get through more than a couple, so I made outlines for short stories. I played along to the Allman Brothers' "Blue Sky" trying to learn Duane's and Dickey's solos. I hadn't the chops, but I kept trying. I'd watch whatever sitcom reruns I could find. I'd weep while Redd Foxx staggered about clutching at his heart, proclaiming it's "The Big One."

I had a few speaking engagements set up. My first trip was in late September to DC to participate in the PEN/Faulkner Gala at the Folger Shakespeare Library. To prepare for riding the Acela, I stayed up all weekend. That Sunday, I took a late morning train to the capital.

I disembarked and made my way from the platform to the great room. Even though it was a Sunday, the station was busy. Bright sun shone through the skylights and large windows. I thought I'd get a cup of coffee, sit on a bench, and relax for a while. I stopped, scanned the vendors for a café, then realized I didn't know where I was supposed to go.

I got coffee anyway and sat in the center of the station and watched people coming and going. I noticed that there were a lot of light-skinned Black men—most wearing suits and carrying briefcases. I made a point to make eye contact with each and nod or mouth hello as they strode past.

After about fifteen minutes, I thought I should come up with a plan. I searched my bags and guitar case for a printed itinerary but couldn't find one. I tried to remember my contact's name or the hotel where I was staying. I remembered that I had the original email document, so I called Michaele. She wasn't at home when I reached her. We had a quick chat. She giggled about my absentmindedness, asked if she should leave what she was doing and go home. I told her not to—that I was enjoying my afternoon and that either someone would call or come looking for me or I'd eventually remember.

I waited in the sunny atrium for another thirty minutes then called Dominic. He answered after the first ring as though he were waiting for my call. I told him my predicament. I was about to ask him to search my Hotmail account, but before I could he asked me for my password. In between jokes, inquiries as to who the hell thought it was a good idea to bring my ass down there, I supplied him with keywords for the search. He found the message after a few tries and read it aloud. He punctuated every few sentences with a cackle or comment about how ridiculous they were for inviting me, how ridiculous I was for accepting. He finally got serious, though, and told me to crush it. He found my contact, hotel address, found it on the map, gave me multiple routes. Asked me if I knew about the dinner that evening, told me that I had plenty of time to get to the hotel, shower, change, and meet the car downstairs. He half joked, half warned about manners and protocol. He said I should, on some level, take this trip seriously.

"Did you write your piece or are you going to freestyle?"

"Oh yeah."

"You got time."

"Yes. Time." I wanted to quote "Burnt Norton" but I just barked the title instead like Jackie Gleason. He signed off with "Way to go, Ralphie Boy."

I called my contact. I couldn't tell if she was relieved or annoyed. I convinced her that the hotel was close enough, and I could get there on my own. I walked the half mile southwest. It wasn't a chain, but it was upscale. One entrance, two bellhops, a concierge, and three people behind the check-in counter, waiting, it seemed, just for me. I went to my room, swept it twice. I turned on the TV to a football game, set the alarm, stretched out on the bed, and spent the second half pleasantly between sleeping and waking.

I woke before the alarm and immediately began intense calisthenics. Then I went out for an easy run in the late afternoon light. Somewhere in the last mile, I remembered the next night's reading. Twelve authors at the Folger, all taking five to seven minutes to share their thoughts about twilight. I was sure they'd brought me in for prose, but I decided to write a poem—a very serious, very formal poem. Not angry—grave. Austere. I sprinted the last quarter mile, and without cooling down drank two espressos. Back in my room I did various sets of push-ups. I'd jump up, rest, scribble notes on the hotel pad, and read them out loud. Then I'd dive back down more.

The sun was going down. I took a shower. I saw what I'd soon write—not the words and lines but their shape on the page, as though they were backlit forms—silhouettes behind a yellowed page.

I tried a few more push-ups, but I was shaky. I was hungry. I remembered Karen Carpenter and how her starved body had eaten itself until all it had left was her heart. I thought about my lineage of bad pumps. I listened for an arrhythmia. When I got like this, Mike had always reminded me that I didn't have one of those. *"You're a goddamn horse, dude."* Twenty-five years of *"You're a goddamn horse."* I'd tell him that I had cocaine-scarred chambers and reference athletes who'd dropped dead. He'd note that my father and grandfather's trouble could've been environmental—coincidental—not congenital. *"You've had so many EKGs that they would've found something long ago."* When he saw that I was still worried, he'd calmly tell me to check my pulse. After several low readings, he'd ask, rhetorically, *"Okay?"*

I told myself I was fine. The phone rang again. My car was there. My suits were still wrinkled. The only shirt I could use was the one I was wearing. I turned on the shower, hung my suits up, and began dabbing at my shirt. I muttered insults at my reflection.

I steamed my clothes as long as I could. I creased my pants, spit shined my shoes, dressed, and descended to the lobby. The driver was waiting by the rear passenger-side door. I shook my head, mouthed an apology. He smiled "no problem," opened the car for me, and we were off.

We drove along the first leg of my run. It was dark now, but I could still see the buildings change every few blocks: well-kept or decrepit, micro shantytowns or gypsy stops juxtaposed with monuments near and far. Some people moved with certainty; some floated. Lost. Along the way, I wrote my poem in my head. Around Dupont Circle to the Avenues of States, people and ambassadors, I drifted between what I saw outside and in. I tried to twin the two, first with words then with what seemed a silent, bluesy prayer. By the time the driver pulled over, all I wanted to do was find a quiet place to hum until I could find or be found by the lyrics to that song.

A staffer greeted me at the door. She bowed awkwardly, then gestured for me to follow her through the mansion's foyer, dining room, and parlor and out the French doors to the patio. She pointed weakly at the opening in a stone wall. "It's a nice night." She tried to sound buoyant but formal. "They're having drinks in the garden."

I walked in, found, greeted, and thanked the hosts. There was a shadowy tree in the back. I made for it and hid there for a while.

I was beginning to believe I was invisible when a man who looked like Sonny Liston approached me with a tray of Collins glasses. They were filled with a chartreuse drink. I hesitated. He nodded at the glasses. I leaned toward them and tried to sniff without him noticing.

"They're good."

"I'm sure."

He pushed the tray forward as if encouraging me to take a deeper whiff. When I did, he smiled and moved them closer to my nose.

"They're clean."

I raised and cocked my head.

"Just lemonade."

I took one.

He asked me who I was and why I was there—how I liked it and where I was from. After a few minutes I did the same. He was reluctant to say much, but after gentle prodding he talked about his current life in DC and the Bush administration.

He went back to work. I felt disproportionately lonely as he walked away. I stepped back into shadow.

We were called in to dinner. I answered most of the questions I was asked with "That's interesting, I admire their work" or "I've never thought about it in that way. I'm not sure if I can answer that right now." And yes or no as needed. On my way out, I had a Black conversation with a Black couple about a Black writer they loved, but I thought little of. A few more yeses or nos, some cryptic answers and I was gone.

I watched TV until dawn, slept for an hour, ran, showered, and was waiting out front when my ride came. A PEN volunteer drove me to the high school where I was supposed to read and answer questions about my book and what one had to do to be a writer. Instead, I lectured on misoneism: the imagery in "East Coker" and "The Dry Salvages." I think they liked it. Rather than delivering it like a frigid Anglican, I treated the poetry like material for my stand-up routine. The kids seemed engaged. Some asked thoughtful questions and most, I think, enjoyed my analysis of the mechanics of a particular line or stanza. *"Does he ever tell us what Krishna meant? What the fuck?"* I received sincere applause.

I had the rest of the morning and afternoon to myself. I walked, watched people, and took notes until I thought it was time for me to begin writing something formal. I headed back toward the hotel, stopped at a coffee shop, and read through a few pages of notes. I liked some of the lines but most of them seemed silly. I thought it might be better if it were prose, but after a paragraph, neither it nor I were any better. So instead I sat in the sun, did the crossword in the newspaper, and listened to the traffic go by.

A few cups later, I was up again. Jumpy from the coffee. I skittered around and then back to the coffee shop repeating, "O, the burdens we put on words." I sat and continued with "The alleged, transitory power . . ." I copied it a few times. Crossed it out. Wrote it again. I snickered, cursed, stabbed the page with my pen, then packed up and left.

I was hurrying back to the hotel when I passed a Kinko's. It seemed right, so I went in. I sat at a terminal, took out the Quartets, opened to "The Dry Salvages," movement IV. I decided to write a poem. I didn't see myself, anyone or -thing at twilight. I was on the deck of a ship. Wind. Rain. Swells that were growing with each rise and fall. I felt that electricity again, but this time it was a thrill. My ship was pitchpoled by a freak wave and then I went under. I knew that I should die at sea. I laughed.

I thought Elisabeth would appreciate the humor of my epiphany. I would write her a poem:

Lady, whose office stands on lower Broadway,
Pray for all those who are in D.C. Kinko's, those
Whose business has to do with books, and
Those concerned with public social deaths
And those who must suffer them.

Repeat a prayer also on behalf of
Children who have seen their fathers
writing poems, and not recovering:
Nothing much makes sense here,
Queen of Black Cat.

Also pray for he who rode on trains, and
arrived at fancy dinners, amidst wine and face-lifts
And embalmed ladies who, though he tries, will not reject him
Or wherever cannot reach him the sound of any other place
but here.

I printed it, marked it up, and typed in the edits. I pasted it into the body of an email. "SOS" was the subject line. I tried to think of a reason not to send it. Nothing. Off it went.

I left Kinko's and was bounding like I'd always thought Whitman would in a shopping district. Elisabeth called. I told her I was looking for a shirt and tie. She laughed. I laughed too because I pictured myself searching the city's dumpsters, gutters, lost and founds for my lost items. I was going to suggest that we drop the literary stuff and begin a career as a comic duo.

She told me she liked my poem. And I told her it was a joke. That I was killing time. That I was jazzed and I needed to burn off some of my coffee mojo. She asked how it was going, and I went on about cocktails and dinner—how I'd joined the "Pet the Artist" circuit.

We laughed for a few more blocks. She asked, "What are you reading tonight?"

"Who knows?"

"Aren't you worried?"

"About what?"

I found a department store and tortured a salesman by holding him captive as I deliberated over shirts and fussed about ties. I couldn't make a decision. I finally picked a black shirt and a slightly textured black tie. I ran back to the hotel, dumped my stuff, tore the pages of notes from my pad, spread out on the desk and bed, and wrote two drafts of my formal poem for the reading. I jogged back to the Kinko's, typed, printed, edited, and retyped. I mailed a copy to myself, printed it out, and sprinted back to my room. Then I pressed my suit, showered, dressed, and met my car outside.

The driver was a different man from the previous night, but he seemed to know me. He was large, light skinned, and gentle voiced. "We have some time." He hummed. "Have you seen much of the city?" I told him I hadn't, so we took a winding tour to the Folger. It was an overcast night. The car was new and quiet. We didn't speak. I leaned against my door. We passed black iron fences, limestone monuments, and, at what seemed to be regular intervals, the silver river. The flat revealed hidden luminosity in each surface: green glassiness in the iron, rough diamonds, gold dust, and crushed mother-of-pearl in the dusky rock facades, a sapphire undercurrent in the water. When we got to the Folger Theatre, I exited the car quickly and shut the door before he reached the curb. We shook. I handed him the tip. He took it and nodded. We both smiled. Then he quickly scanned me—shoes to collar.

"That's a great suit."

I thanked him and he dispatched me with a quick salute.

There were dozens of people climbing or waiting in groups on the stairs. While buttoning my jacket I casually ascended, crossed the threshold, and entered. The party was to my right in a voluminous oak-clad hall. The hall was nearly full, peopled with seven or eight score. Most of them were gathered in the center of the room, while some waited at makeshift bars that were set up along one wall. A few singles and couples studied the paintings and busts. The far end, though, was empty. I wondered if I could move through the party unnoticed.

I made it across with only one woman—a smartly dressed septuagenarian—seeing me. She was more than twenty feet away, but as I passed she turned. I was compelled to stop. She wasn't much taller than five feet but second by second she seemed to grow and, without moving, close the distance between us. I didn't know where in the space we were. I knew no one else could see us. Her eyes were black. Her skin was pearl. She had mercury-blue hair. I felt my blood pump my muscle. I could taste steel in my mouth. That electric current was there in my lungs. It grew and spread throughout my body with every breath and heartbeat. I felt humbled and powerful.

Then it was over. I was back in the hall, back on the floor feeling as I had when I entered. The woman across the room was small again, over there, on the edge of the party. I glided toward the clearing. No one saw me.

I watched the party from that end. Some people who wandered past me quickly looked my way as though something flashed in their periphery, or they perhaps heard a whisper. One sleeveless woman allowed her hands to slowly drift along the suddenly raised down of her forearms. And standing seemed to gently go to sleep. I recrossed the hall, the foyer, and threshold, and I left. I walked along the middle step of the wide stairs to the southeast corner of the building and sat. Cars pulled up. People exited them and climbed the stair. The sky was gray. There was little chance of seeing a sunset. Night would come suddenly. I had to go back in.

I'd killed enough time on the stairs so that there wasn't any left for introductions. All twelve authors were gathered up and briskly led through the crowd. Backstage, we were briefed on how the night would proceed. We were to read in alphabetical order. After we were done, we were to take our seats around the stage.

I sat and looked from the floor safety lights to the dark rafters to the catwalk and down the long, thick ropes back to the floor. Then I stared at the curtain hem, the light and shadows on the worn stage floor. I thought about how a stage, light, and sound design can transform an ordinary space—even a decrepit one—into a train station, the deck of a ship, how it could summon a dead king in the night. I closed my eyes and saw myself out there. Then I saw nothing but could hear my voice in my head. Like someone talking in another room while you're falling into an afternoon nap. Then no voice, but I could see again. I was in the poem. My other senses awoke to the last of a day in the dying summer. I heard my name.

I walked to the dais and looked out over the audience, up to the balcony. I remembered that my third-grade teacher and first deep love, Ms. Cozy, had told me to hit the back wall with my voice. I thought of the river beyond. Something told me to look down and left. There was Jim Lehrer. I had watched his news report with my father. I liked him almost as much as Cronkite. I thought I should begin with a curse—something Richard Pryor would've said: "I want to talk about fucking." Instead, I told a PG story about my old Boston neighborhood, an angry Doberman, and how there were portals—only I knew of—that appeared at twilight and through which I could escape. I'd come out by the train yard or the weed field where the abandoned house had burned down or somewhere in between—no place I'd stay or be kept—until the dog had left.

I think I got laughs. I know I laughed. I breathed as though to signal the joking was done and read a long discursive poem about DC about how standing in front of a methadone clinic you can see tent cities, desperate citizens, and the capitol all in one look. It railed against popular notions of magic and somehow arrived among the reeds and blackish waters of Buzzards Bay at twilight:

> *I cannot see you clearly*
> *The dying light will not allow*

I don't know how long I stood. I saw the marsh, but I was inside it and I couldn't find my way out. The wind was howling, and it was getting dark. As I walked to my seat, I wondered if I resembled someone feeling his way through the muck and reeds.

Dinner. I'd emerged from the grimpen, but was only at its edge in a night fog. The dimmed chandeliers were like the lights of boats and buoys. The other people like driftwood and dark waves of sand.

I didn't think I behaved strangely, insulted anyone, or embarrassed myself, because I do remember two-handed goodbyes. Though they could've been thanks, blessings, or farewells as though I was about to take a journey from which it was almost certain I wouldn't return. I suppose I didn't: night on the steps, car, limestone city, hotel.

Nothing morning. I awoke in my suit, stuffing everything into my bag. I walked down to the station for my early morning train. I boarded. Nothing.

I came to when the train abruptly stopped. The conductor announced that we'd be delayed. We were in the middle of a Delaware power plant, surrounded by electric transmission towers. It was a beautiful morning—clear and dry now—but there were large puddles in the gravel and hardpan. My fellow passengers were reading, working, or manipulating their BlackBerries. Some seemed harried, others even desperate, but none of them seemed crazed—driven to any extreme, high or low. I thought, *I can do that.*

So I got out some papers I hadn't planned on grading until the coming weekend. I told myself to be calm. I had twenty three-pagers and so, with a one-minute transition between each and a five-minute break every five, I'd be done with half by Penn Station.

I did the first paper quickly—under ten—and the next only marginally slower. I lost that time, however, with the third and fourth and slogged my way through the last. I didn't write the obligatory critique on the back of the last page. Later. I would do it all later. I reclined my seat but stacked all of the essays and, as if to keep a promise, held them against my stomach.

I looked out the window. A company pickup bounced toward me along the access road. Splashing across a puddle it turned left through a gate and into the field of evenly spaced—about twenty-five yards apart—pylons. I followed it to another puddle, which from where I sat looked like a seepage—water not from above but below. Even though the truck had easily traversed it, I wondered if it had done so over a shallow strip. There were at least ten yards on either side and there could be a sharply sloped floor or even a deep trench under the reflective but still dark surface.

I realized I was weeping. I would've wiped them, but I liked the way my tears felt and tasted. Like sea water, at first, but then muddy puddle. It was strangely comforting. I wondered why. Perhaps it was the sun on the still-troubled water, the steel towers. I heard Aretha singing "Bridge Over Troubled Water." I wondered if there was a bridge somewhere just out of sight.

I got hit by that current again. It stayed with me. It filled my stomach and made my torso hum. I tried to ignore it. *Why was the water troubled?* The water, no matter the body, was the saving grace. Sailing to the edge of the world, shipwrecked, drowned, lost at sea forever, I'd only have to negotiate the wind and chart the stars. I could be gone so long that there'd be no place to return to. I could sail past the edge of memory.

The current grew. I doubled over and flexed my core. In my head, I was speaking in tongues. I said aloud, "I can't live like this." Someone cranked up the voltage.

The conductor announced something about "problems up the line." I wanted to throw my papers and run through the car wall. I watched myself sprint atop the mud and gravel, through the gate, to the water's edge, and disappear before crossing. Again and again, until finally I crossed. I saw myself running. I thought I was making for the far boundary, but I stopped at the base of the last tower and looked up. My perspective switched; now I was looking up the pylon to the power lines. Then I was among the cables, standing on a steel cross-span between the terminals.

The current ebbed then ended. I sat upright and wiped my face. But I could still see from the tower. I could feel the wind, the pulse in the line, the sun, but I felt the sun through the train window. I closed my eyes. I saw myself dive from the tower, invert, go down.

The vision repeated. Each time, though, it would last a little longer. Each time I came closer to hitting bottom: *"I can live like this..."* Every dive: *"I can live like this"*—in the middle of the air. But eventually the train hummed then jerked and we started moving again. The conductor apologized. We picked up speed. First the feeling diminished, then the vision, until I couldn't sense either. We were out of the power station, accelerating up the coast. I kept trying to retrieve it, but with every attempt it became more fragmented and dimmer. By Philadelphia, I was scared it was gone forever. I wept from Trenton to Newark. When we reached Penn Station, I was numb. My head was full of mumbling voices. They were all trying to tell me different things—some cautioned, others mocked, a few offered what sounded like apologies and condolences. One muttered a prayer I didn't recognize.

We were in the tunnel when I heard my voice tell me to stay on the train. I sat up straight though and started packing my papers. I stood up, yanked my bag off the rack, and bulled my way to the exit. While waiting for the train to stop, I repeatedly told myself to shut the fuck up. On the platform, up the escalator, through the bodies and clamoring station, I listed what I had to do that day—that week. I charged onto Seventh Avenue and east-northeast to Hunter. Every block I grew angrier. I was glowering at everyone, bumping everyone in my path. A taxi turning onto Sixty-Fourth almost hit me. I stared him down as he honked and didn't move until he stopped. I dared every driver thereafter into even coming close. At Hunter, I shamed a group of loitering students who were blocking the entrance and once inside the elevator, I cowed a very large but very young man into turning that thing down. It took only a few floors for me to apologize. He said not to worry, that it was his fault. He was spaced out. We reached his floor. We shook hands, and he apologized again. The door closed. A thundercloud rolled through my guts and shot lightning into them as it passed.

I exited, ran to the bathroom. I waited for a colleague to slowly piss and shuffle to the sink, wash his hands and check his hair, all the while lazily bemoaning the semester. Finally, he moseyed out. I couldn't make it to the stall so threw up my bile in the sink.

The next weeks I hung on.

On Fridays I'd sit in my dark office until seven then walk five blocks downtown to a news shop where I'd buy two car magazines, a

Snickers, and a Planters Peanut Bar. Then I'd descend the levels to the Brooklyn-bound F, walk to the far end of the platform, and wait for a train with an empty last car. I'd eat my candy and read about Ferraris and Porsches I still believed I'd someday drive.

My mother never made excuses: get up, get out. When I thought of her, I felt selfish, weak, and stupid. Work. Children to house, clothe, and feed. Debt x stays debt x. Even if it becomes 10x you still get up. Get out. Work. Even though she did—and I'm not exaggerating—anything she could to give us everything she could to become doctors, lawyers—whatever—she always said, *"I don't care what you do. Dig ditches. Collect trash—as long as it's honest and it pays your bills. That's alright with me."*

I wanted to go to her—not in anger and not to blame—I wanted to ask her if I was any of these things. I wanted to ask if I'd failed her and everyone—all the people who'd sacrificed so much to give me so much. People who'd known far worse than me.

I wanted her to tell me what was wrong with me. But I didn't even know how to ask. I didn't know how to say *I'm sad. I'm scared. I'm confused.* I'd have to say more than *I feel lost.* I didn't know how to ask anything of anyone. I didn't know how to say *I just need some peace.* But wasn't peace the problem? In peace I knew how bad I was, how wrong I was. In peace I believed I deserved the relentless churning in my guts and howling in my mind. In peace I had to live an unlivable life—and live it well. But I couldn't: I never could. I couldn't live with pretending I could read off the page or spell, or that my senses weren't in constant conflict with each other. I couldn't live with having been raped, I couldn't live with being chased and beaten. I couldn't live with cuffs on my wrists and a gun to my head. *"I'll fuck you in the mouth and throw you in the river. You little nigger fag."* I wanted someone to tell me it was real—or not.

But I couldn't ask and I couldn't say. I hadn't made it. Whomever it was that I thought I might be had been lost a long time ago.

In mid-October I decided to be right by the new year. All I had to do was last. I could make it to Halloween and take a break. After that, I could make it to Thanksgiving. I would get to semester's end by willing myself into a frenzy. But at night I was too restless to even sit and during the day I could barely move. When I was at school, I wanted to go home. When I was at home, I wanted to go anywhere. I didn't want to be alone. I wanted to be with Michaele but I didn't know how. I couldn't perform health for the kids but I needed their health near me. Ella was six. Sometimes when she should have been in bed she'd come find me in the dark. She'd sit beside me, place her hand on my wrist, lean against my arm, and stay until she fell asleep.

Sometimes, all you can feel is your distance and sickness rather than how close you are to love, or how deep you are within it. In those moments and in the days that followed I wished I didn't feel so helpless. I wished I didn't need help. I wished I was a better man. I wished I wasn't breaking. But love can seem such a rare thing in this world that when we feel it we fear it cannot be real. Alone or together all we can trust to hold us as one is pain.

3

I was sprinting when I came out of my reverie about the last year. I'd been running through the streets of Kansas City for almost two hours. I felt fantastic. I was fast and strong. And though I'd compressed almost a year of review in a relatively short time, I thought I'd accounted for all of it. I thought I'd figured it out. There was nothing to figure out. I was okay.

I slowed to a trot for the last few blocks and I cooled down in front of the Savoy. I didn't think much of it. A bright young woman had replaced Karloff at the front desk. She tooted hello as I jogged past her to the stairs. I did only a quick room check before I showered. As I dressed I decided that after the students, I'd pack my things and check into an uptown hotel. I changed. I had another hour before my ride, so I left the Savoy and crossed the street to the coffee shop, I had a few shots of espresso. While waiting, I wrote my editor a note.

Ahoy Schmitz—

Kansas City: The Hotel Savoy smells like my father—pork chops, smoke, mold, and whisky.
    It seems I've stumbled upon another ragged edge of the earth—or, the unfolding, in-folding world.
    Must run—I'm off to talk to schoolchildren about a life in the arts, the balancing act on the endless string.
    As always,
    Thomas

> "I see again my schoolroom . . . Everything is as it should be, nothing will ever change, nobody will ever die."
> —Nabokov, *Speak, Memory*, 3–7

I was to talk to a high school English class. My host picked me up. She was easy to listen to. Her car was clean and free of psychological clutter. She was excited about the program and to have me visit. As we left the city and crossed the border to Sumner, Kansas, she told me how she came to be here and meditated upon where she might be going.

I can't recall much of the class. I do remember the Q&A was productive. Many of the students' questions were excellent. One girl had annotated my book and quoted passages. She commented on how she'd recognized similarities between my writing and the styles of my literary ancestors. Their teacher moderated well. He didn't seem threatened. I liked him. We talked well past the bell. While signing their books, I had individual exchanges with nearly every student. I didn't want to leave.

My host suggested that I explore uptown. I could shop and eat at one of the famous Kansas City steak houses. From there it was a nice walk to the Nelson-Atkins museum, and since I was a New Yorker I'd appreciate traveling by foot. She dropped me off at the Plaza, but as she drove away, I felt my energy drain. The sun was hidden. I was wearing only a T-shirt under my coat, and I felt the winter.

I spent an hour looking for jeans, tanks, tees, underwear, and socks. Just in case I had a bedbug problem. I figured I could seal the plastic shopping bag with duct tape or maybe tie it off with some inorganic cord. I spent another half hour talking with the young woman who assisted me about her life in Kansas City. At first she praised her hometown, but then she asked me to take her back with me to New York. She'd be our au pair for room and board. I told her to stay. She'd find the same nothing there—only more nothing. Then I asked her about steak houses, and she pointed to the front of the store—vaguely south—and before turning away said that it didn't matter, "they're all the same."

It was almost two, and my hands were shaking. I set out to find meat.

The restaurant looked like a garish wedding hall. It was empty, too. Even so, it took five minutes to be seated. I suspected I was being ignored because I was Black. And when I was led to the back room I was sure, but the maître d' sat me at a large table by the only window. He clasped his hand, bowed his head, and smiled.

We went to restaurants like it when my father had money and felt like being a father. Perhaps the presence, as Mike suggested, *had* been my father and, as he had while living, tried but failed to be a benevolent one. My father—no matter the eatery—had always let me order anything and as much as I'd wanted. It gave him pleasure to watch ten-year-old me devour the king's portion of prime rib. If he spoke at all he'd say, "You're my hungry Horace," and laugh.

I ordered two appetizers and a twenty-ounce steak with potatoes. The calamari looked like chopped digits and the beets, kidney filets. The salad had olives, red onion, and an unnaturally colored creamy dressing, but I ate it all anyway.

I finished quickly and used the gap between courses to try to remember the past fourteen hours. I hadn't drunk or turned into a lycanthrope, but I'd seen and heard things, and real or imagined they'd frightened me.

When the waiter placed my entrée down, he chuckled and shrugged. "You can eat, man. I'd be full already." I told him I had an eating disorder, reminded him about my missing popovers, requested steak sauce, preferably A-1, and got into my lunch. When he returned, he didn't speak and instead left me to my orgy.

The meat was ordinary, but I didn't mind. Somewhere, my father was worried about me and eating would assure him that I was okay.

Halfway through my porterhouse I wrote:

Steak & notes.

—I don't feel last night. I can't dismiss what I'd believed—felt, but I can't make sense of it. I should, again, write about them, but I know I have to define and characterize each—an encyclopedia of monsters. Ghosts are a subset, because they're a combination of living and dead, past and present, spiritual. I remember what Mike said about my father and his—

—Are ghosts memories?
—Why are monsters evil?

—It's not people. I've never been afraid of burglars or prowlers. Like some errant knight, I worry about them. Children need protection every time and everywhere. It's folly not to protect that which can't be replaced.

—My family and friends think I fear nature. Not true. I wish there were still dinosaurs or mammoths. I wish there were wolves in city parks. I search for coyotes and snakes. But I don't want to be pointlessly maimed or killed. I don't want to be dismembered by a crocodile, gored by a bull, mauled by a bear, gutted and eaten by anything wild. I don't want my tissue predigested by viper or spider venom.

—There's no reason *not* to repel the certain anguish of loss.

—I fear monsters. They're everywhere: in the cellar, on the stair, under the bed, in the closet, on the other side of the shower curtain, in the attic, on the roof. They're in the wood, the thicket, the meadow, the marsh, the dunes. They're in and under the waves, they wait, sleepless, out at sea.

—But they're more, or less, than claws and jaws. They're almost something I recognize, almost something I can name. They're in peoples' promises and lies, their empty affects and affections. *Whispers in farther rooms.* They're in my reassessment of our pasts. My second sight of our further actions.

I finished my notes, bagged the book, forced down the last half pound of my steak and the remaining hardened popover. I thought about my father's sickness and death and wondered if I was mourning him.

I left and followed my pale shadow east. I started trembling again. I wished I could run, scream, drop on the sidewalk, for someone to find me and rush me to a hospital. Maybe they wouldn't ask me about my addictions and sedate me. Maybe after a few hazy days of drugs and testing they'd find something so rare and strange that no one there could address. They'd have to send me to Boston or the Mayo Clinic. There, the doctors would devise a treatment. First though, they'd have to detox me—twenty-eight days in the fancy junkie ward. I'd miss the semester, be clean for Christmas. In spring, I'd rehab my atrophied limbs. Summer. Then fall, a wellness plan. I didn't care what the disease was, I wanted it to be nameable—something blood tests or CT scans would confirm. I wanted something real. I wanted a visible scar—scalpel and suture—a sign on my flesh.

But there was nothing, just lunch, and that loose wire which each minute carried more current into my stomach. I turned to Eliot, *Wars, wars, wars, wars*. The sun came out and darkened my shadow. I stopped and leaned against a wall. I looked up, west to the pale, yellow horizon. Cool fire. Gentle smoke. I knew I had to go there. I heard wings. They were leather, but they weren't coming for me. They were me—or a part of me. I felt a surge of power. I flexed my back muscles then spread them—contract and expand. I exhaled—"War." I felt myself lift, hover. I began gliding east. I closed my eyes. I saw the horizon behind me: rolling clouds, frozen light. I saw me: a dark figure flying into it. My insides settled. My mind calmed. I was well again.

The feeling lasted until I was outside the Nelson-Atkins. Inside, there was only a security guard. Not a single visitor. I walked along the central corridor not looking at the art or other people. I found some in the rooms of the main hall, but they didn't seem to notice me. I drifted to the modern wing. Many of the paintings seemed puerile. They seemed careless, vapid, and cynical. There wasn't anything behind the shapes and colors. Rather than contain some roiling force, the forms obscured an emptiness. If I could've gotten angry and had a sharp edge in my pocket, I would have sliced every Pollock there.

It got worse as I walked past the color wheels and grids—read the plaques that explained what the artist's intentions were. I circled back to the front room where a high school group was filing in. Their teacher—whom I immediately hated—gathered them in the center and in too loud a voice announced: "Thank God we're out of all that oppressive religious iconography."

He looked up and saw me staring at him. He blanched.

"It's a scam. They're all frauds." I pointed to him. "And he's too stupid to know it." I spat. "Good luck." I stared him down, waiting for him to do something, but he didn't.

I reentered the old wing and wandered through a series of small rooms. I stopped in the Caravaggio exhibit and stared at the dark angel who I knew needed my protection and blessing and love.

But it was time to go. I couldn't save the angel. The charge in my guts was back. Outside, I started running downtown, but I couldn't keep it up for long. I heard Fats Domino singing "Kansas City." I saw his piano, then his hands. I saw planes of different sizes ascending and dropping. Some were on fire. I saw the inside of what I knew to be Pap Finn's cabin. I heard the lone owl in the woods. I heard Pap pleading to the angel of death: "Leave a poor body alone." I heard hundreds of screeching swallows massing before twilight. I could see everything from every point of view—omnipotence to tunnel vision. I don't know if I yelled, spoke, or whispered, "Tramp, tramp, tramp—please leave me alone."

I know I took a taxi for a few blocks. I materialized in crosswalks and on corners puzzling at street signs. I found the jazz museum, and it was a heartbreaking shambles. I started running back to my hotel. I tried to envision my swan dive, train crash, drowning, or disappearance. But whenever I did it was overrun by scurrying bedbugs.

I saw a CVS and knew that I had to buy boxes of the heaviest trash bags and rolls of the thickest tape, go back to the Savoy, and sheathe every fabric surface in my room with plastic. I also knew I should douse my body and hair with rosemary, garlic, and tea tree oils. It didn't matter that there were missing floor tiles or that the lights were hanging, single bulbs, or that the shelves were half empty and disordered. I gathered what I needed and stood in the checkout line. It didn't matter that this CVS had shelves of hard liquor behind the cashier—or that most of the people, construction workers or winos, were lining up to buy a bottle. I kept to the plan. I ran back to the hotel. I anointed my body before entering the room. Inside, I sealed the sofa, chair, bed, and carpet. I emptied the shampoo and used up the soap to clean my hair and body. I didn't use the towels. While I drip-dried, I searched the TV for bugs.

My reading was in a voluminous room that made the large crowd it drew seem sparse. The carpet muted everything, the mic and PA made it seem like a tedious lecture was coming, and high above fluorescent lights cast a yellow-green curse over us all. I think I was unremarkable. The dinner was unremarkable too. At first there were pleasantries, polite comments, and long silences. I think I might have looked like the dog who believes eye aversion is a form of camouflage and pretends no one can see him. But the guests, about twelve people, a mix of Black and white, seemed warm and thoughtful. They acted as if we were all old friends at a reunion. They talked and laughed and didn't seem troubled that I didn't say a thing.

When dessert was served I was ready to talk. The table happily included me. I wanted to explain my silence but they all seemed to agree that I was shy. They were happy I'd grown comfortable with them. "Some of us can be a little intimidating." I was willing to at least consider: *Maybe they are. Maybe it's okay to be afraid—even of small things.* And so, I joined the party and I felt better than I had in a very long time.

Some of the younger folks had planned to go to a bar. I didn't want the night to end so I went. Something happened on the drive though. I thought, perhaps, that it was the abrupt transition from inside to out, from the warm light of the dining room to the dark, cool night. I didn't feel *sick* but sad. I wondered why it was so hard for me to stay present with people and why on some level inside me I always felt the pull to leave.

The bar was a cigar lounge. I decided I was going to smoke. I think I spent a half hour in the humidor, not looking at anything, just staring. When I finally sat down with the others, they were engaged in a literary conversation. I couldn't join. They all seemed so far away. They talked. I puffed on my cigar and followed the smoke to the ceiling. I felt a sudden, growing grief.

Back at the Savoy, I got buzzed in. I even smiled at Karloff as I briskly walked to the stairs. I choked when I entered my room. I saw all the taped-down trash bags—white, green, and black. I locked the door and began tearing them up. I tried to do it in a rational sequence but sprang about haphazardly. It seemed that for each bag I pulled up another took its place. I stopped in the bedroom and stood. I paced around rubbing my forearms, picturing someone to call, somewhere to go, but I could only mutter, "The night. The night. The night night night night." But the meter didn't work—nor did the long *i*'s, phantom *g*'s and *h*'s, or the *t*'s' bite.

I heard something in the hall. I looked up. The door was open. I was certain I'd closed and locked it. There was something awful out there, something that had stood behind me waiting. I couldn't see past the doorway. The corridor was black. I thought to get the iron, but I knew that wouldn't help, nor would the hardback chair. I started to whisper, "Who . . . ?" I stopped and shuddered. I didn't want anything to answer. I knew I wouldn't be able to bear its voice. Not it—*them*: they were massing in the hall, on the steps, downstairs, and outside. They'd come all night, wave after wave, until I was gone.

I was sobbing now, but I walked to the threshold, stood, and stared into the darkness. Nothing. I shut the door but didn't lock it. Instead, I moved back to the middle of the room, knelt, and waited.

I don't know how long I stayed like that, but when I came to, I was still crying. I knew the hall was empty. There wasn't anything outside the door. I was alone in the room. Now, all of the haunts were inside me—constant shock and bellyful of dread. I was muttering, "I don't want to die." And "I have to die."

Then I wasn't in the room. I was aflame, plummeting at a sharp angle. I could sense the dark earth rushing to meet me. Then I was on all fours, on fire, beating my arms, shoulders, chest, and temples to put it out. I couldn't feel the blows, but I could see the flames jumping off me. I thought I heard me screaming so I held my breath until I knew it was safe to exhale. I inhaled and it cooled me. I could control the flames. I lowered them until they were out and I was an ember. My muscles pulsed a deeper red, my blood hissed and steamed, my skin tightened, thinned, cracked, melted, and reformed. Then it cooled and hardened. I didn't know what I'd become. But I was strong. I pushed my hands against the floor and my back to the ceiling and knew I could level the building if I wanted. I could see my face up close. It was new bronze. I was breathing through my open mouth. My tongue was out—a hot, red bolt. The point, a glowing spearhead. I was that until morning. I was packing my bag when I *awoke*. I'd already cleared the room. I finished packing, called a cab, said the serenity prayer, and checked out.

There was only one no-name coffee vendor at the airport. I knew their offerings would be poor. But I was invested in staying safe, and that meant modifying some, if not all of my behaviors. I bought a large. It was ridiculously hot and irretrievably burnt, but I double-cupped it, found a kiosk, printed my boarding pass, and headed for the security check.

The line was single file and fifty people long. My coffee was undrinkable. I had to throw it out but the nearest trash can was thirty feet away. I was about to hustle over to it, when three people lined up behind me. I thought I'd ask my neighbor if he'd hold my place, but he was twiddling his BlackBerry and wouldn't look up. I waited for him to finish his missive. Several more people joined us. They emailed, texted, and ignored each other. Most were pinched and grumpy. I thought that if I strayed from the queue—even a few feet—I'd have to ask permission of everyone to my rear. The line wasn't moving. I was sick of holding the acrid brew. I left the line, threw it out, and defiantly strode back. I glowered at the few who noticed until they looked away.

It took fifteen minutes to reach the x-ray machines and another five to pull me aside, recheck my body, and search my bags. I angrily searched for my gate, fumed when I learned it had been switched, and was shocked when I learned that rather than two hours, I had less than a half before departure. While I hurried to the gate, I searched for more coffee. I passed a Dunkin' Donuts stand and a Seattle's Best. I gambled that I would find something better but didn't.

My flight was delayed. There'd been severe winds earlier and the planes had been backing up for hours. The airline was confident that the worst of the weather had passed and we'd be among the first to depart.

I went to the far end of the gate and sat in the last seat of the first row. I was suddenly hungry and exhausted. I felt the beginnings of a caffeine withdrawal. I had time, so I thought it best to go back to the dunker for a few espressos. The room, though, was filling, and I knew I'd lose my seat. I watched how the wind whipped the vests of the ground crew and made the plane rudders wave. The gusts rattled the large pane of glass before me. I found it strangely pacifying and I fell asleep.

I woke up with heart palpitations and what felt like a cracked skull. I stood so quickly that a few nearby travelers shot me curious looks. I heard a bawl, looked out the window, and saw an empty luggage train almost crash onto its side. Inside, people sat on the floor and leaned against the walls. Our flight had been delayed another hour. I grabbed my bag, stumbled through the crowd, and escaped to the hall.

I found the Dunkin' Donuts and drank three doubles. I bought my usual supplies. Walking back down the hall to the gate I couldn't picture where I could possibly eat any of it. I opened, sniffed, and closed the smoothie. I didn't want any of it. I thought I should give the bags to someone, so I stopped at the restrooms and leaned against the wall. I waited for an opening, but even the people who seemed like they might have been receptive passed by too quickly for me to act. I slipped into the men's room, waited until I was alone, and threw everything away.

My seat was gone and there were only a few spots left on the walls. Stepping over the legs and bags I slowly headed for one in the far corner. I leaned back and looked outside. I struggled to use the rocking planes, doomed workers, and helpless debris to free myself from my mind and body, but they wouldn't comply. When I tried envisioning riding the storm, everything outside melted like a stuck film frame in an old-style projector. It threatened to ooze through the glass.

I took out my notebook and scribbled sentence fragments and partial quotes. I wanted to cross it all out, but I had to keep going.

> Living between ~~these places,~~ these times "... among the breakage ..." in that moment ~~of being either swallowed by the abyss or swallowing it: this is my balancing act, my struggle for~~

Outside, the ground crew looked as if they were in a hurricane. I wrote more:

> ~~I used to think that what I wanted was some form of revenge, against whatever slight—real or imagined—that I'd ever endured, no matter the size. But now as they assemble in my head, a din created by their call and my response,~~ I ask nothing of this world—money, fame, position. All I hear, in my private chambers is my repeated plea for mercy. Mercy. Mercy.

I put away the notebook, but I couldn't stop saying mercy. When I closed my eyes I saw it written on the insides of my lids. They called first class to board. I opened my eyes. I felt like I was looking through a violently shaking camera. Mercy. I thought that I might not ever say another word again. Mercy. Mercy. Mercy. Accelerating until it was almost no longer a word but a sound, a cyclone whipping around my brain, which if I didn't stop would strip my mind of everything I'd ever known, and there'd be nothing left but mercy. I searched for anything: a poem, a song, my children's faces and voices. But every thought and memory was caught by the wind and whirled beyond my recognition.

Section by section. They called us to board. I stayed in my corner. There were too many people for two planes. I was feverish, suddenly delirious. Legless. I wanted to sit but knew if I did, I'd never get up. I tried focusing on what I'd written, but it was inscrutable. I lumbered to the back of the line.

The agents made the final boarding call. I looked back over the seats. I couldn't remember having been there. I looked forward to the tunnel and tried but failed to conceive of a plane. I watched the agent check people's boarding passes. For a moment, I was entranced by the rhythm of her mouth and her hands: "Hello." *Take. Tear.* "Thank you." But I was jarred out of it when a man fumbled with his. It started again. I was trudging in a bog with giant hands pushing down on my shoulders. As my body moved slower, my mind sped up. I opened my mouth to call out for help, but I just started saying it again faster than ever: *Mercymercymercymercymercymercymercymercy.* The current and dread surged out of my stomach into my chest, bowels, and balls, through my limbs to my digits, up my spine and into my skull. Then it stopped, and I couldn't feel anything. I didn't know where I was in space—if I was on my feet or the ground. The voices around me were muted and garbled.

A new wave built. I knew it wasn't the flu. I knew it wasn't fatigue. It wasn't the past, current, or future bills. It wasn't a professional or personal identity crisis. It wasn't OCD, dyslexia, or any other cognitive dysfunction. It had nothing to do with being a drunk, the child of drunks, or a survivor of abuses and traumas. It wasn't the Hotel Savoy, the parasites in the fabric, or the monsters in the hall. It wasn't my blood sugar, or the fact that I was about to fly home and honestly didn't know who, what, or where to be when I got back—if I got back.

I was crying, openly. I felt like I was being swallowed and eaten from within. "Mercy." I was saying it again. I was starting to go numb, perhaps brown out, when another wave hit and was closely followed by a stronger one. All I could do was clench my jaw, wrap my arms around me, and wait. This was the beginning and it would get worse because it was the Hotel Savoy, the past year—my past life. I couldn't live with *this*. I'd never be able to live like *this*. Yet *this* had brought me here. I was about to fly into the tail of a storm and nothing—not art, magic, God, my wife, or my children—could stop that. The gale outside was making the jetway shudder and moan. I let go. I waited to be carried away. I felt, for a breath, relief. But I'd gone nowhere. It all came back and I knew I was insane.

Mercury Days

The darkness that was gathering outside has just rolled in over me. The darkness within is rising from the deep. I'm shrinking in between. It's not sadness: it's living between dread and the arrival of that apprehension. It's pummeling and eviscerating. It's unrelenting. Each time it comes, I know if I survive what's left of me will never be good enough. Right now, it doesn't matter what brought it. In these mercury days, the ordinary might seem catastrophic and catastrophe, mundane. No matter the initial or following event, I end here: I want to die.

I'm writing because I know there are others who've felt this and who are perhaps suffering it now: that solidified despair, concentrated, dissolved and run through your lymph and blood; the visceral plummet; the surge and gag in response to all those questions and answers. You must undo everything that's been done, but you lie flaccid, forced to watch the worst of your days play behind your eyes.

I want to tell you how it comes for me, how it's a part of me, how it leaves me unfit to love or be loved, how it seduces and demands that I go. I'm writing this for those who've lost their beloved in shadow; to those whose friends, lovers, siblings, parents, or children have killed themselves. I'm writing to tell you that I'm still here. I want to die, but I'm always trying to stay.

1

The staircase of my house is a switchback that is bolted to footings that run two feet below the cellar slab. From there, it rises four stories to the top floor. Under the first landing is a hollow—a cage framed by fourteen-gauge steel studs and joists—that functions as an unlit, unfinished crawl space. It's dark, cramped, and inhabited by centipedes and spiders. For the first two weeks of December 2007, I lived there.

I'd gone mad in the fall. By December, I was hiding from my wife and children. I couldn't let them see me. I couldn't see them because I loved them. Love for another in that state is the most pain I've ever felt. I've lost, and I've grieved and not grieved. I know why I feel sorrow. Madness, though, while writhing in it, has no motive, origin, or end.

My senses would almost always trigger a memory. Fond or awful, my brain would grab, spin, and twist them grotesque. Any taste was poison—any ache, cancer. Sometimes a notion could become so concentrated by this process that it would become a dense, burning core around which I'd orbit. Then it would suddenly disappear, leaving an emptiness whose pull I couldn't escape. I traveled around a greater entity—*the unmoved mover*—the center of a greater pain. And this system was a small part of a universal sorrow, which created, encompassed, and destroyed everything.

Even a hint of love or sex in a magazine ad, a couple holding hands or bickering on the street—would make me question my marriage. I'd review our twenty years, then jump from month to month until I couldn't help but begin a forensic investigation for signs. Was it me? Drunkenness, megalomania, and frigidity. Or her. I'd start over—large time to small, small to large; imaginary, faceless men, or specific ones. The only way to stop myself was to weakly ask Michaele and double over waiting for her answer, but it was as if I were confessing to some crime for which I was desperate for absolution.

Her answer, ironically, should've been: *"You're crazy."* Even though I was, she'd never say it. When she gently but firmly reassured me, I'd feel a horrible mix of shame and relief. The obsessive loop would terminate, and I'd hover in momentary blankness. As my consciousness returned, I'd hope that the loop wouldn't start again, or if it did, I could obsess about something else. I couldn't, however, help searching for the pain.

It would start again. I'd try to resist by mumbling, *"Crazy crazy crazy."* That would fail, so I'd pant, *"No no no,"* or *"Please please please."* Then I'd see James Brown on his knees, his attendants wrap him in his cloak, lift him, and help him to the wings. As in his concert footage, the godfather would tear himself away, throw off his cape, turn, and with the beat, will himself to center stage: *"Please please please . . ."* I'd watch him drag himself back to where he'd fallen. Then outside a car would honk, or someone would flush the toilet, or I'd hear my breath. I'd remember the original obsession and it would start again.

When I wasn't obsessing about my wife, I was humiliated by my impotence. Attempts at exercise were another kind of emasculation. If I tried to run or even take a brisk walk, I was numb footed, clumsy, and short of breath. When I tried to lift, my arms were like dead tentacles. I wouldn't do push-ups in private because, even alone, I was embarrassed. I couldn't break a sweat or pump a muscle. Rather than triggering an adrenaline rush, I was instead left with small, empty caves in my head, stomach, and bladder. I'd find a dark, quiet space, mutter, *"Please,"* and hold on.

Alex could hardly speak to me, and Miles would try to disappear. My madness was far worse than negotiating my anger. I think they'd have chosen that man over what I'd become. I can see myself then—dragging, mumbling if I could speak at all. I could tell they wanted to help, but they didn't know how. When we met in the kitchen or hall, they'd pause as though waiting for instructions. But I hadn't any, and we'd part more confused and afraid than before. They were losing their father to something nameless and incurable, and they didn't know how or why.

Every morning, Michaele checked my eyes to see if I was there. I rarely drank water, ate, or slept. I seldom changed clothes or washed. Nothing was worth the effort. Drinking meant pissing and eating meant chewing. Personal hygiene was for the benefit of others. Sleep meant lying on the couch in the fetal position obsessing or waiting for nightmares.

I know now that I looked like I'd given up. I resented Michaele for trying to help. I couldn't see that she was torn: the household had to function; she had to protect the kids from me, but she also had to reassure them that I was okay. And in the moments when I needed to be with them, she had to trust me. She constantly had to assess and reassess how to care for me—how to have a calm affect, how to be both present and removed. Much of our marriage's success had to do with our opposing temperaments. She was in charge during peacetime. I managed crisis. But during the greatest crisis we'd ever faced, I was useless. I was leaving her, and while trying to stop me, she had to prepare for life without me.

The first week of '08, we repeated a daily ritual. I'd sneak upstairs from the cellar. She'd wake up, find me in the den or wandering the house, check my face, and ask if I was alright. I'd lie. She'd ask again. I'd nod. She'd go help the kids. I'd isolate and wonder why she couldn't help me. I could see how badly it hurt and frightened her that I was so far beyond her care and moving further every day. But I understood she had to let me go and hope I'd return. I also knew that in some way it might have seemed like I didn't care anymore—that I wouldn't let her help because I wanted to leave her. She was part of the pain and the cure. The only way I could be near her was if she constantly reassured me that she'd loved me, only me, always. I needed her to stay away but be so close that she could be a part of me, feel what I felt, share the mantra—not for her sake, but for mine: *Please! Please! Please!* But I also knew how selfish this was. *"Nut the fuck up, you fucking puss."* Or: *"What did you expect—this is the cost of love?"*

I had things to do. I had taken a semester's leave. I had a book to write. Magazines and journals were soliciting work. I owed it to my family. I owed it to my friends. I wanted to get early tenure. I had the chance to do it all, and I wouldn't squander it.

First, I had a commitment at a literary conference in Key West. The organizer was inquiring about my travel plans and became worried when I told him that I wasn't flying but rather driving the fourteen hundred miles. Michaele intimated that it might not be a good idea. She'd recently been to Key West and referred to it as one of the most "boozy dropout places in the nation." She also had good reason to believe I wouldn't return. When she finally shared her fear, I told her I'd take a wingman. The only logical choice was Mike.

He told me he'd do anything I needed. By the time we organized our departure, it was almost too late to drive. A thirty-hour desperate romp sounded perfect for me—temporary oblivion, public speaking, and a constant unthreatening companion, but I relented and searched for airline tickets, which were of course double what they'd been months earlier. The morning before I was supposed to arrive when Michaele asked, "How are you?" I finally answered, "Not good." She watched me tear up and told me, "You're not going."

My agent agreed with Michaele. She offered to call the organizer, but I thought I should do it. I tried to explain, but it was a brief conversation that was primarily silence. I finally told him it was a medical emergency, and there was no way I could attend. Though he told me I was a major draw and that all the programs had already been printed, he said okay and wished me well.

This left me free to completely break down. *It* returned and in a more pernicious form. I didn't wait for Michaele to ask but told her, "I don't feel good." The cycle started again. Suffer, bottom, wait and fear, forget. Each bottom was lower. I wasn't allowed time to recover. Even when I'd forget, on some level I'd remember.

Michaele told me I needed help. I agreed. It couldn't be her or Mike. I knew I had to call a family friend who had a history of family mental illness.

The friend seemed to be expecting my call. Rather than being ashamed I felt comforted by this. I told her my mind was failing. She suggested we meet. On consecutive mornings we did. The first was an extended triage during which I told her all of my symptoms. She assured me I'd get better—that *"this will pass."* It ended with my secular confession. Although I don't recall what I revealed, she, again, insisted I would be well.

I felt relief for a while, but by dinner I was in pieces and had only a fragmented memory of what seemed to have happened days before. I called her again. She again seemed to have been waiting and told me to meet her the next morning at Starbucks in Brooklyn Heights.

She recommended I read Kay Redfield Jamison's *An Unquiet Mind*. I hadn't read much nonfiction concerning mental illness, but I decided to go look for it. It was something to do and shopping for a book was a challenge. I found it within an hour at the first shop I stopped at and had nothing to do for the rest of the day. So I wandered along the East River in the cold. That morning I felt better, perhaps in anticipation of, even briefly, feeling better, but when I arrived for our meeting and saw her sitting I knew something was different. I sat, tried to speak, but couldn't.

She let me stare for a long while until she spoke. "Here's what I think you should do." The first step was to call Michaele. The second was to leave Starbucks and meet her elsewhere because people we knew were eavesdropping, and this was none of their business. The next step was to get me to a psychiatric emergency room.

We walked silently to a diner. I ordered food and didn't eat it. Michaele came, looked at me, and went ashen. She turned to our friend and immediately understood how bad it had gotten and how much worse it would get. Still, even with her scholarly and empirical knowledge, obvious compassion, and clear plan for us to call her family friend who ran the Columbian Presbyterian ward and for the three of us—right then—to take a taxi there, I knew part of Michaele and all of me wanted to refuse. Our friend wasn't going to back down. The only compromise she was willing to make was that we go on our own. "Don't think about it. Go now."

Michaele and I left the diner and drifted a few blocks. She eventually hailed a taxi. We rode over the bridge and north up East River Drive.

The New York Presbyterian Psychiatric Emergency is at Sixty-Eighth Street and York Avenue. I didn't want to be driven into the cul-de-sac. The taxi stopped at the entrance. Michaele paid. We walked through the sliding door together, alone. She seemed more frightened than I'd ever been. I was going to quote Faulkner for her. She needn't worry. I was afraid, but I wasn't a coward. And if I survived, I knew I would never be afraid again. But I knew saying it wouldn't help her. It would sound empty—or crazy—so I kept it to myself.

In triage, the electricity was gone as was the dread. I was conscious, but I wasn't thinking of anything. I sensed that I was doing something gravely important. In the small, dim antechamber, I answered the nurse clearly. I think I managed a joke. I felt the same when they unlocked the ward door and I was led into another small room. This time there was a security guard. He asked for my watch. I gave my phone and valuables to Michaele. A nurse came in, handed me blue Styrofoam hospital clothes, pointed to the bathroom, and said I could change in there. I wanted to tell her, *This is a mistake,* and that I was me, but she looked at me as if to preemptively state, *No, it isn't,* and *No, you aren't.* And then I was ass-out in a two-piece in lockdown. I don't know if I somehow smuggled it inside, but I had Jamison's book with me.

Even with psychiatric emergencies there's a lot of waiting. There was nothing therapeutic about that place: not the indigents or the mix of body odor and disinfectant, not the plexiglass, chartreuse fluorescent lights, or colorless institutional paint. I stood up, walked to the security desk, and stood in the doorway. The guard looked at me quizzically. I knew he wasn't going to listen to a word I said. Certainly not *I want to leave*.

I didn't know the New York State laws concerning voluntary institutionalization. I had a vague idea that I could only be kept against my will if I was deemed a threat to others or myself. I tried remembering what I'd told the intake nurse. I wondered how she'd received my jokes—if she'd thought of them as jokes. Had I mumbled, repeated myself? Had I seemed coherent? Had I told her I wanted to die?

I was lucid—more than I'd been in months. I was no longer concerned about my past or present but rather where I'd be next. I was locked down now, and I knew if I stayed I'd be taken behind other doors, lost behind thick bureaucracies, and it might be a long time before anyone could get me out. I thought about fights to be reimbursed by insurance companies or to extract my car from a New York City tow pound, how institutions want to keep their money and take not only yours, but also your time. Worse, no one you encountered had any stake in any of this: they're not shareholders or vested senior management. Perhaps, at best, being helpful and efficient engagers, their position, their purpose is obfuscation. The longer it takes to get past them the longer they keep their jobs. I remember believing that because I thought about these matters I was in control of the situation. It would take some time and explaining, but I'd get out: I'd tell whoever was in charge that I felt better. I didn't need to reveal anything other than the events of the past few years—David, my father, sudden quasi-celebrity—was more than enough to emotionally tax anyone. I occasionally demonstrated bland, light masochistic tendencies. And I was a multi-trauma survivor. I simply needed to get into therapy, rest, and adapt to my new life: everyone gets the blues.

They let Michaele in the ward. I don't know how long she'd been waiting alone on the other side of the door, but she hadn't received any report on my status. I tried to look at her warmly, but I must have been a shock. I probably looked cold, devilish, or darkly comical in my hospital garb.

Unable to mask her sorrow and terror, she asked how I was and what was happening. I told her, Okay, better, and not much.

"They haven't done anything. I haven't spoken to anyone." I gestured at the hallway then went silent. I realized that it didn't matter what I did or didn't say. It wouldn't have made a difference: a negative diagnosis at this point wouldn't be much different than a positive one. It actually might have been worse.

Michaele leaned against the wall and scrutinized the ward, the vacant folk wandering in the hall and lying in the rooms. I sat on the gurney and opened the memoir.

After several pages, a young, petite intern approached, introduced himself, and asked me to accompany him to a room across the hall.

I leaned against the examination table. He stood just inside the door. He held a folder at his waist, which I thought ridiculous. He opened it. I could see he'd googled me and printed whatever public information he'd found. At the top of the stack was the *New York Times Book Review*. I wondered for a moment if that was what I looked like, until I remembered my blue uniform. He caught me looking at his cards. There was a long pause, which I enjoyed. I smiled a ghoulish, empty-eyed smile and waited.

"So, you've been having trouble?"

I wanted to ask, *Are you an idiot?* But I refrained. Instead, I told the doctor, "It's a curious thing, the phrase 'out of your mind,'" that it was my normative state. "My trouble, now, is that I'm in a way, in part, deep in it. More than I've ever been." He didn't respond. "It's not a good environment, Doctor."

He asked me to describe what I was feeling.

"Not feeling, only. It's what I'm thinking, too." I told him I didn't know if my thoughts triggered feelings or the other way around—or if they occurred simultaneously. Though considering the limitations of my state, I probably wasn't capable of realizing the phenomenon in totality.

"I have . . . perhaps this is the best way to convey: I have aesthetic theories."

He raised an eyebrow.

"About writing, Doctor."

He nodded.

"A writer must present sensorial information to the reader in an organized manner. Top to bottom, bottom to top, etcetera."

He seemed interested, so I continued.

"The reader, at the end of the descriptive passage, need feel that they've experienced the image, all its qualities, at once. In full." I waved to signal this was common knowledge. "But their *apprehension* or *experience* is a lie."

"How do you mean?"

I cut him off, annoyed. "Consider an equation, addition, a sequence of numbers. I ask you, 'What does two plus two equal?' You answer, 'Four.' I say, 'Add four.' You reply, 'Eight.' I then say, 'Add eight.' You respond, 'Sixteen.' I give you more numbers and finally stop. You have the final sum. Yes?"

He nodded.

"If I list enough, can you remember every equation? No. In a sense, they've disappeared. You're left with the answer."

I wanted to continue and tell him what I was seeing inside my head and floating in the room—numbers, plusses, and equals, on and on. Not gestalt, the sum isn't greater than its parts. But that sum, now, is more than a sum, a product that can be factored—though, not to its origins. This is ambiguity. But I lost track of my theory. I thought to try another example but knew it would probably confuse us both.

He waited, then commented, "That's a very interesting theory."

"Not really." I studied my hands. They looked and felt strange. I caught him watching. I cracked my knuckles. "Learning to do so is akin to developing early gross motor skills."

"Well, I think it's fascinating." He paused. "But we're off topic. What's going on?" He tried to sound casual, as if appealing to my lay sensibilities would relax me. I wanted to hurt him.

"I'm watching my mind fail, Doctor."

"Explain."

"It's simple. I can see my . . . let's call it, to appease the materialists . . . brain failing." I glared at him. It was stupid to be belligerent, but I knew that he'd already concluded what was wrong with me—that my lecture had proven a hackneyed theory. He, no matter the cost to me, had to pay for his conclusions.

"You're troubled by my claim. That I can see my brain?"

No answer.

"You've compiled information about me? You know I'm a writer?"

"Yes." He seemed vulnerable. I wanted to make him wriggle.

"You're beginning to think that I'm suffering from clinical depression, and while that is a dire circumstance, I might have a once-latent, now-active schizophrenia."

"I don't think so."

"Now you think I'm paranoid."

He shook his head.

"Data prevails, Doctor, not preconceived notions."

He nodded again, trying to appear composed.

"It's complicated, Professor Thomas."

"Really, Doctor, for whom?"

He neatened his sheets, closed his folder, told me somcone would be with me shortly and I could return to the hall.

I sat on the gurney next to Michaele and replayed the encounter until I was sure I'd committed it to memory and could recall it to use as a defense.

I kept reading Jamison. Michaele and I were next to each other physically—but distant in every other way. Sometimes I knew she was doing everything she could to stay away from me, but mostly I knew that I was impossibly remote. When she looked at me, it seemed as if she couldn't see me. Not my body but where I was inside—if I were there at all or if some other entity had displaced my spirit and had taken its place.

I began looking up from the book, hoping she'd look back. At first, I thought about winking, but that would've looked . . . crazy. I had to talk—tell her—but I didn't know where to begin. Past to present? Present to past? I hadn't rehearsed it, and I couldn't extemporize because I knew, eventually, I'd get lost. Worse—lose her. I thought of an introduction: *This is beyond me, but I will try. If I fail, even utterly, don't think of it as my diminishing power but rather a story larger than any I've told. I will eventually catch up—adapt—to its demands. Think of this as an excavation. I have, am, a collective of strata—strange creatures in different layers of decay, many of which are unnamed or have been mistaken for other things: more bird than lizard, warm-blooded, not cold.*

And this was great material for the book. Think about it: *The Broken King.* Think of Oedipus, Odysseus, Christ. Men who had been mistaken for one thing but were another, who had another purpose, but I couldn't get past any of the initial thoughts. I wound up singing in my head: *"Hark, the herald angels sing glory to the broken king."* I varied the voicing each time, sincere to shocking to desperate, after which I'd continue with sudden and increasing sadness *"peace on earth . . ."* closing on *"mercy mild."*

I attempted to quiet my mind with Jamison, but it was now written in a different alphabet. So, I tried to settle on one point in the past—something I could tell Michaele, myself, and the doctors who would soon break their meeting and announce the name of my ailment and the cure for it. I had to remember something, because trying to sit in the hall on the gurney next to her, I'd feel sick again.

I fell in love with her on the beach. It was a gray late afternoon in September. We'd walked quietly through the smell of the ripe, wild grapes and past the large but still pale rosehips that lined the boardwalk. We sat midshore on the dry, firm sand. The tide was moving out and the wind that always came at the close of day made whitecaps atop the current. I was thinking of the nor'easter and of the still and changing movement of the sea—not thought really, nor sense, but rather a quiet, strong roll of apprehension and wisdom. I had been a mannish boy, and the poverty, abuse, violence, and death that had always threatened to keep me a spent, desperate child now rendered me a gentle, grown, and soulful young man. She seemed older, too. But we were so young—the age when our first order comes around again, and innocence and experience are for some moments at peace. I looked at her—an English rose, an American beauty—so sure in the mounting bluster. So scared. It was the first time I honestly looked into someone's eyes—not furtively, enraged, or defiant—and so I was open to receive that dark, deepest love. And I think it was the first time I'd been seen or perhaps been at peace while being seen. I didn't know how we'd gotten here. I knew we probably didn't have a chance. We held hands. We would go home soon and have tea. There was going to be a storm.

Now, sitting on the gurney, I tried to look at her in the same way. The wind and the water, the old and the new sickened each other. In her eyes I thought I saw a trace of anger and bottomless fear.

I might have been gone for a while. The ward was hazier, as though someone was planting dry ice in all the rooms, but I could read again.

I was finishing a section on lithium when their meeting broke. The door opened and a blonde woman—a little older than me—burst into the hall. She clapped like a quarterback breaking the huddle and declared, "Let's rock and roll!" Michaele gasped and snapped, "No way." As the shrink and her team strode down the hall toward us, they passed us and began entering the various rooms asking each occupant—rhetorically—how they were and were answered with croaks and moans. One said nothing. An older disheveled man left his chamber and began shuffling between the walls. Though his clothes were filthy, he still wore them. Most of the others had their clothes as well. They all seemed beyond reach, muttering reports from wherever their minds had gone. Michaele and I looked at each other.

The staff made way for the doctor as she exited the last room. They formed a phalanx in front of us. The doctor stepped to the fore and spoke loudly.

"Mr. Thomas?"

I stared through her.

Louder. "Professor Thomas."

I didn't like her voice or the shape of her open mouth. I squinted and cocked my head to the side. She imitated me, so I righted mine. I could feel Michaele tense her body and heard her hold her breath. I pursed my lips and cocked my head again sharply. It made the doctor flinch. I could feel myself returning. My eyes, I think, turned on.

Though the sickness was worse than ever, I knew that fucking with her, at least temporarily, would give me relief. Michaele moved closer and slid in front of me. I thought I'd do her one better by reminding the healers who their father was, but I stayed quiet. The doctor, however, in order to see me, leaned to one side and said again, "Professor Thomas?" Louder. Now a question. I jumped on her sentence.

"I'm crazy, not deaf."

She stepped back, blank faced. Her charges murmured and shuffled. I found and stared at the intern who'd interviewed me until he looked away. I turned back to the doctor, who was now incredulous. She pointed at my book.

"Why are you reading that?"

"Why wouldn't I?"

I stared at her until she blinked then looked down.

"Professor Thomas, we'd like to help."

She waited for me to demonstrate some physical or verbal contrition, but instead I glared and ran my tongue across my top front teeth and raised an eyebrow.

She did her best to ignore my antagonism.

"Professor Thomas, you appear to be in distress." She went on to list my symptoms and paraphrase my narrative as though she were a judge listing my crimes—the rigged jury behind her. No verdict—just my sentence. "We'd like to keep you here—"

Michaele cut her off. "Why?"

The doctor cleared her throat and pretended to search for the words.

"We need to stabilize him. And in order to do so he needs to be monitored."

Michaele had seen enough psych wards, worked with enough patients, questioned their detainments. I found it darkly funny that rather than me being legitimized by her race and class, she was tainted by mine. She was—to them, despite my credentials—ignorant and powerless. She was hackled and openly belligerent in a way I'd never thought she could be.

"You want to drug him."

Nothing.

"You're not going to."

The doctor paused to think of a counter. The debate was done, but my wife wasn't going to stop. Growling and barking about my rights, how long we'd waited, having had my clothes taken away, their professionalism. How there was no "damn way" our children would ever have to visit their father in a psych ward. She listed the drugs that I would never be forced to take. I wouldn't have fucked with her.

"We're leaving."

"I'm going to put in a call to the chief of the unit."

"We're leaving."

The doctor looked at me, but I was "leaving" in my own fashion. I shrugged and did my best to smile. They left. Michaele sat next to me with her arms folded, fuming.

After thirty minutes, the doctor—with two lieutenants—returned with a brown jar, a business card, and paperwork. The release forms, outpatient clinic information, and Zyprexa, "a mood stabilizer."

"Mood stabilizer?"

The doctor responded, addressing me, though. "It's an antipsychotic, which at low dosage, what you'll take, is a mood stabilizer." She paused. "We need you to stay here for a little while longer to see how you react."

Michaele asked me if I wanted to. I sensed a brutal episode nearing. "Sure." I popped one and hoped, silently, it would hit immediately.

Michaele snatched the clipboard and began filling out the forms. While the doctor told me about how serious my condition was and that I couldn't take it lightly, I struggled against doubling over and screaming, "It's back!"

She noticed my distress because she asked, kindly, "How are you doing?"

I told her my stomach hurt because I hadn't eaten all day. She nodded, told us she'd be back soon. I waited until Michaele and I were alone then slumped. The sorrow welled up. The whirlwind started. I felt that I'd pass out but also never sleep again. I began obsessing about infidelity and death.

Twenty minutes later, the Zyprexa hit. My body began to tingle, and I thought my brain was slowly being smothered by thick, warm foam. It frightened me. The loop seemed to be disappearing and I had one more brief fright as I thought I would be smothered by it. I even briefly tried to fight to keep the vicious cycle going, but eventually everything in my head made way for a droning hum. The doctor checked me, made sure that I was going to the outpatient clinic the next day. Then we were free to leave.

Strangely enough, we stopped for dinner at a Neapolitan pizzeria. I ate. Michaele didn't. We must have looked like a couple that had just broken up. We took another silent cab ride home.

Michaele sat with me as long as she could. She fell asleep. I assured her that the medication was working and that I was much better. She should go to bed. I went to the den. I thought I owed everyone that much. I couldn't stay there long. I had six hours until my next dose, and I knew I wouldn't be able to mark that time in any relative comfort. I went out walking and tried focusing on being unfocused. After an hour, I realized that I felt nothing inside. Then there was a light splash of relief, which I took a moment to recognize for what it was. I felt a wave roll up. I braced for it, but it was gentle, and I was compelled to trust it.

I found myself at the mouth of the East River. Back then, Red Hook was still empty. Under the moon and behind the taillights of the garbage trucks, the old dog pack still ran. To my right was the Statue of Liberty, the tip of Manhattan, and, traveling north in my mind, the late lights of the island. To my left were the Verrazzano straits, the narrows, the bridge, the reach, and then, the open sea.

I imagined a loon cried. That wasn't right; it was a gull. They were out there now with me. I heard the creak of a boat's wooden deck. I was almost senseless—no lap, no wind, no brine—but I knew all the sea sounds in their absence. I knew the drift and fixity of the stars, and I sailed the empty wake of the water and the wind. Winter night on the Atlantic—there was going to be a storm.

I was back on the shore, crying, and I hadn't any idea why. I walked through the projects where the cops waited, but they ignored me. Still over a mile from home, I suddenly felt tired and sore, so I started running. I was dizzy and shuddering, but I kept on. I knew if I stopped, I'd die. Behind me in the distance, the water called, so I ran faster.

Once home, I went down under the stairs. I repeated, "I want to die." I wouldn't listen. I wrapped my body around my sickness and refused to let go. I vowed I wouldn't be locked up again. I wouldn't die drunk. I wouldn't die crazy. To live, I'd cling to this and never let go.

2

In fifth grade, my class was required to keep a journal. A few times a week we started our day with ten minutes of writing. Whatever the day and report I'd begin or end with either "I'm depressed," "I'm angry," "It makes me angry," or some variation of that theme. My teacher, Mrs. Aronson, would, while the others went out to recess, ask me to stay behind. She'd pull a chair up to her desk and ask me to sit. She'd leave my journal on her desk or place it on her lap. Either way, she'd run her fingertips along the edges as if she were about to open it, but she never did. Sometimes she'd ask how I was doing, others she'd wait for me to speak. I'd answer, "Okay." Or match her quiet with my own. She would smile, watery eyed, then let me go.

I'd go outside and watch the other kids playing Four Square, tag, or kickball. The cool girls rarely played. Instead, they huddled together pretending not to notice the games, how the cool boys fared.

I was always asked to join the games. I'd usually play, but sometimes I'd hover near the fretful, screaming boys. If they asked me again, I'd insult and mock them until they started crying.

Minutes later, I'd feel awful. Back in class, I'd watch whomever I'd hurt sit wounded and begin constructing an apology. That feeling would grow through the day and evening. I'd have no appetite for dinner, I wouldn't be able to concentrate on my homework, and no matter how important the assignment was, I wouldn't finish it. I'd neglect my clarinet. I'd lie awake most of the night envisioning my music instructor sighing with frustration, my teacher shaming me as though I weren't the author of those lonely missives to myself. I'd disappoint my buddies who were waiting for more of my cruelty. I'd let the scenes repeat until

I was trembling with shame and dread. Finally, they'd fade, leaving me in an exquisite melancholy, which I felt was right.

Otherwise, I'd find a remote place in the playground or in the airlock between the sets of double doors and stand disorientated by hazy, amorphous apparitions in my peripheral vision and the muted yells of the kids outside and aural hallucinations—barely audible mutters, whispers, and moans.

There was something—or some things—larger, which made me feel too much or too little, which seemed to predate me, which would live after me. I sensed that I needed to *be* more or *feel* more than it.

I used to gloss or jump over childhood events that I deemed narratively irrelevant. I've done that with the weeks of follow-up after my ER visit. I don't want to know how little I remember, or, I don't want to know how little I understood. I don't want to know how little control I had. I don't want to know where and what I might have been and where and what I am now.

And right now it seems foolish to recall and assess: it's *impractical*. And it seems dishonest—a pursuit conceived under the influence of illness. Rather than grounding, that practice seems to be my preparation for departure for a full flight from reality. I don't want an answer. I want more questions. I don't want surety. I want greater doubt.

I choose not to review because I'll reveal to myself and to you a set of beliefs that perhaps once served a purpose, but are now antiquated, even dangerous. My disease has progressed past their ability to contain it, or I never was really doing what I thought I was.

But even this exercise seems dishonest. It's circuitous and driven by a desire to remain in psychological and emotional stasis. So I'm left without a practice to either access the past or to let it go. I know I went to multiple follow-up sessions, but I was in shock, sleepless, and heavily medicated, so the events aren't really there to be reviewed. There's a gap in me. Something happened within it—is still happening, over which I've no control and I feel a retroactive vulnerability and ever-present danger. It feels like I'm actually and potentially being violated. But, again, here I am, now. My notions colliding with themselves, wondering what to say, how to say it, if the struggle to do so is worth it—if it's really a struggle at all. Once I was in northern Vermont for a fellowship and walking alone over deep, densely packed snow. I was headed west. And to the north, about a quarter mile away, high above me, just behind the tree line, I thought I heard a wolf howl. I turned and looked up. Suddenly I was blind and deaf and had no sense of where I was or had been and I apprehended a missing link in my evolution. I needed someone to tell me what had happened, but I was alone. The wolf couldn't tell me, so I decided it was winter lightning.

I've rarely had anyone to talk with about this, or any other private phenomena. I get lost in corroborating it with myself—which I've never, honestly, been able to and with each failure I feel myself fading away. I get found in depicting it for others, but as the story ends, so do I. It's been hard—living like this—talking and writing at people. I want to share, I think at times I have, but right now, I don't know. I tell myself, as comfort, it's surreal, or unreal, but mostly I just feel sick and alone, and of this I'm sure.

So, I talk to myself or I talk to others who either aren't or never were here. Or I think about other experiences conveyed over the ages. Back in my room in Vermont, the practical response was to consider Paul and the line of thinkers and doers from epistles of the metamorphosed zealot to John Newton's "Amazing Grace" and settling on Dr. King's "Letter from Birmingham Jail."

But for the analogy to have traction I'd have to have been one person before and another after. I would have to have gained purpose, sight, and action. I think that in those early weeks I lost some part of me—something strong, whole, and good—that I'll never recover. The man I was is gone, but worse, the man I'd wanted to be is too and I don't even remember who that might have been.

Dishonesty is an untenable state. We feign ignorance when knowing and claim knowledge when unaware. We must be hypervigilant of being discovered and constantly attend to our omissions and additions, our subterfuge we conceal from ourselves. It's always easier to lie. Others forgive me, but I don't. I run to and hide from my own judgment.

Writing about the past evokes too much pain. I'm afraid to admit what I did and didn't do—what was done to me. I'm ashamed to admit I've never been able to control my behavior and that the lightest touches hurt. I told you that I'm writing this to you, for you, perhaps even with you—even for us. As soon as I tell you though, the impulse to do so fades and with it the belief that I'm sincere. I don't know what I'm saying, who I am, or if all of this is myopic self-pity given some credence because it's now documented that I'm sick. I want someone to tell me. I want to trust, but in my experience there's no one I can.

My mother used to ask us, "Why haven't I cracked up?" I didn't understand that it was a rhetorical question. I'd stand there dumb and wondering if her visible fissures and faults were the causes or effects of a deep heaving and breaking.

Somewhere, though, in her tone—exasperated or Socratic—was the answer: *Get real and get tough.* While my father couldn't or wouldn't deal with anything, my mother dealt with everything, and so she didn't have time to address her own needs; there was no *self-care*. I know she suffered from depression, but it was buried beneath so much trauma, alcohol, stress, and responsibility, that even now it seems attempting to treat it would be cowardly indulgence.

When I was older and she'd ask, "Why haven't I cracked up?" I'd answer in my head, *You already have.* But there she was, and I thought I could see her life in full and in the moment: brief joy, born and erased by acute and chronic pain. But she still fed us and loved us with as much of herself as she could offer.

In my first daily sessions when my new doctor asked how I was doing, I couldn't answer. I couldn't answer any of her questions: "How long have you been feeling like this?" I'd try, but all I could do was start to think about the question—a month, a year, a life. I felt I was wasting her time and that I was disappointing both her and Michaele, who sat beside me, helpless. If I could do it over again—a perverse notion—I would've said that in this moment, it was that I didn't know. But she'd say, "That's time." The session was over, and I felt I'd accomplished nothing. In future sessions, she didn't press though. Sometimes I would just nod my head and smile. I might have said some funny things. I remember her laughing. She'd tell me I was okay and that it was time. I was getting better at ignoring invasive thoughts—by day, at least—and beginning to enjoy the company of others. It was a little over a week since I'd come to the ER and I was almost *back*. My doctor said at the end of each session, "You're going to be okay." And I'd leave believing it.

Back at home, I realized I couldn't live under the stairs, so I moved up to the den. I spent nights there, forcing myself to be interested in the books I once thought sacred. Now they confused me.

So, I played my electric guitar, unplugged. At first, I was happy to quietly strum with my thumb. Then I'd try a nuanced R&B rhythm or a country lead. I'd feel *okay*—even forget myself. Then I'd try to play something beyond me—Mick Taylor's solo in "Winter" or Dickey's part in "Blue Sky." I'd try for hours to connect with my fingers, but no blues would come—not the way I felt them. I'd feel the compulsive, alcoholic *more*, the mounting OCD, then the self-loathing that I'd had such a ludicrous aspiration. So, I'd place my guitar out of reach and sit rigidly on the couch until dawn when I got to take a pill.

I tried sleeping in my bed again. It was difficult, but I accepted that it wasn't Michaele but me. I was envious that she could sleep and felt abandoned when she did. I was ashamed of my thoughts. I didn't want to talk about them. I didn't want to hurt or frighten her.

After a few nights of chronicling the life of my inner child, I started cutting myself—my hips, back, and between my toes as I had done as a kid. It didn't do anything, so I started imagining my body. I'd always been dysmorphic, and the mirror rarely offered an honest reflection. In my mind, I could see fat and bloat, so I'd starve and binge and purge.

I had to punish myself for the pain I felt and punish myself for being so weak as to feel pain, then punish the punisher, and so on. I contrived that my break was a willful, sinful act (or that I'd always been this way and that sin was my condition). The intercession, though, wasn't divine, but rather self-inflicted torture, which is really a wild flight from God.

When I was an adolescent, I'd talk to my friends. Sometimes talking worked. Mostly, though, it was the time spent together. We'd make or discover a plan, ride the T into Harvard Square to search for posters in the COOP, browse through the collections in the comic book store, grab pizza at Pinocchio's or an Elsie burger and eat on the Brattle Street Mall. We'd sit outside of Au Bon Pain and watch the chess matches while listening to the skaters clatter their boards over the bricked sidewalks.

When we could drive, we would cross the New Hampshire border for fireworks or pick a town and feel our way on the back roads to find it. One week, Chris Bowen and I decided to sample every McDonald's in Eastern Massachusetts to find the best French fries and cherry pies, and then we set out to collect a tray from each. We never completed the task, but we kept in motion: B-side mixtapes of our favorite bands or albums we'd just discovered. Yes, often we were ridiculously stoned, playing air guitar along with *Hendrix in the West*, screaming, "No fuckin' way!" when Jimi turned feedback into supersonic jets and missiles, explosions and shockwaves. "No fuckin' way, dude!" was all we could say. Anything else would come out like a donkey honk or a geezer wheeze, followed by hysterical laughter. Chris would have to pull over, too. When he was composed again, he'd drive a few car lengths and it would start over again. "I am so fuckin' baked. I'm stoned out of my tits!" We'd blindly search for the nearest highway—east, west, north, south—it didn't matter as long as he could drive without sharp turns or having to stop. We'd pop in a mellow tape—folk, blues, or soul—and with aching heads and burning throats try to find our way back home.

I never felt that I was running from hurt and darkness. I was running with it—high, tripping, drunk, all three, or even clean. It and I were, together, a place I belonged—a diner, thrift store, the foothills of Mount Monadnock, and the rocky beaches of Cape May, counting the cherries in a cherry pie. *I could live like this.*

I could live like this in blackouts and withdrawals, in patrol cars—any kind of trouble, real trouble made *it* real or connected me to others—real or unreal—who felt as I did. I was Orpheus without Eurydice, Achilles without Patroclus, Cool Hand Luke, the Little Drummer Boy. I was Robert Johnson or Willie McTell or Otis by the dock of the bay.

It had always been like this. But I'd always gotten over it—most of the time.

I was growing suspicious of my psychiatrist. Though she hadn't said it, I thought she had been trying to imply that I was bipolar. I remembered that I suffered from anxiety and perhaps panic disorder. I had the history to prove it—late night ER visits that had started when I was a teen and first tried getting sober. My distrust made me angry. My anger distracted me from the fact that I'd been so sick. I knew I needed to stay medicated but I thought I could be done with therapy. I had an out. My insurance only covered five or six sessions with my psychiatrist. I had to transfer to the outpatient clinic and see a social worker. I didn't want to go.

But I went. She was young—just out of social work school. I didn't say much the first session. She told me that I was safe and could "open up" to her. The next sessions I did—or I thought I did. She told me that I was speaking metaphorically. I wasn't in the classroom and instead of explaining myself by proxy of archetypical characters I should speak about my own experiences and feelings. I asked if I could tell her about the things I imagined—what I saw when I thought. "Of course." She said. "But I want you to start with something you remember and how it made you feel."

So I did. For the next few sessions I freestyled about my father, racism, and sexual abuse. I told her that when I reflected on "particularly painful events" I'd imagine myself wandering the Arctic, joining the French Foreign Legion, or sailing into rogue waves far out at sea. I told her that in sixth grade I tried to ask out Nooni Hamerlin and she was mean to me. We'd just moved to Newton and I was in a new school. I wore the same thing every day—a disintegrating gray too-small cotton Patriots sweat suit that my father had given me. I secretly changed into it every morning on the way to school. At recess I said, "Can I ask you something?" I thought she rolled her eyes, held her nose. She walked away and joined her girlfriends. They started laughing. I kept wearing it though. Every day after school I'd walk down to Newton corner, to the Mass Pike overpass. Through the cyclone fence I watched the traffic. I'd try to make myself cry but couldn't and I'd wonder why. I'd feel the links loosen, the gaps of the metal widen. I remembered the peace I felt when I thought I could fall through.

My therapist looked like she was grieving. After a long and uncomfortable silence she asked, "How long have you been having suicidal ideations?" I'd never realized that there was a connection between imagining and desiring death.

I left her office after that session and wandered the blocks to Central Park. For the first few, I regretted not having challenged her. I should've told her that I'd never tried to kill myself. Yes, one could interpret my drinking as having been a death wish, but one could also see it as a desire to live—an antidote to what I wouldn't accept as a terminal disease, a recklessness that depicted how much I wanted to feel alive. Except I was too young to understand that death was . . . real. If she questioned that analysis, I'd posit that I'd spent much of my drinking years trying to get sober.

If she was right, then I'd been having them as long as I could remember. I never tried to construct them, rather they'd appear. I never thought of them as epiphanies. Until I knew what they were—clinically—they were images, sensorial answers to questions I hadn't known I'd asked, responses to prayers that I didn't know I'd uttered. I walked and wandered and searched for what I'd tell her in the next appointment, but I found it hard to think clearly long enough to form any thesis—even for myself.

I entered the park and made my way to the zoo. I wanted to be near the polar bears. They were much more compelling than anything I was grappling with. I didn't want to write. I was afraid to, but I knew it was the only way I'd have a chance of organizing my thoughts. I watched the bears dive and paddle in the turquoise water. I took out my notebook.

—On annihilation

I want to die? Or is such an exercise indicative of, at very least, curiosity—there's something I seek? I'm on the brink. To do or not do is to die? "Every action is a step to the block, to the fire, down the sea's throat."

I couldn't write anything else. Rather than organizing my thoughts they became scattered and vague. The swimming bears were ragged, dirty, and restless. Their water was toxic. I didn't know where I'd go, but I had to leave.

I stumbled south down Fifth Avenue past the landmarks—public and private. At Twenty-Third Street, I cut over to Broadway and headed for Union Square. When I got there, I traced the perimeter of the park twice and settled near the playground at the north end. It was cold and blustery but sunny out, so I was surprised, saddened even to find it empty. I sat on a bench by the gate. As soon as I did, I remembered why I had to keep moving. I didn't want to move, though. I was tired and ashamed of being bullied by a feeling. So, I bent over, jammed my elbows into my sides, and waited until the feeling passed and I could walk when I chose to.

I'd made it through another attack. It was just past noon, which meant I had two hours to go until school pickup, followed by a ten-minute walk home, perhaps another ten if we stopped at a deli or drugstore for a snack or even thirty to forty-five for a couple of slices and some homework. We could even pick up groceries. I could start dinner, listen to everyone's day, have tea with Michaele, eat, and watch a couple of kid shows, do bath and books. I'd have to find some way to keep moving or sit and brace for the next surge—four hours—then I could take a pill, fight the urge to pop more, wait thirty minutes for the encroaching dullness, and for the next thirty feel it as it crept and grew until I was—almost entirely—it. I'd turn on the TV and search for anything to watch as long as it was sexless.

3

By late January my brain was working *better*. That better mostly allowed me to obsess about futility. I could, I found, defend myself against my therapist. I'd minimize the damage of each session by adhering to a rigid schedule. I couldn't fake wellness for the entire appointment, but I could break it up into small pieces: be three to five minutes late, appear harried for two more; two or three minutes of greeting and pleasantries; a minute of duplicitous silence during which she'd think I was being reflective or stuck. Just as she'd inhale to ask a question, I'd point out something I liked, found flawed, or wasn't sure of. *"I like your shoes. I smell vinegar: Did you have salad for lunch?"* I'd point at her coffee cup: *"You're a tea drinker, no? I've been cutting down on caffeine. I've been sleeping better—funny how I never thought that it might be part of why I can't sleep."*

I'd scan the walls and comment on the paint—color and application. I'd keep this up—for as long as I could, hopefully ten minutes. Then I'd start quoting and lecturing on aesthetics, form and function, function and form, Baldwin's sacred and profane, Al Green and soul, protest and carnal love.

If that wasn't enough, or if she wanted to hear about me, I'd talk about how I was struggling with my writing, how I couldn't find or manipulate the vehicle to transport the content. I couldn't concentrate long enough to write much. "I'm out of shape." But every day it was getting better.

When she asked about my home life, I'd fabricate conversations I had with Michaele and plausible breakthroughs and conflicts with the kids. I'd never talk about money. But like lockdown, it was hard to remember what I'd said, and it was difficult to plan what I was going to say. Finally, she'd glance at the clock above my head, ask about my meds, and try to summarize the hour. I'd do my best to leave with a nod and a smile.

Somewhere outside, I'd lose the smile and feel the dread again. And I'd walk. I'd almost always be on the verge of crying. On days when I didn't have therapy, I'd still get on the train to Sixty-Eighth and walk north or south on First Avenue. Then after a mile or so, I'd turn west and eventually south toward Union Square. I'd want Elisabeth to call me, but even when she did, I either wouldn't answer or I would tell her I was somewhere else. Heading downtown, I'd avoid walking past the Grove offices in case she happened to be looking down onto Broadway—just the same, though, I wanted her to see me passing by.

Day by day, my walks got longer. I'd concentrate on my footsteps and my breathing. I'd imagine I was part of the city's consistent rhythm: inhale on the one, footstep on the two; exhale on three, footstep on four. But after a few days of that, I started feeling crazy again: the beats, the regularity, began to conjure the frightening apparitions I'd seen and heard in the months before. Once I'd get home, I'd lock the door, hide in the bathroom, and run the water so my family thought I was doing something normal. I'd lie about having come from the gym. I'd gather books, papers, pads, and pretend to work.

I started traveling with Alex's iPod. I pinched an expensive pair of earbuds from an electronics store, set the music to shuffle, and roamed Manhattan listening to random songs. More than half the songs were "mine," many of which I hadn't remembered loading. Some I didn't like. Alex was twelve and had twelve-year-old, intolerable tastes—partially. I didn't, however, skip any of his pre-tween nonsense. It was my way of countering obsession—my own method of cognitive therapy. Instead of getting angry or dismissive, I concentrated on tuning them out—or, closer, I constructed a barrier between them and me through which I couldn't hear except for the bass pulses and drum vibrations that one might hear from the other side of a wall. Better yet—cocktail clatter. These listening sessions reminded me of how as a child I'd protected myself from sensorial overload—almost. My coping mechanisms weren't broken; they were misdirected. I didn't need to compartmentalize my brain; I needed to make it a compartment. The outside world was fucked—not me. Or I could try to once again, permanently, be apart from it. There wasn't a middle ground. Everyone else was wrong. There were only extremes.

One afternoon, though, I was walking down Broadway to SoHo when Nick Tremulis's "A Man's Way Out" came on. He was a friend of a friend. I'd met him almost twenty years prior in the East Village. I was in a bar, young and drunk and about to give up on my dream of being a folk-blues sensation. A rock trio was playing. They were good, but their sound system was weak, so the band's music sounded impotent. No one was paying much attention to them anyway. There were rumors that Nick was coming. He'd, in fact, been there most of the evening.

Late into the second set, the front man called Nick up to play a couple songs. He'd been sitting only a few barstools away from me. He walked up to the platform and picked up a maple-necked black-and-white Strat. He was wearing a leather jacket and vest and a top hat, which on most anyone else would've looked idiotic. I could tell as he tuned that I was going to hear something remarkable. I did. The sound was richer, louder, and more aggressive—as though they'd plugged into a new set of larger amps. He tore through a blues piece—almost recklessly but with a control that makes certain musicians simply better. He stood still while he played—eyes closed, back slightly arched, sloping more when he soloed. I'd seen Muddy Waters, Albert King—some of the great performers of the last fifty years—and that night, Nick rated among them.

I didn't meet him that night or see him again, but after a few years when I was visiting my friend who knew him, he wanted to play me a cut from an album Nick was working on. I had to leave, but he insisted I listen. "One cut," named "A Man's Way Out."

> *Bold thoughts of killing you*
> *I said killing you*
> *This wall ain't no place that you choose*
> *You turned these fine boots into slaughterhouse shoes*
>
> *Do you know how it feels, man*
> *To know you ain't worth a damn*
> *And pushed to the side like a plate*
> *To make room for coffee and angel food cake*
>
> *Won't you give a man a man's way out*
> *A man a man's way out*
> *Won't you give a man a man's way out*
> *And I'll go*

    It was like hearing something written by Neil Young and Leonard Cohen, sung by a crooner who was backed by The Band—not there, there, then gone. Guitar followed by the opening refrain, the second verse suddenly underpinned by horns, say, and muted trumpet, which drop out for the two lines to be replaced by a distant pedal steel. The horns come back with the chorus.

    The next time through—first the slide, then the horns, but always central that thumbed, hesitant guitar—which sounded like it was being played by one who's only recently mastered the chords. His voice part hopeful but mostly resigned.

    For a good while after, I was ruined for other music. I never got a copy and kept forgetting to make one. Finally, I thought that it might be best to forget it.

    Years later, I found the song on iTunes. While I was waiting for the light at Houston, it shuffled on. I paused it, turned around, headed north a few blocks to Washington Square Park, sat on a bench, and listened to the four-minute song for almost an hour. I got up and continued listening while I slowly walked home.

    Nick's song became "it" for me: the answer. It wasn't didactic or instructive. If it was at all cathartic, it was that the song was so painful to hear it relieved me of any hope of future health. It was an ironic comfort: anguish was real, profound even. Grotesque. It wasn't metaphysical or philosophical. Thought wasn't the trigger for physical pain; nor had my brain broken my mind. The word was flesh and the flesh was word. Together: they were too big to contain with thought or action. I realized—fighting, fleeing, or capitulating—that I'd lost a long time ago, but this fact didn't sadden me. I didn't despair.

If it had been an LP, I would've worn out the grooves. I played it for hours each day—played it in part. Start. Stop. First chord. Stop. First word. Stop. Play until chorus, until the horns or the pedal steel slide, five, ten, twenty times before letting it finish. I shared it with others. No one cared about its merits. They'd say, "That's great," or "That's so sad." I didn't lament that no one really got it. It was my song anyway. Not a proxy. Not a prayer. Just a song.

I walked the streets start to finish, point to point. I'd once carried Eliot. Now I carried this up and down the avenues and streets in my "slaughterhouse shoes."

I started playing guitar again. I'd sit up with my unplugged electric at night, strumming with my thumb and whispering the lyrics or humming the melody. And as I did when listening, I'd start and stop, sometimes because I got it wrong—flubbed the strum, missed the change or the note (usually flat)—or because my performance sounded like mumbling crap. My hands would tremble or my voice would crack. I'd sit back and idly pick and wonder if I should write my own song, but I'd only manage a few words, so I'd go back to playing Nick's.

I began to wonder about the *you*. Was it Michaele? My shrink? The hospital? My insurance company who wanted a clinical diagnosis? Or, of course, me?

I knew then that my therapist was right. I'd always wanted to die.

The first suicidal ideation I clearly remember was when I was four. I was walking with my mother to pick up my brother and sister from school. It was an unseasonably warm spring afternoon, but my mother's dress code was calendar and not weather based. Since it was well before Labor Day, I was in my Calvert's painter's pants.

We'd just crossed the driveway of McNamara's concrete company. I always looked down the rough path to the enormous piles of sand and gravel and listened to the rumbling. We were always careful there, though, because the orange cement mixers and dump trucks made frequent entrances and exits.

When crossing the street, my mother uncharacteristically decided to jaywalk. That day, she took my hand and pulled me off the sidewalk. North Harvard was two lanes and at rush hour could be busy. The traffic never stalled but rather sped up. Travelers used it to avoid jams and shorten the distance between Allston and Harvard Square or Watertown. They took advantage of its relative openness and often roared up and down it at half again—sometimes twice the twenty-five-mile-per-hour speed limit. And unlike today, weren't required to stop for pedestrians in crosswalks.

Nothing was coming from either direction, but she rushed to get us across the street. She led. I trailed. When I was about to cross the centerline, I slowed. The yellow paint on the blacktop made me think about a fight I'd seen just days before between a hornet and a bumblebee; they'd rolled and twisted and stung each other's undersides.

I stopped on the crest. The exposed quartz and embedded glass sparkled. My canvas navy Flyers had metal eyelets and white rubber toes. I heard the rumble of an oncoming truck. I twisted free of my mother's grasp. She snapped, "Come on!" But she didn't turn or stop. I turned and saw the truck, now fifty yards away. I took two side steps to the middle of its lane, poised like a shortstop. Thirty yards. There was nothing but the grille and the chrome bulldog jutting from the hood. The truck driver blew his trombone horn. My mother screamed my name and grabbed my shirt with one hand and my arm with the other. I remember that there couldn't have been nearly enough time—and wondered how something so big with a horn so proud and deep could have brakes that whined so high. She dragged me to the gutter the dump truck bellowed past. We were still in the gutter. My mother cocked her arm and waited, open-handed, the other hand around my wrist. She was squinting against the sun, the look on her face a combination of rage, horror, and joy. I wanted to hug her—then lie down in the warm, dusty gutter and go to sleep.

4

Elisabeth called to "check in." I did a terrible job of trying to assure her I was okay. After a short, almost silly exchange, she asked if I wanted to get coffee. I didn't hesitate to agree. I winced, though, when she asked if an hour was okay. I wanted to say no, that I had to talk to her immediately, but I didn't know how to tell her.

Obviously, I should've been writing all this, but I couldn't. I couldn't tell her that I could no longer write. I didn't want her to think I had writer's block—that wasn't it. I had plenty to write out, I knew the form—the macro- and microcosmic—the sequence of the chapters to the arrangement of words—the words alone. I wanted to tell her and the only meaningful way to do so was to write it.

We met outside and sat on a bench near the southeast corner of the square. The park and surrounding streets were full. All I did for the first several minutes was avoid looking at her and pretend to be preoccupied with the lunchtime clamor. I didn't know how to start. The more she waited, staring, the less I had to say. The more I thought about it the more anxious I became. I began wondering if I were sick at all. I listened to my voice in my head. No words: all I heard was a whine. So that's where I started.

"It's not so bad. I'm okay." To which she leaned in and looked at me with deep concern. She stared like that for a minute, leaned back slightly.

"I'm worried about you."

I wanted to quote my first doctor: *"You'll be okay."* I wanted to remind her just how low I'd been. But also wanted—needed—to tell her that I was awful. Nothing had changed. In fact, in many ways I was much worse. This wasn't an acute episode but rather a chronic condition. "It's always been this way. It'll always be this way." But whatever *it* was was impossible to get out. It wasn't a thought or emotion but rather a near-stagnant vision and physical sensation and though it was excruciating to suppress, I knew that it would be worse to fail.

But even if she could listen, hear, and understand, I knew—as I feared for Michaele in the hospital and my children at home—that it was insane for her to risk her time on me, even a small part of it, for what to me, every moment, I feared was a futile endeavor. I had two choices: beg her to save me or tell her to let me go.

I wanted her to go, so I could disappear. But I knew she wouldn't, so I turned away from her and watched the taxis and delivery vans fighting for lanes on Park Avenue South. I knew she would wait there for me to return. I thought I could distract her with a story or meditation while I made my escape, but ironically I was whole—one body, one mind.

"I don't want to be here."

She straightened. Shook her head. She seemed ready for this moment when she'd be able to reason with me. She had a list of things I had to live for—my family, friends, career—but I was ready for that and sat unmoved, which spooked her and caused her to repeat her reasons. She lost track of her assertions and spoke each out of the original sequence, growing more worried with each recitation. The more impassioned she got the more numb I became. By the time she stopped to check if anything had reached me, my only sensation was of being lifted up by a force that would soon take me out of the world.

She could see it, too. Each of her reasons, for me, was a reason to leave and accelerated my ascent. I didn't want to tell her because I knew it would intensify her plea. I didn't want to hear her voice or mine. When she paused again, I just told her, "No."

She reached out and lightly took me just below my elbow. Not a grasp or a reassuring touch, but somewhere between and more for her perhaps than me, as though she needed tactile proof that I was still there. I looked down and laughed.

It had an effect—though I don't know if it was the one she'd intended. She'd stopped me in midair—made me, even, forget that I'd wanted to leave, caused me to laugh at her, given me some time out of my mind. While it hadn't made me want to live, I hadn't for those minutes needed to die.

I could've stayed in the park well into the evening, even followed her home like a stray. I took my arm back, waited a quiet second—we both did—to see if I'd be carried away, but I wasn't. We tacitly agreed that for the moment I was safe. I said thank you and goodbye, then descended into the station to get the train home. At the last stop in Manhattan, my teeth clattered and my body shivered uncontrollably. I knew it was useless to put on my coat. Under the East River, the sick hole in me reappeared, but this time it felt like a crumbling tunnel under filthy water. I replayed our afternoon until I lost control and I was forced to watch and listen to it—a film loop at 10x speed. We stalled just off the Brooklyn shore. I sat wishing I could erase, burn, unlive the day, and that she'd never known me at all.

People have told me that they're glad *Man Gone Down* ends happily, but I've always thought its close is, at best, ambiguous. It still seems to me a novel-length suicide note, and that is the dominant autobiographical content. Now, however, I know rather than the protagonist's, it's mine. After completing his tasks and journey, he sits with his family, broke, in a borrowed car, spent. He stares through the windshield into the night, then turns and looks at his children. He hopes that his boys are protected by sleep and dreams. His daughter, a toddler, blows him a kiss. Perhaps it's to welcome him back, but considering the mood and tone of the scene, she could also be saying goodbye.

I don't blame the reader for an optimistic interpretation. It's probably my failure not theirs. Whatever the case, that late January of '08 I realized—more deeply—why I frightened Michaele, caused Elisabeth to repeat her list of reasons to live, and rattled my shrink: most people don't want to die.

Michaele had long ago conceded that I was inherently and experientially unique. Elisabeth wasn't ready to openly admit it because to do so meant that I was alone, unreachable, and that no one knew what to do with me. My shrink, who I now openly called the Witch Doctor, had remarked weeks before that not many people could clearly and calmly articulate their insanity while being so and that even retrospectively it was a very difficult thing to do.

But I wasn't living with my words, at least not those I shared with them. I rarely remembered what I'd said. When I did, I seemed incoherent. With Michaele, I knew that I sounded angry, paranoid, defeated, or all three. I'd learn later, though, what was bizarre—chilling even—was that I was lucid. I made sense of the senseless in words and actions. I'd move slowly, either stiffly or limply, and I'd find her watching me—or my husk. She'd search for me—my eyes—which were always, I'm told, watery and almost lifeless. When she asked how I was, all she got was a cold reporter who unflinchingly informed her of what was going on inside.

"In there," I was trying to talk to myself. That voice wasn't anything like the one she heard. It was scared, restless, even manic. In there, I was living multiple lives. Where I once had multiple personas for the public, I now had only one. And I now had to manage them—inside—and they refused to conform to my will. I knew I wasn't schizophrenic, but I had to admit that I had a severe personality disorder.

Inside were the remains of past lives—not necessarily the most recent—that were in the foreground; those which sometimes stepped to the front and tried to remain there; those which I'd lost and found, forgotten and remembered, pleasant or horrific; those which though I'd "lived" them, I'd no knowledge of having done so. And was just now becoming aware of—latent lives.

There were things inside me I'd thought I'd resolved years before but hadn't addressed. Things I thought I'd understood but was only obliquely beginning to; things I'd understood but hadn't the means to convey to myself or others; things that I could've but for whatever reasons hadn't; things I'd said and related; things I'd said that had been rejected or ignored by others and the worst things that had been heard and celebrated.

I realized Michaele's fears hadn't much to do with practical matters. They weren't selfish questions: how she'd handle domestic life. They were basic: How will I live without my husband? How will my children live without their father? I knew she believed that she'd rather live with a piece of me than nothing at all, that she hoped I'd find the others and make myself whole, and if not then regenerate from that piece, but as I neared my destination—loving her with whatever I had left—I knew that the only way we could be together is if we both were in pieces.

If we stayed together, we'd have to make a new pact—a second marriage—neither of us could break anymore, we'd have to maintain our current conditions. I knew we couldn't and believing we could was weak, letting go of strength. Together, we could minimize the damage for everyone.

There was Elisabeth, too. She was devoting too much time to me—usually when I was at my worst. I knew she was worried about me when we didn't meet. Unlike with O'Reilly and Dominic, I had never and would never be able to give her anything. She'd tell me I'd given her "The Book" and had more books to offer. I wouldn't tell my shrink about this. I didn't want her to suspect that I'd any intentions of hurting myself.

I stopped listening to Nick's song because I loved it. It seemed to love me too and so I didn't want it near me. It's the blues but I was willfully trying to make it hurt me. I didn't want my sickness to bleed into it. It deserved better.

I could "hang on" until Alex's birthday on the tenth, Ella and my mother's on the sixteenth. Valentine's Day could be a break too. Miles's came after spring. That was too far away to call.

I kept walking the city. Now I listened to Dylan, Van Morrison, Marley, and Sam Cooke. "I Dreamed I Saw Saint Augustine." "Astral Weeks." "Time Will Tell." "The Hem of His Garment." Over and over. Part of a song. An entire song. The four in a row. Sometimes I'd feel safe. I'd remember that I once felt joy. I remembered that there were long stretches of time—perhaps years—when I hadn't been afraid. But then I'd remember that I'd lived under my stairs and believed that my family hadn't noticed. It hadn't been that long ago. I needed more time. My therapist and I needed to patiently find the right medication. We were only trying to keep me stable. I didn't want to be stable. I wanted that ecstasy that allowed me to think, act, and believe. I wanted to remember what it was to be without the dread of being. I remembered effects without causes. Causes didn't matter. It didn't matter why it seemed I wanted to shoot myself in the head. It only mattered that I hang on and the only things that kept me here had been unearned exuberance, rage, aggressive buoyancy, a twisted kind of joy, or frenetic love.

5

One day in late February after I'd sat quietly through therapy, I was leaning on the Helmsley Building at Sixty-Ninth and York. I was strangely energetic, not angry or manic but focused, grounded. I decided I didn't want to write my book. Instead I'd leave my bag there on the sidewalk—computer, books, pads—for someone to find, pick through, and deliver to Elisabeth. I was sure they wouldn't keep anything and that they'd give her everything intact. She could sort it all out—the fragments of the past years, the emails, letters, notes. But I didn't want her to publish it in my book, rather I wanted her to include it in her own memoir about her professional life. I saw the book in my head. I saw her typing, editing, and reading. I remember that I started tapping my foot to the beat of the city bustle and nodding my head on the upbeat. I was sure it was time to kill myself. I didn't feel euphoria. I didn't have any epic visions. I would go home and gather every pill in our medicine cabinet, a rope from the cellar, walk to Prospect Park, find a secluded place, tie the noose, string the branch, swallow the drugs, wait until they almost took me, then hang myself.

I left my bag, stood, and walked to the curb. I'd never been so sure about an act. I recited, "Every action is a step to the block, to the fire, down the sea's throat." This act wasn't nihilistic: I felt alive and free. That feeling, however, only lasted a few moments. As I waited for the light, I started to grow afraid and confused. I wasn't at the crosswalk and would have to jaywalk, which seemed impossible, so I drifted north along the curb for a space between the cars into which I could wade. Nothing. The cars were grille to bumper. I stopped and looked across the narrow avenue—more fearful. I spoke the Lord's Prayer. As I reached "for thine," the light changed. I looked down into the window of a dark blue Chevrolet. I finished the prayer. The window lowered and in the opening were two brown, kind faces. The passenger was an elderly woman; the driver was much younger. Both were crying. The younger leaned toward me.

"Excuse me, sir," she called.

"Yes." I thought I hissed.

The cars behind started honking, which caused the older woman to sob.

"We need your help."

"Okay."

She reached across the older woman's lap and opened the door. "Please help my mother."

Now the horns were constant and accompanied by motorists' curses and yowls. As I held my hand up—I might have imagined it—they quieted. I helped the mother out of the car and onto the sidewalk. She didn't seem able to talk, so I looked back to her daughter. I expected her to ask me to take her to one of the medical buildings, but the mother spoke.

"I need money."

I knew she didn't mean from me. I pointed north. She nodded. While closing the door her daughter called out, "Chase."

I waved, looped her mother's arm in mine, and started walking.

Inside, she pointed to the ATMs and leaned against the counter. She handed me her purse and gestured for me to open it. She searched for and produced her bank card, which she handed to me. She nodded toward the machines. "Please." She'd stopped crying.

She whispered her PIN. I walked across the foyer and inserted her card. She instructed me through the menus until I'd withdrawn $200. I gave the bills to her, returned her card, and walked her outside. Her daughter was double-parked, enraging both north- and southbound drivers. I helped her mother into the car. She thanked me and pushed a twenty-dollar bill into my chest. I declined. Wordlessly, she insisted, but I backed away, closed the door, and turned south. I saw my bag still leaning against the wall. I retrieved it. Walking downtown on York Avenue I knew I had to live.

If I were to live, nothing I felt could matter, only that which I knew. And I knew I could only live in service of others. What one could've called going mad had really been a conversion experience. I was now a hero.

So, every weekday morning, I traveled to the Upper East Side. I'm not sure why that neighborhood other than habit. I didn't wear a coat or carry a bag. I had a small Moleskine in my front right pocket, an ultrafine Sharpie in my pack. On Zyprexa and Cymbalta, in my T-shirt, I searched for ways to help.

There's not much overt criminality there, so I used my powers to help nannies and the elderly. I was a crossing guard, I helped with grocery bags, I carried strollers up and down subway station stairs. Sometimes I glared angrily at those who catcalled women, but mostly I hovered above the streets in a medicated haze until spring.

6

I'd forgotten that months before, we'd planned a trip to Los Angeles to visit old friends Sarah and Glen. I'd known Sarah since high school and Glen had become one of my closest friends. I'd always felt comfortable enough to raid their refrigerator. They had three children too—all close in age to ours—the ten of us always had a blast together.

They'd moved west ten years prior. I'd been excited to go; we'd booked our flight the past summer. But a few days before our trip I got pneumonia. It frightened me when I realized I could stay home alone because of it. And I wanted to. Michaele pleaded with me to go with them. I did.

I think I carried myself well. My family seemed relieved and unafraid of my presence. Glen, Sarah, and their three sons seemed happy I was there. I didn't participate in any of the family outings though. I mostly drove around LA alone. I continued marking time until Easter Eve. When it came, I watched movies with the boys. They all went to bed. I announced I'd work for a while and set up at the kitchen table. I whimsied about drinking, taking all of my medications, and going for a last swim—or of waiting outside for that mountain lion I'd been hoping for. Fortunately, each ideation was paired with actuality. My death wishes were insane. I was ashamed that I didn't consider what it would do to my family if they woke up to a bloated corpse or bloody carcass.

I didn't know what to do. I didn't know if I could or should tell Michaele, Sarah, or Glen that I couldn't think of anything but dying.

I couldn't feel much of anything other than its pull. I tried saying it aloud to myself, but I'd feel grotesquely sad and be reminded that I'd told others about the bank, that I wouldn't have been there talking to them without the intercession of an ordinary angel. But they couldn't know what it meant—the privacy of salvation. I knew I had to keep this to myself but not from myself, because I no longer wanted to practice partitioning. I wanted to be unfolded, creaseless, bigger, and not so crazy. I wanted to thank God by making myself holy. I no longer wanted to proffer the broken love of a mad soul.

I didn't want to be afraid anymore.

It was three o'clock. I wanted morning to come so I could make breakfast for everyone, but I kept repeating Rilke's "I want to be with those who know secret things." But who, other than my maker and I, knew secret things? And even these things, now, were secrets to me. I didn't know if it was God's will that kept it so—protected me from me—or if it was my will that rejected becoming whole.

I sat at the kitchen table scribbling and typing, reading and staring, praying and questioning. Dawn came and I slept upright until the rose broke white. Christ didn't come for coffee. I went outside. He wasn't by the pool, nor was his visage reflected in it. I suspected he wasn't down on Ventura Boulevard, or anywhere over the Valley. I couldn't tell if being tired made me sardonic, or if it did the opposite, but I remember as the day went on I felt somewhere inside a distant grief for something profound that I couldn't quite recall. That night Sarah grilled a lovely flank steak and I didn't need to intervene. I even poured her wine.

The next day I had a meeting with my Hollywood agent. She was warm, smart, engaging, and seemed to be interested in my thoughts. I wanted to tell her everything. I didn't. I wanted to sit by a window in her office all day. I had to leave, of course, so I clung to the feeling of someone being sincerely kind.

I had a call with the editor of a magazine scheduled, so I found a Starbucks and waited. She was going to give me notes on an essay

I'd written. On the phone, she said, "It's a little dark." But she had helpful tips to brighten it. I paid close attention to her but struggled to incorporate edits, so I barely remembered or understood. I wanted to tell her that I'd written it in another life, but I kept my mouth shut until we signed off.

I needed food and sleep. I left Starbucks and thought I'd walk to the pier. When I arrived at Ocean Avenue I looked across to the beach. It was invitingly empty, but it was still cold, and I wanted to bake the remaining pneumonia out of me. I stood waiting among the homeless, those who'd been pushed west as far as they could be. For a moment, I had the beginnings of an essay on the perversity of manifest destiny, but I couldn't organize the chronology of migrations or separate the movement of seeking from the movement of flight. Cavalries and cutlasses, locomotive-driven bison killers, lynching, choking dust. And then the idea just seemed so stupid. As soon as I demeaned my thoughts, it seemed the only thing to do was to cross the avenue, look out on the Pacific—such a strange ocean—and imagine me gone.

Styron writes, "Most people in the grip of depression at its ghastliest are, for whatever reason, in a state of unrealistic hopelessness, torn by exaggerated ills and fatal threats that bear no resemblance to actuality." But what of the other ills? The "realities" alien to him? Madness, at times for me, has been a reprieve from circumstances that cannot be dulled or stilled, that don't trill along the wire but rather are the wire and the poles—and remain when the lights go out and are all that remains when they come back on. The underworld is a sanctuary from the irreducible horror. No one ever came in the dark hours, and no one wanted to be with me—all of me—in the light. It seemed the only thing there at the world's end was the chance to walk off the edge. And while many call it a selfish act, perhaps the onus couldn't be on me. Perhaps my final freedom required the selflessness of those who loved me, to give me the life that was not my own so that I could take it.

And that was just it: *I didn't want it.* I walked back to the Starbucks and leaned against the building. It seems there's always a suicide note behind my eyes or on my lips. I must leave the hurt for now. I stay for a moment and then another. I leave—even briefly—any notion of my value or my lack thereof. I neither quantify nor qualify myself. I'm neither part nor sum. I forget everything that anyone has asked of me or told me except to please stay.

Somewhere past Malibu I pulled into a gas station and parked. It was midafternoon. I still had plenty of time to make it back to the house for dinner. I got out, sat on the warm hood, watched the traffic, and listened to the seabirds and the surf. The sun and metal quickly baked the chill out of me, and when I felt I had enough reserve warmth, I got back in and continued north on Route 1.

One night nine years prior, while staying with a friend in Topanga, I'd heard a cougar in the night. The next morning, I'd woken to find a western diamondback on the patio. I wanted to be among them, so I drove for ten to fifteen miles and turned east on what seemed to be a major road. I'd hoped to avoid the freeway and find my way to the edge of the state park, drive northeast along its border until I found Ventura Boulevard, and cut through the Valley's enclaves until I was home.

I turned east up a short, steep rise, then coasted down a long, steady descent into the canyon. The blacktop was smooth, and the putty and rusty hills, the sage and scrub were vibrant and clean under the bright blue sky. It was quiet. The sun was on my back. The road wound north and east past an occasional house or store. I repeated, "I can live like this." And: "But not like this." Marking time between distractions and highs: that wasn't living. My life was more than intermittent torpors and epiphanies. I had my family, friends, and at least a few pages that showed me I might still write. I had the top down. I had motion, the sun. I knew there were wildcats and rattlers up in the hills.

I had my failures and regrets, too. I had memories that were still hurting me, and I knew they always would. I had my misfiring head and my uncertain body. I had a book to write, which in my current state was beyond me—at least the book I thought I must write.

I knew I had to surrender my will because I didn't know anything other than that my mind would show me no mercy. I tried imagining—out there beyond the sage—that there was a way to surrender without capitulation. I remembered the feeling of both beautiful and awful things and that I'd continue to struggle with either or both. I knew what dying would do to me. I knew I'd continue waking up in dreamworlds, underworlds, worlds between worlds, and nightmares. I knew I'd get sick again—not slowly but suddenly and prompted by nothing. I knew there was no defense against it. What would I do to stay? I wondered what the cost would be to others. I wondered how many people I'd hurt in trying to stay.

It's what I had—all of it. It's still, always, what I have. Among the hills, for the first time in a long time I didn't think in terms of blessings and curses. I wasn't a portal to anything cosmic or redemptive. I wasn't a villain or a saint. I wasn't anything either I or anyone else could flatten or reduce to chemistry—be it wiring or story. Testimony would come later. I wasn't desperate in that moment. That was a start. Good enough for now.

I've gone numb while the world's been on fire and burned when it's gone cold. I've felt mercy as wrath, hope and fear as the same. I've believed that the next moment must be the last of me. I know the darkness inside and out will gather and roll and a voice that might be mine will say, *"Just go."*

I'm in the darkness now. It calls me deeper. I will not go. In these mercury days, there are too many reasons to live and die. I stay because I don't know what's next.

Sometimes all I can do is survive.

I suspect that I will always feel sad and alone, even in the best of times. But this is the pain of being whole not broken. This isn't the pain of living. It's the pain of believing I have to die. This is the pain of the now. So stay, stay, stay with me here and know that in this moment, again, I am not afraid.

Acknowledgments

With Love & Gratitude to everyone who helped me stay:

Cecil Alexander, Miles Fowlkes, Ella Sweet, and Ezekiel James

Padraic Michael O'Reilly, Dominic Anthony Taylor, and Al Maeda

Sara Rempe

Tracey Thomas and Larry Hosmer

Michaele Wylde

Sarah Morse and Glen Mazzara,
Robey Newsom
Elise Cannon

Lisa and Russell Houston

Maria Massie

Alexandra McLean, James Regan, Laura Raffa, Mauro Premutico, Leslie Marshall, Julian Nestor, Judy Maeda, A.Van Jordan, Stephanie Bower, David Baird, Geoff Sands, Elena Kugler, Oscar Cantu, David Yamada, Marianne Rempe, Deirdre O'Reilly, Eamonn O'Reilly, Shokry Eldaly, Crystal Granderson-Reid, Kenyatte Reid, Patty Neagle, Aaron Stanton, Samareh Eskandaripour, Yvonne Paine, Ben Russell, Robert Penn, Nicholas Tremulis, Pieter Van Tol, Tufic Thompson, Julia Bannon, Brendan O'Connor, Sylvie Rabineau, Lauren Szurgot, Kim Wiley Paul Yamazaki

Frank Kirkland, Elizabeth Beaujour, Kelvin Black, Collin Craig, Rebecca Connor, Donna Masini, Gavin Hollis, Jeremy Glick, Jeff Allred, Janet Neary, Amy Robbins, Paul McPherron, Alan Vardy, Nijah Cunningham, Barbara Webb, Elizabeth Nunez

Everyone at Grove Atlantic for seeing this book through.
Deb Seager
Katie Raissian
Amy Hundley
Judy Hottensen
Gretchen Mergenthaler
Mike Richards, Sal Destro, and everyone on the production staff for all the extensions and revisions.

My friend and ally, Morgan Entrekin

Laura Schmitt is brilliant.

And Elisabeth Schmitz, my editor, who wouldn't let me fail.

Still: "Many rivers to cross" but always "coming in from the cold."

Permissions Acknowledgments

From "Little Gidding," "Burnt Norton," "Dry Salvages," "East Coker" from *Four Quartets* by T. S. Eliot. Copyright © 1936 by Houghton Mifflin Harcourt Publishing Company, renewed 1964 by T. S. Eliot. Copyright © 1940, 1941, 1942 by T. S. Eliot, renewed 1968, 1969, 1970 by Esme Valerie Eliot. Used by permission of HarperCollins Publishers and Faber and Faber Ltd.

"The More Loving One," copyright © 1957 by W. H. Auden and renewed 1985 by The Estate of W. H. Auden; from *Collected Poems* by W. H. Auden, edited by Edward Mendelson. Used by permission of Random House, an imprint and division of Penguin Random House LLC. All rights reserved.

"Mulatto" from *The Collected Poems of Langston Hughes* by Langston Hughes, edited by Arnold Rampersad with David Roessel, Associate Editor, copyright © 1994 by the Estate of Langston Hughes. Used by permission of Alfred A. Knopf, an imprint of the Knopf Doubleday Publishing Group, a division of Penguin Random House LLC. All rights reserved.

Lyrics from "A Man's Way Out" by Nick Tremulis. Reprinted with permission from Nick Tremulis.